T0385978

MALE DESIRE IN HITCHCOCK, DE PALMA,

PSYCHO SEXUAL

CORSESE, AND FRIEDKIN

DAVID GREVEN

UNIVERSITY OF TEXAS ⩔ AUSTIN

Copyright © 2013 by the University of Texas Press
All rights reserved
Printed in the United States of America
First edition, 2013

Requests for permission to reproduce material
from this work should be sent to:
Permissions
University of Texas Press
P.O. Box 7819
Austin, TX 78713-7819
http:// utpress.utexas.edu/index.php/rp-form

The paper used in this book meets the minimum requirements
of ANSI/NISO z39.48-1992 (R1997) (Permanence of Paper). ∞

Design by Lindsay Starr

LIBRARY OF CONGRESS CATALOGING-IN-PUBLICATION DATA
Greven, David.
    Psycho-sexual : male desire in Hitchcock, De Palma, Scorsese, and Friedkin /
by David Greven.—1st ed.
        p. cm.
    Includes bibliographical references and index.
    ISBN 978-0-292-75676-2
    1. Masculinity in motion pictures. 2. Homosexuality in motion pictures.
3. Hitchcock, Alfred, 1899–1980—Criticism and interpretation.
4. Hitchcock, Alfred, 1899–1980—Influence. 5. De Palma, Brian—Criticism and
interpretation. 6. Scorsese, Martin—Criticism and interpretation.
7. Friedkin, William—Criticism and interpretation. I. Title.
    PN1995.9.M46G746 2012
    791.43'653—dc23   2012026244

doi:10.7560/742024

First paperback edition, 2013

For my inspiring students, whose love of movies deepens my own.

CONTENTS

S EVERAL PEOPLE HAVE SHAPED the thinking that has gone into this book. I wish to acknowledge Donald Spoto, whose book *The Art of Alfred Hitchcock* was an early influence. Reading Spoto led to the incisive and inimitable writings of Robin Wood, whose work has profoundly influenced my own. I want to thank Robin for encouraging me to write what would become my first published article on Brian De Palma, an essay on *Snake Eyes* that appeared in *CineAction*, and for his kind mentorship and friendship in the years that followed. I also want to acknowledge Pauline Kael for her extraordinary example of passionately committed criticism over the course of several decades. She was not a Hitchcockian by any means, but, in her kindness, she wrote me a letter when I was a teenager in response to one I sent her expressing my desire to be a film critic and full of undoubtedly eloquent panegyrics to *Vertigo*. Advising me to get the best possible education that I could, she encouraged me to pursue my critical aspirations if my passion for movies "was still as intense" after college. I have tried to take her advice, and I hope that this book demonstrates that.

Several professors in the Department of Film & Media at Hunter College of the City University of New York were inspirations to me when I was an undergraduate. Ivone Margulies taught an avant-garde film class that still lights up my critical faculties; I also very fondly recall her kindness. Though he was pretty tough on my homework, Richard Barsam, whose class "Cinematic Space" I had the honor of taking, taught me a great deal. Martha Gever's class, "Sexualities and Media Representation," radicalized my thinking. Steve Kruger, my faculty mentor for two successive McNair Fellowships, led me through the ins and outs of queer theory during this period as well. For early encouragement about my critical aspirations, I want to thank Bruce Goldstein, the extraordinary repertory film programmer for Film Forum, especially for those long train-ride conversations from Inwood, New York, so very long ago.

My graduate education at Brandeis gave me access to unforgettable intellectual experiences. I want to thank, especially, Paul Morrison for galvanizing insights into sex and culture, Mary Baine Campbell for her inspiring intellectual example, Eugene Goodheart for telling me once, "you have the capacity" (those words meant a great deal to me coming from Gene), and the dream team of Michael T. Gilmore, Wai Chee Dimock, and John Burt for turning me into an Americanist. As ever, I thank Timo for his invaluable friendship, too.

For their truly penetrating insights into portions of the manuscripts at various stages, I am indebted to Tony Williams, Magnus Ullén, Richard Allen, and Sidney Gottlieb. Obviously, any mistakes or infelicities in the completed work are entirely my own. I want to thank Ann Kibbey, the brilliant editor of the journal *Genders*, for her support over the years. *Genders* published a shorter version of Chapter 4, "Misfortune and Men's Eyes," on De Palma's early comedies, and I am very grateful to the anonymous readers for their incisive feedback. A shorter version of Chapter 1, "Cruising, Hysteria, Knowledge," on Hitchcock's 1956 remake of *The Man Who Knew Too Much*, was published in the *European Journal of American Culture*. Similarly, I want to thank the anonymous readers at EJAC for their insights. I also thank the journal *Cineaste* for permission to quote from my reviews of Eyal Peretz's *Becoming Visionary: Brian De Palma's Cinematic Education of the Senses* and of Richard Allen's *Hitchcock's Romantic Irony*, both published in the Summer 2008 issue.

All of the illustrations in this book are film stills from Jerry Ohlinger's Movie Material Store. I want to thank the JOMMS staff for all of their tireless efforts to procure the requested stills.

None of my understanding of film would be possible without the movie-loving enthusiasms of my friends Viki Zavales and the Zavales family, Robert Simonson, Ben Schreier, Rick Cole, Steve Paltsios, and many others. My partner Alex Beecroft remains my critical touchstone at every turn, in all ways, for every occasion, through a variety of media experiences and in every aspect of my life. I want to thank my movie-loving family as well—my mother and my aunts for their love of Old Hollywood glamour; my brother Mike for his love for Hitchcock, especially *Rear Window*; and my father for taking me to the theater to see

Vertigo when it was re-released in the 1980s (my life has never been the same since), and for buying me the Spoto book, which was on sale at the concession stand of the D. W. Griffith movie theater. I am confident that my younger brother Ozzy's daughter, Mia Rose, is going to grow up to be a film scholar and fan in the proud Greven tradition.

I want to thank the amazing online De Palma community for their brilliant insights and friendship over the years, especially Peet Gelderblom, Geoff Beran, James Martin Moran, Keith Uhlich, Michael Crowley, and Bill Fentum.

Last and by no means least, I want to thank the students for being such acutely perceptive readers of movies as well as movie lovers. Words fail me when I think of the brilliance of their critical example. So many students have made such a significant impact on my movie-related thinking, but I want to make a special point of thanking James Bogdanski, Lyman Creason, Tristan O'Donnell, Brian McCarthy, Devon Butler, Julie Pereira, and Zach West for their friendship and erudition.

PSYCHO-SEXUAL

N THE OPENING MOMENTS OF Alfred Hitchcock's cold, cunning 1954 masterpiece *Rear Window*, the camera, mobile with a pure cinema life of its
own, roams about the apartment of L.B. Jeffries—"Jeff"—played by James
Stewart. It's a hot summer day, and the jazzy music in the background adds
to the sultriness. An action photographer for magazines, Jeff, his leg in a cast from
a work-related injury, is asleep in his wheelchair as the camera examines some of
his possessions for clues to his identity, pausing deliberately to focus on various
objects, especially some framed photographs. As if crawling into Jeff's apartment
from the outside, the camera scales the building, comes in through the window,
stares at the perspiring Jeff, then scans the length of his seated body, particularly
the extended cast in which one of his legs is simultaneously immobilized and
erect, an apt metaphor for his version of masculinity. The movie camera then
looks at the photographer's crumpled camera on a desk, presumably destroyed
in the accident in which Jeff broke his leg. Deepening the import of the images
of broken-legged Jeff and the broken camera, we see a framed photograph of a
car as it flips over in an auto race; unmistakably, the image of the cylindrical car
with two large wheels along either side recalls a penis and testicles. But, given that
this is an image of the accident in which Jeff broke his leg, and that one of the
wheels is coming loose from the car, the photograph evokes castration as much
as it reassures the spectator with the presence of the phallus. In one of the other

photographs, a mushroom cloud climbs out of the frame; if we see a continuation of phallic / sexual imagery here, we might read this as a sign of orgasm, but also as a statement that male orgasm is apocalyptic. Next, we turn to a framed photograph of a smiling blond woman, her hair cut appealingly short. But the framed photograph is in negative film. This negative image in a frame is then juxtaposed against the actual image of the woman, on the cover of a magazine. That we see the negative image of the woman first seems to me significant. That the image is framed is also significant. Jeff can only see "negative" images of women, which does a lot already to explain his mysteriously contemptuous disposition towards his girlfriend, the beautiful, witty fashion model Lisa Carol Fremont, played magically by Grace Kelly. Moreover, Jeff frames his negative image of a woman, proudly displaying his own caustic, acidic take on sexual difference and perhaps sex itself. That the "normal" image of Woman appears on a magazine, and that this magazine is the top one on a stack of what are presumably more copies of the same magazine, signifies the mass production and circulation of normative images of gendered subjectivity. That this image is of a woman emphasizes difference, emphasizes the gendered distinction between the male subject and the female photographic object. Gender is the work of the age of mechanical reproduction.

Of particular interest to me is the allegorical value of the distinction between the framed negative and that stack of magazines with the normal, real-life image. If we take the frame as an allegorical representation of the cinematic image—the frame within the frame—and the magazines, with their innumerable identical images, as the social order's normative image of gendered identity, a model of sameness and normality endlessly reproduced and mass circulated, we can understand that Hitchcock is setting up a decisive, illuminating contrast between his own framing of women, and, for that matter, men, and the mass production of women and men as first and foremost visual personages, images of gendered selves. Subjectivity is created entirely from the outside in and is indistinguishable from the visual representation of it.

Hitchcock's negative images of women—and of queer subjects—have preoccupied a great deal of critical treatments since the 1980s. Though she frequently qualifies, amends, and problematizes her views of Hitchcock, Tania Modleski finds Hitchcock's films rife with "lethal misogyny."[1] This seems to me a powerful and apt phrase even though I disagree with her about its presence, or the meaning of its presence, in Hitchcock. Misogyny is lethal: it promotes the devaluation of women, leads to the permissiveness of violence against women, and generally has inescapably dire consequences. Yet in Hitchcock, misogyny, while at times the director's own, much more frequently emanates from the characters and the situations. Further, directorial and audience identification is generally with the female protagonist. Indeed, I would argue that the female protagonist in Hitchcock is consistently viewed from a sympathetic perspective, though also, to be sure, an ambivalent one. Let me add also that I believe Hitchcock treats his queer characters with sympathy, and with an even greater curiosity.

As I discuss in Chapter 1, a tension exists in Hitchcock's representation of femininity and queerness that the films actively thematize. A pattern exists in Hitchcock films that I call "the feminine versus the queer." This contest almost always ends up ruling in favor of the feminine. If considered in relation to the representation of queerness, the feminine in Hitchcock comes to seem especially validated and supported. But then again, in comparison to his treatment of heterosexuality—which is to say, the normative gendered and sexual standard—Hitchcock's treatment of queerness comes to seem more radical. Queerness in his films constantly challenges the presumptions, strictures, and moral enforcements of the hetero-normal world.

Hitchcock's films share with Freud a resistance to the view of heterosexuality as "natural," as the self-evident basis of normal human life. That, as Robin Wood would point out, is their value. In a startling statement on the subject of homosexuality in a footnote in *Three Essays on the Theory of Sexuality*, Freud notes that "the exclusive sexual interest felt by men" for women is, from a psychoanalytic perspective, "also a problem that needs elucidating and is not a self-evident fact based upon an attraction that is ultimately of a chemical nature." Freud debunks the mythic naturalness of heterosexuality here, asking us to see it as no less strange and mystifying than homosexuality. "All human beings are capable of making a homosexual object-choice and have in fact made one in their unconscious."[2] One of Freud's signal contributions to a queer understanding of human culture and sexuality is that desire has no one true object and no aim. Despite the binding strictures of heteronormativity, no less restrictive a regime for those who desire the opposite sex than for those who desire the same sex, sexual desire is neither authentically, naturally, or originally heterosexual, nor is it inauthentic, unnatural, or a poor imitation of an original sexual design when it is homosexual. Freud and Hitchcock challenge heterosexual presumption in their refusal to treat sexuality as a place of reassuring refuge. Throughout his films, Hitchcock makes male-female sexual relations pointedly confused, tortured, exhausting, contentious, a sadistically erotic struggle. He refuses to allow us to experience man-woman sexual relations as anything but a befuddling problem that needs serious explication.

Negative Images: *Frenzy*

As I will demonstrate, my major focus in this book is, first, on the representation of masculinity in Hitchcock's films and, second, on the influence of this representation on several important filmmakers of the 1970s, specifically Brian De Palma, Martin Scorsese, and William Friedkin. I argue that in Hitchcock, American masculinity, especially from the late 1940s forward, is founded on pre-dilections for voyeurism, anxieties over homosexuality, and a growing fascination with pornography. In turns, these predilections, anxieties, and fascinations inform the films of the 1970s, especially where masculinity is concerned.

A metacritical vein runs throughout this book, a concern over certain directions that film studies has taken since the 1980s. In its current state, film studies can be summarized as following two directions: ideology without beauty, and beauty without ideology. As I will explain, this impasse in critical practice is organized around the crisis over "negative images" within the culture wars that date back to the 1980s. As part of my effort to reorient discussions in film studies related to issues of gender, sexuality, race, and the ethics of representation on the one hand and aesthetics on the other hand, I will also be addressing the "negative images" controversy. I can think of no better example to begin with than *Frenzy* (1972).

Frenzy marked Hitchcock's cinematic return to English shores after several decades of Hollywood filmmaking. While there is much to discuss in this comparatively overlooked and highly important film, for our purposes the sequence in which a woman, Brenda Blaney (Barbara Leigh-Hunt), is raped and murdered is the most significant in the film. It is, arguably, the most harrowing sequence in Hitchcock's oeuvre and contains what is, undoubtedly, the most painful, horrifying image in it: the medium close-up of Brenda Blaney after she has been murdered by the ginger-haired, dandyish serial killer Robert Rusk (Barry Foster). Only *Psycho*'s shower-murder sequence contains images of sexualized violence of comparable difficulty and disturbance, and I would argue that *Frenzy* goes even further in this regard.

Brenda is the ex-wife of Richard Blaney (Jon Finch). Yet another of Hitchcock's wrongly accused male protagonists, Blaney will be accused of her murder as well as those of the other women killed by Rusk. Rusk will also kill the lively, loyal Babs Milligan (Anna Massey, who also portrayed the one victim to survive Michael Powell's 1960 film *Peeping Tom*), who stands by Blaney once he is accused. Blaney is, without question, one of the least attractive and sympathetic of Hitchcock's male protagonists. While Brenda has pity for Blaney, taking him out to her club for dinner, she astutely realizes that, in emotional terms, he's bad news. A former RAF pilot, Blaney now works at a lower-class pub, from which he gets fired as soon as he appears in the film. On a perpetually short fuse, he blames his woes on everyone else, including his now much more successful ex-wife, who runs her own business, a dating service. Unbeknownst to Blaney, Brenda slips him money to live on, which he discovers when a man in a homeless shelter tries to steal it during the night. Meanwhile, Rusk gambols about, the merry, loquacious owner of a fruit and vegetable store (eerily reminiscent of Hitchcock's father, a greengrocer), cheerfully clapping his friend Blaney's shoulder while offering him fresh fruit, advice, and money to help him out. That Blaney and Rusk share a deep-seated rage, which they reveal and act out in distinct ways, is part of the film's message; Hitchcock's doubling of them draws attention to their differences but more saliently to their similarities. Blaney directs his rage outwardly, fulminating at everyone; Rusk keeps his murderous rage private, unleashing it only with the women whom he rapes and then kills, choking them with a piece of his apparel that earns him the title "the Necktie Killer." While Blaney is not a murderer, his unpleasantness stands out in the Hitchcock canon, notable for its skeptical disposition toward straight screen masculinity. Clearly, Rusk unleashes at least some of the rage that Blaney feels as well, just as the psychotic Bruno Anthony does for the apparently normal, all-American tennis player Guy Haines in *Strangers on a Train* (1951). "I'd like to wring her neck," Guy says of his troublesome wife; Bruno wrings her neck. Male doubling in Hitchcock collapses the desires of each male into one, which has important implications not only for murderous, misogynistic violence but for homoerotic desire as well.

That indelible, terrible image in *Frenzy* of the dead Brenda, raped and murdered by Rusk, continues to demand analysis. In one of the most incisive of her readings of Hitchcock films—which, as noted, are complex in their understanding of his ambivalence towards femininity—Modleski challenges the criticisms of Hitchcock's depiction of the rape and murder here as too graphic, lacking his former discretion:

> Of course, one might ask why, if a sordid crime like rape/murder is to be depicted at all, it should not be shown "in all its horror." In fact, it could be argued that the stylization and allusiveness of the shower scene in *Psycho* have provided critics with the rationale for lovingly and endlessly recounting all the details of its signification in the very process of self-righteously deploring its signified, the rape/murder.[3]

Astutely, in my view, Modleski, who doesn't flinch from calling Hitchcock misogynistic when she feels it is warranted, points out that it is the very graphicness of this rape/murder that reveals and critiques its barbarism.

Far from a discrete or "suggestive" depiction of sexual violence, the representation of the rape-murder is, however, deeply stylized, in no way offering "documentary realism." Rather, it offers and mixes a number of realistic and stylized maneuvers.[4] The way the scene is cut; the manner in which its temporal duration is alternately extended and compressed; the deeply odd behavior of Rusk, alternately moaning, "Lovely," and shrieking, "Bitch!"; the close-ups on Brenda's face during the rape, as well as her heartbreaking gestures, such as trying to pull up her bra when Rusk yanks it down; and that final, horrific, simultaneously re-alistic and deeply stylized image of her in death all add to a curiously dreamlike atmosphere during the murder, a mixture, as we find in dreams, of the lifelike and specific and the singularly bizarre.

Of the many ways that Hitchcock could have shown us the aftermath of the murder in *Frenzy*—such as the austere overhead shot he gives us of the murdered Marion Crane, slumped over the bathtub, in *Psycho* (1960)—he chooses to give us a shockingly gross, unseemly, and, I argue, pornographic shot of the dead woman. She stares right out at the viewer, wide-eyed, as if made to look on the spectacle of her inexpressible violation forever. Grotesquely, her tongue lolls out of the corner of her mouth. An image redolent of the Surrealist canon, it seems to suggest the opposite meanings from its content. Her expression makes her look coarse and weirdly bawdy, as if she were enjoying this pornographic spec-tacle with lowbrow humor.

This image is the ultimate violation imaginable to a person after death: it mockingly distorts the horrific nature of what she has suffered into a come-dic, crudely sexualized image of her in death. Laura Kipnis argues in *Bound and Gagged*—a study that is notably sympathetic to the often maligned genre and its viewers—that the lure of pornography is its central fantasy that women enjoy sex with the same impersonal crudeness that men do. Within this grotesque image in all of its horror, *Frenzy* critiques the analogous fantasy that women actually "want" to be raped.

What I want to suggest about this image is that, while it may actually reveal something about the director's personal perversities, to use that term with point-ed looseness, it more acutely conveys something about his films generally, Hitch-cock's public, celebrity persona, and their shared cultural status. Throughout his films, Hitchcock makes a game of murder. It is the inspiration for the most cun-ningly storyboarded and shot sequences in film history; it is the darkly humorous subject matter of his direct address to the audience on a weekly basis at the start, end, and in-between moments of his television series *Alfred Hitchcock Presents*; it is the darkly humorous subject matter of Hitchcock's mordant, joke-filled speeches at public events, usually award ceremonies ("As you can see, scissors are really the best way," said after a clip from 1954's *Dial M for Murder* is shown in which Grace Kelly stabs her would-be killer with these typically feminine, sewing-kit implements).

Pauline Kael, no supporter of the Andrew Sarris–*Cahiers du Cinéma* auteur theory that was enshrining Hitchcock in the 1960s as a great director and one of the many critics who revolted against the revolting *Frenzy*, once wrote of the film as "rancid." I find this description especially apt, though not in the way that Kael uses the term, for a movie that shows us both the rotten core of the Hitchcock film and thematizes food and its nauseating aspects as metaphors for sex, lust, and sexualized violence.[5] For what *Frenzy* does is rip off the veil of politesse that shrouds the Hitchcock film.[6]

The hideous shot of the murdered, tongue-lolling Brenda is the ultimate negative image, fusing horror, exploitation, and pornographic film—lowbrow art par excellence—representations of femininity in its graphic display of a gruesomely killed woman character. Yet this negative image—precisely for the ways "it looks at you," in the words of Wheeler Winston Dixon, for the way the image returns the gaze, and so assaultively—also conveys the horrific nature not only of this especially traumatic moment but of all such moments in Hitchcock's films, even those generally considered light entertainments. Dixon discusses those moments when a film "acts upon us, addressing us, viewing us as we view it, until the film itself becomes a gaze, rather than an object to be gazed upon."[7] The returned gaze can produce moments in which "film structure watches us," when we "feel the look of the image being turned against us, surveilling us, subjecting us to the 'look back' of the screen."[8] Though Dixon does not discuss Hitchcock in this study, focusing instead on artists such as Andy Warhol, surely this moment in *Frenzy* in which Brenda stares at us so assaultively is one of the most significant moments of the returned gaze in the cinema.

A woman in death haunts Hitchcock's cinema, as it will that of his most ardent and imaginative screen disciple, Brian De Palma. In much the same way that the murdered Brenda is violated anew by having her expression in death so distorted, the murdered Sally in De Palma's *Blow Out* (1981) will be violated after death, her wrenching screams used to plug up an auditory hole in a cheapjack porny horror film named, tellingly, *Co-Ed Frenzy*. Watching Hitchcock's *Frenzy*, one gets the impression that he, in his old age, had grown tired of camouflaging his subject. Here, Hitchcock breaks through decades of studio- and self-imposed repression, going further even than he did in the revolutionary *Psycho*, the film that created the genre of modern horror, in exposing the utter grimness of the human potentiality for violence and the ways in which this potentiality so often takes the form of violence against women.

While many critics have found the violence against women in Hitchcock's films to be expressions of Hitchcock's own violent attitudes towards women, to be acts of violence against women, I would argue here against simplistically reading the films biographically to begin with, but more importantly against drawing an equivalence between what is represented and what is being expressed by a film: a simple point, perhaps, but at the same time a controversial one in the quarters of identity politics.

Identity Politics, Ideology, and Critical Practice

The "positive images" argument—the belief that representations of oppressed groups such as women, queers, and those of nonwhite races and ethnicities should cast these identities in an affirming light—wielded for the last three decades in academic cultural discourse has disturbingly blunted and distorted not only many works of art but a great deal of critical thinking. In challenging the "positive images" argument, my work intersects with that of critics such as J. Jack Halberstam, Richard Dyer, Ellis Hanson, and Sabrina Barton, who have all made similar and persuasive cases.[9]

One of the difficulties of challenging the "positive images" argument is that many of the concerns undergirding it are quite legitimate ones. Matters of feminism and queer/transgendered rights are of no less pressing importance now than they were in previous decades, and race representation has lost none of its urgency as a concern, to say the least. One part of the turn against the "positive images" debate, in terms of film theory, has been challenging the stronghold of Laura Mulvey's theory of the male gaze, articulated most clearly and forcefully in two articles of boundless influence: "Visual Pleasure and Narrative Cinema" from 1975 and its sequel, "Afterthoughts on 'Visual Pleasure and Narrative Cinema' inspired by King Vidor's *Duel in the Sun* (1946)." Feminist as well as queer critics have challenged the Mulvey model of an unchanging, essentialist cinematic representation of "Woman" as well as any stable, coherent understandings of the gaze—the screen protagonist's, the spectator's, and both at once—as white, male, and heterosexual.[10] While I have often chafed against Mulvey's constrictive paradigms, there is still much that is useful in these two essays, to say nothing of her considerable body of later work, which remains, along with the shifts in her critical positions since the early 1980s, comparatively unexplored.[11]

In large part, however, the necessary challenge to Mulvey that has been conducted in the past two decades has taken the form of an opposition to the theoretical framework through which Mulvey articulated her theories of femininity, masculinity, and the gaze. As exemplified by *Post-Theory*, the reader that they edited, David Bordwell and Noël Carroll have led a movement toward the appreciation of film aesthetics that directly opposes the psychoanalytic methodologies so central to film theory in the 1970s and 1980s.

In many respects, the stronghold of psychoanalytic/semiotic approaches in film studies did indeed demand a revision and a resistance, especially the centrality of the concept of the phallus in Lacanian theory. Yet instead of revising and reimagining the uses of psychoanalytic theory—despite its limitations, an insightful methodology for the study of gendered identity, desire, and the emotional experiences of sexual subjectivity—the post-theory camp has dispensed with it

8

altogether.[12] With this dismissal of psychoanalysis has come a de-emphasization of issues of gender and sexuality in film studies within the approach embodied by critics such as Bordwell and Carroll.

The case I make for difficult artists like Hitchcock and De Palma and against the "positive images" argument is also quite distinct from the kind of work José Esteban Muñoz does in his important study *Disidentifications*. Whereas his focus is on the ways that queer artists of color have simultaneously worked within and critiqued the dominant culture, I argue for the importance of dominant culture to the ways that cultural, sexual, and raced subjects make sense of our lives. Those who occupy subjectivities relegated to the margins of culture—women, queers, the nonwhite, the economically disenfranchised—at times also seek out and locate representations of resonant and meaningful importance within dominant culture, in this case popular culture/Hollywood, rather than in alternative forms of creative expression. Speaking as a multiracial gay man from an immigrant, working-class background, I know that I have spent a lot of joyously frustrated time sifting through the endlessly accumulating evidence of how the dominant culture sees me to make sense of how I see myself. I humbly offer as evidence of the unpredictability of art and representation and reception the fact that I, as someone with a Haitian mother and a Hispanic father, neither of whom were born in the United States, find Hitchcock films indispensable to my understanding of the world and to my love of popular culture.

In my case, Hitchcock films, as well as the others discussed in this book, are especially significant in terms of understanding how gender and sexuality shape both American constructions of subjectivity and the experience of subjectivity in gendered and sexual terms. Moreover, Hitchcock's skeptical disposition towards normative sexuality, embodied by heterosexual romance and marriage, makes his work consistently interesting to me as a queer, multiracial male who, while fascinated by the iconic, mythological images and narratives of normative sexuality (I couldn't be as passionate a fan of Hollywood otherwise), sees them always as iconic and mythological rather than, as they are so often purported to be, the essential, unchanging truths of human existence.

Hitchcock, Classical Hollywood, Homosexuality, Genre Film

To return to the central issue at hand, Hitchcock and his influence over the New Hollywood, this book takes the conflictual relationship between heterosexual and homosexual masculinities that Hitchcock stages in several works, but most definitively in his 1960 film *Psycho*, as a template for the exploration of masculinity in the films of the 1970s. Much of the homosexual content in Hollywood film, at least until the twenty-first century, has remained allegorical, suggested rather than explicit, a vexing, indistinct presence rather than a directly stated threat.

Nevertheless, we can track the historical emergence of an explicitly represented homosexuality in Hollywood film. It was in the Cold War 1950s that the gay rights movement first gained prominence in the United States, through groups such as the Mattachine Society. It was also a decade in which homosexuals were persecuted in a newly organized and public way as a national threat linked to Communism, the decline in public morals, and a crisis in American masculinity. Hollywood responded in kind with increasingly more obvious, though still resolutely coded, representations of homosexuality.

Though bowdlerized, film adaptations of stage plays with homosexual content—*Tea and Sympathy* (Vincente Minnelli, 1957) and numerous adaptations of Tennessee Williams, especially *Suddenly, Last Summer* (Joseph L. Mankiewicz, 1959)—heralded the advent of a self-consciously queer cinema. Moreover, numerous films from the period functioned as queer allegories—*Red River* (Howard Hawks, 1948), *Fear Strikes Out* (Robert Mulligan, 1957), *The Strange One* (Jack Garfein, 1957)—while other films evoked homosexuality by drawing on real-life controversies involving it (Richard Fleischer's 1959 film *Compulsion*, based on the Leopold and Loeb case, as was Hitchcock's *Rope* before it and, after it, Todd Kalin's *Swoon* [1992]).

By the time we get to the 1960s, these suggestively queer films gave way to a veritable explosion of films with explicitly gay content: *Victim* (Basil Dearden, 1961), *The Children's Hour* (William Wyler, 1961), *Advise & Consent* (Otto Preminger, 1962), *The Sergeant* (John Flynn, 1968), *The Detective* (Gordon Douglas, 1968), *The Boys in the Band* (William Friedkin, 1970). They formed a pattern that continued unabated throughout the seventies, in significant films such as *Dog Day Afternoon* (Sidney Lumet, 1975), in which Al Pacino's hapless bank robber tries to get the money for his boyfriend Leon's sex-change operation, and another Pacino homo-vehicle, *Cruising* (William Friedkin, 1980), to which we turn in Chapter 6.

While many classical Hollywood films demand analysis from a queer perspective, I focus on Hitchcock as the representative of a welter of issues related to sexuality because of his undeniable influence on later filmmakers, particularly in the New Hollywood era. While Hitchcock's homophobia has been amply discussed by many, his homophilia has been considerably less discussed, a lapse I attempt to redress. In addition, I challenge the view of Hitchcock as misogynistic while also arguing that any discussion of queer sexuality in his work must also consider the representation of femininity.

Far from being the exclusive intertextual domain of Brian De Palma, Hitchcock's films were central to the aesthetic and cultural poetics of the New Hollywood cinema of the 1970s. This claim is a point of departure for a larger one. Many critics have noted the fixation with American masculinity in the period's filmmaking; I argue that what undergirded this fixation was a preoccupation with homosexuality.[13] Further, I argue that it was through a larger agon (or conflict) with Hitchcock's cinema that filmmakers conducted their investigation of American masculinity, one that focused on its fissures and failures. Homosexuality emerged as representative of these and also as a potential new direction for American masculinity to take, not without serious risk but also treated with surprising, fascinated interest.

While homosexuality informs several important New Hollywood films, it is only intermittently treated in explicit fashion by them, though when it is, as in William Friedkin's *Cruising*, it is subjected to documentary-like "realism." Diegetically, homosexuality is relegated to the margins, yet shown to be a pervasive, implicit threat registered within the larger crisis in masculinity at the center of so many 1970s films. Not just registering this crisis, New Hollywood films strove to make sense of the shifting, unstable state of masculinity in the decade, and, I argue, used Hitchcock's anxious representation of masculinity in the Cold War era as a template for their own investigations.

Establishing that issues of intertextuality are fundamental to an understanding of New Hollywood film, I claim that the triumvirate of male sexual anxieties—voyeurism, pornography, and homosexuality—at the center of several significant Hitchcock films became newly relevant in 1970s filmmaking. Comparing Hitchcock's *Rope*, *Strangers on a Train*, *Rear Window*, *The Man Who Knew Too Much*, *Vertigo*, and *Psycho* to important 1970s-era films, I argue that New Hollywood filmmakers seized upon Hitchcock's radical decentering of heterosexual male dominance, devising contemporary narratives of heterosexual male ambivalence that allowed for, at times depended on, an investment in same-sex desire as well as an awareness of its dangerous, pernicious seductions.[14] Homophobia in both Hitchcock and the New Hollywood is informed by an attendant fascination with the homoerotic that emerges from scenes of gender crisis and disorganization that are rife in both the Cold War and New Hollywood eras. The question of Hitchcock's intertextual relationship to the New Hollywood is intricately large—an entire book could be written on the formal transmission, uses, innovations, and developments of Hitchcock's aesthetics and techniques in 1970s filmmaking practice. And, to be sure, the question of the representation of gender, sexuality, and also race and class in Hitchcock's films and those of the New Hollywood will continue to demand a great deal more attention and expansion than I can provide here. By considering some very specific issues—namely voyeurism, homosexuality, and pornography—as overlapping concerns in Hitchcock and the New Hollywood, and how these relate to masculinity, I believe that I am opening up a discussion that will continue in myriad ways, not just in my own work but in that which will follow it.

The genre film emerges as a particularly interesting and useful form of queer address. While genre per se, treated by many critics over the years, is not my chief focus here, it is important to note that it is in the genre film—horror, suspense, comedy, the western—that a queer presence exerts a particularly insistent while almost always allegorical power. What unites the majority of the films that I discuss in this book is that they are works within a genre Hitchcock innovated: the psychosexual thriller. (I also discuss De Palma's early comedies.) This queer presence emanates from the points at which normative masculinity breaks down, falters in its own performance. What I call elsewhere "gender protest"—a resistance to or a collapse in gendered identity—opens up possibilities for non-normative desire as well. Scenes of gender and sexual crisis—and American masculinity just about always seems to be in crisis—open up possibilities for queer desire, but the crisis itself often seems to emerge out of a conflict over sexuality.

Inordinately and provocatively concerned with gender—its boundaries, its performance, its pressures, its development, its impact, its endurance—genre makes up its own rules, often existing outside of and venturing to places untraveled by realistic modes of narrative production. The special nature of the genre world, the ways in which it structures reality as an emanation of a particular sensibility unique to itself, allows for an unusual range of desires and anxieties to be suggested and suggestively present. Freed from the strictures of realism, genre allows for the testing of social and logical limits in ways that enable queer potentialities.

Be it the shape-shifting capacities of a sci-fi alien, the undead regenerative power of the horror monster, or the propriety-blasting excessiveness of gross-out comedy, the propensities of genre film for the defiance of social and natural laws make it a fertile, perhaps ideal place for transgressions against the cultural codes that regulate both gender and sexual identity, as well as sites for the exploration of anxieties over these codes.

Moreover, I argue here that it is often the films deemed most problematic, even offensive; the representations that trigger the most controversy and condemnation; the directors whose offscreen reputations get read into their work in ways that make their work indefensible to many, that on occasion make the boldest and most challenging statements about gendered identity, in particular about hegemonic masculinity, which they very often undermine if not altogether topple. The negative images—of women, queers, and other races—that have been the preoccupation of identity politics and other forms of activism have very often been more revealing, urgent, poignant, and exciting than the concomitantly bland, anodyne, safe, "progressive" image of oppressed identities. This book challenges the "positive images" argument—the insistence that images of underrepresented and oppressed minorities must be positive—that has blocked understanding and appreciation of all of the works under discussion here.

That startling, framed negative image of the woman in Jeff's apartment is so much more arresting, bewildering, and provocative than that stack of magazines with her normal, sunny, "positive" image on them. Taking this pointed contrast as a defining allegory, this study explores a variety of negative portrayals. Hitchcock's representation of women and queer subjects; De Palma films and their representation of women; *Taxi Driver* and its purported misogyny and racism; William Friedkin's apparently deeply homophobic *Cruising*—negative images all—are reconsidered for their political value and aesthetic importance. While Hitchcock is solidly still established as "the Master," and in some ways needs very little critical help to be taken seriously, I will establish here that his representation of femininity and queerness still needs more illumination. While *Taxi Driver* is certainly a famous, iconic film, it has been faulted for its representation of femininity and racial difference. De Palma's films, though given very serious treatment by Eyal Peretz in 2008 and the subject of a major retrospective at BAM (the Brooklyn Academy of Music) overseen by the film director Noah Baumbach in April of 2011, continue to need critical reevaluation, now more than ever. Peretz, despite the strengths of his study, runs the risk of seriously distorting De Palma's work, particularly in that he overlooks almost entirely the psychosexual themes at their center. And though Friedkin's *Cruising* is no longer the reviled work it once was, I believe that careful reexamination of it reveals not only a less homophobic film than it was once perceived to be, but also a resonant exploration of the psychosexual foundations of homophobia.

Defining the New Hollywood and Redefining Film Authorship 13

Before proceeding to the book proper, it is necessary to define my use of the term "the New Hollywood," a controversial concept within studies of Hollywood film of the 1960s and 1970s. As Derek Nystrom helpfully lays these controversies out,

> The mid-1970s . . . gave birth to the New Hollywood, which established what Thomas Schatz calls "the blockbuster syndrome," in which high-budget, high-concept, saturation-booked, multimedia-marketed, spectacle-oriented films (such as Jaws [1975] and Star Wars [1977]) provided, as they continue to provide, the U.S. film industry with at least some of the economic stability it lost after the end of the old studio system. Other critics, of course, emphasize an earlier, different New Hollywood, the so-called Hollywood Renaissance of Francis Ford Coppola, Martin Scorsese, and Robert Altman, and others. For these critics, the years between 1967 and 1976 marked a brief but glorious time during which Hollywood produced a body of work as narratively, visually, and politically adventurous as that of the European art cinema—an aesthetic flowering that was cut down to the industry's shift to blockbuster filmmaking.[15]

Nystrom goes on to discuss the confluence of national and class politics in the United States as reflected by these films, an important and often overlooked aspect of their cultural work.

As Robert Kolker puts it, *Bonnie and Clyde* "opened the bloodgates" to a new era of graphic cinematic realism.[16] For my purposes, the New Hollywood signifies the period of Hollywood filmmaking from Arthur Penn's controversial breakthrough hit *Bonnie and Clyde* (1967) to the commercial and critical failure of De Palma's *Blow Out* (1981), which signaled the demise of publically championed personal filmmaking as resonantly as Penn's film did a new public appreciation for such personal visions and for new cinematic truths.

I think it's misleading to cut off the period of the New Hollywood at the point where the blockbuster began to appear. Spielberg's *Jaws*, for example, is a spiky and arresting work, and his even more spectacularly blockbuster-ish *Close Encounters of the Third Kind* (1977) is as mesmerizingly "personal" as key works of the early 1970s. As the example of Coppola's first two *Godfather* (1972, 1974) films enduringly confirms, blockbusters were capable of being expressively idiosyncratic. More importantly, the New Hollywood period signifies an era in which self-consciously quirky, singular, vexing movies were sought out and commercially supported by the public. Often times, the films that excited audiences did so, in their eyes, strictly as commercial entertainments—I doubt that most people going to see *Carrie* (1976) or *Saturday Night Fever* (1977) believed they were in for serious works of art. Nevertheless, the New Hollywood period reflects an openness to the personal vision that was never seen before and has not quite been seen since.

14

The failure of De Palma's deeply personal *Blow Out*—the ur-example of the potentialities of the thriller form—seems to me particularly evocative. The film teems with many preoccupations of the films of the 1970s—paranoia, conspiracy, political scandals, and graphic sexual images. And like many 1970s films, it is a downbeat film with a sad (deeply sad, to be sure) ending. I am fairly convinced that if *Blow Out* had come out in the 1970s, it would have been more successful. By the 1980s, family entertainment, goofy comedy, and cartoonishly hypermasculine stars and action films were beginning to rule the day, a reign that endures. This is not to suggest that plenty of good-to-great films were not released in the 1980s, and, of course, after this decade, only to suggest that the 1970s were a far more sustained period of urgent cinematic work.

In many ways, the chief legacy of Hitchcock in the New Hollywood is his trick of combining idiosyncratic and artistic filmmaking with commercial savvy. Some of the films of the 1970s, distinctively made by creative and singular personalities, also managed to be wildly entertaining. I would argue that this is Hollywood's most distinctive contribution to world cinema—the work of serious and demanding art that is also a work of pleasurable and heady entertainment. Unabashedly I remain in the mode of critics who see the New Hollywood as an aesthetic Renaissance, as my readings will, I have no doubt, evince.

In a wonderful assessment of the significance of Tom Gunning's work on Fritz Lang, Adam Lowenstein writes, during the course of a reading of Hitchcock's *Frenzy*, that the significance of film authorship lies in

> interpretive practice for the audience, and for the critic. The author exists as "an invitation to reading . . . precisely poised on the threshold of the work, evident in the film itself, but also standing outside it, absent except in the imprint left behind." What anchors Gunning's study is the firm belief that reading this imprint constitutes a valuable act of scholarship, one that allows audiences and critics to engage authorship by detecting interwoven patterns across a director's oeuvre—an encounter not with the biographical author, but with the "language of cinema" as negotiated between viewer and director. In other words, the author's revenge is not reasserting absolute mastery over the meaning of his or her films, but suggesting a set of terms, a number of possible identifications, with which audiences make meaning from those films. To take these identifications seriously as a critic does not automatically denote ideological irresponsibility, where cinema's inscription in larger discourses is simply ignored—instead, it attends to the complexity of acts of reading within such discourses, where cinema's coming-into-being between director and viewer is a living negotiation rather than a predetermined certainty.[17]

This passage seems to me so poignantly apt and so incisively true that I offer it as a description of the spirit in which the present book was written.

As I discuss at greater length in Chapter 3, film studies has largely moved away from the aesthetic and from the model of evaluative criticism—the writings of Robin Wood being the pinnacle of this critical model. Film studies has instead embraced the non-aesthetic, pursuing a cultural studies model in which either the modes of film production or the implications these modes have for viewing practices become the central focus. In terms of the latter, these questions are often embedded not only in ideological concerns but also assumptions about the ideological dispositions of the reader—which is to say, properly leftist ideological dispositions. Or, as in the case of the post-theory school, the question of aesthetics assumes a new and binding importance, but at the cost of resolutely eschewing ideological concerns.

In my view, these two main directions in film studies are both frustrating and worrisome. In many ways the present book is an attempt at an intervention. While I do not agree with all of his positions—I am particularly opposed to his restrictive "therapeutic" model of film, which leads him to undervalue films such as Hitchcock's masterpiece *The Birds* (1963)—Robin Wood remains, for me, the gold standard of film criticism. He was a critic who was able to bring ideological concerns to bear on his analyses of film while also being critical and evaluative and, perhaps most resonantly, deeply personal.

At the same time, the writing of Pauline Kael remains a touchstone. As will become quite clear, I very frequently disagree with Kael's positions. I even disagree with her specific defenses of Brian De Palma, a foundation that few of us who write appreciatively about De Palma would be able to do without. I find her dismissal of Hitchcock's importance as a serious filmmaker—as opposed to being an expert entertainer, which Kael did celebrate him as—frustrating. Most of all, I find that Kael was at times perversely indifferent to the political ramifications of works (except when she wasn't, which could lead to penetrating political analysis, as in the case of her review of the 1971 Don Siegel film *Dirty Harry*).

Kael is influential to me because of her openness to art and the experiences of moviegoing. Academia remains, dare I say it, a bastion of the middlebrow elitism that Kael challenged throughout her career. To my mind, the "positive images" argument stems, though complexly and not in clear-cut ways, from this middlebrow stance, though in a much more evolved form. Wood and Kael are an emboldening yin and yang, he providing the seriousness and the scrupulousness, she the charm, sexiness, and play that I believe are also endemic to the moviegoing experience. (Of course, his wit and her seriousness have been undervalued.) Throughout this book, as I attempt to navigate controversies in critical practice, these critics will be my guiding stars.

Chapter Descriptions

While many Hitchcock films lend themselves to my thesis, in Chapter 1 I begin with a discussion of a film that has not been commonly read as significant to Hitchcock's queer themes: Hitchcock's 1956 remake of his original *The Man Who Knew Too Much* (1934). I discuss two major aspects of the film: the allegorical depiction of homoerotic encounters—in a word, cruising—through espionage; and the woman's position, figured as both paranoid and astute, within frameworks of simultaneously explicit and disavowed knowledge of homosexuality. The film submits the normative model of the heterosexual couple to a rigorous analysis that entails explorations of each member of the couple's respective struggles with gender and sexual expectations. The film allegorizes homosexuality as both a threat to and a potential freedom from the strictures of normative gender identity against which both of the protagonists chafe.

I then turn, in the next two chapters, to *Psycho*. My reading of *Psycho* is central to the claims I make about the relationship between Hitchcock and the New Hollywood. I argue that *Psycho* brings into much clearer articulation the themes of voyeurism, homosexuality, and pornographic viewing that had been developing in Hitchcock since at least *Rear Window*. It is precisely this welter of psychosexual disturbances that informs the representation of masculinity in films by De Palma, Scorsese, Friedkin, and others.

In Chapter 2, I discuss Hitchcock's characteristic use of the double and how he deploys this Expressionist figure in his depiction of the confrontation between Norman Bates and Sam Loomis. In contrasting these male characters, one representative of sexually suspect psychosis, the other of gendered and sexual normalcy, Hitchcock blurs the lines between them, creating effects that will inform future depictions of American masculinity. I also discuss the effects created by crosscutting the men's encounter with Lila Crane's exploration of the Bates house. While Lila Crane has been read positively as a lesbian character, and also as Carol Clover's prototype for the "Final Girl," I demonstrate here that Lila is a more ambiguous figure, tied to social repression and the law.

In Chapter 3, I discuss *Psycho* as a key text in the development of mainstream pornography. Here, my focus is on Norman's voyeuristic staring at the undressing Marion Crane. Just as the book without a title on its spine that Lila Crane examines in Norman Bates's bedroom evokes pornographic viewing, so too does Norman's spying on Marion before she takes her infamous shower. Infusing these pornographic motifs with additional levels of intensity and dread was the increasingly public threat of homosexuality within the Cold War context in which Hitchcock's related themes gained a new, ominous visibility. What emerges in *Psycho* is a tripartite monster—voyeurism-homosexuality-pornography, a cluster of psychosexual anxieties that would prove to be of enduring influence precisely as this cluster. Hitchcock's film is crucial in linking an emergent homosexual identity to a new kind of pornographic masculinity enabled by the increasing prominence of pornography in American life.

In Chapter 4, my focus is on Brian De Palma, his significance as a director who very self-consciously reworks Hitchcock's films, the critical reception of De Palma's work, and, most centrally, on three early De Palma films—*Greetings* (1968), *Hi, Mom!* (1970), and *Get to Know Your Rabbit* (1972). I read these films in light of De Palma's interest in the dynamics of the homosocial, an interest that permeates his body of work. While this critical perspective does not settle the question of De Palma's purported misogyny, it does contextualize it. De Palma's overarching interest in male relations is a key aspect of the political critique of patriarchal masculinism in his films. Though made before his Hitchcockian phase, in these comedies De Palma already begins working through the concerns that define the later films: voyeurism, sadism, betrayal, misogyny, and the role played by pornography in the shaping and the experience of male subjectivity. Revisiting the early work of Judith Butler, I argue that De Palma presages Butler's key paradigms: that gender is a performance that functions through reiteration and citation, and that homosexuality plays a key cultural role as an imitative copy to a straight original.

17

By examining the relationship an embattled and ostensibly straight masculinity has to the larger culture in De Palma's draft-dodger Vietnam War–era comedies, I make the case that De Palma's films illuminate the precarious psychic structures of white straight manhood, which can only be maintained as an intelligible identity through homosocialized rituals in which homosexuals, women, and non-whites are rendered perpetual threats to white-male group identity. De Palma's treatment of women, I argue, must be understood within these larger schemas of male gendered and sexual anxiety and social conflict.

Chapter 5 offers a critical analysis of, arguably, the greatest film of the 1970s, Martin Scorsese's *Taxi Driver* (1976). While the film has repeatedly attracted critical commentary, I explore some less well-charted aspects of it, in particular its intertextual engagement with Hitchcock, specifically the films *Rear Window*, *Vertigo*, and *Psycho*. *Taxi Driver* rearticulates Hitchcock's themes of a male subjectivity that is indistinguishable from homosexual anxiety and pornographic visual desire. I address the issues of misogyny and racism in the film, challenging the view that the film expresses these attitudes and arguing that, instead, it confronts and grapples with them. I also explore the film's well-known thematization of paranoia while revisiting Freud's tripartite schema of jealousy, homosexuality, and paranoia. I argue that *Taxi Driver* reworks Freud's theory, locating paranoia within anxieties over gender performance and sexuality, not only that of its protagonist but also of the other characters, and a prolonged state of grief that is steeped in gender nonconformity.

Two of the most controversial films to emerge at the end of the New Hollywood era are the focus of the final two chapters. In Chapter 6, I reexamine William Friedkin's film *Cruising* (1980), a film about an undercover New York City detective who investigates a string of murders in the gay sadomasochistic-leather community. Long denounced as a deeply homophobic film, *Cruising* has not been given its critical due until very recently, other than Robin Wood's early defense of it. I argue that, far from being a homophobic work, the film critiques homophobia by pursuing the Hitchcockian play of male doubles in its representation of straight and queer masculinities. The film's constant play between the symbolic and literal is a crucial one. Though its documentary value has been newly appreciated, the film is as determinedly non-mimetic—nonrealistic—as it is self-consciously realistic. To take it as an attempt at a realistic representation of gay life is to ignore the film's much broader exploration of the psychosexual dimensions and foundations of American masculinity. None of this is to say that *Cruising* presents an attractive or nuanced vision of gay life. But within its often-negative portrayal lies something more challenging: a provocation to contemplate queer male desire in unfettered forms within a larger homophobic culture.

In Chapter 7, we return to the cinema of Brian De Palma. De Palma takes the relay between terror and humor in Hitchcock to a new level of postmodern play. But he does more than that—whereas in Hitchcock the humor very strategically alleviates the terror, in De Palma it is the very relationship between terror and humor that becomes the drama. The tension between the two modes is never more fully sustained or thematized than in *Dressed to Kill* (1980), a film that self-consciously reworks Psycho by drawing out its pornographic themes. Revisiting the film, often denounced as misogynistic, I discover a playful, moving, and feminist reinterpretation of *Psycho* that focuses on female pleasure, frustration, and sexual independence. In *Psycho*, women are forced to submit to the dictates of capitalism in order to procure marriage (or such is their fantasy), but in *Dressed to Kill* the question of marriage no longer holds sway, and women can act on their desires for sex and money—sometimes with disastrous consequences, but also in ways that defy constrictive cultural constructions of femininity and female sexuality. I address as well issues of De Palma's intertextual cinematic aesthetics and his own version of the feminine versus the queer, a pattern that I argue can be found throughout Hitchcock's work. In De Palma, the feminine versus the queer emerges as a contest between sexually and economically enterprising women and men who are either murderously conflicted by their gender identity or more comfortably defy conventional gender typings. In the Coda, I return to the question of negative images and critical practice.

HITCHCOCK, GENDER, AND THE NEW HOLLYWOOD

CHAPTER ONE

CRUISING, HYSTERIA, KNOWLEDGE
The Man Who Knew Too Much (1956)

C URIOSITY AND SUSPICION, sympathy and distaste, attraction and repulsion: these simultaneously held attitudes inform Alfred Hitchcock's treatment of queer sexuality. While a great deal of ink has
been spilt on the phobic aspects of their depiction, my aim in this
book is to explore the "attraction" side of Hitchcock's representation of queer
characters, often his most interesting, magnetic, sympathetic, and enigmatic. As I
begin to develop here and discuss at greater length in the next chapter, any analysis of queer issues in Hitchcock's work must take into account his representation
of heterosexual femininity—not only because Hitchcock's conflictual identification with his women characters is the most highly charged aspect of his work,
which is to say, its chief point of directorial investment, but also because a telling
competition exists in Hitchcock films between heterosexual women and queer
characters, usually though not always males, though his queer male characters
are my focus here.[1] Locked in a fatal dance of rivalrous desires and ambivalent
sympathies, both strive to gain narrative control while fighting to stay alive. To
discuss the relay between female and homosexual desires is to intervene in the
critical impasses within both feminist and queer theory approaches, which tend
to focus either on Hitchcock's female or his queer characters but rarely discuss
the complex interactions between them. In discussing their intertwining fates, we
gain insights into the director's ambivalent identification with both.

Still contested but generally conceded examples of Hitchcock's homosexual male figures include the lover-killers of *Rope* (1948); Bruno Anthony (Robert Walker) in *Strangers on a Train* (1951); Leonard (Martin Landau) in *North by Northwest* (1959), henchman of the suave villain Vandamm played by James Mason; and, of course, Norman Bates (Anthony Perkins) in *Psycho*. I begin this study, however, with a film that is not commonly read in these terms, *The Man Who Knew Too Much* (1956), an American remake of Hitchcock's original 1934 English film.

The 1956 *Man* covertly evinces the thematic importance of homoerotic attractions and homophobic defenses against them in Hitchcock's work. Once interpreted along these lines, it can also be read as a template for several New Hollywood films of the 1970s, a cinema profoundly influenced by Hitchcock and, like his work, a cinema of paranoia. In particular, the themes of gay-male cruising and also the vulnerability of heterosexual men to being cruised that would be of such fascination to directors like William Friedkin had a surprisingly powerful intertextual precedent in the '56 *Man*. Hitchcock's depiction of normative American masculinity as beset by gendered and sexual anxieties—a thematic element in several of his films—provides a template for the New Hollywood representation of masculinity, which also has implications for the films' analysis of race-related anxieties and conflicts.

In an extraordinary sequence in Hitchcock's undervalued *Torn Curtain* (1966)—linked to *Man '56* and *North by Northwest* (1959) in a homoerotic triptych of Hitchcock scenes from these films in the 1999 art installation *Phoenix Tapes*—Paul Newman's Michael Armstrong, a seeming defector to East Germany and a secret American spy, enters the Museum of East Berlin in order to elude the suspicious bodyguard assigned to watch over him, Gromek (Wolfgang Kieling), a shabby, greasy, oddly endearing man in a leather jacket whose chief attribute is a memorably strained penchant for American slang. Exhibiting the experimental uses of sound that characterize his early films such as *Blackmail* (1929, originally made as a silent film, and then reworked to become England's first talking film), Hitchcock narrows the soundscape down to the deliberate, staccato footsteps of the two men in parodistic pursuit, one of the other, one of escape from the other. Their footsteps hauntingly echo within the strangely empty, depopulated, and vast museum.

Given that Hitchcock attempted to incorporate the homoerotic intrigue of the "Cambridge spies" scandal of 1950s England into *Torn Curtain* but was forced by the studio to drop this theme, his depiction of the two men alone and engaged in shadowy games in the museum can be plausibly read as his attempt to register homoerotic tensions through allegorical means. As Richard Allen has noted, the scene in the museum can be interpreted as a coded depiction of gay-male cruising.[2]

If Hitchcock does indeed represent gay cruising here, as I believe he does, what is particularly notable about the allegory he devises is its staging of queer male desire as oppositional patterns of chase. As Michael Armstrong attempts to elude Gromek, Gromek follows and tries to catch him in the act of counter-spying. The very oppositionality of their movements tells us a great deal about Hitchcock's understanding of what the sexual pursuit of one man by another might look and more importantly *feel* like. On the one hand, their opposed purposes reflect a fundamental conflict, rivalry, alienation, or repulsion. On the other hand, the very oppositionality of their positions can be read as a form of erotic entanglement, warfare, or gamesmanship, the erotically charged relay of pursuit and escape emerging as a metaphorical courtship or a metaphor for desire itself. What helps to keep these themes allegorical is the unthinkability of an actual sexual pairing between the men, the nonstandard physical presence of Kieling in the role of Gromek ensuring this.

If we consider Freud's contention that desire has no object, and the larger psychoanalytic understanding of desire as self-perpetuating, a force that keeps itself

23

The American family confronted by difference on
several levels: *The Man Who Knew Too Much* (1956)

endlessly alive by constantly deferring the achievement of its goals, the men's fruitless chase comes to seem especially significant, an elaborate exercise in desire's constitutional unsatisfiability. As Lee Edelman discusses in Lacanian terms in the context of Hitchcock's *North by Northwest*, "Thus aligned with the law's prohibitions that keep its object out of reach, desire is desire for no object but only, instead, for its own prolongation, for the future itself as libidinal object procured by its constant lack."[3]

As an allegory of desire and its inherent frustrations, the museum sequence in *Torn Curtain* also reflects the homophobic strictures of the era in which the film was made (which is not to suggest an escape from such strictures in our own era). As I will show, the cruising-spying metaphor in *Torn Curtain* has precedents in previous Hitchcock films, especially Hitchcock's second *Man*. This film provides a surprisingly revealing glimpse into the director's attitudes towards homosexual desire and gendered anxieties, generally and within the specific context of the Cold War 1950s. My analysis engages with Robert Corber's work on homoerotic and homophobic tensions in Hitchcock's films of the period, but takes a largely distinct view from Corber's.

Strangers on a Train provides a remarkable precedent for *Man '56* and its elaboration of a pattern of rivalry that, I argue, is essential to Hitchcock films.

As will happen in *Man*, the woman observes—with increasing suspicion, skepticism, frustration, and feelings of genuine unease—the man who is the object of her romantic interest engaging in a mysterious and erotically charged relationship with another man that plays out like a *public* flirtation or a seduction. The woman's triangulated position between two men whose strangely intimate relationship, the intimacy of which each man denies with varying degrees of intensity, she steadfastly and suspiciously observes becomes in both films a key means of perceiving a threatening homoerotic potentiality in everyday relationships between men. In *Strangers*, Guy Haines (Farley Granger) keeps telling his fiancée, the senator's daughter Ann Morton (Ruth Roman), that he "hardly knows" Bruno Anthony (Robert Walker); in *Man*, Ben McKenna (James Stewart) meets Louis Bernard (Daniel Gélin) by chance on a bus on which the McKenna family rides to Marrakech. The woman is shown to be the center of a structure of paranoid knowledge—which she can and cannot possess, which she possesses even as she is told that her suspicions are entirely unfounded—through which the open secret of homosexuality can be simultaneously revealed and denied.

Specifically, the point in Hitchcock's films at which feminist and queer theory concerns most dramatically overlap is in the competition they stage between female and queer characters. The opposition in Hitchcock films between femininity and queer sexuality, staged across his body of work, can be summarized thusly: the independent, unclassifiable young woman vies against a queer character, usually typed as fathomlessly evil, for screen dominance, a struggle appropriately rendered as a battle to the death. *Shadow of a Doubt* (1943) is the most explicit rendering of this implicit struggle.

Something that Lee Edelman does not explore in his provocative but frustrating (for several reasons) reading of *North by Northwest* is that the conflict in the film that motivates Leonard to squash Roger Thornhill's (Cary Grant) hand beneath his feet as Thornhill hangs precariously from a cliff on Mount Rushmore is Leonard's rivalry with Eve Kendall (Eva Marie Saint), an American spy, for the love of the villain Vandamm (the peerlessly urbane James Mason). As happens in *Strangers*, the ostensibly straight man, Vandamm, punches the queer man, Leonard, in the face when the intensity of his desires for the "straight" man becomes too apparent. *"Leonard?"* Vandamm incredulously asks when his henchman points and then fires a gun at him. The gun was Eve's, the same gun she used to throw off suspicions when her cover was blown by "killing" Thornhill, and it fires blanks. Leonard successfully deduces Eve's ruse. Firing the woman's blanks at the

An intimate exchange between *Strangers on a Train*: "From A to G . . . Criss-cross!" Does the inscription on Guy's lighter also stand for "Alfred to Granger"?

object of his desire, Leonard attempts to demonstrate not only the woman's duplicity but also her powerlessness, her lack of phallic potency. At the same time, he shows off what he calls his own "woman's intuition."

When Vandamm punches Leonard, repeating Guy's gesture toward Bruno from *Strangers on a Train*, the act has multivalent force. It seems motivated as much by Leonard's animosity towards Eve as it does by the threatening intensity of his desires for Vandamm (who may feel similarly towards Leonard). Leonard lifts—tears off—the veil of mystery that conceals woman's sexuality and her carnal arts. Woman's vaunted sexual mystery and her seductive powers undergird the entire structure of heterosexual desire, organized around constructions of women's sexuality as enigmatic, hidden, and inscrutable. If female sexual powers can be decoded, so too can the heterosexual sexual order be exposed, undermined, and destabilized. That Leonard has no sympathy for the woman's social position confirms his status as villain, but he pales in this regard to Vandamm, more obviously typed as heterosexual, who immediately decides to throw the exposed woman out of the getaway plane. "Such matters are best disposed of from a great height—over water," Vandamm decisively remarks.

That the pattern of rivalry between heterosexual women and queer characters occurs so frequently in Hitchcock's American films is highly significant; yet it was a theme already present in Hitchcock's English films. In *Murder!* (1930), the innocent heroine sacrificially takes the fall for the murder committed by the man she loves. As most critics have concluded, this film uses race as a metaphor for homosexuality. The murderer's shame over his mixed-raced heritage appears to motivate him to commit murder, yet, palpably coded as homosexual, what he seems most acutely conflicted over is his sexuality. There is an extraordinary sequence during a trapeze act in which ghostly images of the falsely accused woman, Diana Baring (Norah Baring) and the man trying to prove her innocence, the juror Sir John Menier (Herbert Marshall, who would go on to be a dependable support to Bette Davis), besiege the murderer's consciousness and, apparently, conscience, since he plummets to his death. These images, paired expressionistic close-ups of Man and Woman, suggest a psychic heterosexual normativity that cannot be resisted or ignored and that ultimately imposes a kind of self-immolating order on the queer murderer. Hitchcock's American films consistently stage the battle adumbrated in *Murder!* between heterosexual female desire and queer desire. There are variations to this general theme, of course, but in just about every significant Hitchcock film from *Rebecca* (1940) to *Torn Curtain* (1966) this conflict—which I call *the feminine versus the queer*—informs the narrative. (Queer must be taken loosely and capaciously as a term: it can mean homosexually inclined, but generally refers to anything that can be seen as non-normative, resistant to the trappings of the social order, to normative structures such as marriage and family, linked to productivity, rationality, and smoothly functioning cultural systems.)

In *Rebecca*, the heroine's movement towards heterosexual fulfillment, becoming a successful wife, is consistently thwarted by the housekeeper Mrs. Danvers. In *Shadow of a Doubt*, the heroine discovers that her mysterious uncle is a serial killer: her love for him is confronted by his own deeply held, murderous misogyny. In *Spellbound* (1945), the young psychiatrist Constance Petersen and the aged and secretly sinister Dr. Murchison war over the fate of a young, tormented, beautiful man, John Ballantyne. Made a year later, *Notorious* makes its heroine's desire for the male protagonist the chief drama of the film, a desire which her sexually ambivalent husband seems not only to share but in which he wishes to partake, commenting himself on how handsome he finds Mr. Devlin (Cary Grant). In *The Paradine Case* (1947), a carnal and duplicitous woman who has murdered her husband appears to compete with a man who, it is strongly suggested, was her husband's wartime lover. The complementary films *Rope* (1948) and *Strangers on a Train* (1951) each star gay actors and each concern a homosexual relationship that is shown to be in opposition to a preexisting heterosexual one. In *Dial M for Murder* (1954), the scene in which the jealous husband blackmails a shady ex-classmate into murdering his wife is suffused with homoerotic intrigue and suggests a different kind of blackmail, the blackmailing of a closeted homosexual. Blackmail comes up again in *Rear Window*, released the same year, in which James Stewart feels erotic passion for Grace Kelly only when she joins him in his zeal to expose a murderer: the killer Thorwald believes that James Stewart's Jeff is attempting to blackmail him. The 1956 remake of Hitchcock's original 1934 version of *The Man Who Knew Too Much*, as I will show, creates a conflict between the shadowy intrigue of a spy attempting to seduce an American physician into his covert operations and the knowing, suspicious resistance of his wife. *Vertigo* (1958) is an extraordinarily complex negotiation of the feminine versus the queer. In this film, one man's false narrative entraps a failed heterosexual couple—Scottie and Madeleine/Judy—in its duplicitous logic; one could argue that the hero falls in love primarily with another *man's* narrative, the villain's plot; the woman, doubly victimized, must negotiate both of their rivalrous desires. As I have suggested, in *North by Northwest*, the smoothly charming villain's allegiances appear torn between his duplicitous double-agent girlfriend and his homosexual henchman Leonard; in the meantime, the film renders its presumably heterosexual hero a profound blank, a man without qualities easily mistaken for someone else, the kicker being that this someone, given the name George Kaplan, doesn't even exist. *Psycho* (1960) is the ultimate version of the feminine versus the queer, as the film violently bifurcates from a feminine into a queer narrative. If, as Lee Edelman has suggested in *No Future*, the titular avian menace of Hitchcock's film *The Birds* (1963) suggests queer sexuality, their opposition to the heroine's desire for the hero certainly fits neatly into the pattern we have been developing; moreover, the fair lady/dark lady contrast in the film between Melanie Daniels (Tippi

Hedren) and Annie Hayworth (Suzanne Pleshette) has striking lesbian overtones, especially as they emanate from Pleshette's ambiguous, husky-voiced sexuality. In the 1964 *Marnie*, the troublesome character of Lil Mainwaring (Diane Baker) was a homosexual man in the original novel by Winston Graham; certainly, her opposition to Marnie in the film retains a queer dimension in the character, as dark Lil seems excessively preoccupied with and fascinated by blonde Marnie even as she schemes against her. And in *Torn Curtain*, the famous scene in which Paul Newman and a farmer woman kill the agent Gromek, who discovers the protagonist's secret identity as a counterspy, is preceded, as I suggested, by one of the most exquisite renderings of homosexual cruising in Hitchcock's canon, Gromek's pursuit of Michael Armstrong in the museum. The murder of Gromek is an allegory of the annihilation of queer villainy, by the feminine, on the one hand, and by the heterosexual couple, on the other. The pattern of rivalry between a threateningly independent femininity and an often villainous queer sexuality emerges as the defining psychic structure of Hitchcock's films.[4] The implications of this pattern are broad, and continue to resonate in critical discussions of the films. The pattern has its masculine version as well—*Strangers on a Train*, *Rope*, the "Ben" narrative of *The Man Who Knew Too Much*, *North by Northwest*—but it is never as emotionally resonant because of Hitchcock's far more cathected identification with the female character. Throughout his films, Hitchcock stages a peculiar tragedy: the inability of transgressive female and queer energies to coalesce and correspond, to form a unified resistance to the normativity that threatens them both. The films foreground Gramsci's theory of hegemony: minority groups pitted against each other so that no unified opposition to structures of power can be organized.

The complexity of Hitchcock's treatment of homosexuality has not always been apparent to critics. Favorably discussing *Murder!*, Eric Rohmer and Claude Chabrol, in their famous book *Hitchcock: The First Forty-four Films*, write:

> In *Murder!* the homosexual kills when unmasked. Unlike the protagonists of *Rope*, or Bruno Anthony (Robert Walker) in *Strangers on a Train*, he considers himself abnormal and is aware that his vice is a defect. But he is also incapable of loving, and he is interested only in escaping the consequences of his crime. When Hitchcock gets around to probing the problem of homosexuality in the two other films, we will become aware that his condemnation of homosexuality is justly based on the impossibility of true homosexual love: since this love is only an imitation, it is condemned to nonreciprocity. Diana [the wrongfully imprisoned heroine of the film] loves the homosexual, since she allows herself to be convicted in his stead, but the homosexual doesn't love her, since he permits her to do so.[5]

28

That *Murder!*'s villain is only concerned with escaping the consequences of his crime is an arguable point, but that is another matter. One of the chief goals of my work on Hitchcock is to problematize the Rohmer-Chabrol reading of homosexuality in his work, to say nothing of their reading of homosexuality. In key ways, Hitchcock's treatment of homosexuality resists the disappointingly homophobic cast of these famous critics who would become even more famous directors. If we owe much to the *Cahiers du Cinéma* critics who initially called attention to Hitchcock's brilliance as a filmmaker, they also have much to answer for in their portrait of Hitchcock's moralizing opposition to homosexuality.

But accounting for the depth and sympathy in Hitchcock's treatment of homosexuality is no easy task, since these dispositions are inextricable from his negative images of queer figures. Overall, it is more accurate to say that the homosexual figure is treated ambivalently, rather than as a black hole of amorality and sociopathic indifference, in Hitchcock's films. The sheer prevalence of homosexual figures and tropes in them attests to the films' insistence on representing alternatives to dominant, normative codes of heterosexual representation. The point that I would emphasize is that homosexuality as a threatening possibility, particularly in Hitchcock films from the 1950s forward, emerges as a reflection of larger fears related to normative gender roles and sexual identities—that both were breaking down and losing their structural integrity.

Man '56 and Transatlantic 1950s Homophobia

In the 1934 version of *Man*, an English couple, Bob and Jill Lawrence (Leslie Banks and Edna Best), are vacationing in St. Moritz, Switzerland, when their daughter Betty (Nova Pilbeam) is kidnapped. The kidnapping of a child during a family holiday is also at the center of the 1956 *Man*, but this time the family is vacationing in Morocco (on their way to Marrakech at the start of the film) and the kidnapped child is a boy rather than a girl. The remake has been described by Donald Spoto as "Hitchcock's warmest film . . . really full of love."[6] Genuine emotional warmth is quite palpable here; indeed, at key points the film is emotionally overwhelming. But a clinical quality, an attitude of detachment, also informs it.

This attitude comes through most strongly in Hitchcock's treatment of the relationship between the protagonists, the married couple at the center of the film, submitted to analysis as a heterosexual couple, as gendered individuals, and as parents. A preoccupation with the disturbing aspects of the couple and the family links both the '34 and '56 versions of *Man*, but these disturbances are explored much more directly in the latter. Through its depiction of the McKenna family—Ben, a physician (James Stewart), Jo, a famous singer turned housewife (Doris Day), and Hank, their son (Christopher Olsen)—the remake registers the gendered anxieties inherent in national constructions of the American family in the 1950s, refusing any stable understanding of the model. Rather than present-ing the family as a "normal" one whose coherence is disrupted by the interna-tional espionage plot that ensnares them, the film presents the family as always already incoherent, beset by anxieties that are not contained by the reclamation of the kidnapped child and the happy closure it ostensibly provides. The perva-sive anxieties are already very much present before the disaster of the kidnapping ensues.

In my view, the film foregrounds the heterosexual couple's dissatisfactions with their own subservience to compulsory gender roles and uses the threat of queer sexuality as a metaphor for these dissatisfactions. While the film's queer metaphor has a homophobic dimension, I argue that, in showing that regimes of gendered and sexual normativity are intimately *complicit* with queer sexuality, Man makes the case that institutionalized heterosexuality organizes itself around the rigorous policing of both homosexual threat and any deviation from steadfast codes of gendered identity. Man suggests that gendered normativity is a compul-sory social construction, a constantly embattled state that must be perpetually defended and scrupulously maintained.

An important aspect of the film's critique of normative gender roles is its con-struction of motherhood, which critics such as Corber have read as misogynis-tic. Disputing this view, I offer a close reading of the film's depiction of Jo as a mother, arguing that the representation of her maternal ambivalence registers dissatisfactions with normative gender roles assigned to women. Analogously, Ben's growing attraction-repulsion to encroaching homoerotic energies signals discontentment with postwar codes of American masculinity. Narratives of crisis and disaster, such as the kidnapping here, open up new avenues of possibility, as Patrick E. Horrigan observes. "Catastrophe," he writes, "makes people free to discover capacities within themselves that were, until then, unimaginable."[7] The disaster in Man allows Ben and, much more resonantly, Jo to discover such as yet unimagined capacities in themselves, a process of discovery with great relevance to the themes of gendered and sexual discontentment that are central to the film.

As with many Hitchcock films, Man '56 figures homosexuality as a pervasive, gnawing anxiety within dominant culture. The anxious ambivalence towards mothering from Jo and the homoeroticism that threatens to engulf Ben do not exist in isolation in this film; rather, they form a relay that positions Jo, Ben, and the film itself at an alienated remove from the strict adherence to gender and sexual norms that are seemingly embodied and upheld by families like the McK-ennas. Given Hitchcock's oeuvre-long fixation on both the terrors of American Mommyism and the threat of homoerotic passion, it is unsurprising that Man would foreground and link both themes.

Man's subtextual queer themes reflect and may even be a response to actual transatlantic political events. Homosexuality in the United Kingdom would not be decriminalized (for adults over 21) until 1967. The 1950s were a time of great and shifting struggles for gay rights movements in both the United States and the UK, as "homophile" movements to end homophobic oppression gained momentum while diligent campaigns, typified by McCarthyism in the United States, specifically targeted gays as enemies of the state who must be ruthlessly routed out and punished. In 1953, the trial and eventual imprisonment of Edward Montagu (the 3rd Baron Montagu of Beaulieu), Michael Pitt-Rivers, and Peter Wildeblood for committing acts of homosexual indecency caused an uproar that led to the establishment, by the Home Office minister Sir Hugh Lucas-Tooth, of a 1954 committee to examine homosexuality. The Wolfenden Committee's report, which came out in 1957, recommended the decriminalization of homosexuality, but this would not occur until ten years later.[8] In the United States of the 1950s, prominent people such as the great literary critic Newton Arvin (who, at one point, had a romantic relationship with Truman Capote) were persecuted because of their homosexuality.[9]

Most relevantly for the present argument, important linkages exist among spying, espionage, blackmail, and homosexuality, linkages that the 1950s rendered intensely visible. In the early '50s, two members of the "Cambridge spies," Guy Burgess and Donald Maclean (the others were Kim Philby and Anthony Blunt, an art historian who advised Queen Elizabeth), key figures in British intelligence who were also secret spies for the KGB, defected to Russia, which an embarrassed England grudgingly revealed to the public. Burgess and Blunt were homosexual; though a married and ostensibly heterosexual man, Maclean had many homosexual affairs. The scandalous defection of Burgess and McLean crystallized popular associations among homosexuality, Communism, and treason, triggering witch hunts for gay men in the British foreign service and intelligence agencies. England's gay panic cross-fertilized with the United States's own, influencing U.S. McCarthyism, equally determined to rout out hidden gay employees and other enemies of the state. As I will demonstrate, *Man '56* can be read as an allegory for national homosexual panic that circulates the public linkages among homosexuality, espionage, and a fearful foreignness.

Leaving Normal: The Perversity of an American Family

In the first scene of the film, on the bus to Marrakech, the family is shown sitting at the back of the bus, in apparent unified contentment. Little Hank then wanders up the aisle. The bus comes to an abrupt stop, and Hank, about to fall, grabs onto an Arab woman's veil and accidentally yanks it off. The ruckus that ensues between the irate Arab husband and the McKenna parents, Ben and Jo, is smoothed over by Louis Bernard (Daniel Gélin), a darkly suave Frenchman who, like the English couple the Draytons, will defy expectations. The failure of communication between the McKennas and the Muslim man is the first of many such moments that emphasize the tendency for the main characters to find themselves at cross-purposes with their surroundings, the people they encounter, and with each other. Once the Arab man has been quieted down and returns to his wife, Bernard explains the situation to the McKennas, informing them that Hank violated the religious sanctity of the Muslim couple by exposing the wife's face. This episode sets the plot in motion, providing a means whereby Bernard and the family can meet. But it plays a subtle symbolic role as well—this film will be an extended act of revealing "true" faces, perhaps especially the woman's; of tearing off the veils of social identity.

With subtlety, the film suggests the emotional gulfs that *already* exist among the McKennas before Hank is kidnapped. Unusual, discordant small moments abound in this film. The seismic tensions within the adventurous cheer of this American family on a holiday would appear to have their roots in the essential conflict between Ben and Jo—formerly Jo Conway, a musical theater star who performed in major cities such as New York, London, and Paris—over where the family will live: Indianapolis, their current home where Ben is a family doctor, or New York City, the location of Jo's successful former career.

Ben asks Bernard why the Muslim man was so angry, and after Bernard offers an explanation, Jo turns to her son and says: *"Hank?"* This moment is only a flyspeck, yet it is notably odd. Is Jo, however mildly, chiding Hank, though he has only inadvertently caused harm? As Olsen plays him or, more likely, as he was directed by Hitchcock to appear, Hank actually looks terrified by the severity of his mistake. (He gets over this fairly quickly, making jokes about inviting the Frenchman Bernard over to devour the troublesome snails in their American backyard: "We did everything we could to get rid of them. We never thought of a Frenchman.") And since the McKennas themselves appear to have no knowledge of Muslim customs or of the specific nature and gravity of what Hank accidentally did, it is unlikely that Hank would have known to avoid doing such a thing. In expressing astonishment at Hank's actions, Jo implicitly assigns the blame to her child while absolving herself and Ben of any culpability. A surprising sense of disjunction emerges—each member of this family is on their own as a social agent. Notably, Ben and Jo will be decisively separated at one point, each pursuing their own courses of action. Jo's independence will be treated with equal measures of suspicion and sympathy. The suggestion made mildly here that Jo focuses more on her image than her child, is more interested in her own status *as* social agent than in her role as doctor's wife and mother, only grows stronger over the course of the film and deepens the pathos of the famous Albert Hall sequence.[10] If the film consistently oscillates between judgment and empathy in its treatment of Jo, an ambivalence towards female agency characteristic of most Hitchcock films, at the same time it is in Jo that the film finds its emotional center and dramatic focal point, Ben receding in importance as she gains depth and complexity.

Part of the film's simultaneously essentialist and subversive representation of Jo is its investment in her "feminine intuition," as it was once called. Unlike affable but apparently innocent Ben, she immediately detects a disparity between Bernard's deft inquisitiveness—his skill at drawing out information from Ben in their very first conversation about where the McKennas live, their professions, and their travel itinerary (spanning Europe and Morocco)—and what he is himself willing to reveal. As James Stewart plays Ben, his open willingness to discuss their personal lives has an undertone of panic—but it is a panic that derives from an eagerness to please and probably to impress a sophisticated European, not from an awareness of having his privacy skillfully invaded. The perspicuity with which Jo deduces that there's something "funny" about Bernard is concomitant with her instantaneous alarm at him. She has an uncanny acuity—from her own embattled position within the film's difficult negotiation with modern American femininity—for apprehending the multiple layers of intrigue in seemingly casual conversation, for sensing the "strangeness" within Bernard's solicitation of Ben. The film's political MacGuffin, the assassination/espionage plot, is rather evanescently sketched here, even for a Hitchcock film. The many levels of intrigue at work suggest a larger network of unclassifiable, unnamable tensions. *Man* endorses Jo's suspicions by demonstrating that the duplicity she quickly perceives is so deeply prevalent within the narrative as to be all-encompassing. Given that Hitchcock made this film after *Strangers on a Train* (1951), with its obvious homosexual themes, it is not implausible that some awareness existed of the homoerotic valences of a conversation between a "normal American male" and a stranger on a moving vehicle. The film's construction of homosexual threat is enmeshed with its themes of exoticized foreignness and the espionage plot. As I have been suggesting, a tension between an independent woman and a queer character, usually villainous, informs the Hitchcock film. In *Man*, Jo's femininity opposes—and competes against—the increasingly intense and threatening shadowy world of secrets and lies represented initially by Bernard and his homoerotic seduction of Ben.

For the most part, Bernard addresses Ben, not Jo, in his initial conversation with the family on the bus. While Bernard is, here, attempting to get information about the McKennas in order to determine if they are the "suspicious married couple" involved in the assassination plot that Bernard, a French spy, is attempting to foil, in retrospect the scene plays out like a seduction by one man who possesses knowledge of another man who does not. As Eve Kosofsky Sedgwick so brilliantly demonstrated, epistemological matters—knowledge and knowing-ness—are crucial to cultural understandings of homosexuality.[11] In certain re-spects, Bernard, right before Jo's eyes, seduces her husband. This seduction of the American innocent by the attractive foreigner has been a common theme in American culture, present in such classic nineteenth-century works as Haw-thorne's *The Marble Faun* and Henry James novels such as *The American* and *The Ambassadors*; fascinatingly, it has its most indelible cinematic realization in such lonely-spinster-awakened-by-love films as *Now, Voyager* (1942) and *Summertime* (1955). Ben doesn't "get it," but it would appear that Jo does.

I argue that this male-male version of the American innocent/foreign seduc-er theme can be read as a metaphor for homosexual cruising, a theme that is extremely important to the film, which links espionage and spy-game double-dealing with behaviors, mannerisms, and actions that resemble underground same-sex practices. The seductive sharing of secrets between Ben and Bernard resembles coded homoerotic exchange in the Cold War era. Bernard's interest in and questioning of Ben allegorizes homosexual cruising, with its imperceptible-to-the-untrained codes and decoding of other's signals. Clearly, Jo isn't foolish to be suspicious. But what exactly is the nature of her suspicions? "He told us nothing about himself but you told him everything about us," Jo testily observes to Ben. In terms of national sexual and gendered stereotypes, Ben becomes the all-American country rube easily preyed upon by the machinations of the darkly knowing, elegant, polished, skillful, well-traveled foreign seducer. The film draws on longstanding distinctions between American normality and European deca-dence, while also devising a male-male version of the traditional gothic seduc-tion plot in which a suave and suspect man seduces and ruins a guileless young woman.

Bernard's lack of interest in Jo and adamant fixation on Ben is the chief source of Jo's consternation—a fact cogently observed by Ben himself, who jokingly chides Jo for getting jealous because Bernard isn't paying any attention to *her*. Yet, paranoid though Jo seems from the outset, she is shown to be *always* right. Her canny distrust of not only Bernard but also, initially, of the English couple the Draytons, and her realization that Ambrose Chapel is a physical place, not a per-son, are significant details that demonstrate the acuity of her deductive powers.

Jo crystallizes the validity of the associations Freud made among jealousy, ho-mosexuality, and paranoia. If paranoia, for Freud, was a projection onto others of one's own fear of homosexuality, Jo projects her fear of her husband's possible queer desire outward. Along these lines, these may be Jo's fears about herself as well: when she and Mrs. Drayton exchange looks for the first time, they seem locked into the same chilling, exciting paranoid knowledge (figured in Brenda De

Banzie's piercing, intense gaze) that Ben will experience with the other male characters: the open secret of homosexuality, in its power as such, potentially applies to Jo as much as it does to Ben. One remembers what Louis Bernard says, upon learning that Jo is Day's character's name, not that of her son's: "How *different.*"

From the moment dubious Bernard inserts himself into the McKennas' hetero-familial narrative, the film links tensions between Ben and Jo to a threatening homoeroticism. Bernard introduces this homoerotic threat, but many such threats will infiltrate the couple's seemingly normative and increasingly unstable lives. As a metaphor, the homoerotic synthesizes the deviant energies that threaten to devour the family's wholesome normality (homosexuality therefore emerging as the catch-all category for all manner of deviance and otherness). At the same time, it is, as embodied by Bernard, an alluring and dangerously compelling force to which the apparently all-American Ben, much to Jo's chagrin, is mysteriously and continuously drawn. After the dying Bernard has reached out to Ben, pressing his mouth to Ben's ear, and Ben holds his face in his hands, Ben remarks that he "feels funny. Why did he pick me out to tell?" These lines anticipate the devastating ones Stewart's distraught Scottie will direct at Madeleine in *Vertigo*: "Why did you pick on me? Why me?" In *Man*, this question has a somewhat different valence, though the link with *Vertigo* is that Scottie is also someone picked out for secret purposes by another male (Gavin Elster, the villain). Scottie could almost be registering the kind of alarmed and angry discomfort of the ostensibly heterosexual male who chafes against the erotic interest of the homosexual male. Given the Cold War context of the film, a regime in which deviant sexuality was violently likened to threats against the stability, sanctity, and emotional, physical, and moral health of the nation, these ruptures in normative gendered and sexual identities deepen in significance and demand analysis. When the all-American male is made to feel funny in public by another man who leaves, literally, his mark on him, there is cause for concern.

35

Spy Games and Sexuality

Espionage and other kinds of spy games hinge on covert, clandestine meetings, usually at the expense of heterosexual relations. The classic espionage scene shows the husband/lover secret-spy making an abrupt exit from an intimate scene with a woman, to whom he offers a hasty, flimsy excuse before rushing off to meet his contact, the trench-coated government official who will give him his orders, or the clandestine source, a "Deep Throat," who gives him secret information. This classic espionage scene can be read as a metaphor for the closeted homosexual's clandestine sexual liaisons; if read this way, espionage emerges as an inherently, symbolically queer narrative trope.[12] By showing espionage as an irresistible attraction for Ben, drawn inexorably into its seductive realm, the film metaphorically suggests Ben's growing attraction to secrecy and, by implication, deviant forms of intimacy. *Man*'s linkages between espionage and homoeroticism emerge directly from its Cold War context.

In his 1952 reelection as a senator from Wisconsin, Joseph McCarthy, part of a Republican majority in the Senate but not particularly popular with the new majority leader Robert Taft, was assigned the somewhat lowly chairmanship of the Committee on Government Operations. But McCarthy capitalized on the plush resources of one subcommittee, the "Permanent Subcommittee on Investigations," and exploited its "wide discretionary authority to study such sensitive issues as 'export policy and loyalty' and the 'employment of homosexuals and other sex perverts' in the government."[13] The ruthless and unremitting persecution of homosexuals in Cold War America, embodied in the obsessions of McCarthyism, linked homosexuals to Communists as fellow enemies of the American nation, a linkage with decisive significance for *Man*'s depiction of normative all-American identity imperiled by forces of foreign, queer invasion.

The sexual integrity of the American innocent—usually figured in the Cold War context as a male who could be corrupted by enemy forces—would prove to be a vital national concern with profound implications for homosexuals. Sex held (as it no doubt still does) a vaunted position in the strategies used to recruit traitors against the United States government. Homosexuality was thought to lend itself especially well to potential recruitment: "The potential recruit could be a closet homosexual who recently lost a promotion for reasons that had nothing to do with his sexual choices."[14] In a testimonial sure to succor the worst fantasies of the genuine threats to American life during the Cold War, former KGB Chief of Counterintelligence and Major General Oleg Kalugin wrote of Cold War recruitment of foreigners, "The KGB had a department called Territorial Intelligence whose job was to recruit tourists and foreign businessmen . . . [using two main hooks], illegal currency transactions, and sex. . . . Territorial Intelligence would target a foreigner for recruitment, then introduce him to an attractive Soviet at a bar, a hotel. . . . On the sexual espionage front, we usually got the better of the CIA and . . . the exceptions. Territorial Intelligence also used gay recruits to entrap homosexual foreigners."[15]

As John D'Emilio writes, "[I]n June 1950 the full Senate bowed to mounting pressure and authorized an investigation into the alleged employment of homosexuals 'and other moral perverts' in government." Justifying their decision to bar homosexuals from the government, the committee discussed the reprehensible character of the homosexual, who lacks the "emotional stability of normal persons."

The committee also argued that "sexual perverts" imperiled national security. "The social stigma attached to sex perversion" [ensured] that detection could ruin a person for life. [Hence the tendency for "gangs of blackmailers" to prey on homosexuals.] . . . Espionage agents "can use the same type of pressure to extort confidential information." Immature, unstable, and morally enfeebled by the gratification of their perverted desires, homosexuals lacked the character to resist the blandishments of the spy. They would betray their country . . . rather than live with the consequences of exposure. . . . Besides, the committee concluded, homosexuals "seldom refuse to talk about themselves," and foreign agents willing to embark upon clandestine liaisons could easily extract sensitive information while preserving blackmail as a last resort.[16]

Hitchcock's career-long trope of *Blackmail*—the title of Hitchcock's, and England's, first sound film, from 1929—finds new resonance in *Man* as the threat of exposed homosexuality, not just in terms of Ben's identity but in the myriad ways in which the open secret of homosexuality, as D. A. Miller and Eve Kosofsky Sedgwick, respectively, developed the term, threatens to pour out, from multiple sources, before him and Jo. And in Ben's increasingly hysterical behavior, he threatens to relinquish the "emotional stability" that lends creditability and coherence to his performance of normative manhood. Moreover, the all-American male film protagonist of Hitchcock's film endangers his family and nation by exhibiting a queer avidity for "talking about himself."

"And What Exactly Is It That *You* Do, Mr. Bernard?"

Jo's ambivalence over her roles as wife and mother, her uncanny knowingness, and Bernard's homoerotic threat emerge as key, interrelated themes. The nighttime scene, simmering with an odd tension, in which Jo and Ben entertain Bernard in their hotel room, visually stages the erotic relay of the film. As Hitchcock pans across the main hotel room, which leads out into a balcony, we see a rather louche Bernard artfully leaning against the door frames of the balcony. His liminal position, half in the room, half on the balcony, enshrouded in a seductive darkness, perfectly encapsulates his dark, sensual threat to the bright normality of the family's life. We see Ben, making his tie in the mirror, looking rather self-contentedly over at Jo and Hank, but craning his neck in a manner that suggests a strained and even impossible kind of looking; Jo is tucking Hank in, singing to Hank as she makes the bed; Hank accompanies her in song and whistle, touches that will be crucial to the climax of the film. Standing in the room though we never see him enter it, a rogue element in this familial scene, Louis Bernard is an inorganic detail that jarringly sticks out, *that should not be there*. He is, to use Žižek's term, the Hitchcockian blot, a stain on the image, in this case a queer

37

stain on the image of the normative family.[17] Bernard-as-blot is a piece of a homoerotic Real that can never be seen in its entirety, signaling the unseen, unrepresentable threat of homoerotic potentiality within this familial group: in Ben, in Jo, perhaps even in or around the figure of Hank.[18]

This scene in its entirety is tonally complex. Making the bed, familial ritual par excellence, is joined to the shared song between mother and son. The song stalls the action, as we experience the ritualistic exchange between Jo and Hank that pointedly excludes Ben. As Hank sings, Ben, making his tie in the mirror, wryly remarks, "He'll make a fine doctor!" Ben's joke suggests that he worries that this singing child closely connected to his mother will not properly identify with him—in other words, properly oedipalize—and take up the masculine profession of a physician.

The film then gives us a moment that explicates its central tension between Jo's insight and Bernard's knowledge. Ben surreptitiously shrugs at Jo before she walks out onto the balcony to have a drink with Bernard, as if to say, "Good luck." Provocatively turning the tables, Jo artfully and tensely questions Bernard about *his* private life: "And what exactly is it that *you* do, Mr. Bernard?" she pointedly asks him. Bernard continues to deflect Jo's questions, answering hollowly, "I buy and sell." He telegraphs his determined lack of interest in Jo by mocking her questions with obviously hollow answers. Jo presses, "And what do you buy and sell?" Unruffled, smooth Bernard answers with the confidently cryptic, "Whatever makes the most profit." Bernard almost threatens to "out" the very codedness of his own language, to reveal the strenuous opacity of his responses as code, as subterfuge.

If Jo is paranoid, an idea I will be developing, this scene foregrounds a particular dimension of paranoia: "paranoia is fun, or pleasurable," as Patrick O'Donnell describes it, "because it allows us to perceive a self-referential depth in the fantasy of the totalized world of available objects, folding back into it a kind of personal history, destiny, and temporality that fantasy itself attempts to erase or revise as immediacy," or, to put it another way more directly germane to this moment, Jo uses her interrogation of Bernard as a way of gaining a kind of authority and satisfaction that she is denied in her own roles as wife and mother.[19] Chafing against her constrictions, Jo carefully monitors possibilities that may be afforded Ben, the person who has imposed these constrictions on her. Her grilling of Bernard is, actually, readable as her grilling of Ben and her analysis of what, exactly, might be his potential freedoms.

That Bernard makes an abrupt exit after a mysterious man appears at the door, who scans the room before claiming to have knocked on the wrong door—he is the aptly named Rien, played by Reggie Nalder, a sinister, cadaverous man who will be revealed as the hired assassin—deepens the sense of clandestine assignations between men. Rien, as I will develop, is a significant presence who signals the dark side of Bernard's attractions, though, plot-wise, the two men are fundamentally opposed. He is, embodied by the thin and arch Nalder, a striking contrast to the assassin, Ramon (Frank Volper), in the first version of *Man*, a comparatively bluff, sturdy masculine type. (Ramon's imposing physicality makes it all the more striking that the wife is presented as his rival in this film and also shoots and kills him, to protect and rescue her kidnapped daughter, at the climax.)

Nalder's Rien is most analogously the remake's equivalent to the extravagantly queer presence of the young Peter Lorre—sly, sensual, droll, insinuating, witty, corrupt—as the conspirator and chief villain Abbott in the '34 *Man*. Conversely, his heavy, mannish female accomplice Nurse Agnes (Cicely Oates), whose death he mourns as he holds her dying body in his arms, is matched in the remake by the hard, taut Mrs. Drayton and her even harder young female assistant (who plays checkers with Hank at one point, snapping harshly at him for beating her at the game). In the end, the film reveals Mrs. Drayton to be surprisingly gentle and maternal, once again defying expectations. ("Look," she chides her assistant for her brusque treatment of Hank, "it doesn't hurt to be kind, does it?")

Consistently, Hitchcock uses the same cinematic technique to emphasize Rien's presence in the narrative, another queer blot. Hitchcock dramatically dollies in to close-ups of Rien's sinister smile in the hotel room; when he is revealed in Ambrose Chapel, collaborating with the Draytons; and when Jo spots and recognizes him, in terror, at the Albert Hall. "You have a very nice little boy," he sinisterly and smilingly threatens Jo before the concert begins, amplifying his sexual threat with a note of pedophilia.

After Bernard cancels dinner plans with the McKennas, they go out to dinner on their own in a Moroccan restaurant. This eating scene is one of the most notable in the film.[20] Hitchcock, his expert screenwriter John Michael Hayes, and the actors all convey a slapstick sense of the sheer out-of-placeness of conventional American masculinity in a foreign setting. Ben is shown to be completely ill at ease, either sinking into the low sofas or scissoring across screen space with his impossibly long legs as he shifts seating positions, which he will do more than once. At one point, his crotch bizarrely engulfs Jo's quizzical face as she looks up at him. Ben cannot properly abide by Arab customs while trying to eat his chicken dinner, which the film milks for its full, excruciating comic-humiliation potential. (The scene prefigures Ben Stiller comedies.) As it turns out, the Draytons are sitting behind the McKennas—and once again, Mrs. Drayton sinisterly stares at them, in this film that abounds with penetrating and ominous stares, a recurrent Hitchcock motif.

Ben's position on the sofa as he twists his body around, especially his long and contorted neck, to face them in discussion while sitting in the opposite direction

Hitchcock's original version of *The Man Who Knew Too Much* (1934).
Peter Lorre's queer sensuality shines.

further intensifies not only his physical as well as social discomfort but also his disastrous attempt to maintain forward-facing masculine coherence while speaking from behind, as it were. This thematic of impossible looking is a crucial aspect of a phenomenon in Hitchcock films frequently found in those he made with Jimmy Stewart: what I call *rear viewing*, a backward-focused, aversive, paralytic gaze that defies reality, deconstructs male visual mastery, and in so doing lends itself to queer interpretation. Scottie's oddly strained, contorted posture and craned neck as he sees Madeleine Elster for the first time in *Vertigo*—and the impossible access to her as a visual subject he is granted by the camera's sweeping movements, which denies as it transcends his real position as a spectator—is an even more striking example. In *Manhood in Hollywood from Bush to Bush*, I defined the masochistic gaze as a form of queer looking that reflects prohibitions on queer visual desire, resulting in scenes of the male gaze as impaired, balked, or frustrated. I would insert rear viewing into larger schemas of the masochistic gaze. I return to rear viewing in Chapter 3's discussion of *Psycho* and the pornographic gaze, and also in my discussion of the intertextual presence of *Vertigo* in Martin Scorsese's

Taxi Driver in Chapter 5. Ben's impossible looking in *Man* signifies, in my view, a kind of visual metaphor for his Janus-faced hetero-homo male identity.

Once the duplicitous Draytons, at Ben's comic-desperate behest, join them for dinner so that Ben won't have to keep twisting his head around to speak with them, Jo spots Bernard and a woman companion sitting down at another table. Reciprocally, Bernard spies on the pair of couples having dinner. It is interesting that Bernard's spying entails a voyeuristic fixation on the spectacle of a normality he seemingly, being with a woman himself, enjoys. Bernard's female dinner companion, a woman who seems very much aware of Bernard's clandestine activities, asks Bernard if that is the couple he seeks, to which he responds yes. (Unbeknownst to us at this point, he is actually referring to the Draytons.)

Bernard's calm starkly contrasts against Ben's excruciating physical discomfort as he tries to negotiate his inconvenient body and strenuously attempts to eat chicken with select digits of his right hand, as Mr. Drayton instructs him to do in adherence to Moroccan culinary custom. All the while, Ben, marionette-like, is controlled by Jo's monitoring vigilance. His uncannily inhuman contortions are, in Freudian terms, a somatic compliance—his body registers the twists and turns of his increasing levels of confusion.

The English Draytons are represented through a series of scenes that defy expectations or overturn previous understandings of their character, Mrs. Drayton's in particular. While Mrs. Drayton is ultimately a very sympathetic figure, it is interesting to think of the Draytons together in their role as what Raymond Bellour would call the "shadow couple," which doubles the normative one. The Draytons shift from seeming initially threatening, with their intrusive stares ("Aren't you Jo Conway?" they ask, cleverly "explaining" why they have been staring), to welcome, cheerful, and helpful dinner companions, invited by Ben to sit with him and Jo. Soon, they will be revealed to be even more perfidious than the McKennas could have imagined; far from aiding the couple, they kidnap their child and come close to destroying their lives. It is worth considering here that Bernard, the single seductive foreign man, is revealed to be someone that the McKennas could trust after all, while the less-foreign fellow heterosexual couple, the Draytons, emerges as entirely untrustworthy. Moreover, it is interesting to consider that, while evil, the Draytons are also not interchangeable: while hard and tough, Mrs. Drayton is also shown to care for Hank. With palpable anguish, she eventually and desperately attempts to protect the kidnapped Hank from her husband, who was instructed to kill him. In this manner, Mrs. Drayton truly is Jo's double, the more interesting, courageous, and resourceful half of a married pair.

As Jo complains that Bernard has dumped them in favor of his new date, Ben initially attempts to deflect her complaints, but becomes progressively more vexed and finally nearly belligerent. Having skillfully riled him up, Jo now

41

chastises him for *getting* riled up. As typically happens with food in Hitchcock, the chicken dinner and its metaphorical difficulties organize the entire relay of suspicion, vexation, and violence here. As Ben's vulnerability before seductive Bernard transforms into his desire verbally and perhaps even physically to assault him (another frequent pattern in Hitchcock), he also gives up on proper Moroccan dining customs. In an unseemly gesture, he grabs pieces of the recalcitrant chicken carcass with both hands, leading the waiter immediately to intervene with an aghast *"Monsieur!"* as he instructively pantomimes eating etiquette.

The left hand, in this case, knows exactly what the right hand is doing, even if the right does not. Associated in the Arab world with excrement, being the hand one uses to wipe one's bum, the left hand metonymically signals an open secret, a knowledge known but unacknowledgeable except under duress. This panicked atmosphere points to, I believe, an entire underworld of the forbidden. Specifically, in pointing to the excremental, it evokes the hidden depravities of the sodomitical in a homophobic register. Not only the film's consistent motifs but also the entire discourse of Moroccan-Mediterranean homosexual tourism charges the scene with these associations. In this new, bewildering social world of foreign threat into which the McKennas have plunged, Ben is publicly exposed as someone who simultaneously fails to understand the codes of custom and violates the code in ways that associate him with offensive practices. The eating scene prefigures the key scene in the marketplace the next day in which the full bewilderment and intensity of his odd and disturbing bond with Bernard is dramatically and publicly revealed.

Murder in the Marketplace

The sequence in which Ben, Jo, Hank, and the Draytons wander around the antic Marrakech marketplace, and Bernard, having been stabbed, staggers towards Ben and literally dies in his arms, passing the secret to Ben's ears at last, is important as the culmination to the first thematic movement of the film. As Robert J. Corber notes, Jo and Ben demonstrate a certain disregard for Hank's welfare: the McKennas allow Hank to roam free-range style, and it is Mrs. Drayton who rushes after Hank to protect him once the threat of street violence becomes apparent.[21] The point here is not to fault Jo as a mother, but to establish that the film portrays both Ben and Jo ambivalently as parents and as individuals. At Jo's prodding, the couple, rather languorously ambling through the hot, dusty, sunny marketplace, discuss the ways in which the various medical operations that Ben has performed (extracting tonsils and gallstones, delivering babies) have enabled their lavish vacation. This discussion is the most *explicit* confirmation of the couple's ambiguous morals. As they gaily discuss the profits they have gained through others' pain, their shared relish for what is irreducibly the suffering of others make them the antithesis of the wholesome couple they ostensibly appear to be.

In this regard, Jo's abrupt announcement that she "wants to have a baby" (which seems prompted by the sight of a Muslim woman holding a baby) seems especially jarring. A conversation about having another child isn't typically preceded by a discussion of organ removals. If the film suggests that the McKennas may be unfit parents, this suggestion emerges as a disturbing "truth" spectacularly revealed by both Hank's kidnapping and their complicity with it. Unthinkingly and unhesitatingly, they allow the Draytons to take Hank away from them. Even within the comparative relaxation of attitudes towards child-supervision in the 1950s, their casual disregard for Hank is striking.[22]

As we have noted, Jo signals ambivalence about motherhood but also about marriage. Exemplary of this ambivalence is the way in which Jo coordinates the discussion of lucrative medical ailments. At the start, she speaks with tense merriment, while initially Ben is curiously, even vacantly, silent. But as they continue to speak, Ben grows excited, avidly discussing elements of the same theme; it's almost as if he catches but then exceeds her mania. But then, as she did in the restaurant when she criticized Ben for getting upset over Bernard after *she* had complained about seeing him dining with someone else, Jo now chastises Ben, albeit playfully and with laughter, for speaking so avidly about the very macabre topic that she implanted in him. None of this makes either Ben or Jo, played so well by such expert stars, dislikable, but we do get the opportunity to see the ambivalence beneath their charming teasing of each other. Indeed, what is unsettling about this scene is how playful they are about such an unseemly topic.

If this family is shown to be less than wholesome, *Man* deploys homoeroticism as a sign of the innate deviancy of the McKennas. Right in the middle of the ghoulish discussion about patients and the depiction of the Draytons' increasingly tenacious hold on Hank—paralleling the McKennas' inability to rear their child properly—Louis Bernard appears, having been fatally pursued by a man, himself pursued by the police, wearing the same white robe that covers Bernard. The chase sequence, as brilliantly choreographed as it is brief, with its identically clad pursuer and pursued, and Bernard in "Arab" make-up, adds a thematic of narcissistic doubling to the homoerotic atmosphere. It culminates in Bernard's being stabbed in the back, a reification of the film's themes of betrayal and duplicity. Moreover, the knife sticking prominently out of his back, which the dying Bernard helplessly and hopelessly grabs at, has terrible sexual associations, evoking sodomy as a kind of murderous penetration of one man by another. (These associations will be much more explicitly elaborated by William Friedkin in his 1980 *Cruising*.)

For all to see, Bernard staggers up to Ben, grabs his face, and, with extraordinary intimacy, forces Ben's ear to his mouth and whispers a deadly not-so-nothing to him about the assassination plot. It's like the last, fearless act of a failed lover. Ben is horrified but unable to resist Bernard's final seductive embrace. The shockingly public nature of this scene—underscored by Bernard Herrmann's notably disruptive, jangly music—intensifies the terrible threat of queer sexuality's revelation as such, for all, finally, to see. The nothingness—an anti-life—of *Rien's* cadaverous aspect culminates in the literal nothingness that Bernard becomes.

A powerfully suggestive and disturbing effect occurs here—the transfer of Bernard's make-up from his face to Ben's hands. This was an effect Hitchcock took great pains to capture on film, and it behooves us to consider why it was so particularly urgent for him.[23] In this film obsessed with the flimsiness of appearances and the masklike nature of identity, the ease with which one man's identity can be transferred to another vividly literalizes the work's major themes, themes which have a powerful precedent in classic American literature and its preoccupations with identity's "pasteboard masks," to lift from *Moby-Dick*. If Louis Bernard represents the threat of homoeroticism in the face of the normality of the conventional family, the transfer of make-up from his face to Ben's hands can be read as a transfer of this threat to Ben, now irreparably stained, marked by it, as well. Little wonder that afterwards, Ben, trying, like Lady Macbeth, to wipe the guilt stain from his hands, says, "I feel funny": this transfer becomes metaphorical intercourse between these disparate men shown, ultimately, to be on the "same" side. Their verbal and physical exchange pushes the boundaries of what was cinematically representable, especially in terms of male-male contact, in Hitchcock's era.

As Bernard was fleeing his pursuer, he tripped on a can of blue paint that smeared his white robe. Hitchcock gives us an extreme close-up of James Stewart as Ben listens to Bernard's dark message. Stewart's shockingly blue eyes dart, as always, with the most expressive intensity. The weird, alien blue color of the paint on Bernard's robe finds a strange complement in the blue of Stewart's eyes. Hitchcock creates a collage of colors that link the men, Bernard's brown make-up on Ben's hands, the matching blues of paint and eyes. Colors function here as a metaphor for exchanges between men as well as their visible, literal mark.

Though a full consideration of this aspect of Hitchcock's visual and thematic design needs much more elaboration, the exchange of colors between the men has unmistakably racial overtones as well. Given that Hitchcock made this American film—even though set in foreign lands—in the context of the "separate but equal," pre-civil rights era of the 1950s, the metaphorical intensity of exchanges between white and "brown" bodies, especially with the suggestion made of how easy it is for brownness to "rub off" on whiteness, charges the episode with racial significance and tensions as well. Moreover, within the context of its own plot, the film evokes the entire history of foreign visitors to North Africa and the Mediterranean seeking illicit sexual pleasures, homosexual sex in particular.

It is interesting to contrast the film's staging of the revelation of the spy's identity and his whispering of secrets to that in the '34 version. In the remake,

Hitchcock emphasizes male-male contact. In the '34 version, Louis Bernard (Pierre Fresnay), a friend that the couple Bob and Jill Lawrence make at the St. Moritz ski resort, dies in Jill's arms. Played by the smart, appealingly modern Edna Best, Jill Lawrence is a skillful markswoman who is shown competing at a clay pigeon shooting contest early on in the film. In comparison, drab Bob (Leslie Banks) is a drip who sits grousing with their daughter, Betty (Nova Pilbeam, who will later star in Hitchcock's undervalued *Young and Innocent*), as swankily-clad Jill and Louis Bernard dance.

To get comic revenge on the dancing couple, Bob affixes a piece of yarn from the sweater that Jill is knitting for Louis, which unravels as he dances with Jill, ensnaring other dancing couples in the process. Though played successfully for laughs, this moment suggests an undercurrent of real aggression in Bob that his dyspeptic complaining camouflages. It also establishes, once again, Hitchcock's interest in the ways in which chaotic forces can disrupt the apparent stability and order, as well as the gaiety, of human life. Murder and intrigue infiltrate this comedic and elegant scene of well-dressed revelers dancing away the evening at a fashionable ski resort. A bullet is fired through the window and into Louis Bernard's chest. "Oh, look," he says, with poignant understatement, as he notices the spreading blood on his shirt and collapses into Jill's arms. Whispering his secret knowledge of the assassination plot to Jill, he makes her, not Bob, his secret sharer. Paul M. Jensen observes in his study of Hitchcock's English films that "the banter of Bob and Jill cuts too close to the bone for comfort, and by the time of the dancing, the jokes sound like barely disguised cruelty. As a result, although Bob's trick with the yarn seems harmless, it suggests a real (if unstated) jealousy of Louis and a resentment at Jill's taunting. In addition, by placing this action where he does, Hitchcock contrasts its mundane silliness, Jill's casual ruthlessness, and Bob's immature passivity with something truly serious—a death."[24]

The '34 film places its emphasis on the idea of friendship rather than passion between Jill and Louis Bernard. Coming off the ski slope and presenting himself to Jill and her family at the beginning, Bernard is presented as a friend, not as a potential lover or rival to Bob, though Bob nevertheless expresses irritation with Bernard's presence. That Bernard poses no sexual threat is confirmed, rather than disputed, by Jill's flamboyant and theatrical exclamation at his appearance: "My love!" she says, embracing him. ("My lunch," Bob retorts.) Making a funny show of their "passion," Jill and Bernard make clear that this passion is platonic; they suggest a woman and her gay best friend. Lacking in charm or passion, Bob would appear to be irritable because Bernard entertains his wife, brings out her playful side.

In contrast, the '56 version makes Jo's frustration with Bernard's attentions to Ben a murkier matter. On the way to their hotel, the McKennas see, in an

45

eerie long shot, Louis Bernard laughing fairly uproariously along with the man who had been so incensed at Hank for pulling off his wife's veil on the bus. Jo complains to Ben about Bernard's behavior, and Ben, after deflecting her comments, begins ribbing her about her own jealousy, deducing that she is peeved by Bernard's lack of interest in her. The tripartite schema Freud lays out in his essay "Some Neurotic Mechanisms in Jealousy, Paranoia, and Homosexuality" (1922) illuminates Jo's jealousy. Freud establishes that there are three kinds of jealousy: competitive, or normal; projected; and delusional. Of great interest is his finding that "normal" jealousy is also competitive jealousy and, moreover, "that essentially it is compounded of grief."[25] If we consider Jo's jealousy as a manifestation of her anger toward Ben for having boxed her into a conformist life as a family doctor's wife, we can also understand that this anger stems from a core of grief which proceeds from an awareness, conscious or otherwise on her part, that larger social standards have still more determinedly boxed her in; Ben's control over her career (and with it, the range of her experiences and personal possibilities) only mirrors these larger standards.

Jealousy's grief, Freud theorizes, stems from a "narcissistic wound"; surely, Jo suffers from just such a wound in having had her career ended and her voice symbolically, perhaps even, for all intents and purposes, literally, cut off. The film will restore her voice without restoring her career, but it will also make the restoration of her voice a decisive struggle between her passionate commitment to her role as mother and her equally ardent desire for individual social agency.

Jo also occupies the classic role of the paranoid that is more commonly associated with the closeted homosexual man who angrily denies his own sexuality while accusing others of being gay. Freud's portrait of paranoia as a defense against one's own homosexuality enlarges our understanding of Jo's "different" personality. Day's own "butch" screen persona, exemplified by her title role in *Calamity Jane* (1953), contributes to the subtle portrait of Jo as a potentially lesbian character, as the oddly intense exchange of looks between Mrs. Drayton and Jo suggest.[26] Is it possible that Jo's attentive and shrewd monitoring of Ben's peccadilloes serves to deflect attention from her own "unwomanly" affect and desires?

The film figures paranoia as central to the maintenance and negotiation of the open secret of homosexuality within the constrictive and panoptical context of the Cold War 1950s. Its unusual contribution to this familiar construction of the paranoid response to the transmission and coding of illicit knowledge is that it makes the married woman and mother its apex. A consideration of the relationship between paranoia, femininity, and homosexuality in *Man* leads us to different aspects of these questions than those explored by Jacqueline Rose in her much-discussed essay "Paranoia and the Film System."[27] Rose discusses the latent paranoia in the film system itself and theorizes that the woman threatens to draw it out and expose it because her narcissistic relationship to the mirror stage, figured through the shot/reverse shot structure of films, such as Hitchcock's *The Birds*, is, in Lacanian terms, shot through with aggressivity and paranoia. Paranoia in her view is an inherently feminine "position," whether occupied by the male or the female, because it is characterized by a passive homosexuality. Drawing on but also problematizing Rose's view, J. Jack Halberstam rereads Freud's theorization of female paranoia in his 1911 "Psychoanalytic Notes Upon an Autobiographical Account of a Case of Paranoia," as related to a "mother complex," re-incorporating female paranoia into a system of homosexual panic with which he associates male paranoia.[28] While I appreciate Halberstam's nuanced reading of *The Birds*, I believe that she presents an incomplete portrait of Freud's theory of paranoia and its significance for queer as well as female sexuality.[29]

For our purposes, my chief point of divergence from Rose's argument is that, as the example of *Man* evinces, female paranoia can be resistant and active, and, moreover, alert to and a means of negotiating a potentially, and therefore threateningly, active homosexuality. At the same time, in agreement with Rose, I would argue that Jo's paranoia does return her and the film to a state of narcissistic self-encounter reminiscent of the mirror stage: indeed, the film thematizes her conflicts as a narcissistic crisis. She is made to confront the damage done to her own image of herself; she is made to recognize the intensity of her own desires—career-related, and possibly related to her sexuality—which have been diminished and suppressed by her marriage.[30]

Oddly enough, Ben's potential homosexuality emerges, therefore, as yet another possibility afforded him, even within the stifling homophobia of the Cold War context, simply because he is a man. Sabrina Barton, in her excellent discussion of paranoia, male homosexuality, and their impact on the woman in Hitchcock's *Strangers on a Train*, also notes the importance of Freud and grief to Hitchcock's work. "*Strangers on a Train*," she writes, "seems fascinated by the inevitability of coming to grief, by the inevitability of paranoia in a society that requires the repression of all 'abnormal' desires."[31] Female paranoia is represented as both reactionary and resistant: a means of resisting the inevitability of male homoerotic desire, which threatens to exclude the woman, on the one hand, and of registering the urgency, on the verge of explosion, of both the woman's suffering and of her own desires, on the other hand.

Like the murder Bruno Anthony commits on Guy's "behalf," disguised Bernard's public death and feverish embrace of Ben link the American protagonist with inscrutable, mysterious forces, with intrigue that emanates from secrecy, guilt, clandestine meetings, and covert negotiations now made almost unbearably public. The transferred stain of Bernard's secret life forces Ben to endure the open secret of Bernard's hidden, deviant identity, because now *Ben* shares in this identity, and is, in fact, subsumed by it. The transfer of make-up from one secretive man to another makes painfully clear Ben's attraction, however subtextual, to the very intrigue he was seemingly repulsed by and attempted to elude. Bernard's dying words are suggestive: "A man will be killed." Indeed, it is Ben's coherent, socially normative manhood that is in danger of being killed off.

Hystericizing Woman

The famous sedative scene is crucial to an understanding of Hitchcock's divided loyalties in terms of female representation, a division that, more often than not, comes down more strongly on the side of sympathy with the embattled, anguished woman in patriarchy. This extraordinary scene stands in for the discourse of hysteria that is a crucial component of the construction of womanhood from the late nineteenth century forward.[32] Ben tricks—strong-arms—Jo into taking a sedative before he tells her that Hank has been kidnapped; obviously, he wishes to forestall, if not foreclose, her emotional response to this upsetting news. Telling her that she's been "talking a blue streak" and exhibiting other wild behaviors—an obviously false diagnosis that Jo vehemently protests—Ben uses his professional medical credentials to force Jo to follow his commands. By forcing her to take the pill that will diminish what he expects will be her hysterical reaction, Ben paradoxically hystericizes Jo. The rest of the film will foreground Jo's endeavors to wrest back control over her own identity—control over her own social performance, her own agency, her own life—from Ben. Pathologizing, tranquilizing, and generally attempting to pacify his wife, Ben transmutes her wifely manipulation and control over his emotions into a medico-social masculine control of the unruly feminine, a maneuver with a longstanding history. At the same time, this entire scene tells us much more about Ben's own fears than it does about Jo's emotional life, self-control, or lack thereof. It's almost as if he can only contain his own increasingly explosive passions by pacifying her.

In its initial early form in the foundational days of psychoanalysis, hysteria was, if anything, more commonly known as a male malady than it was a female. In her superb work on the subject, *Mad Men and Medusas*, Juliet Mitchell notes that Freud's famous theory of the "Oedipus complex emerges from an analysis of male hysteria—above all, Freud's own," in reference to his "self-analysis."[33] Mitchell writes that the "repression of male hysteria haunts the theory and practice of psychoanalysis; psychoanalysis must . . . share responsibility for both the so-called disappearance of hysteria in the twentieth century and for our partial understanding of it."[34] Jo's hystericization recalls nineteenth-century scenes of the "madwoman" tended by officious male physicians both bewildered by her ailments and determined to lock down her uncontrollable body through rest cures and other forms of corporeal and psychic immobilization. All of this was charged with the tensions that stemmed from the extraordinary transition taking place:

from female midwifery to the masculinization of the midwife's role, embodied in the male figure of the gynecologist. (The widespread implications of the phenomenon and its development into a crisis that defined late-Victorian femininity is exemplified by the American feminist's Charlotte Perkins Gilman's indelible tale "The Yellow Wallpaper.")

As a physician, Ben both stands in for and recalls the Victorian gynecologist and the emergent figure of the psychoanalyst. The sedative scene indexes the controversies that have attended Freud's and Josef Breuer's foundational psychoanalytic work *Studies on Hysteria* (1893–1895). Like Anna O., one of the first hysterics treated and the person who gave psychoanalysis its most well-known description ("the talking cure"), Jo also, in her torment, victimization, and protest, registers the impact of complex negotiations between men in culture on woman's body and spirit, forever the battleground of desires between men, a structure that Eve Sedgwick in *Between Men*, following René Girard and Gayle Rubin, theorized as triangulated desire. Through her desperately moving resistance to Ben, rebuking him for having drugged her even as she is succumbing to the sedative, Jo recalls the intransigent female hysteric who opposes her own cure, such as Freud's famous analysand "Dora," who "vengefully" terminated her own treatment.

Ben's Contested Manhood

I am going to restrict the remainder of my close reading to the Ambrose Chappell and the Albert Hall sequences. Both of these sequences are key for the development of the film's themes of homoeroticism and maternal ambivalence.

Many intriguing avenues of discussion open up in a discussion of acting in Hitchcock. To focus first on Hitchcock's use of James Stewart, in *Man* he unabashedly conveys Ben's mounting emotionalism, indeed, his own hysteria. In each of the four films Stewart made for the director, the affable, genial star known mythically for his "aw, shucks" drawl and looming American likability assumes an increasingly disquieting affect.[35] As in Capra's *It's a Wonderful Life* (1946) and the Anthony Mann westerns of the 1950s, the Stewart of Hitchcock films embodies and expresses a distinctly masculine rage—a tendency towards apoplectic anger that signifies nothing less than a deep frustration with the threatened state of coherent American manhood. Capra, Mann, and Hitchcock capitalized, in their use of the actor, on the apparent simplicity and guilelessness of the star's popular persona. Seducing the audience into thinking they were safe with unassuming Jimmy, the guy who talks to phantom rabbits (*Harvey*, 1950), these directors forced audiences to endure various levels of masochistic obsession through their uses of Stewart. As Amy Lawrence observes in her essay on *Rope*, "American Shame," Stewart returned from service in World War II, in which he was a wing commander, ambivalent about the relevance of film in the face of what he had seen and experienced in the war, all of which he refused to discuss. The

1950s directors tapped into reserves of unspoken suffering seething beneath his all-American surface. "[N]early all of Stewart's postwar roles are haunted," writes Lawrence, "by an undercurrent of confusion, guilt, and shame that is historically specific but can never be articulated."[36]

Certain frantic, helpless moments in *Rear Window* and the second half of *Vertigo*, in particular, showcase Stewart's access to reserves of torment. *Man '56* does provide such a showcase at certain moments. But given the film's greater interest in Day's Jo, Stewart is almost a supporting character here. While his curious, almost antic nervousness provides an odd undercurrent to scenes in which Ben is ostensibly his "normal," untroubled self, as in his first conversation with Bernard on the bus, and while he does have moments in which he seems to be on the point of unraveling, as in the airport police station scene, overall what Hitchcock seems most interested in making use of in *Man*, in terms of the Stewart persona, is the star's all-Americanness and its implications. Stewart's embodiment of national manhood is strategically deployed as a set of expectations and assumptions which the film can denature, parody, and confuse.

Stewart's Ben is often quite brusque, even rude, and always agitated. He exudes American cultural narcissism in the restaurant, where he can't or refuses to adapt to Arab eating customs. He waves his finger dismissively and angrily at the French police captain after Bernard is killed; with aggressive calm, he tells the British secret intelligence chief that nothing can be done to Jo and him by the British authorities; the guards at the Albert Hall seem more endangered by Ben's hectoring than by the assassination plot. These examples reveal Ben's anger and contempt for established, lawful symbols of masculinity and masculine authority. Given that Ben is such a symbol *himself*, it is intriguing that he so often vents his anger at similar icons. Yet his vulnerability is also deeply palpable: after telling off the British intelligence man, he and Jo have a wrenching fight in which his determination to exert control is revealed as a desperate strategy for simply maintaining it. Even when he manipulatively drugs his wife, his quiet sorrow as he says, "Forgive me, Jo," imbues the scene with pathos.

Man figures American manhood as a monolithic entity under siege. The homoeroticism is the film's metonym for the larger crisis in masculine autonomy and self-control. If we examine the Ambrose Chappell sequence in detail, we can understand the way this sequence synthesizes and, partially, resolves the homoeroticism theme, while also leaving it perilously *unresolved*. Ben, as usual, has gotten it wrong—the Ambrose Chapel he seeks is not a man but a church. His attempt to find and speak to Ambrose Chapel leads him into an encounter with Ambrose *Chappell* the man. This episode of the film is extraneous to the plot. But it is crucial to the film's ideological schema, as well as an unsettling (and cruelly funny) passage.

Ben walks down a particularly desolate street in a particularly desolate area of London. As he walks, he furtively pauses and glances behind him. While it seems that no one else is present in the area, we do hear ghostly, disembodied, reverberating footsteps, which literally explains why Ben continuously, furtively glances backwards. It also reinforces our understanding of his apprehensiveness. As he will do in the later *Torn Curtain*, Hitchcock uses the motif of eerily echoing footsteps to convey an increasingly tense atmosphere between men that evokes homosexual cruising. In many ways, this is the aural complement to the visual motif of the men's clashing shoe styles in the opening of *Strangers on a Train*, perhaps Hitchcock's most openly homoerotic film. The visual fascination with their contrasting shoes culminates in a moment in which the visual cedes to another sense, when the men's shoes touch on the fateful train. Aural, visual, tactile senses of shoes and feet and footsteps: taken together, these representations of particular aspects of men's bodies, apparel, and movements form a collage of homoerotic tensions. Heightening these tensions, perhaps, may have been an awareness of one of the "secret" trademarks of homosexual subculture: the technique of foot-tapping in men's restrooms to signify sexual interest.

But then suddenly a man—the Man that Ben seeks—appears behind him, lending form to footstep. The stranger himself seems hesitant and apprehensive; he looks furtive, guilty. Right before, in his stride, he overtakes Ben, there is a deliberate moment of *shared* hesitancy between them as they anxiously occupy the same physical space. The stranger moves ahead; but then he pauses before a little alley, and now *he* is the one who turns around to stare at Ben, as if both are nervously and urgently hoping that Ben will also go down the little alley with him. This passage plays as a striking realization of the film's increasingly more obvious cruising theme. As if the two men had met in a park, signaled sexual interest at each other, and then, with an excited panic, each attempted to follow the other, tentatively and erratically moving down the street when *we* catch up to them, Ben and the stranger perform a dance fraught with cruisy overtones. Ben could be a closeted gay man who was lured out of his latency by the persistent efforts of a dark French seducer and who now, in London, anxiously explores and experiments with his newly awakened queer desires.

In his study *Queer London*, Matt Houlbrook writes that 1950s cruising "was experienced as an erotic descent into a metropolitan underworld in which men exchanged propriety for a realm of sexual possibility and pleasure. This movement was often represented by discarding middle-class styles of dress, echoing the conventions of social investigation, and disrupting the visual cues of class." Manipulating appearances allowed one to take on "an alternative social identity." Cruising could take place in nocturnal, obscured places but also, more often, in public places, such as parks, both because lonely, isolated men were driven there

51

out of sheer necessity, and because of their "positive attractions. Cruising—like public sex—was erotic and exciting precisely because it generated the electric thrill of social and spatial transgression."[37]

Hitchcock emphasizes the spatial dynamics of social transgression, as Ben negotiates a narrow passageway that may lead to an illicit encounter with a man with whom he has exchanged illicit, cruisy looks. Moreover, Hitchcock uses subjective camera work to make us feel as Ben feels. In an eerie subjective tracking shot (a familiar Hitchcock technique), we see, through Ben's eyes, the narrow passageway ahead of him, adding a weird intimacy to the scene as well as ratcheting up a sense of constriction and potential danger.

Once inside the Chappell taxidermist's shop, the homoerotic energy intensifies, though so does the parodistic comedy. A knowing gnome of a man, the *senior* Ambrose Chappell, approaches Ben, whose insinuating questions, the exact sense of which, in keeping with the unacknowledgeable knowledge-relay in the film, the old man cannot comprehend. Rather pointedly, he tells Ben, "I think I know what your problem is." Then, with an equally significant look of disdain, suspicion, or annoyance, the father calls to his son, the squirrely-looking young man that Ben followed into the shop.

When Ambrose Chappell Jr. (the uncredited Richard Wordsworth), moves towards his father and Ben, it is with the expression and body language of a person who verges on being caught—in my queer reading, in a cruising attempt that has spilled out into public view. Ambrose Jr. tries to get his father out of the way—"get some rest"—an attempt his father both testily rebuffs—"I have centuries of rest ahead of me, *thank you*"—but to which he acquiesces. With darting, anxious eyes and a curiously guilty air, Ambrose Jr. denies knowing anything of which Ben speaks. Ben's comment to Chappell about Marrakech and the information "about" Ambrose he got there from Bernard vaguely but also quite suggestively evokes the underground tradition of the Mediterranean as a place for exotic homosexual encounters. The European appropriation of the region for homosexual possibilities was quite well known by the 1950s.[38] If someone were, indeed, referring to such shared and secret encounters during this period, Ben's insinuating but indirect questions would be just such a register in which they might be brought up.

Ambrose Jr. is like an English Rien. He has the same vaguely decaying air and effeminate nervousness. Ben's rage against him could be the straight-acting closeted male's phobic rage against an unattractive or threatening mirror-image reflection of his own queerness. Adding to the sense of Ambrose Jr.'s imperfectly realized masculinity, he cries out for help to the other workers. The scene that ensues is a burlesque of masculine roles. Ben transforms from the scary physical oppressor to the scared and oppressed as the other workers, and Ambrose Sr., battle against him. But adding to the sense of satire, these would-be rescuers are all of advanced age and decreased height, while still being hardy enough to threaten bewildered Ben, writhing in their grasp.

One rescuer's little jig with a half-stuffed panther is a disorientingly fey, silent-comedy touch. The *pièce de résistance* of this parodistic scene is Ambrose Sr. holding up a swordfish against Ben's throat—a funny phallic symbol that parodies Ben's imperfectly wielded phallic power. (Even more humorously, the older Chappell is not so much brandishing the swordfish at Ben as he is preventing it from being damaged in the melee.) The various stuffed animal predators lend the scene a décor of violence—especially when Ben's hand is caught in a tiger's dagger-toothed mouth—but a violence emptied of real vitality, much like the animals on display. Being stuffed, they represent an embalmed version of male aggression, machismo in a museum, an exhibit of male physical prowess that is now strictly prehistoric. All in all, Ben desperately attempts to avoid getting "stuffed"—British slang for penetrative intercourse, visually represented by taxidermy (anticipating the important thematic imagery in *Psycho* of the sexually enigmatic Norman Bates's stuffed birds)—by this gang of non-virile men. The last shot of this sequence—a quizzical stuffed lion's frozen expression—is an ironic, deflating mock-roar.

Man figures conventional masculine anxieties about the successful performance of virility—protecting those under your care, getting along with your wife, not being hoodwinked by other men, doing, at all times, the right thing, rising up to any challenge, and so forth—as embodied homosexual threats. Bernard, Rien, and now Ambrose Chappell Jr. all "come at" Ben with the dark, sinister proposition of queer knowledge, even as they are in flight from *him*. Between this sequence and the earlier one in which disguised Bernard made a public spectacle of his secret affiliation with Ben, the film offers a striking allegory of homosexual cruising. The Albert Hall sequence will allow Ben to kill the queer messenger and the threatening message he bears, just as it allows Jo to reclaim her rights to maternal femininity.[39]

Mother Courage Screams

Jo, who correctly deduces the real identity of Ambrose Chapel—the church—valiantly demonstrating her admirable, superior resourcefulness, now makes her way to the Albert Hall, which becomes the site of her reclamation of her precariously endangered femininity—of her embattled, nearly lost, and powerfully regained woman's voice. Complexly, her reacquisition of her voice endangers her maternal femininity as it signifies the triumphant regaining of agency—an agency that will itself need to be redressed in the film's climax by being reconceptualized as properly maternal love. The Albert Hall sequence allows Jo to be in charge of her own hysteria. At the same time, it is a horrifying parody of her identity as a stage performer, culminating in a scream that mocks her famed prowess as a singer. Given Hitchcock's oeuvre-long deconstruction of "The Mother," the generally negative images of maternal figures in his work—in dramatically obvious ways (*Notorious, Psycho*), and in less obvious but subtly frightening ways (*North by Northwest*)—his treatment of Jo is interesting for its refusal to demonize her while also showing unsavory aspects of her, such as her morbidity, snideness, manipulativeness, and coldness. To be sure, Ben shares many of these qualities as well.

In an analysis of Day's career, Tom Santopietro writes that "at various stages of her career, Doris Day represented the idealized career woman, the perfect mother, and the longed-for girl next door"; Day "thereby came to personify the very woman Americans wished they knew, or were."[40] As he also observes, Day's star persona "functioned as a role model through whom thousands of women worldwide lived vicariously. Aggressive, tomboyish, yet utterly feminine, she was the most self-sufficient, forward-looking woman in American movies. In short, Doris Day, the most authentic of film actresses, personified nothing less than an authentic American heroine of the twentieth century."[41]

Hitchcock had a tendency to cast actors in roles in which he could either denature their customary associations (casting Cary Grant as the would-be wife murderer in *Suspicion*) or, Pygmalion-like, mold them according to his own designs (Tippi Hedren in *The Birds* and *Marnie*). In my view, Hitchcock used Day to reinforce the idea that Jo was inherently resourceful, a natural leader when placed in a tough situation. At the same time, her gender ambiguity lends Jo a potentially dangerous, nonconforming "masculine" toughness and forthrightness. Given that certain viewers responded to Doris Day as if she were not properly and normatively feminine enough, one wonders if Hitchcock also cast her in the role specifically because of her lack of an obvious, conventionally warm, sensual femininity.[42] Her sexual ambiguity as a star deepens the suggestion of that in the character, given her unfeminine interest in her career.

Day's Jo is a frieze of conflicted 1950s womanhood. The subversive energies of women granted an unprecedented but fleeting freedom during the World War II era were contained within the newly conservative, suburbanized Normality of the 1950s. Women chafed against and resisted—but also had to find ways of dealing with—this containment. The characterization of Jo communicates the difficulties of these negotiations. Just as Hitchcock denatured the star associations of James Stewart, which, to be sure, Stewart himself and other directors sought to do in Stewart's postwar roles, Hitchcock denatures the associations with a certain can-do pluckiness in Day's persona. Jo's struggle over her moral decision during the assassination attempt at the Albert Hall belies these all-American cheerful, commonsensical, and, in their way, also quite tough-feminine characteristics. Hitchcock is interested—and so is Day—in drawing out the anguished uncertainty in '50s womanhood.[43]

One of Hitchcock's greatest sequences, the Albert Hall assassination attempt features the great Bernard Herrmann conducting the aptly titled "Storm Cloud Cantata." (That the real-life composer of the film is the real-life composer *in* the film adds to its thematic of the "open secret.") The sequence synthesizes the conflicts in Jo over her problematic motherhood and her longing for her past career as an artist. Hence the great suspense generated: will Jo reveal what Rien is about to do, risking the possible loss of her son, on the one hand, and knowing complicity in a murder, on the other? In one of Hitchcock's most emotionally direct moments, he allows us access to Jo's suffering beneath the wearisome weight of her dilemma. The camera all but embraces Jo as it closes in on her uncontrollable weeping before Rien shoots. Jo's Mother Courage dilemma is one of the most wrenching moments in Hitchcock. What is extraordinary about the assassination attempt is its effectiveness as a thematic synthesis—it is used to bring both Ben's and Jo's gendered crises to a cathartic head.

Hitchcock handily reinforces Rien's queer sexuality through visual metaphor: he and his date, a young woman—his "beard"?—are shown rising in their viewing box and walking to opposite sides, the parodistic deconstruction of heterosexual presumption. If Rien represents the creepiest manifestation of queer forces that threaten normality, the famous image (repeated from the original film) of the gun emerging from behind the curtains is an interesting intensification of this theme.

The gun, tediously obvious phallic symbol that it is, is denatured as such by its autonomous agency in this shot. Disconnected from though wielded by Rien, the gun becomes a roving, floating phallic symbol, unclaimed by any one male character—a visual suggestion that virile masculine power hovers in the air, is possessed by no one, is up, literally, for grabs.

Rien's implicit wielding of it (later confirmed in shots of him holding the gun), however, suggests a deepening of his thematic queer threat—he has wrenched phallic power away from the person to whom it properly "belongs," the normative and ostensible hero, Ben. Little wonder that Rien and Ben fight over it as they do. The actor who played Rien, Reggie Nalder, as Donald Spoto reports, "recalled Hitchcock's calm and detached manner from start to finish. A Viennese dancer and stage actor, Nalder was acting in his first American film thanks to Hitchcock, who advised him during the scene at the Albert Hall in which he gazes at the man he is to kill, 'Look lovingly at him, as if you're glancing at a beautiful woman.'"[44]

If the assassination attempt has homoerotic overtones, once again we have a version of murder as sex in Hitchcock, this time between men. Strikingly, in one shot, Jo stares upwards at Rien as he puts on his opera glasses to see the man he is planning on shooting. The suggestion, once again, is that Jo spies upon scenes of illicit exchange between men. Moreover, the focus on visuality here—opera glasses exchanged for a long, slender phallic gun—makes nearly explicit one of

55

Hitchcock's most frequently devised metaphors: vision as a form of phallic violence. One thinks of Dr. Murchison (Leo G. Carroll), in a striking point-of-view shot, aiming a gun at Dr. Constance Petersen (Ingrid Bergman), and then turning the gun upon himself and firing, producing a shocking flash of color in a black and white film. If Constance is the triangulated woman between Murchison and "John Ballantyne" (Gregory Peck), the young and troubled man who so troubles Murchison, Jo is equally triangulated here, the obstruction between one man and the one he desires, so lovingly, to kill.

With the climactic cymbal crash imminent, Ben and Jo both engage in their desperate struggles to reaffirm normative gender/sex roles. Ben furiously knocks on every door, looking for Rien, after Jo has pointed him out. (The wordlessness of all this action adds to its suspenseful power.) Their individual but linked struggles to reaffirm their normality reach nearly simultaneous climaxes. Ben wrests the gun away from Rien, who he, in effect, dispatches (Rien falls off the balcony). Jo manages to cry out in time to disrupt the assassination plot (the target ends up with a wounded arm). By manfully wresting the gun from Rien's hands, Ben regains his phallic power, so endangered throughout the film; by instigating Rien's death, Ben vanquishes the insidious power of homoerotic forces that have threatened his hold on normative masculinity.

The climactic face-off with Drayton at the end reignites these anxieties over Ben's male "lack." Drayton points a gun at Ben and Hank, who Drayton has been instructed to kill, using, it should be noted, a rope, which recalls the murder weapon of one of Hitchcock's most homosexually oriented films: *Rope*, of course. While there is little about the sinister nebbish Drayton personally that could intimidate one, with a gun in his hand, he is deadly.

The actual climax of the film, in which Ben knocks the sexually ambiguous Drayton down the stairs (presumably, he dies from a self-inflicted gunshot), concretizes the goal that Ben would appear to have been pursuing all along: not just the reclamation of his son, but also the reclamation of his phallic potency and heterosexual manhood. Analogously, Jo's crying out reaffirms her ability to feel— not just a cold, sedated woman without voice, she screams loudly and publicly, as much as a release from the conflict over her embattled femininity as it is in protest against the attempted assassination.

In this regard, the actual climax, in which her singing penetrates the secret confines of the embassy and reaches Hank's ears, only concretizes her triumphant reclamation of womanly normality. Her voice, once employed in artistic/ careerist endeavor (notice the embassy royals' pained mutual expression at her unseemly high-decibel level—a symbolic judgment of her breaking out of her matronly role), is *now*, in the final sequence, purely the transcendent voice of maternal femininity.

Hitchcock, for his part, never allows these twinned projects of reaffirmed gendered normality to become bathetically celebratory. When Hank runs over to Jo at the end, we see Jo from the back, and the shot ends just as they embrace, as if to cauterize the wound of overwhelming feeling. And in the next shot, back at the hotel room where Jo's friends have fallen asleep, the couple and Hank, the restored heterosexual family, are viewed from a discreet, almost clinical, distance before the triumphant end-credits music peremptorily commences and, just as rapidly, ends. These final moments suggest, to me, at any rate, that Hitchcock felt that restoration of hetero-familial normativity was compulsory and necessary—but that, even so, he wasn't about to congratulate normality's return with any effusiveness.

The People Who Protest Too Much

In Robert Corber's reading of *Man*, he argues that Hitchcock, aping Dr. Spock and his parenting theories, makes Jo an obviously imperfect mother—insensitive, selfish—who needs to become a good mother by the end, and who accomplishes this by reclaiming her natural, maternal role, a process which involves rejecting her career and accepting the "professionalized" role of mother to Hank. I am not in agreement with Corber's readings, though my own and his do at times overlap. On the face of it, my reading is not all that different; after all, I, too, am saying that Jo (like Ben), by the end of the film, has resumed her normative role. I do not strongly disagree with Corber's finding that Jo, in emulation of Dr. Spock's theories, wraps Hank up in a comfortingly maternal, prelinguistic "sonorous envelope": "In the final sequence, her voice no longer signifies Jo Conway, the famous recording star, but the maternal body, and thus it can function independently of her body without posing a threat to the hierarchical structure of the patriarchal family."[45] For Corber, the remake subordinates visual pleasure to auditory pleasure because of Hitchcock's desire to "return the spectator to the imaginary plenitude and bliss of the primordial listening experience."[46] In this way, Hitchcock colludes with the sexist dictates of Dr. Spock, who emphasized woman's role as primary shaper of a child's life and urged women to stay at home, take care of their children, and eschew careers.

While one cannot claim that Hitchcock was completely opposed to such attitudes, neither can one ignore the complexity of the construction of gender roles in Hitchcock films.[47] I would like to offer a less end-directed reading, one that does not view the film's conclusion as its ideological key. The film works hard to suggest that Jo is vaguely dissatisfied with both her wifely and motherly roles, regarding both with ambivalence. The film also shows that, far from being a mere automaton, Jo is independent, canny, shrewd. While Jo's final singing is indeed maternal, signifying that the conservative program has won out, in the end, I think, an important distinction needs to be made regarding the competing, multivalent uses of her voice.

When Jo decisively screams at the Albert Hall, is her voice really that of, in Spoto's words, "the *mother's* cry in childbirth, a liberating cry of anguish and a triumph over death" (my emphasis)?[48] For in screaming at the Albert Hall, Jo is pointedly *not* acting like a mother, but as an autonomous, independent person. Her cry at the Albert Hall is a reclamation of her right to and her possession of womanly feeling, but not, necessarily, of *motherly* affect. It should also be remembered that another woman joins Jo's outcry. "The two great liberating screams of *The Man Who Knew Too Much* (Doris Day's in the Albert Hall, Brenda de Banzie's 'answering' scream in the embassy) must be read on one level," argues Robin Wood, "as the protests of women against masculinist politics and the cruelty and violence that issue from it."[49]

In order to remain fixed in their program to save Hank and facilitate his return, the couple would need to remain silent and impassive. Rien threatens Jo with Hank's death at the Albert Hall, specifically telling her not to reveal her dangerous knowledge about Rien to anyone else. But in the terrible, Mother Courage–like struggle Jo faces, which Hitchcock frames with great sympathy, Jo opts, finally, for a role larger than mothering and being the silent wife. As if it were a counterpoint to the clashing cymbals, a competing piece of shrill, adamant music, her cry cuts through the assassination plot and in so doing signifies her reclamation of an autonomous social role, *independent* of her identities as mother or wife.

Moreover, I would argue that the power of Jo's scream here also substitutes for the phallic charge of the mother's climactic shooting of one of the villains in Hitchcock's 1934 version of the film. Edna Best's character in the original film competed against this man in a clay pigeon shooting contest at the ski resort in St. Moritz at the beginning of the film; it is revealed that he is part of the assassination plot. Whereas he beat her in the shooting contest, she now expertly dispatches him at the climax as he chases after her daughter on the rooftop of the building where the conspirators held her hostage. Within, between, and through the two films, Hitchcock treats woman's agency as active and phallic, as exemplified by the sharpshooter Edna Best and the decisively voiced singer Doris Day.

Hitchcock establishes a contrast between phallic gun and phallic voice with numerous implications. In both films, the wife-mother is an infinitely more interesting, competent, and daring character than the husband-father. Both versions of *Man* are essential works about the woman's place in patriarchy, and her attempts to negotiate and transcend this narrowly demarcated place.

As in psychoanalytic theory, voice is synonymous with phallus. Whereas the mother's gun in the '34 *Man* brought death as well as salvation, in the remake, Jo's voice gives life. In crying out at the Albert Hall, Jo asserts her right to individual choice in a difficult, murderous world as she relegates her roles as parent or wife to subordinate categories. Screaming as she does, she opts for the greater social good instead of her own private desires to regain her son.

On his own gendered/civic mission, Ben, too, by dispatching Rien, reclaims individual (male) agency at the expense of subservience to his fatherly role (while also, as we stated earlier, resolving his gendered and sexual crises). But his reclamation of normative masculinity is treated sketchily, in rapid shots that underscore rather than constitute the momentum of the sequence, indicating a bored indifference to its predictability. Similarly, in the '34 version, the weak-willed and vaguely felt presence of the father undergoes a virilization by the end, but one that is only partial and is never as interesting—or as directly and decisively effective—as the mother's access to phallic ingenuity and power. In the remake, Hitchcock focuses on Jo's anguished struggle as the much more compelling, difficult, and *unpredictable* one.

The genuine terror of the oft-critiqued sedative scene may lie in a different aspect than is usually observed. Perhaps what Ben—and the film—are terrified of is not Jo's volcanic explosion of grief and rage at the loss of Hank, but the *absence* of suitable, satisfying motherly affect—which would then be the full, irrefutable exposure of her maternal ambivalence. Then Ben and Jo both would have to know that what Jo wants, more than anything else, is escape from the confines of her imprisoning roles. To put a slightly different spin on Wood's words, perhaps the terrifying "truth" at the heart of *Man* is that Jo truly *is* the more rational one of the two.[50] In this regard, the more appropriate medical-psychiatric foil may not be Dr. Spock, but Bruno Bettelheim. Bettelheim's 1950s popularization of the term "refrigerator mother" seems apropos of the film's gendered tensions. Speaking from the misguided (and damaging) vantage point that autism was a psychological and not a neurological disease, Bettelheim blamed "refrigerator mothers," who had failed properly to nurture and love their damaged, now icily removed children.[51]

In any event, *Man* would appear to circulate anxieties attendant in the conformist but also unstable 1950s about motherhood, nurture, and the especially dangerous and disturbing maternal ambivalence Jo seems forever on the verge of unleashing. The film's chief terror, perhaps, is the possibility that Hitchcock's cool blonde will be revealed as a refrigerator mother, a terror that informs but also mobilizes the action of this film so obsessively concerned about withheld and exposed forms of incendiary knowledge.

Neither Jo nor Ben is comfortable in the normative gender roles they have been placed in and are forced to embody. The film has its reactionary side, but in the end, in its insistence on exploring the various threats to gendered normativity from within and without, it's one of the most ideologically unstable and

59

unclassifiable films of the 1950s—hardly subservient, itself, to the gendered and moral codes of its era.

I also find it impossible to accept the notion that Hitchcock, so ruthlessly committed, throughout his Hollywood career, to depicting the terrors of American mommyism, would *uncritically* suggest that the state to which we would like to return is Mother's enveloping, sonorous nurture. A desire for return to the mother powerfully informs Hitchcock's films. But it is counterbalanced by a dread of this return, and any reading that privileges one fantasy over the other, each ardently registered, threatens to distort Hitchcock's thematic complexity. What James McLaughlin writes of *Shadow of a Doubt* applies just as pertinently to *Man*:

> It is . . . the perpetual repetition of banal existence of the family which generates the wish to escape and destroy it, which instills guilt for having the wish, which distorts the effects of the wish, which brings near death and a return to the family . . . that elicits Hitchcock's most profound disgust and transforms the family into the great Unsolved Crime.[52]

Man may ultimately fall into the same ideological trap of subversion and containment that some critics have found to be present in Shakespeare's plays. Yet I think that its value—like that of Hitchcock's oeuvre—lies in its simultaneous unwillingness to offer a coherent portrait of gendered and sexual identities and its effort to show the intensity of struggles that ensue over these identities. The film's radicalism lies in its willingness to explore the deeply unsettling and strenuous efforts behind the achievement of apparent normativity.

IN THE NEXT TWO CHAPTERS, my focus is on Hitchcock's 1960 *Psycho*. If it seems strange to move from *Man* '56 to *Psycho*, Pascal Bonitzer crystallizes the logic of the transition:

> *The Man Who Knew Too Much* is already, in filigree, *Psycho*, which seems, in retrospect, to derive from the burlesque scene with the taxidermist and, above all, from the motif of the mother's voice which acts upon the son at a distance, through the incongruous song "Que Sera, Sera."
>
> The vocal bond between mother and son in *The Man Who Knew Too Much* is the seemingly innocent expression of a normal, maternal and filial love, and also the sole safety line of a boy who has been kidnapped and whose life is in danger. In the light of *Psycho*, where the mother's voice has entered the son, tears him apart and possesses him in a murderous fashion, one cannot help but find even the normality of the ordinary, typical American family slightly disquieting.[53]

CHAPTER TWO

"YOU ARE ALONE HERE, AREN'T YOU?"
Psycho's Doubles

THROUGHOUT HITCHCOCK'S work, he makes use of the figure of the *doppelgänger*, or double, to contrast and explore many distinct kinds of subjectivity. The theme is a direct borrowing from the German Expressionist cinema that continued to inform his work to the end.[1] My focus here is on Hitchcock's specific uses of the double to highlight the similarities between the ostensibly normal, sane male protagonist and his nemesis, the villain. What undergirds this comparison is the deeper one made between straight and queer masculinity. The thrill-kill male lovers versus their presumably straight mentor Rupert Cadell in *Rope* (1948); the casting of the gay actor Farley Granger in the straight role and the straight actor Robert Walker as the queer villain in the 1951 *Strangers on a Train*; the queer perversity of Leonard (Martin Landau) in *North by Northwest* (1959), and, in its own way, that of the debonair villain Vandamm (James Mason) contrasted against Cary Grant's protagonist Roger O. Thornhill, whose middle initial stands for nothing and whose initials together spell ROT. These pairings/doublings work to undermine stable, coherent understandings of screen masculinity, depicted in Hitchcock as neither straight nor queer, neither normal nor perverse, but all of these qualities at once.[2] Hitchcock's doubles draw out the narcissistic and homoerotic elements inherent in the figure of the double as Otto Rank famously theorized it. In his famous study of the double in psychology, folklore, and literature, Otto Rank argued that the double is a transformation of one's own narcissistic self-love into "the feared and loathed other of one's own desires."[3] Hitchcock takes his characteristic use of the double to a new degree of critical urgency in his 1960 film *Psycho*. The striking physical similarities between Sam Loomis (John Gavin), Marion Crane's boyfriend in *Psycho* (1960), and the Mother-obsessed Norman Bates (Anthony Perkins) will be our focus here.

One of the first challenges we face in any argument about Hitchcock's queer sensibility is the perception within certain critical quarters that Hitchcock was homophobic. D. A. Miller's definitive late 1980s essay "Anal *Rope*" and Lee Edelman's *No Future*, from 2004, serve as markers for this longstanding view (even though Edelman also frequently employs Hitchcock tropes as examples of the queer death drive—the subversive queer embodiment of the very negative, anti-life forces homophobically associated with queerness—he advocates). While Robin Wood frequently and forcefully problematized such a view of Hitchcock, Richard Allen, in his masterly study *Hitchcock's Romantic Irony*, has made the best recent case of which I am aware for the non-homophobic quality of Hitchcock's approach to queer themes. Allen argues that the early nineteenth-century concept of romantic irony, most eloquently theorized by the German Romantic Friedrich Schlegel (1772–1829), forms the aesthetic sensibility of Hitchcock's work. This "continual self-creating interchange of two conflicting thoughts," in Schlegel's words, becomes in Hitchcock a "composite mode, suspended between the ideal and its opposite."[4] If the model of the heterosexual couple is crucial to Hitchcock's cinema, "what defines Hitchcock's presentation of heterosexual romance as an ideal is the manner in which it is entwined with its opposite—human perversity."[5] The "logic that unites romantic love and human perversity or life and death in Hitchcock's works is the both/and logic of romantic irony in which romantic love and human perversity are at once utterly opposed to one another and yet also, paradoxically, closely identified."[6] Allen describes Hitchcock's cinema as an oscillation between masculine and "ludic" (playful), and feminine, emotional styles. He contextualizes Hitchcock's famously perverse humor, his "prankster sensibility and fondness for obscene jokes," as part of Hitchcock's playful visual style that functions as "punning displacement of sadistic sexual content that is at once asserted and denied," "a masculine aesthetic" that illuminates both Hitchcock's "relationship to male sexual aggression" and to his consistent fascination with homosexuality, which Allen links to the intersection between Hitchcock's films and the cultural afterlife of the Victorian dandy and Oscar Wilde's indelible real-life performance of this role.[7]

Allen, in a view that corresponds to my own, makes it clear that Hitchcock is not homophobic. Rather, he seeks to displace perversity into *form*. "Hitchcock," Allen writes, "is not concerned to demonize homosexuality. His interest in these characters lies in staging the performance of a gentlemanliness beneath which the darkest secrets are harbored in a manner that renders them alluring and often sympathetic."[8] One thinks immediately of Hitchcock villains such as Ray Milland's cuckolded former tennis-player husband in *Dial M for Murder*, plotting Grace Kelly's murder and then, appearing to be the most loyal spouse, defending his wife against any hints of suspicion during the murder investigation, even as he secretly frames her for the murder. Once his perfidy is exposed at the climax, he elegantly offers and makes drinks for the victims of his plot and the detective assigned to the case.

The significance of such urbane-malevolent figures lies in Hitchcock's own developed authorial identity: "Hitchcock's persona is . . . a self-conscious, ludic performance of Victorian English gentlemanliness that combines the austerity of Pater, the self-publicity of Wilde, and the roguish wit of a cultured Cockney."[9] If Hitchcock's masculine aesthetic exposes masculinity as always already a performance, his feminine aesthetic, on most vivid display in masterpieces such as

The lover-killers of *Rope*. Farley Granger looks tormented, but John Dall basks in his diabolical triumph.

Rebecca and *Vertigo*, expressing itself in "camera movement and mise en scène," registers "the full intoxicating allure of human sexuality."[10]

Psycho does not register the full intoxicating allure of human sexuality—to put it mildly. I say this even as I note that the film opens with one of the most sexually charged scenes in American movies up to this point, Marion Crane (Janet Leigh) and Sam Loomis (John Gavin) in various states of undress in a hotel room. This scene and certain key moments later enunciate, as I will elaborate in the next chapter, a new pornographic awareness in narrative film. But human sexuality, perhaps because it is now framed in pornographic terms, has been deadened. The "decline in the sentiment of sex" that Henry James observed in the late nineteenth century has considerably deepened by the time of *Psycho*.[11]

Hitchcock has often been compared to the antebellum Southern American writer Edgar Allan Poe. In my view, Hitchcock has even more in common with the antebellum New England writer Nathaniel Hawthorne, whose works similarly abound with murderous doubles and homoerotic narcissism. But to pursue the valences between Hitchcock and Poe, the words of one of Poe's finest critics, Allen Tate, come to mind as equally descriptive of *Psycho*. As Tate observes of Poe's masterpiece of the short story genre, "The Fall of the House of Usher," "The mysterious exaltation of spirit which is invariably the unique distinction of his heroes and heroines is not quite, as I have represented it, bodyless. *It inhabits a human body but that body is dead. The spirits prey upon one another with destructive fire which is at once pure of lust and infernal.*"[12] (Emphasis mine.) Indeed, if anything, Tate's description is more pertinent to *Psycho* than it is to "Usher," whose heroine, Madeleine, provides the name for the cool siren indelibly played by Kim Novak in *Vertigo*. Sex has happened in *Psycho*, but we arrive at its aftermath and in a world in which sex seems inconceivable. Intimacy and connection here seem just as unthinkable, their flickers of possibility stamped out. Clamped in our private traps as moviegoers, we watch as the characters attempt to claw their way out of their own, none of us ever budging an inch.

My focus in this chapter is on the confrontation Hitchcock stages between Norman Bates and Sam Loomis. Their encounter is not only crucial to this film but would prove to be fundamental to the New Hollywood representation of masculinity, equally fascinated by the juxtaposition of "normal" with perverse, or, in a word, queer masculinity. This pointed comparison, as we have noted, occurs in several Hitchcock works that anticipate *Psycho*, the most important precursor being *Rope*, a film that demands critical reappraisal.[13] As Richard Allen argues, it is a comparison that is central to Hitchcock's work generally. But in no other film does the juxtaposition between the apparently sane and straight and the perverse and the queer have greater intensity or resonance.

Psycho puts into motion a series of anxieties bedeviling culture that *must be confronted*: female desire, queer desire, and normative masculinity's dependence on what it repudiates to construct its own identity. In my view, the film is the site of a fatal rupture between the classical Hollywood woman's film and modern horror. Briefly put, the most frequent narrative of the woman's film is a young woman's struggle with the marriage plot—will she retain her independence once she finds love, romance, and marriage, or will she avoid marriage in order to retain her singular personality? At the same time, the woman often maintains a fraught relationship to her own mother, who simultaneously wants to see her daughter married and to keep her by her side. *Psycho* is the template for the most conventional narrative of the modern horror genre that it spawned: an emotionally damaged and homicidal male maintains a fierce devotion to his mother even as he goes about murdering various women; indeed, it is precisely this inordinately intimate mother-son bond that provides the basis for the killer's monstrous and violent desires. In *Psycho*, the story of the mother-obsessed and homicidal young man supersedes the initial narrative of the independent woman struggling with romance and marriage.[14] Along these lines, the film is the most dramatic staging of one of the defining conflicts in Hitchcock's work, *the feminine versus the queer*, which we discussed in the previous chapter. Some key examples of this pattern are Charlie's conflict with her Uncle Charlie in *Shadow of a Doubt*; the increasingly tense and heated conflict between Janet and the maliciously witty Brandon in *Rope*; and Jo's attempt to trick Louis Bernard into "revealing" himself in the 1956 version of *The Man Who Knew Too Much*. In *Psycho*, the feminine versus the queer pattern takes on an especially dramatic character. The film stages a conflict that, as I have argued elsewhere, will be central to modern horror, especially in its slasher thriller form: a battle between a female avenger and a queer monster. It might be said that what the woman stands in for and avenges, ultimately, is the heterosexual sexual order.[15] I will explore the significance of the contrast Hitchcock draws between the scene of hetero-homo male *doppelgängers* and Lila's investigation of the Bates house, which foregrounds the woman's appropriation of the masculine investigator role.

Splitting the Difference

At the climax of *Psycho*, John Gavin's Sam says to Perkins's Norman: "You are alone here, aren't you? It would drive me crazy." The line is more than sexually suggestive; it's downright cruisy. It's not just lines like these but also Gavin's surprisingly insinuating delivery of them in the scene that startles. In its own way, Perkins's pointedly clueless, or anything but, response is equally interesting: "Now, that would be rather an extreme reaction, wouldn't you say?" Mutually uncomprehending and accusatory mirror figures, these double men reflect each other's potential for violence and self-disavowal. "You look frightened," Sam says.

65

"Have I been saying something frightening?" Norman's response characteristically deflects and reveals: "I don't know what you've been saying." If queerness, as D. A. Miller and Eve Kosofsky Sedgwick established, is tied to regimes of knowing and the open secret of homosexuality—which everyone "knows" about but can never explicitly acknowledge, hence the secret's unyielding hold on the imagination and power to shape discourse—what is interesting about the exchange between Sam and Norman is Sam's position of being the one who *knows*.

"He knows, he knows!" Farley Granger's Phillip explodes at the climax of *Rope* when James Stewart's Rupert Cadell verges on discovery of the dead body of David Kentley, murdered by Phillip and his lover Brandon (John Dall) and contained in the chest upon which they served dinner to guests that included David's father. The closeted homosexual and the heterosexual interlocutor, the one in the position of seeing through the closet door and who attempts to decode and reveal the homosexual secret, conduct a profoundly tense and complex relay of knowledge and not-knowing. The closeted one knows his own secret and carefully monitors the levels of awareness and knowingness on the part of others; but the interlocutor, the one who wants to drag the closet case into the light of day, also *knows*: he conducts stealth missions, charges conversations with ironic levels of *double entendre*, heightens interpersonal encounters with multiple layers of meaning. In short, the straight male interlocutor makes latent content manifest; he exposes to light, or attempts to do so, the entire system of sexual secretiveness. (Of course, the straight interlocutor can just as easily be a "she," much like the relentlessly inquisitive and troublemaking Lil Mainwaring who pursues the titular heroine in *Marnie* in order to expose her sexualized secrets.)

Indeed, the closet case and the straight interlocutor are the ultimate doubles, each charging their exchanges with myriad levels of intrigue and double meanings. The men at the climax of *Psycho*, in their asymmetrical relationships to knowledge and knowing, in their mutually tense and conflicted but also mutually exclusive positions within this epistemological schema—Sam believes that he knows what Norman "did to get" Marion's money; Norman knows that Mother killed the girl; Sam believes that money drives Norman's passions; Norman knows nothing of the money but all about the murders—are each the other's secret sharer, each the other's mirror image in their respective but similar acts of self-concealment and subterfuge.

James Naremore observes that for Sam and Norman's conversation, "Hitchcock repeats the compositions he had used earlier for the confrontation between Marion and Norman. He poses the characters symmetrically, on either side of the registration desk, and once again achieves a 'doubling' effect: Lila of course resembles her sister Marion, but for the first time we realize that there is an odd physical resemblance between Sam and Norman. Both are tall, with dark hair and eyes, their profiles set off against one another. Sam, however, is not birdlike; in fact, he reminds us of a strapping, 'healthy' version of Norman. [In the course of their argument and struggles,] the movie seems to be verging on psychomachia, as if Norman's potential consciousness, his possible daylight existence, were forcing itself upon him."[16]

The contrast between normal and insane—or straight and queer—masculinity in *Psycho* indexes the film's series of pointed contrasts, emphasized by visual motifs of splitting, such as the telephone pole that bifurcates the screen when the highway cop with the dark sunglasses wakes up Marion, asleep on the side of the road. These include the casting of physically similar actors (Leigh, Miles; Gavin, Perkins) to play the central female and male roles. What is, finally, the near indistinguishability of the males underscores the greater sympathy we have for the queer male monster, especially in the scene in which Sam grills Norman for "what you've done with the money, and what you did to get it," as if Mother-bound Norman were in it for the *money*. Up until the climax, the audience identifies with Norman far more than Sam, and also, I would generalize, finds him a more sympathetic character. Sam is ostensibly presented from the start as the red-blooded heterosexual male figure, in bed with his beautiful blonde lover. If his sexual potency is implicitly registered at the start, more significant is the film's depiction of Sam's failure to satisfy Marion emotionally, which has a decisive impact on her future decisions and implications for the film's overall representation of relations between men and women. Waffling about the ever-looming marriage question, Sam tellingly responds—to Marion's earnest line, "I haven't even been married once yet"—"Oh, but when you do, you'll swing!" This is one of the numerous *double entendres* in Joseph Stefano's brilliant, maliciously witty script. It's difficult not to imagine the literal swinging of a person who has been hanged. (In Hitchcock's England, capital punishment was always carried out by hanging until the punishment's wane in the early 1970s.) Sam not only treats Marion's needs cavalierly but also hints at her murder, a grotesque substitute, to say the least, for the fulfillment of her erotic and romantic wants.

It is the queer Norman who nurtures and listens to Marion, and also provides insight into her plight: "What are you running away from?" Horrifyingly, the intensity of his sexual and gendered torment is such that he also murders her. But for much of the film, we are strongly encouraged to believe that a third party—Mother, the enemy, after all, of the independent heroine—has done the killing. Hitchcock draws our attention to the physical similarities between Gavin and Perkins in order to undermine our assumptions about what makes one man sane, the other psychotic; one sexually normative, the other non-normative. It is precisely this splitting of male identity, this conflict between men and their queer doubles, that will take on a powerful and endlessly revised life in the New Hollywood.

67

The split image of Gavin and Perkins summarizes the tradition of darkly beautiful, tremulous young men in Hitchcock films. Throughout his work, it is the dark young man in particular who either evokes or embodies queer masculinity in one form or another: Ivor Novello in *The Lodger* (1927), Gregory Peck in *Spellbound* (1945), Louis Jourdan in *The Paradine Case* (1947), Granger in *Rope* and in *Strangers on a Train*, Montgomery Clift in *I Confess* (1953), and, most acutely of all, Perkins in *Psycho*. Peck, Jourdan, and Granger are all beautiful, dark young men tied to the threat (and reality) of violence; the beautiful, dark Clift in his role as a young priest is locked in a male-male conflict with an older man and murderer who wants to expose Clift's secret. *I Confess* is especially interesting because the young man's secret is knowledge of the *older* man's evil (Clift hears his confession of murder, but the murderer, perversely taking on the role of the straight interlocutor, relentlessly pursues and threatens to expose the priest).

There are other male physical types in Hitchcock, but his nervous brunets need more recognition than they have received (which also goes for the dark women in his films—such as Ingrid Bergman, Suzanne Pleshette, Diane Baker, and, in certain scenes in *Marnie*, Tippi Hedren—who are perpetually obscured by his cool blondes). That the majority of the actors playing these roles were themselves gay or bisexual—Novello, Granger, Clift, Perkins—adds to the queer valences of such figures. The scorching darkness of Gavin and Perkins—the contrast between intensely black hair and pale skin, allegorical of the splitting/doubling of masculinity and its straight/queer split as well—will manifest itself again and again in New Hollywood film.[17]

In staging a conflict between normal and perverse types of masculinity, Hitchcock stages a conflict between the idea of heterosexuality as normative and therefore desirable and queerness as non-normative and therefore undesirable to the point of being loathsome. In staging these conflicts, Hitchcock questions the foundational ideas and biases that undergird them, problematizing what is and is not desirable as he calls attention to the fissures and instabilities within normative models of sexuality and gender—the crazy cracks in the edifices of the normal. In *Psycho*, Norman's lonely and isolate queer psychosis is contrasted against the embattled woman (Marion), the female investigator (Lila), the straight male (Sam), and versions of the heterosexual couple. Perhaps most acutely of all, it is against the heterosexual couple, either synecdochically (Marion without Sam but headed to him) or implicitly (Lila and Sam), that Norman's isolate perversity is contrasted. The heterosexual couple, of course, always already represents the definitive and defining split of sexual difference. In this film, as in Hitchcock generally, the heterosexual couple represents a deeper, gnawing, finally inescapable set of anxieties about the social order itself. The social order, the film ominously suggests, is in the process of being split wide apart, alternately in danger of disintegration (as

A disoriented, amnesiac Gregory Peck holds a razor over the sleeping Ingrid Bergman in *Spellbound*. Hitchcock's darkly beautiful young men are associated with violence and emotional anguish.

Louis Jourdan
and Alida Valli in
The Paradine Case.
She has claimed
his body, but his
heart belongs to
her murdered
husband.

Montgomery
Clift in *I Confess*.
His crime is
ambiguous, but
his punishment
is severe.

Hitchcock's heterosexual doubles: Janet Leigh and John Gavin in *Psycho*

PSY-FI

Psycho contrasts the solitary, queer Norman Bates (Anthony Perkins) against the hetero-sexual "shadow couple" of Sam Loomis and Lila Crane (John Gavin and Vera Miles).

figured in the car sinking into the swamp) and of mechanization (the murdered woman's body contained within and on some level fusing with a car that, in the final image, looks like a grinning death's-head).

The negative images that abound in the gay male repertoire of the twentieth century and well into the twenty-first concentrate in the central image of the mother-obsessed male homosexual. (Consider Wes Craven's *Scream* franchise, the fourth film of which came out in 2011, obsessed with mother-obsessed queer killers.) In American psychiatry, Freud's theory has historically been thoroughly misrepresented, its complexities ironed out into pathologizing prescriptiveness. Elsewhere, I have challenged these pernicious applications of Freud's theory of male homosexuality as well as conventional denunciations of it as homophobic, arguing that it contains elements that remain useful to the understanding of male sexuality *generally*, particularly in that heterosexual as well as homosexual males can identify with the mother rather than the father within and/or as a result of the Oedipus complex.[18] Just as Freud's theory of male homosexuality (and, for that matter, of lesbianism) has been taken as a negative image, one that has pathologized and injured queer people, Hitchcock's vision of the queer male in *Psycho* has been apprehended as homophobic, qualities deepened, apparently, by its Freudian cast.[19] While my intention is not to repeat my previous arguments, I do want to establish that Hitchcock, like Freud, has too complex a view of sexuality generally, including queer sexuality, to classify his views as phobic. Indeed, given that, other than Marion, the character we identify with the most and feel most intensely for is Norman, and given the ways in which Hitchcock problematizes the queer/straight divide in cinematic male sexuality, I argue that, *on balance*, even if it contains phobic elements, *Psycho* is a queer film in its challenge to normative regimes of sexual order.

Sam's Body

Hitchcock famously begins *Psycho* with a series of panoramic, helicopter-shot views of Phoenix, Arizona, that move from the general cityscape to the specific hotel room in which lovers lie in a post-coital moment. Specifically, it is Marion Crane, in a white bra and skirt, on the bed; standing *above* her is Sam Loomis, her indecisive lover, bare-chested and wearing black pants. It's an impressive chest, chiseled though not excessively so in the gym-maven way that we are now used to, hairy but again not excessively so. With his hunky chest and gracefully, smoothly muscular arms and dark good looks, John Gavin's Sam is a prime cut of *Hunkus americanus*.

73

The visibility of Sam's/Gavin's upper body has not attracted the critical attention that Marion's/Janet Leigh's undress has. Even Robert Samuels in his excellent *Hitchcock's Bi-Textuality* makes no mention of Sam's equal state of undress or half-dress.[20] This oversight probably owes to the fact that bare-chested male characters are sometimes present in classical Hollywood (think, for example, of Johnny Weissmuller's genial jungle-bound Tarzan or William Holden in *Picnic*). Classical Hollywood films, however, rarely *opened* with a sight of such palpably visualized masculinity. We are invited to look up at Sam's screen sexiness, from the position usually reserved for someone about to perform oral sex. We are made to look at Marion lying on the bed, the tips of her bra tautly pointed upwards; but we are also made to look at Sam from the waist down, and specifically at crotch level. Indeed, in one shot, he simply *is* a lower body, a body that begins at crotch level.

Paradoxically, by being clothed and hidden by Sam's dark trousers, the lower half of his body is activated as a site of mysterious, tangible sexual interest. If no drop-trou will or could occur in such a film—as opposed to Gus Van Sant's shot-for-shot 1998 remake—that we are made to see Sam as naked from the waist-up and clothed from the waist-down alerts us to what we do not see as much as what

John Gavin as Sam in *Psycho: Hunkus americanus*, circa 1960.

we do, the hidden parts of his body.[21] If anything, these hidden parts are more alluringly eroticized through their obfuscation. Lying on the bed and snuggling with Marion, Sam's chest is again palpably visible, and Marion's caressing of it becomes our caressing of it. The low intimate level of their voices adds to the sense of very private exchanges; there is a kind of dreamlike, or simply post-coital, languor in Sam's responses that is also unusual for a Hollywood leading man. The scene feminizes him as much as it emphasizes his masculinity, making him seem, at moments, soft and sluggish.

Marion's point of view dominates the film in its first half, or, to put it more properly, the film oscillates between its own point of view and hers, both perspectives reinforcing as they contrast with each other. For example, the film follows the line of her gaze in her bedroom as she gets dressed and stares at the $40,000 in the envelope, but then also turns to the left to focus on the open suitcase in the process of being packed. The ominousness of the camera's deliberate movements simultaneously reflects her agitation and determination and communicates its own alarmed, knowing, yet fascinated interests. In her car, Marion's internal point-of-view dominates, as we hear the other characters' concerned or angry words from her perspective, rather than cutting to actual scenes of these characters talking about her.

Marion's point-of-view, rather than that of any other character save for Hitchcock's camera, dominates the first half of the film. Therefore, her perspective on not only her own but the couple's joint predicaments shapes the entire opening scene. If what is being racily foregrounded here is a new screen sexiness, the sexual desire in the foreground is *hers*, not Sam's. While the audience is invited to stare in titillation at the half-clad Marion, it is more importantly, given the emphasis placed on identification with Marion, made to desire Sam along with her. Vicariously, we are made to experience her physical intimacy with Sam, as well as her longing for greater and more sustained intimacy. Put another way, to the extent that our sexual interests are being solicited here, they extend fully to both man and woman.

If for critics such as the influential Raymond Bellour these opening moments evoke the primal scene, the mythic event of parental intercourse which is witnessed by the very young child, what is of great interest are the numerous ways Hitchcock devises to undermine the heterosexual logic of such scenes. In the first use of the *doppelgänger* motif in the film, Hitchcock frames Marion and Sam in the same shot, standing and facing each other. With her white blouse on, Marion physically matches Sam with his white shirt on, the mirror behind them enhancing the impression and effect of narcissistic doubling. One aspect of Janet Leigh's taut, controlled, urgent, and witty performance that has not often been commented on is its gender fluidity and ambiguity. In some shots, especially in this opening scene, Leigh's Marion looks more boyish than womanly, evoking Kim Novak's gendered ambiguity as Madeleine Elster in *Vertigo*.[22]

In a gorgeous reading of the shot that ends the scene, Raymond Durgnat observes that the image of Sam looking down at the floor, as Marion leaves after saying, "And you need to put your shoes on," evokes German Expressionism, a forlorn image of defeated man.[23] To take Durgnat's point further, we can posit that Sam's posture signs the expressionist figure of the double. As an image that evokes the double, Sam anticipates and will extend Norman's own series of doublings, of personality, body, and sexual identities.

Flashing forward, I want to call our attention to the shot of Sam and Vera Miles's Lila Crane sitting in *his* office in his hardware store, a scene that replicates and doubles the famous one between Norman and Marion earlier when she eats, "like a bird," the dinner of sandwiches and milk he prepared for her. In the hardware store, household objects such as rakes loom menacingly above this male-female couple, just as the stuffed birds of prey do in Norman's office. Lila sits in her chair, coiled and pensive; Sam looms above her, standing (like one of the menacing objects?), but looking much calmer. The cheerfulness with which he tells her that they should just sit tight, relax, and wait for news and the broad, handsome-bland-American-man smile he gives her are odd and confusing touches. Do they indicate his shallowness? They do seem to signal his surprising lack of urgent concern for Marion. (Was he really worth all of the trouble she went to? Is it possible that even the money would have really made a difference to him?) In contrast, Miles, in a tightly controlled performance, makes Lila a small bulldozer of determined force. Her urgency contrasts tellingly against his lack thereof, as it alerts us to what a weird character Sam is (though no weirder than the intensely dour Lila).

Sam's cheerfulness within this tense scene is a kind of interior, one-character doubling, his affect jarringly juxtaposed against the increasing panic and awfulness of the situation. Hitchcock refuses to allow us to view Sam as the masculine embodiment of stability, of moral, emotional, and demeanor-related normalcy. The film continues to deepen the impressions made in the first scene of Sam as someone who sits on reserves of barely untapped violence, as his explosion over his frustrations with his father's debts and the alimony checks to his ex-wife, "living somewhere on the other side of the world" (much like, in another way, Mrs. Bates and, soon, Marion), doubly suggest.

All of which is to say that when Sam and Norman are doubled in their climactic confrontation near the film's end, we have been well prepared to see these male characters as similar: doubles, mirror images, effectively one and the same. The small burst of violence in Sam in the first scene (when he complains about his debts) and the sexual ambivalence that he displays link him subtly to Norman. The forces that seem to be holding him back from marrying Marion can be summarized as the past's tyrannical hold over his present life. Norman, tethered as well to the past, reflects, to a horrifying extreme, Sam's predicaments. At the same time, Sam's particular problems prefigure what we learn of Norman.

Mirror Men and Shadow Couples

If Sam ostensibly provides the normal counterbalance to the psychotic Norman, there are key ways in which Norman is the more sympathetic character. In contrast to Sam, Norman seems much more genuine, openhearted, and sensitive, especially in the early scenes between him and Marion, even if it is in one of these early scenes, the famous shot/reverse shot conversation of them in the office, that his full menace begins to be apparent. In part, Norman's likability comes through as a result of the extraordinary delicacy and complexity of Anthony Perkins's performance in the role. Perkins's star image would become indelibly linked to the queer/psycho male identity Hitchcock constructed. Yet it is also the case that Perkins's 1950s roles—particularly *Fear Strikes Out* (Robert Mulligan, 1957), in which

76

he portrayed a real-life emotionally unstable baseball player locked in an oedipal conflict with his unrelentingly critical father, played with memorable relentlessness by Karl Malden—anticipated his Hitchcock turn; Hitchcock made use, in other words, of an incipient unsettling intensity in the Perkins persona.[24]

Whatever else he may be, Norman is more responsive to Marion—more interested in what she has to say, in *her*—in their first motel scene than Sam is shown to have been in theirs. Norman's murder of Marion in the shower has often been read as a metaphorical rape, the substitution for the sexual act he wanted to but could not commit. At the same time, the shower scene has been taken as the ultimate negative image of woman—defenseless, murdered for her moral failings, even though she has decided to "step out of her private trap," to cleanse her spirit as she does her body. Yet the murder maintains a much more complex metaphorical relation to other aspects of the film, if it is to be read as chilling sexual metaphor. The shower murder does not merely "enact" Norman's balked sexual desires, but also reflects other disquieting dimensions of male sexuality in the film. Sam's sexual ambivalence and potential for violence; the authoritarian blankness and ominousness of the highway cop (Mort Mills) with the black sunglasses; the odious tycoon Tom Cassidy (Frank Albertson), from whom Marion steals the money, and his desire to use Marion's "fine soft flesh" to replace it (albeit, a line said from within Marion's own apparently self-hating mindscape); the disgruntled, vaguely indifferent older sheriff, Al Chambers (John McIntire), who seems decent yet blank; and the psychiatrist, Dr. Fred Richman (Simon Oakland), who takes an almost sadistic glee in narrating Norman's story from "the Mother," as evinced by his callously theatrical response to Lila's question about whether or not Norman killed her sister: generally speaking, masculinity is depicted, when not bumbling, as alternately troubled and menacing in *Psycho*.

This is a film in which doubles deliriously abound. Cassidy and George Lowery (Vaughn Taylor), Marion's boss, double each other, each man linked to Marion's finances, the one odious and sloppily seductive, the other worried and kind, allowing Marion to go home for the day after she claims to have a headache. (Then again, maybe not so kind, after all: Lowery does not air-condition the office, even though, as Cassidy coarsely says, "It's as hot as fresh milk.") Other doubles include the private investigator Arbogast (Martin Balsam) and Al Chambers, one intently interested in finding Marion, the other not so much; Sam and Bob (Frank Kilmond), his nondescript, inquisitive hardware store assistant, who Sam yells at to "run out and eat" his lunch when Lila arrives; the authority figures of the highway cop, staring at Marion from behind those blinding dark sunglasses, and the psychiatrist, whose pomposity has made the denouement scene the embarrassment of an otherwise austerely well-designed film. (Oakland's performance may be more responsible for this pomposity than Joseph Stefano's script; in the Van

Sant remake, the unshowy Robert Forster makes the psychiatrist's monologue sound reasonable.) These authority figures should help, rescue, and illuminate, but end up failing utterly in their purported missions. Then there is "California Charlie" (John Anderson), the used-car dealer, and the highway cop, men who suspect Marion looks "like a wrong one" but do not further investigate the matter, much less help her. All of these male doubles—contrasted against the female doubles of Marion/Lila, Mrs. Bates/Marion, Mrs. Bates/Lila, Mrs. Bates/the sheriff's wife (Lurene Tuttle, who whispers the line, "In bed," and gives sexual matters a hushed look of disapproval, linking her to sex-phobic Mother and, as I will show, to Lila), and other variations. The idea of an essential split in identity, its essential doubleness, is consistently reinforced visually and thematically.

In terms of masculinity, the doubling reinforces the idea that masculinity oscillates between modes of violence and of kindness, which is itself, I argue, an allegory for a straight/queer masculinity, albeit in its most conventional form. While doing something ostensibly necessary, Sam's interrogation of Norman at the climax seems sadistic rather than moral; we're much more squarely in Norman's camp here (as it were) than we are in Sam's. Hitchcock pairs these physically similar actors/characters as he did Marion and Sam at the start, drawing our attention in haunting ways to their narcissistic mirror sameness. Sam walks by Norman's office, making sure the coast is clear. Standing there, staring at him, precisely as if he is waiting for him, is Norman. Once he has corralled Norman, Sam surreptitiously gives Lila a signal that she should make her way to the Bates house.

Hitchcock's blocking of this scene is extraordinarily suggestive. Framed in the doorway, these two male doubles occupy a shockingly small amount of screen space that *forces* them into physical intimacy. Or, perhaps, it is Sam that does the forcing. Preventing Norman from leaving the office and catching Lila as she darts away, Sam places his body directly against Norman's. Indeed, Norman looks *down*, crotchward, in surprise.[25] In his white shirt, Norman now wears a top remarkably similar to that which Marion wore in the opening scene and in the office. Sam, in his dark jacket and tie, presumably wears what he wore as he walked into that hotel room with Marion before we discovered them in post-coital languor. All in all, "the end answers the beginning," but not as Raymond Bellour's insightful but resolutely heterosexist schema would have it.

For Bellour, the Hitchcock film is exemplary of classical Hollywood's insistence on narrative closure; the end of the film resolves a problem set up at the start. Hitchcock must find a means of containing the unruly threat of unlicensed female sexuality that Marion represents at the beginning of the film, when we voyeuristically perceive her illicit lunchtime sexual tryst with Sam. The film will transform her feminine illness of "neurosis" into Norman's male malady of "psychosis," thus providing masculine closure through scopic schemes of voyeurism to an initially feminine narrative.[26] Our peering into Marion's sex life transforms into Norman's voyeuristic gaze, explicitly rendered as an act of looking that objectifies Marion as a sexual spectacle, and finally into the full revelation of Norman's "male" psychosis, to summarize Bellour's argument.

For all of their structural brilliance and influence, Bellour's readings of Hitchcock are inescapably heterosexist, especially in his insistence on reading Hitchcock films as versions of the Oedipus complex that produce male characters who have resolved theirs by the end: learned to *identify* with rather than compete against the father and to desire a woman *outside* of the family. *Psycho* commences with a heterosexual primal scene, yet it is with a highly charged pair of same-sex conflicts that Hitchcock brings the film to a climax: the contrasting and paired battles between Sam and Norman, on the one hand, and, on the other hand, Lila and the dead/living Mrs. Bates, whose uncanny presence pervades the Bates house. Hitchcock resolutely decenters the inaugural image of the heterosexual couple through his strategic doublings: Sam/Lila, in Bellour's words the "shadow couple"; Sam/Norman; and, indeed, the doubling of all of the other characters with the isolate Norman.

The reception desk that separates the heterosexual couple from the solitary male in the office (an echo of classic American literary figures, such as Melville's famously intransigent scrivener Bartleby) functions as yet another object that bifurcates the screen. I refer to the shot, near the end of the film, of Norman behind the desk, checking in the incognito Sam and Lila, who are surreptitiously planning on "searching every inch" of the Bates Motel. In contrast to the vertical split-object of the telephone pole on the road where the highway cop wakes Marion up and interrogates her, the desk is horizontal, but functions in a similar manner, as an emblem of division and split subjectivities, here, between the heterosexual couple and the isolate, queer male. That this "heterosexual couple" is, as Bellour points out, a shadow of the real heterosexual couple with which the film began only reinforces the overall queasy sense of deadened and hollow relationships.

"We're going to register as man and wife," Lila says in the car as they drive over: the shadow couple plays at being the normative couple, a play deepened by the gender ambiguity of Vera Miles as Lila, the toughness and even iciness she brings to the role. The key point is that Norman's queer subject position is contrasted against their ostensibly normative one. Hitchcock then stunningly reconfigures this contrast as one between the male doubles of Norman and Sam and the isolate female investigator (Lila in the Bates house). Superseding the split between the heterosexual couple and Norman, the doubling of the paired men and the solitary woman inverts this prior split and further emphasizes gender and sexual ambiguity: the threatening homoerotic pairing of two male characters and the gender-bending acquisition, on the part of Lila, of the masculine role of the investigator. As Laura Mulvey points out in "Visual Pleasure and Narrative Cinema," the investigator is traditionally the male role. It is he who penetrates the mystery of woman, obsessively following her and trying to figure her out, as Scottie does with Madeleine in *Vertigo*. (In my view, that film is a *critique* of these paradigms, not a perpetuation of them.) This investigative penetration is linked to voyeurism, which, along with fetishism, is one of the two means male characters have for dealing with the overwhelming castration fears embodied in the female form. In *Psycho*, Lila becomes a kind of voyeur as well as investigator, penetrating the mystery of Mother and her house as well as of Norman.

One of the unexplored aspects of Bellour's reading of Sam and Lila as the shadow couple—the couple that serves as *doppelgänger* to the original heterosexual couple of Sam and Marion—is that *Sam becomes his own doppelgänger*, his own shadow, just as one heterosexual couple becomes another's mirror image, implying a series of sexual masquerades and a deep psychic instability within the normative structures of sexuality, valences that are characteristic of Hitchcock's representation of the heterosexual couple. This self-doubling and splitting off of Sam's own identity and roles in the film all imply an essential fragility in his heterosexual masculine composure, one that allows for the possibility of queer dimensions to his character. Sam's questioning of Norman is, as I noted, surprisingly cruisy at first. He asks, "You are alone here, aren't you?" Then, he slouches against the counter and adds, "Would drive me crazy." Sam, as Gavin is positioned in the frame, slouches to such an extent that his image is *not* captured in the mirror that hangs, most significantly, behind him. Symbolically, Sam has placed himself in such a way as to be undetectable and to have eluded surveillance. In a pre-Stonewall, homophobic environment, and, I would add, afterwards, the mythic "sneaky gays" have had to use just such stealth maneuvers of verbal play—in a most apt phrase here, *double entendres*—as well as physical hints (unostentatiously or absently scratching one's crotch, for instance) to signal sexual interest. These covert signals could, of course, once properly understood, be rebuffed, but could also always be denied. While my argument is not—exactly—that Sam is "gay," I do find it interesting that he acts in a manner that is so sexually suggestive. What counts most here, I think, is a strategic and eerie blurring—who should be the object of our sexual gaze in the opening scene, Marion . . . or Sam?; who is the sane and normal and therefore always already heterosexual male subject here? Not Norman to be sure, but perhaps not Sam, either. As I noted earlier, the interlocutor, the one attempting to penetrate the mystery of the closeted person's sexuality, and the closeted person both share a highly charged space of sexualized knowledge and intrigue. At the very least, Sam's interrogation of Norman has a queer edge because of the sexual intensity of interrogation—especially the insinuating kind on display here—itself.

The blocking in this scene is significant. Sam/Gavin's slouched posture—matching and amplifying the somewhat insinuating, lazy way that Gavin delivers the line, "Would drive me crazy"—in this first shot of the men talking on either side of the reception desk is remarkably sensual, almost louche; it is simply not a conventional leading man's physical position, especially when speaking with another male character. Norman, for his part, is also oddly positioned, with his left leg raised, his foot presumably on a ledge within the rear portion of the desk. In the next shots, in which Sam's interrogation of Norman grows more and more intense, he stands erectly opposite Norman. Yet now his image is captured in the mirror. The symbolic valences shift: it is as if the mirror now *contains* the secret between them that the first shot of their discussion on either side of the counter only whispered. The mirror reifies their thematic doubling as visual fact.

Sam's interrogation of Norman doubles Arbogast's in the same room. Outside the horizontal office, looking up at the looming, vertical Bates house, and noticing the figure of Mother in the window, Arbogast asks to see Mother, and, once rebuffed, taunts Norman by saying that if he were indeed hiding Marion, he would have to know that she was only using him. In response to Norman's defensive contradictions and line, "She might have fooled me, but she didn't fool my mother," Arbogast responds, "This is not a slur on your manhood." Between them, Arbogast and Sam are, indeed, a slur on Norman's manhood, and he on theirs, if we consider the dictionary dimensions of the term:

1 a : an insulting or disparaging remark or innuendo : aspersion
  b : a shaming or degrading effect : stain, stigma
2 : a blurred spot in printed matter : smudge

These dark-haired, normal/perverse masculinities leave a stain on the image of normative American manhood, one that spreads out over its cheerful, progress-minded, smiling, obdurate face. Sam seeks to shame and degrade Norman into confessing his crime, eerily tantamount to wringing the confession of the crime of his desire from the offending closeted/cruising gay man.[27] "Where's that girl you came here with?" Norman asks, and well he should—where, indeed? The question could be read in many ways, but at least one way to read it is as a challenge to Sam and the heterosexual presumption and privilege he hides behind in this office made for hiding. In other words, Norman, turning the tables whereby Sam questions Norman's sexuality, might be asking: "Where's that girl you came here with—and why are you trying to seduce me and not her?" For his part, as if exposed, Sam begins to taunt Norman about his relationship to his mother. He decisively shifts from the oddly seductive and homoerotic position he maintains at the start of the scene to that of a much more stereotypically straight male character who derides Norman for his mama's-boy leanings—correctly deducing these as urgent while also grotesquely misreading Norman's obsessions as monetarily motivated.

Norman, for his part, is a doubled character in heterosexual terms as well as queer ones. Audiences at the time, especially given Perkins's matinee idol status, and given that the film came out long before Perkins's own homosexuality, or bisexuality, became public knowledge, were eager to see Norman as Marion's rescuer and, potentially, romantic interest. Indeed, the film, a very different one, to be sure, could have played as a very unlikely love story, a romance between two lost souls who each rescue each other from respective private traps. It is fascinating to consider how often the film plays around with these audience expectations, and how careful is its oscillation from hetero and queer typings of Norman.

As the endless slasher-horror films made in its wake will reinforce, *Psycho* is primarily a cinematic expression of the widely known Freudian theory of the male homosexual who overidentifies with his mother and her desire. The most undeniable nod to this Freudian construct is the shot of Norman going up the stairs to Mother, swaying his hips. Norman goes into Mother's room, attempting to coax her into letting him hide her in the basement, his fumbling speech a variant, as are the long pauses, of the stuttering that generally characterizes it. No sooner does he speak than Mother snorts at him in derisive laughter. "Heh heh heh. I'm sorry, boy," she says caustically. "But you *do* manage to sound ridiculous when you give me orders." Norman responds, after his initial fumbling, "*I'll carry you, Mother*," and now he sounds cold and determined, as if marshalling his masculine strength. And as he does carry Mother, the usefulness of the overhead shot now becomes quite apparent: we can see Norman carrying Mother downstairs but *cannot* see that she is a skeletal corpse animated only by Norman's voice. In this one scene, Norman moves fluidly and weirdly from the swishy gay male to the male who stands up to Mother and dominates Woman.

Earlier, the shot of Norman carrying the shower-curtain-wrapped dead Marion out of the motel room grotesquely inverted the iconic image of the man carrying his bride over the threshold into their new home. It also, poignantly, in my view, represents the child-caregiver's relationship to the aging parent. More than any other referent, the moment establishes that Norman cares most compassionately for women after he has killed them. It is a heartbreakingly bare moment as well as one of great intertextual resonance, given its relationship to related moments in other Hitchcock films.[28] In perhaps the ultimate reversal, it is the queer Norman who overpowers the ostensibly strong and stalwart heterosexual male Sam, conking him on the head with an object. Sam can only overpower Norman once he is *feminized*, dressed up as Mother. Knocking Sam unconscious in the parlor, Norman assumes the more properly masculine role, just as Lila does as the investigator who solves the crime. By the time *Psycho* has ended, with Norman's face, Mrs. Bates skull-face, and Marion's car-body-swamp face hideously merged into one, identity itself, gender itself, sexuality itself, have all been so radically denatured that doubling as a way of life comes to seem a reparative strategy for a relentlessly riven world.

The Feminine Versus the Queer: Lila as Double

Hitchcock contrasts Lila's exploration of the house with the increasingly tense discussion, with menacing homoerotic undertones, between the doubles Sam and Norman. The doublings in the film reinforce one another: the menacing encounter between Sam and Norman ratchets up the drama of Lila's exploration of the Bates house; her investigation of this nightmarish domain reflects, refracts, and ironizes their psychic duel. While her solitary journey stands in poignant contrast to their conflictual pairing, her encounter with Mrs. Bates is another kind of fraught same-sex confrontation. These same-sex pairings now double each other.

We have been discussing the pattern of the feminine versus the queer in Hitchcock's work. *Psycho* is the most stringent exploration of this rivalrous relation. In his essay "How Queer is My *Psycho*," Alexander Doty has helpfully and rightly rescued the character of Lila from critical oblivion. I believe, however, that the film's depiction of her is a much more ambivalent one than Doty suggests. While she may indeed be a lesbian figure, a sympathetic character, and an exciting representation of femininity overall, she isn't quite so heroic, in the end.

Approaching and entering the Bates house, Lila becomes at once the investigator and Carol Clover's famous figure of the "Final Girl," who survives to do battle with the slasher-film monster. First, Lila investigates Mother's room, during which she experiences a terrifying moment in which she gasps at what appears to be another woman in the room—Mother, perhaps—but turns out to be Lila's own reflection in a series of mirror images. The following scene, in which Lila investigates Norman's childhood room, is much more extraneous to the plot. But it has its own urgency and logic, and, I argue, it sets the stage for the central conflict of modern horror: the showdown between the heroine and the queer monster, the *locus classicus* of gendered warfare in the slasher horror film from which Clover draws her theory of the Final Girl.

In my view, Clover does not pay sufficient attention to the *disciplinary function of the Final Girl*, who is a feminist icon in that she defeats the monster on behalf of all of the genre's slain women as well as herself, but is also a reactionary figure who purges the film of its unruly, non-normative gendered and sexual aspects, in a word, of its queerness, embodied by the monster, almost always represented as a male who is both a social misfit and sexually dysfunctional.[29] Lila's inspection of Norman's childhood room is an exquisite example of the Final Girl's oddly disciplinary function.

As Lila investigates Norman's old room, we see everything through her gaze, through shots of her pointedly looking at objects in the room and the shots of the items themselves, seen through her gaze. The objects, deeply telling, include: a boy doll, at an odd tilt; a bedraggled stuffed rabbit, one of its ears forlornly bent; a child's unmade bed, in stark contrast to the hyper-fastidious cleaned sheets and made beds Norman insists on, week after week, for the motel (he cleans the motel rooms even though guests haven't checked into them, grossed out by the "creepy" smell of dampness; his fastidiousness and the creepy dampness have obvious sexual overtones); a record player turntable, with a record of Beethoven's "Eroica" symphony in it (This is a puzzling detail that seems punningly placed to suggest "Erotica." On the one hand, this is a sexual joke, but it's also a joke related to Norman's inadequate gender performance. If Beethoven initially intended this symphony to honor Napoleon Bonaparte's war campaigns, and "eroica" is Italian for "heroic," there is very little that is conventionally masculine or "heroic" about Norman.); and lastly a book with an untitled spine, which Lila handles, turns up and down, and looks inside.

This book, as presented in the film, could simply be something innocuous (say, an album of family photos; but then again, in the Bates family context, what could be *less* innocuous?). Donald Spoto has noted, however, that Victorian pornography was printed in books with no titles on their spine.[30] Doty further reminds us that Robert Bloch's original novel revealed that this was a book of pornographic pictures.[31] Hitchcock ends Lila's inspection of Norman's childhood room with Lila's reaction shot as she peers into this illicit volume, whose contents we are not allowed to see. But we can guess at their illicit nature through the quietly alarmed expression that grows on Lila's face.

Norman incapacitates Sam, knocking him on the head with an object, and now races into the house to look for Lila. The shot of his furious progress up the stairs is the first one in which he unambiguously provokes terror in the audience in a conventional horror-movie monster manner. He could be the scary serial killer now. If the shower murder horrifically symbolizes the film's decisive splitting of the woman's narrative from that of the horror male's, which supersedes her own (I will further discuss this split in the next chapter), it is in this moment that *Psycho* unambiguously transitions from female melodrama to horror movie, a passage further symbolized by Lila's literal descent from Mother's bedroom to the lower, chthonic reaches of the house, the *locus classicus* of the horror movie being the basement or some other hidden, obscure, subterranean, infernal place. (It could be a seemingly abandoned or empty shed, a hut out in the woods, or some other secret and prohibitive space, such as the attic or the bedroom closet as well as the basement in the terrifying 1974 Canadian slasher film *Black Christmas*, directed by Bob Clark.) If Norman was momentarily frightening in the parlor scene with Marion—leaning forward, with frozen, deadened, yet intensely incensed eyes on his line, "You mean a madhouse? An institution? My mother there?"—we may have been able to shrug this moment off, as we do odd, outré moments in life that radically defy expectations. And, with sickening effectiveness, the movie has shown how desperately we cling to an onscreen protagonist by so effortlessly shifting our allegiance to Norman once Marion has been killed. At midpoint, he became the figure of identification and also sympathy, harassed and dominated by a tyrannical and murderous old woman. And we felt for him as Sam mercilessly grilled him. But now, in the shot of Norman racing up the outdoor stairs, the film finally achieves the slickest genre conventionality—Norman is now purely menacing monster.

Almost immediately, however, we are back into the realm of the Hitchcockian uncanny in which nothing feels or looks conventional. Norman's odd position, once inside the house, at the foot of the main staircase; the odd, birdlike, but also robot-sentry manner in which he moves his head, shifting it to one direction, then another—Better to hear Lila? Or to let us know that he means business?—before racing up the main stairs, not realizing that Lila is behind these on the short lower staircase leading to the basement, all contribute to the strange and unsettling atmosphere.

Lila now descends into the chthonic recesses of the fruit cellar. As in the modern horror films to follow, *Psycho* foundationally sets up a confrontation between the Final Girl and the queer, mother-obsessed monster. The basement, that Freudian metaphor for repressed desires and the unconscious, is at once dead Mother's barren womb and the "fruity" zone of queer fecundity—an anus that breeds horrifying anti-life, that, indeed, gives the dead figure of Mother an obscene, uncanny semblance of life. If there are both undeniable misogynistic and homophobic elements in this schema, what is more palpably present is a savagely skeptical disposition toward the apparently wholesome joys of family life, the house providing an architectural metaphor for its layers of repression, cruelty, and decay.

If the tension between the queer male and the "woman who knows too much" about his predilections, a theme we found already to be at work in *The Man Who Knew Too Much* of 1956, finds a startling development in *Psycho*, this conflict also has a much broader set of implications. Doty reads Lila as "a brash, heroic dyke" who must meet her mirror image in the distorted queer image of transvestic Norman. Donned in Mother's attire, wielding the knife, Norman is ultimately disabled by Sam, who bursts in to save the heroine. Resourceful and heroic though she is, even Lila, Doty notes, cannot escape the "queer apocalypse" of *Psycho's* end.[32]

I am in appreciative agreement with Doty about Lila's significance in the film and very much admire Miles's performance, here and elsewhere, especially in

85

Hitchcock's *The Wrong Man* and John Ford westerns. I read Lila differently, however. There are a series of tensions surrounding her that have troubling resonances. As James Naremore observes in his *Filmguide to Psycho*, "After we have seen the film several times, Lila's explorations of the Bates mansion begin to look like some sort of violation. At first we have the titillation of discovery and suspense, but later we are aware of Norman's anguish. Hitchcock cuts back and forth between Sam's relentless questioning and Lila's investigations, until the madman begins to look like a trapped insect. Nevertheless, the camera in these sequences gives most of its sympathy to Lila, becoming her eyes as she climbs the hill" and enters and inspects the house.[33]

Others have also noticed the oddness of Lila's characterization. In his essay "Is there a proper way to remake a Hitchcock film?" Slavoj Žižek writes, "While watching *Psycho* for the twentieth time, I noticed a strange detail during the final psychiatrist's explanation: Lila listens to him enraptured and nods two times with deep satisfaction, instead of being shaken by the final confirmation of her sister's meaningless death. Was this a pure contingency, or did Hitchcock want to suggest a strange libidinal ambiguity and rivalry between the two sisters?"[34] What makes Lila a less-than-fully positive figure for me are her associations with a culture of repression and sexual hygiene. Lila may be, in certain respects, a queer heroine. But, more pronouncedly, she is the embodiment of normativity. While she is excitingly forceful and active, she is also harsh and humorless, an unyielding presence. When she peers into the pornographic book, as she does into his room, Lila is not only invading Norman's secret space—his closet, if you will—but implicitly rendering judgment on it. Perhaps this is the quality that Žižek picks up on—Lila's associations with the law and a culture of repression. If Žižek's reading is valid, Lila identifies with the institutional rhetoric and diagnostic power of American psychiatry, certainly, by the time this film was made, a repressive regime. (I say this as a passionate Freudian. Freud in his complexity was not embraced by American psychiatry, but was, instead, plumbed for his most conservative positions.)

One could argue, of course, that Lila admirably maintains her composure in this scene, keeping her grief private—not allowing it to be exploited by the faces of male power encircling her. For that matter, Sam, though he seems somewhat more discomfited than Lila, doesn't go into hysterics, either. The real heavy in the scene is the pompous psychiatrist, who treats the death of Marion as an incidental part—to be glossed over with theatrical rhetoric—of his master narrative. ("Did he kill my sister?" Lila asks. "Yes—and no," the psychiatrist responds.)

To be sure, Hitchcock, as is his fashion, regards the woman's journey, plight, and endangerment with sympathy, and that disposition, combined with Miles's intelligent intensity in the role, make Lila both compelling and an important audience identification figure—far more so than, say, Sam. Overall, this is a complex representation of femininity. Yet Lila is also figured as a hygienic presence, which reinforces her associations with repression and the law. It is she who notices and picks out of the toilet—the first to be seen flushing in a classic Hollywood film and, indeed, according to its makers, any Hollywood sound film—the piece of a paper on which Marion's scrawled cash amount figures are still visible, subtractions from the $40,000.

This gesture emphasizes Lila's associations with control, money, hygiene, anality, and sadism at once. If money, as Freud theorized, is excrement, and if the anal stage is associated not just with excrement but with sadistic mastery and control, what Lila presides over are the psychic messes of other people, including their excessive, non-normative desires and emotional states. In other words, Lila is the person who cleans up other people's shit. On the one hand, she provides a correct, orderly counterbalance to the unruly Marion's wayward desires. On the other hand, she provides a corrective contrast to Norman, his unseemly desires as well as his inadequate performance of gender identity. A great deal more needs to be said on these last points, to be sure.

An excitingly modern woman and an avenging feminist angel, Lila is also a figure who ensures the reestablishment of the normative order by ridding it of its agency-seeking, nonconformist women and queer, sexually non-normative men. While it cannot in any way be ignored that Norman Bates is a serial killer of women (and men) who must be stopped, it is nevertheless also true that Lila emerges as his judge and vanquisher. Staring into that pornographic book, is Lila Norman's queer sister—or is she an anticipation of the anti-gay activists who emerged in the 1970s, an Anita Bryant peering, aghast, into the depravities of queer men?[35]

Surely, this last must be a wild overstatement. But if we consider that the kind of male figure that the Final Girl, of which Lila is the prototype, most often annihilates is sexually non-normative—as Carol Clover theorizes in her readings of such films as *The Texas Chainsaw Massacre* (Tobe Hooper, 1974) and its sequel (Hooper, 1986), even as she discusses the resistant potentialities of the Final Girl, and even as she more emphatically treats the Final Girl as the cover behind which male spectators can hide, thereby disavowing their own masochism—her role, however counterintuitive it is to consider it this way, must, on some level, be tied to and supported by regimes of sexual normativity. Her killing of the monster is a purgative act that supports the gendered and sexual status quo. If the knowing woman had been a sympathetic figure in previous Hitchcock films, here she emerges as a more suspect one. She metonymically represents the forces of law and order that exposes Norman's gender-bending psychosis to the light of rational justice. At the same time, Lila does not kill the monster. Moreover, she is the woman who fights for other women and avenges her sister. All in all, Lila is fascinating precisely because she is so complexly drawn—by Miles, Hitchcock, and the screenwriter Joseph Stefano—and because her functions in the film are so difficult to pin down.[36]

PSYCHO SYNTHESIZES the thematic of queer male sexuality in Hitchcock's previous films while also establishing a remarkably influential precedent for cinematic masculinity, in the modern horror genre most prominently, but also generally in the movies to follow. *Psycho* established a confluence among voyeurism, homosexuality, and the emergent technology of pornography, as signaled by the risqué early scene between half-clad lovers in the hotel, Norman's peeping at the undressing Marion, and Lila's scrutiny of the pornographic book. As these modes began to inform masculinity, they also rendered it fundamentally split, divided against itself. In its prophetic synthesis of these tensions and trends, *Psycho*, I argue, creates a postmodern male subjectivity that will prove to be a template for the masculinity that the New Hollywood, influenced so resonantly by Hitchcock, will create as a group portrait.

CHAPTER THREE

BLANK SCREENS
Psycho and the Pornographic Gaze

A FTER ITS FAMOUS OPENING SERIES of helicopter-shot, panoramic vistas of Phoenix, Arizona, Alfred Hitchcock's 1960 film *Psycho* gives us an illicit view of post-coital lunchtime lovers in a hotel room, he shirtless, she in her bra and half-slip. "The sex angle was raised," François Truffaut remarks in one of his famous interviews with the director, "so that later on the audience would think that Anthony Perkins is merely a voyeur. If I'm not mistaken," Truffaut continues, "out of your fifty works, this is the only film showing a woman in a brassiere." Hitchcock confirms that his choices reflect his awareness that the "audiences are changing."[1] Through such innovations as the bared brassiere, the film announces itself as daring and modern, "a new— and altogether different—entertainment," as the poster for the film, which shows Janet Leigh in her white bra and half-slip only, proclaimed. Determinedly breaking taboos in terms of what can be shown and inferred in a movie, *Psycho* shows us more than movies had before: more flesh, more violence, and for the first time in American film, according to its makers, a flushing toilet.

Hitchcock may have been teasingly manipulating the audience, as was his custom. But in no Hitchcock film is a character "merely" something as momentous as a voyeur. Voyeurism emerges as one of the major themes of Hitchcock's mature work, from the 1950s forward. In *Psycho*, the comparatively teasing, playful evocation of voyeurism in *Rear Window* (1954)—which certainly prefigures the later film's bleakness—takes on an especially anguished and murderous character. Viewed, at the film's midpoint, by Norman Bates through the peephole in his office, Marion Crane is clad in a black bra and black half-slip, in contrast to the white undergarments of the first scene. She wears the color of her sin—the infamous stolen $40,000. If we stick with this moral framework, as Hitchcock himself did, one might ask about Norman's sinful spying. Hitchcock will show us that Norman is in a hell of his own making.

In any event, Norman's pornographic voyeurism does not lead him to pursue Marion romantically or sexually. Indeed, if anything, it presages his murder of her. Moreover, and this is a crucial point, Norman's illicit looking at Marion does not proceed from any clear-cut, defined sexual orientation. It is a kind of sexually blank, though intimidating and invasive, looking. If *Psycho* foundationally indicates a new sexual openness, part of this openness is the inference of pornographic viewing in certain key scenes. Indeed, *Psycho* heralds the emergence of the pornographic gaze in mainstream narrative film. In the Hitchcockian context as well as in many of the films that have been inspired by his work, the pornographic gaze is associated with these qualities of blankness and violence at once, and, most palpably, an overwhelming sense of isolation. *Psycho* frames the pornographic in its incipient emergence in narrative film as a symptom of what ails American men. Hitchcock figures the pornographic gaze as the domain of men whose empty looking matches their emotional, sexual, and social emptiness. It is Hitchcock's depiction of the pornographic gaze as indicative of social and sexual disconnection and emptiness that will prove so influential for later films.

Drawing a Blank: Pornography and Eros

As John Orr puts it, "for Hitchcock Eros is usually inseparable from love. The opening of *Psycho* may be steamy but there is also a deadness in the knowing solitude of its lovers, an excess of familiarity where love and Eros are dying simultaneously."[2] The damaged, decaying, and dying levels of love and eros in *Psycho* characterize both heterosexual and homosexual possibilities. *Psycho*'s representation of masculinity as fundamentally split, with its implications for a fraught hetero-homo divide, and its themes of voyeurism, homosexuality, and the emergent technology of pornography, figured as reflective of a larger deadening of social ties and individual subjectivities, will be endlessly repeated in the New Hollywood, as the following chapters will show. If the cinematic output of the New Hollywood was, indeed, male-dominated, as Peter Krämer has argued, the very term "male-dominated" would undergo a thorough and unflinching critique. Shown to be the locus of national sexual and gendered anxieties, American manhood in the films of the 1970s inherited the murderous conflicts attending masculinity in *Psycho*, conflicts shown to be no less murderous in the post-studio years. Through Hitchcock's influence, these conflicts would be given a newly urgent treatment.

In the previous chapter, I focused on the climactic exchange between Norman Bates and Sam Loomis that is intercut with Lila Crane's exploration of the Bates house. Here, my focus is on Norman's voyeuristic staring at the undressing Marion Crane. Just as the book without a title on its spine that Lila Crane examines in Norman Bates's bedroom evokes pornographic viewing, so, too, does Norman's spying on Marion before she takes her fateful shower. Infusing these pornographic motifs with additional levels of intensity and dread was the increasingly public threat of homosexuality within the Cold War context in which Hitchcock's related themes gained a new, ominous visibility. What emerges in *Psycho* is a tripartite monster—voyeurism-homosexuality-pornography, a cluster of psychosexual anxieties that would prove to be of enduring influence precisely *as* this cluster. In order to make sense of *Psycho*'s multi-pronged significance and its influence, one must discuss it from numerous angles: its relationship to Hollywood history, its intersection with the emergent technologies of pornography, and its impact on subsequent cinematic representations of gender and sexuality.

While contemporary film studies has more than rightly challenged the Mulvey-model of the heterosexual male gaze in the classical Hollywood cinema, it is undeniably true that, given the strictures of the Production Code, the films of classical Hollywood revolve around—at least, this is their manifest sexual content—the heterosexual desire that ostensibly motivates all film narratives of the period. A number of insurgent factors began to topple this heterosexual reign. The collapse of the studio system in the 1960s, a shift heralded by Hitchcock in his independent, TV-crew-helmed *Psycho*; the increasingly public Cold War threat of homosexuality; the increasing visibility of pornography; and the incipient stirrings of what would become a full-blown, if short-lived, Sexual Revolution all helped to create a postmodern Hollywood as well as viewing subject. Synthesizing or anticipating these shifts and tensions, *Psycho* is central to the development of a postmodern masculinity, and within that emergent model the relationship between the pornographic and male sexuality is inextricable.[3] One way of looking at the issue is to consider pornography as the outcome of sexuality in postmodernism—which is not to imply that the longstanding history of pornography is a postmodern creation, but, instead, a phenomenon that postmodernism made prominent.

In my view, Hitchcock and the other filmmakers I treat in this study offer critiques of pornography, rather than simply exploiting its provocations or perpetuating its most exploitative proclivities. At the center of this critique is the almost uniform presentation of the pornographic as an emotional, spiritual, and even physical deadening. The pornographic deadens the viewing subject as well as the subjects being viewed, rendering the pornographic gaze a state of blankness. One could call all forms of sexuality in *Psycho* blank, the work of rigid forms against blank screens, to evoke George E. Toles's superb essay on the film, "If Thine Eye Offend Thee . . ."[4] Linking Hitchcock's film to works by Bataille and Poe, Toles observes that they achieve their "respective forms of pornographic intensity by impersonally rendered shocks" organized around "the same obsessive significance" of the eye as metaphor. Open mouths and gaping toilets further allegorize the eye.[5] Rabidly potent and just as rabidly lifeless, the monster of *Psycho* is this all-seeing, all-knowing, utterly blank and unfeeling eye.

While I concur with Toles, I believe that a specific set of concerns informs and perhaps even produces the blankness of *Psycho*. The incipient and intensifying pornographic awareness that comes to define male sexuality is enmeshed, inescapably, with the growing visibility of homosexuality. In a way, it is precisely homosexuality coming into ever more explicit, enunciated focus—both culturally and in Hitchcock films—that produces what is perhaps the most striking blank in *Psycho*, male sexuality itself. Indeed, as if implying that the homosexual male's fraught bid for representation was becoming increasingly undeniable, Hitchcock compromises by evacuating sexuality from the male subject altogether. Like the woman-suit-making serial killer Jame Gumb in Jonathan Demme's 1991 film *The Silence of the Lambs*, very much in intertextual engagement with *Psycho*, Norman Bates is a queer male subject whose queerness is not registered through any explicit reference to his sexuality, even though, at the same time, he has inescapably been read as "the homosexual."[6]

The coldness that characterizes sexuality generally in *Psycho* has its underpinning, in my view, in a growing contemporary understanding of sexuality as a commodity that one could purchase like a deluxe new luxury item. If there was a stifling, indeed suffocating, dimension to 1950s suburban-family-oriented constructions of sexuality, the incipient Sexual Revolution, with its promise of sex without such constraints, also had its dangers, especially when this revolution became tethered, along with everything else, to the market. These patterns had already been established by the time *Psycho* was made. As James Gilbert astutely observes,

> In many respects, for men, at least, the sexual revolution had already begun by the 1950s. Patterns of sexual behavior in both men and women had, as sexologist Alfred Kinsey discovered, changed rapidly, particularly after World War I. . . . In some respects, it took Hugh Hefner and *Playboy* magazine to demonstrate the potential of these findings. Hefner's magazine, which celebrated and exemplified the "Playboy philosophy," captured a huge amount of attention in the late 1950s and early 1960s. It advertised an alternative male sexual ethic offered up as

traditional and virile, but existing outside and beyond marriage and middle-class norms.

Hefner's genius was to recognize that sex could be sold overtly and above-board as an item of modern consumption. [While he didn't publish hard-core porn or promote prostitution], he did . . . make sex another consumer object associated with leisure pastimes and personal consumer products, almost a coffee table commodity.[7]

Psycho links pornography to a culture of consumerism that reifies all human subjects, or at least attempts to do so, into dead objects animated by monetary desire, empty shells stuffed with money.[8]

Smithereens: The Woman's Film and Anti-Capitalism

Psycho's critique of capitalism jaggedly intersects with its metatextual assaults on studio-era Hollywood. In her black undergarments that contrast against her white skin, Marion, seen through the peephole, is an allegory for the cinema itself. *Psycho* is the last black-and-white film Hitchcock would make, and in many ways the last work of classical Hollywood, with its particular formal elements, decorum, and constrictions in terms of content and acceptable subject matter. Indeed, *Psycho* kills off classical Hollywood, a formal and cultural maneuver that is allegorized by the murder halfway through the film of the protagonist played by a major star, Janet Leigh.

Hitchcock was killing off a particular kind of moviemaking associated with the Production Code. He was also killing off, as I began to argue in the previous chapter, a particular genre, the woman's film, which the first half of *Psycho* revisits. If we see the woman's film genre, which appears to fade away in the 1960s, as principally engaged in the conflicts faced by an independent, intelligent young woman, specifically her relationship to the question of marriage, *Psycho* offers a variation on the woman's film narrative, with Marion taking marriage matters into her own hands, stealing the money in order to buy her way into the marriage industry. Taking romantic matters into her own hands by taking the money placed into her hands by the odious Cassidy, Marion attempts to buy happiness as well as love, companionship, and emotional and sexual fulfillment. Marion Crane, in other words, attempts to manipulate the capitalist social order to her own ends, not to beat it at its own game, or even to game the system, but simply to enter into it. In the process, she applies its philosophies of reification—of turning everything from passions to bodies into things—to her own life and desires.

Marion takes Catherine Sloper's threat to her tyrannical father, in *The Heiress* (William Wyler, 1949), to its logical extreme. Dr. Sloper (Ralph Richardson) forces the shy and credulous Catherine (Olivia de Havilland) into telling her secretly

Sexual Aberrations of the Criminal Female: Janet Leigh's Marion Crane in
Psycho, a new-style woman's film that transitions into the horror genre.

mercenary suitor Morris Townsend (Montgomery Clift) that her father will cut
off her inheritance if she marries Morris. (She will still have her mother's inheritance, but overall much less.) As accurate a judge of character as he is cruel to
Catherine, her father turns out to be right about Morris's true nature. Catherine
discovers Morris's perfidy for herself when, after she tells him about her reduced
inheritance, he then abandons her on the eve of their planned elopement. Seeing
her grief-stricken, her father, now dying, promises to restore her full inheritance.
But Catherine retorts that she may take all of his money and procure marriage to
Morris with it. "If I am to buy a man," she challenges him, "I would prefer buying
Morris!" Marion Crane, the protagonist of a new woman's film that blows the
genre to smithereens (which Hitchcock will reconstitute in *The Birds* and *Marnie*,
especially), not only threatens to buy a man with money but actually attempts to
do so. (Catherine decides to live life alone. But she coldly takes her revenge on
Morris when he returns. "He has grown greedier with the years. First, he wanted
my money. Now, he wants my love, too. Well, he came to the wrong house. And
he came a second time. I shall see to it that he does not come a third." She certainly does, refusing to come to the door as he furiously pounds at it in the closing
image.)

That Marion ends up not just dead but hideously murdered literalizes, in particularly grotesque fashion, the ways in which the social order renders its subjects dead precisely by enflaming their desires through the promise and allure of money's possibilities.[9] Conversely, Lila and Sam's insistent belief that Norman has killed Marion for the $40,000 she stole further confirms the film's view that all desire, sexual and otherwise, springs from the desire for material gain. *Psycho* comes horribly close to making Norman a kind of romantic figure precisely because his desires, however corrupt, are not linked to capital but, instead, to the ties that precede the entrance into the capitalistic Symbolic—the obsession with the pre-oedipal mother and her sexuality, which the child assumes to be phallic (hence the fantasy of the phallic mother). In Lacanian terms, the subject must renounce the mother in order to enter the father's realm of language and law, which Lacan calls the Symbolic order. These thematic patterns in the film are grimly synthesized in Marion's line to Sam in the early hotel scene: "They pay, too, who meet in hotel rooms." Even here, when Marion is attempting to get Sam to see that she is suffering, just as he is with his interminable debts, she can only do so by appealing to his sense of economics, by, in a word, turning herself into a commodity for his emotional consumption.

Skin Shows: *Psycho* and the Emergence of Pornography

In *Screening Sex*, Linda Williams writes that the "illuminating point for our discussion of how American movies began to show adult sexual knowledge is that this knowledge is rarely grasped in a single 'aha!' moment. Sexual knowledge seems to be that which initially breaks in on us from the outside before we are ready for it but which also sets itself up in us as a kind of inner foreign body—an 'internal alien entity' that provokes excitement."[10] In terms of sexual knowledge and the gradual mass infiltration of the pornographic into American culture, I argue that small moments in films, particularly those poised between the studio and the post-classical Hollywood eras, are the indicators of a growing awareness of the pornographic. *Psycho* has several of these small moments, such as the one in which Lila Crane picks up a book with no title on its spine in Norman Bates's room and looks at it with a subtly alarmed look. As we have established, Victorian pornographic books had just such untitled spines, and, moreover, the filmmakers were very much intending for this moment to evoke a scene of pornographic reading.[11] I argue that a pornographic awareness suffuses this film from its racy start with a post-coital scene between scantily clad lovers.

In an essay in which he describes the flourishing of the feature-length hardcore narrative porn film from 1967 to 1972, the year *Deep Throat* "thrust it into the center of the cultural stage," Eric Schaeffer argues that this period was "merely an entr'acte between reels of essentially plotless underground stag movies in the years 1908 to 1967 and the similarly plotless ruttings of porn in the video age (emerging in the mid-1980s and continuing to the present)."[12] Most saliently, Schaeffer notes that

> [I]n the late 1960s and early 1970s, the adult film industry did not exist in a vacuum. Hollywood was being influenced by, and influenced, the producers and exhibitors of sexploitation films, and they, in turn, were jockeying for position with the insurgent manufacturers of 16 mm hard-core films. . . . [T]he hard-core feature developed as a reaction to conditions in the adult-film marketplace, in addition to more obvious social conditions. The hard-core feature was certainly not a predetermined end.[13]

I share Schaefer's sense of the cross-fertilization of the pornographic feature film and the studio feature film, though I see the depth of the former's influence on the latter as indicative of the destabilization of the classical Hollywood studio system, its increasingly desperate need to stay relevant in the face of the growing threats of television, youth culture and shifting audience tastes, and the gathering social unrest that led to the civil rights, feminist, and gay rights movements. The confluences between the pornographic industry and mainstream Hollywood require an extensive historical account, but we can establish that the mainstreaming of pornography, and its attendant shifts in Hollywood filmmaking practice, began to happen in the 1950s. The growing visibility of homosexuality and pornography were linked to a larger openness about sexuality in American culture that presaged the Sexual Revolution.

As noted in the Introduction, films with increasingly explicit homoerotic/homosexual content indicated a widening awareness of alternative sexualities.[14] At the same time, other films were challenging the limits of the Production Code generally, such as the scandalous *Baby Doll* (1956), about a child bride and her brutal husband, directed by Elia Kazan and written by the great gay playwright Tennessee Williams.[15] Teasingly, the tagline for the poster of Stanley Kubrick's 1962 film version of Nabokov's scandalous novel *Lolita*—about a man who loves an underage girl—was "How did they ever make a movie of *Lolita?*" Above the tagline, Sue Lyon in the title role licks a suggestive lollipop. One could argue that heterosexual pedophilia in the classical Hollywood era, especially in its decadent late stage, heralded the heady if brief period of the mainstream hard-core narrative. Linda Williams's phrase "the frenzy of the visible" is apt here on many levels. The varieties of sexual experience were becoming increasingly more visible in American film in ways that intersected with the growing visibility, availability, and even cultural and social prominence of pornography. Hitchcock's *Frenzy* (1972) was, not incidentally, released in the same year as *Deep Throat*. A more graphic version of the psychosexual terrors in his previous works, *Frenzy* is a critique of an increasingly visible culture of sex and its attendant anxieties and potential for violence.

The earlier *Psycho* was an incipient critique along these lines. One of the key episodes in the film vividly evokes the scene of pornographic viewing. In his darkened office, alone after Marion Crane leaves, Norman Bates takes down a painting that depicts the biblical story of "Susanna and the Elders" and stares through a peephole into Cabin 1. In this famous story, a chaste young woman bathes and is spied on by two old men who then try to blackmail her into having sex with them. The story is overdetermined as a Hitchcock motif, containing, as it does, so many of his signature themes. There is a long tradition in Western visual art of reading this biblical narrative as a rape scene, and this painting joins the number of classical rape paintings that adorn the back wall of Norman's office, all of which signal the history of anti-woman violence, and that this hideous history is being made in the present. Norman voyeuristically observes Marion as she undresses. He watches as she bares down to her black undergarments, in pointed contrast to the white bra and half-slip she sports in the opening scene.

Like the solitary male viewer who surreptitiously sneaks into pornographic theaters and who will come to embody the rise of such venues in San Francisco, Los Angeles, and, especially, New York City's Times Square, scenes of illicit viewing that will be on ample display in several of New Hollywood films, Norman Bates stares at the spectacle of female sexuality secretly, illicitly, and anonymously. Peeping Norman simultaneously recalls the solitary male viewer of early peep shows and anticipates the later porno-arcade viewer who pops quarters into a machine to get a porn film running, though here he watches without paying—it is Marion who will pay the price for his scopic greed.

In Gus Van Sant's frustrating, far from uninteresting, occasionally brilliant, and also often quite literal-minded shot-for-shot 1998 remake, Norman Bates (Vince Vaughn) masturbates as he stares at Marion (Anne Heche) undressing. In a surprising touch for a gay filmmaker, Van Sant fixes Norman's sexuality as heterosexual by having him bring himself to orgasm while watching Marion in erotic *dishabille*.[16] Not so in the queerer, more ambivalent Hitchcock original. Norman stares, to be sure; but then he puts the painting back on the wall and stares dead ahead in the *opposite* direction, with a clenched, fixed, angry, or, perhaps, simply mystified expression, and heads back up to the house and to Mother.

Staring intently now in the *opposite* direction from the spectacle of woman, Norman inhabits what we can identify as one of Hitchcock's most consistent tropes: *rear viewing*, an aversive, backward-focused looking that refuses the visual mastery of the Hollywood and pornographic screen both, and that as such has important queer implications.[17] I touched on rear viewing in Chapter 1 as

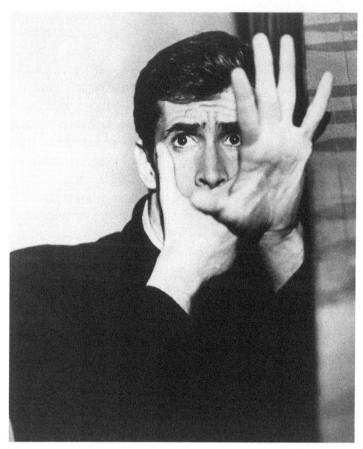

Norman Bates
repels the gaze
as he wields its
power.

a thematic that is frequently found in Hitchcock's films with James Stewart. In his essay in *Homographesis*, "Seeing Things: Representation, the Scene of Surveillance, and the Spectacle of Gay Male Sex," Lee Edelman calls such "disturbances of positionality" in representations of male-male sexual contact "behindsight."[18] I would identify rear viewing as an aspect of the masochistic gaze, which I theorized in *Manhood in Hollywood from Bush to Bush* as a mode of spectatorship in which vision becomes an impaired, frustrated, or delimited act. The masochistic gaze is relevant to any understanding of the cinematic representation of looking and vision, but particularly to queer inflections of them, given the system of prohibitions on queer desire. The masochistic gaze is a representation of repressed homosexual voyeurism that, as such, signals the very problematic relationship that it works to obscure, the queer subject's relationship to a visual object of desire. The most succinct cinematic example that comes to mind is Matt Damon's Tom Ripley looking from a strained, averted angle at the naked Dickie Greenleaf of Jude Law, dripping from having emerged from a bath and standing before a mirror in Anthony Minghella's brilliant screen version of Patricia Highsmith's novel *The Talented Mr. Ripley*. As *Psycho* illuminates, the queer subject's relationship to a visual object may not have such comparatively readable, identifiable desiring markers, qualities, or characteristics; Norman avidly looks at Marion from his non-normative voyeuristic vantage point without a definitive sexual purpose or agenda.

What *Psycho* thematizes here is, I would argue, a kind of queer viewing that is organized around heterosexual spectacle. Norman's rear viewing is an expression of ambivalence over this spectacle and the desired body of a woman. Though he himself performs the act of looking, invasively voyeuristic looking at that, there is another sense in which it is heterosexual spectacle, figured as the transgressively viewed and desirable woman, that always already looks at him. This is not so much Wheeler Winston Dixon's useful theory of the "returned gaze" as it is the panoptical Foucauldian gaze, albeit understood in terms of heterosexist social control. While I do not frequently speak from a Foucauldian basis, Foucault's theory of surveillance seems quite appropriate here when it is specifically situated in regimes of normative heterosexuality that monitor and maintain the heterosexual male viewing subject. On some level, males are always already staring at undressing women, enflamed by desire that is incited by visual pleasure. Norman is both submitting to a construction of his own gendered identity and sadistically wielding his right to the male gaze. But my argument is that, even if both of these aspects are authentically felt parts of his gazing performance, neither amounts—necessarily—to an experience of heterosexual desire, even if both figure heterosexual male dominance.

While it is entirely possible that Norman is, as the psychiatrist puts it in his infamous denouement speech, "touched by her, aroused by her," entirely possible that Norman "wants" Marion sexually, it is also entirely possible that he does not, that he feels no desire for her, indeed, feels nothing at all. (It is this potential "nothing" in the heart of *Psycho*'s pornographic gaze that Martin Scorsese will take to its breaking point in *Taxi Driver*.) Primarily, his looking inhabits and projects a blank nothingness.

Though Hitchcock doesn't, and couldn't, show Norman masturbating, certainly the scene suggests the scene of masturbatory pornographic viewing, or, in Magnus Ullén's description, "masturbation as a mode of reading."

> Pornography's persuasive element is . . . highly conspicuous—photographic pornography, indeed, comes with an inherent graphicality so forceful it would seem well-nigh impossible to doubt the truth of what it depicts. The ideological nature of this truth, it is important to observe, does not derive from some hidden meaning located in the pornographic discourse. Instead, it is a product of porn's

ability to persuade us that it can annul its own fictivity: that it can become a reality which is literally lived *through* by the reader, in that s/he consumes the reality made available by the discourse the very moment s/he experiences it. Pornography automates the persuasivity of rhetoric.[19]

Ullén's reading stems from a larger argument that critiques Linda Williams's reading of pornography as subversive. He argues instead that whatever is subversive, or seen to be this way, in pornography is dependent on historical and cultural context. For example, when homosexuality is no longer seen to be aberrant by the dominant culture, gay and lesbian porn will no longer be seen as a subversion of the dominant culture but as just more porn. While I concur with Ullén's nuanced and provocative argument, I want to take it in a different direction. What Hitchcock does in *Psycho* is suggest that live human beings have become reified as pornographic objects. He had begun to articulate this theme with mature force in *Rear Window*, but now takes it much further.

If pornography is endowed with the ability to "annul its own fictivity," as Ullén puts it, the porn viewer also has the ability to annul the fictivity of pornography. One means of doing so is to make other *people* fictive in the manner of porn. Jeff in *Rear Window* and Norman Bates transform other people into pornographic objects. Norman not only violates Marion Crane in this voyeuristic manner, annihilating her agency, but also physically annihilates her in the shower. A symbolic killing off of the person prefigures an actual act of murder.[20]

One specific dimension of the emerging technology and lifestyle of pornography is relevant to our discussion of pornography throughout this book. "Stag" films—in Ullén's description, "short, sexually explicit films the length of a reel, produced between 1915 and 1968, and shown to private gatherings of men"— have generated a great deal of critical thought. No doubt, they were deeply influential not only to the eventual mainstreaming of pornography in the 1970s, exemplified by the release of *Deep Throat* into mass-market cinemas, but also to the development of a postmodern American masculinity.[21] Thomas Waugh has greatly enlarged the critical understanding of the stag film, noting its crucial importance to the development of a homosocial male identity.[22] As I will be demonstrating in the chapter on De Palma's early comedies, pornography's ability to form and shape group male identity is highly significant. Films such as *Psycho*, however, do not derive from the male homosocial stag-film setting in anything but a general way (though as such the stag film provides a hardly unimportant precedent). Rather, *Psycho* evokes the scene of solitary pornographic viewing in the porno-arcade that will become the *locus classicus* of male despair and disconnection in the New Hollywood cinema.

In a 2008 article, Amy Herzog documents the history of the porno-arcade.

100

As Herzog notes, the "rise of the modern-day peep arcade in the 1960s is subject to much mythologization. Coin-operated motion picture 'peep' machines were hardly a new invention at that time, with Kinetoscope and Mutoscope parlors dating back to the late nineteenth century." Herzog explains that what "changed in the 1960s, however, was the scale and ambition of the peep industry and its visible intrusion into the public sphere."[23]

The "Panorams" of the 1950s—which "consisted of a large wooden cabinet and a ground-glass screen on which the film was rear projected, maximizing visibility of the musical shorts in the restaurants and bars in which the machines were installed"—were converted into machines for individual customers. "Despite the musical origins of the format, the peep loops were silent, and the machines contained no curtains or doors, such that the body of the user remained fully visible to the outside (paradoxically, unlike the body of the performer on film)."[24]

Of particular interest to us is the symbolic sexual value of numerous aspects of this technology, its innovations, and its growing importance to how viewers—presumably mostly male—experienced pornographic images. Of importance, too, is the visibility of the viewing male body and the invisibility of the performers. While we see Marion through Norman's eyes, what is most significant about the scene is that *we see Norman seeing*. Indeed, Hitchcock's extreme close-up of Norman's eye—we can practically count the number of his eyelashes—isolates the male eye as a distinctive new cinematic figure.

Psycho allegorizes the transformation of peep-show viewing into an increasingly public phenomenon and experience, in venues such as restaurants and bars, that made the peep-show viewer visible. But at the same time, *Psycho* presciently prognosticates peep-show viewing's later transformation into an increasingly *private* experience, emphasizing the isolation of the male spectator. The image of the solitary voyeur before the sexual spectacle in Hitchcock's film eerily anticipates the New Hollywood's scene of male anomie par excellence: Travis Bickle, alone in a random sea of other men, watching a pornographic screen with no clear-cut desiring intention. Hitchcock begins a dialogue about the role of pornography—which, in its hard-core mainstream form especially, was a galvanizing and maddening synthesis of transgressive vision and technologically enhanced constructions of sexuality and spectatorship—that will be painstakingly maintained in the films of the 1970s.

Psycho, then, occupies a shifting middle ground in the history of pornography. The voyeuristic Norman is liminally poised between the visible pornographic viewer of the 1950s and the later, hidden viewer of more elaborate venues for watching pornography, such as the peep-show arcade and the porn theater. Through directorial touches such as the extreme close-up of his ocular organs,

Hitchcock emphasizes the voyeur's own body. *Psycho* literalizes the male gaze by reducing it to an actual, bulbous eye. Hitchcock exposes the male gaze to scrutiny, as opposed to merely reproducing, perpetuating, or facilitating its apparent mastery over the visual regime. New Hollywood films, similarly focusing on the bodily presence of the pornographic spectator, will also subject the gaze to critical inquiry.

Psycho derives transgressive thrills from the illicit nature of what Norman sees through the peephole. Of course, *we* already saw Marion in this state of undress at the start of the film; Norman is only catching up here to our own illicit gaze. When Norman stares through the peephole in his office, a business space transformed into the private space of pornographic viewing, what is being allegorized, then—held up to our critical scrutiny—is our own specular subjectivity. Marion has no awareness that she is being viewed. In this regard, she is *unlike* the performer of the pornographic film, who knows that she is being filmed, but *like* that performer when captured on film, locked within the diegetic space of the filmic event, and perpetually subjected to the gaze of the viewer. The living Marion could just as well be the non-living but perpetually animated figure within a pornographic film (or any other kind of film, for that matter). Living people, viewed pornographically, and pornographic figures have become indistinguishable. Adding to these philosophical quandaries, of course, is the ultimate deception of the film medium: that Marion, or any other character, is actually a "living" person. All film objects are, after all, dead objects, given the semblance of life through light.[25]

102

Issues of misogyny clearly inform these dynamics, as Marion, like Miss Lonelyhearts in *Rear Window*, is violated through a devouring male gaze, a symbolic violation that prefigures the ultimate literal and physical violation of murder (Mrs. Thorwald's in *Rear Window* as well as Marion's). Hitchcock is providing a means of critiquing this spectatorial misogyny by placing it within a larger, increasingly ominous context of shifts in spectatorship. Films such as *Rear Window* and, with more explicitness, *Psycho* explore the development of modern forms of sexuality within an increasingly visual and technologically advanced social world.[26] Just as the protagonist of the earlier film, Jeff, uses his neighbors seen through his pointedly rear window as objects for sadistic visual pleasure, in that he derives pleasure from his dominance over their almost marionette-like activities, amplified by his various visual enhancements such as telephoto lenses, binoculars, and cameras, *Psycho* figures male viewing as sadistic, as power over a defenseless viewed body. (I will discuss the Freudian basis of my reading of voyeurism as sadistic in greater detail in the next chapter.) Moreover, it is one of the first and most explicit cinematic depictions of male viewing *as* pornographic. *Psycho*, *Rear Window*, and *Rope* together and with increasing focus portray an emergent pornographic male spectatorial subjectivity that, I argue, has important queer dimensions. Pornographic heterosexual male eye cult and homosexual male eye cult historically merge in the new scopic regime of pornographic visual frenzy, and Hitchcock's films reveal the process and effects of this merger.[27]

In *Rear Window*, James Stewart's Jeff, given a beautiful girlfriend in Grace Kelly, is ostensibly depicted as heterosexual. All of his viewing would appear to proceed from the vantage point of heterosexual desire. As soon as we note this, however, we remember that Hitchcock problematizes every aspect of Jeff's heterosexual desire, not only through his chilly treatment of Grace Kelly's Lisa Fremont but also through such devices as the monstrous, engulfing close-up through which she is diegetically introduced. It threatens to engulf the viewer along with Jeff, and is certainly reflective of Jeff's ambivalence over her character and the sexual difference she represents. As always with Hitchcock, we are at the same time made to empathize with the female experience of the male protagonist's ambivalence. Expertly limned by Kelly, Lisa's palpable pain makes it impossible to share in Jeff's disdain toward her. Indeed, she is increasingly sympathetic and likable, he disquieting and off-putting.

Rear Window explores the homoerotic as well murderously homophobic potentialities in male-male looking. The look that the spied-on wife-murderer Lars Thorwald (Raymond Burr) returns to the spying Jeff, one man behind a glass screen looking with recognition at another; the nightmarishly cruisy scene in which Thorwald meets up with Jeff in his apartment after they have exchanged looks, both reinforce the theme that terrible repercussions come when one man looks at another. Thorwald's attempt to murder Jeff is a kind of violent allegory of the promise of sexual intercourse/conquest contained in cruising. One man catches the avid eye of another; they meet up; violence ensues rather than sexual ecstasy. The blocking of the actors, their torturous physical intimacy as Thorwald tries to kill Jeff, strangling him as he throws him out of the window, is charged with sexualized violence. *Rear Window* offers its own variation on the theme of murder-as-gay-sex in *Rope*, significantly broadening its implications for male sexuality generally. Both films thematize the inherent violence of the gaze.

The 1948 *Rope* begins, as both *Rear Window* and *Psycho* do, with an illicit camera movement, a voyeuristic invasion of the private urban space of an apartment from the outside in, through a window. We are made to witness a scene of male-male intimacy that is also a scene of murder: a young man being killed by two of his friends, also young men, who, with shocking tenderness, hold and explore his body in its death throes.

The dead body of this young man becomes something like a pornographic spectacle for the killers, Brandon (John Dall) and Phillip (Farley Granger), who organize a party around it, forcing the guests to be unwitting spectators to their "ugly murder," as their old headmaster, Rupert Cadell (James Stewart), puts it.

In *Rope,* James Stewart's Rupert Cadell hypocritically denounces
the queer ideology he instilled in his pupils.

Ugly murder allegorizes the ugliness of gay sex; at the same time, dead bodies
become a source of anxious spectatorial pleasure, as the young men, Phillip in
particular, incessantly stare at the chest in which David Kentley's body is stored.
Indeed, these averted, sidelong, obsessive, anguished, incessant looks at the chest
convey a powerful sense of masochistic pleasure.[28] A chain of related anxieties—
desiring looks, murderous violence, dead bodies, necrophilia, masochistic pleasure—links these astonishingly like-minded films, the former Hitchcock's first
film in color (*Rope*), the latter his last in black and white (*Psycho*), suggesting that
the sexual significance of each film was registered on a formal level, as *Rope*'s famous experiment with the ten-minute take and *Psycho*'s experiment in audience
identification with the film star further reinforce.

Rope, however coded it keeps such matters, strongly suggests the homosexual
relationship between the murderous lovers, and represents the murder they commit as some form of gay sex or homoerotic release within its stifling homophobic cultural moment. *Psycho* however, as I have been arguing, is most notable
for its overall sexual blankness. Moments such as Norman's voyeuristic looking

at Marion do not proceed from a clear-cut basis of heterosexual desire (though many have, indeed, read it this way), but it also does not have the same coded homoerotic logic that informs *Rope* or Minghella's *Ripley*. (When Dickie stands, with his back to Tom, staring with averted eyes at Dickie's wet, glistening backside, it is after Tom has asked Dickie in the bath, "Can I get in?" and been rebuffed. "I didn't mean with you in it," Tom says, attempting to recover his dignity or to refute his suggested desires.) At the same time, Norman Bates's blankness does not imply an absence but, indeed, a proliferation of sexual possibilities. To give a sense of their sheer range, let me offer a few speculations about these possibilities, which are, of course, only speculations.

Norman could, indeed, be looking at Marion with sexual desire. He could be getting really turned on by her as he spies on her undressing. That possibility is the one Naremore explores in his account of this moment: "We cannot help but admire her body as she casts aside the dress; when her hands go up to remove the slip, the males in the audience watch expectantly, sharing in Norman's secret desires . . . some of the audience are as interested in the half-naked woman as he is—they have happily looked at her twice before, and now they itch with expectation that she may finally cast aside the brassiere."[29] I admire Naremore's candidness here as much as I do his work generally. But clearly, his heterosexual presumption ("the males in the audience" who can be counted on, *en masse*, to salivate over Marion-as-sexual-spectacle) needs a revision. And this revision comes from Naremore himself, who notes that Hitchcock, even as he facilitates the heterosexual male gaze, creates a "certain detachment," that "teases us, inviting us to become aware of our own relation to the photographic image."[30] I argue that Hitchcock's characteristic infusion of a metatextual awareness in the viewer, as decisively deployed here, radically enlarges—and at the same time quite utterly denatures—the potentialities of erotic looking.

On behalf of the heterosexual male viewer whose desire has been enflamed by repeated glimpses of an undressing woman, Norman could very well be looking at Marion with sexual lust. At the same time, however, any other possibility is just as valid, given how carefully Hitchcock creates the sense of anything-or-nothing in terms of reactions to female sexual spectacle. He could be looking at her to *test out* his responses to a naked woman. He could be looking at her with ambivalence, or even with disgust. He could be looking at her and wishing he were looking at a man undressing, instead. (He could be seeing, for that matter, a man undressing as she undresses.) She could be his serviceable *substitute* for the naked body of a man. He could be looking at her in an attempt to feel something in him stirring. Or—and this is the scariest proposition of all for our culture—he could be looking at her and experiencing nothing, absolutely nothing, at all.[31] As I have argued elsewhere, the possibility of a "man beyond desire"—a man who does not pursue sexual experiences and may not even experience sexual desire—has historically been a vexing, exasperating, and frightening prospect to American culture. The sexually inviolate male has a relevance to queer sexuality in that he, too, is cut off from the normative demands of the social order, which determines adult genital contact within marriage as a necessary achievement for all individuals.[32]

What finally fixes *Psycho* as a representation of the pornographic gaze is the subjectlessness of Norman's looking. The emphasis is on Marion undressing, not on what Norman experiences, rendered impenetrably enigmatic. In the words of Franklin Melendez in a different pornographic context, we can say that *Psycho* "reduces the viewing subject's engagement to an abstracted, almost subjectless activity: looking. This theoretical (rhetorical) effacement of the viewing subject constitutes a crucial move that vividly captures the degree to which mediating technologies determine our experience of the image."[33] The point is that we do not know, and have no way of knowing, what Norman feels as he looks at Marion, or even who Norman *is* when he looks at her. In *Psycho*, competing and oddly correspondent tensions coalesce. The pornographic viewer who blankly regards scenes of the sexual is at the same time an emergent queer subject and the postmodern male who sees all sexuality as simulacra: a series of citations, an unceasing procession of rote cultural tropes.

106

Norman Bates prefigures the pornographic viewer of films such as *Taxi Driver*. Travis Bickle, alone as always, stares blankly at the screen in the porn theater, his looking, like his identity, itself a blank screen. This image of modern despair, linked to the image itself and to the depiction of pornography as a deadened and deadening spectacle, finds its powerful precedent in *Psycho*, which reduces the pornographic subject to a blankly ravenous and anonymous eye. While earlier works such as Steven Shaviro's *The Cinematic Body* and many readings in contemporary porn studies emphasize the ecstatic libidinal potentialities of pornography—its engorgement rather than the familiar psychoanalytic preoccupation with lack—and while pornography's potential vitality and subversiveness are undeniable, the movement to embrace pornography as radical has, at times, run roughshod over the genre's equally relevant associations with decaying social ties and psychic anomie, associations that *Psycho* and certain key New Hollywood films obsessively thematize. They represent pornography as an expression of the deadening of male psyches, which has grim consequences for those who wield as well as fall under the male gaze, and results, in part, from a phenomenon we can call *pornographication*: the compulsory submission to pornographic sexuality that defines our long cultural moment from the 1960s to the present.

Hitchcock's notably ambivalent representation of sexuality—his sense in films such as *Psycho* that sex is dead, or a kind of deadening—is what makes his

Hitchcock, significantly posed between the failed heterosexual couple and the queer male.

cinema enduringly interesting and useful to a queer theory analysis of sex in the cinema, not because queer theory is (or should be) inordinately obsessed with death-tinged Eros, but because the denaturing of the master narratives of sexual fulfillment (courtship, romance, marriage, reproduction) in Hitchcock's films is a form of resistance to their compulsory logic.[34]

To return to Truffaut's discussion with Hitchcock about *Psycho*, one notices how rarely Truffaut—despite his always penetrating understanding of Hitchcock's cinema—presses Hitchcock on his occasional remarks about his own motivations for making films or for creating certain aspects of them. Here is a telling example, from their discussion of the first scene in the hotel in *Psycho*:

F.T. . . . If I'm not mistaken, out of your fifty works, this is the only film showing a woman in a brassiere.

A.H. Well, one of the reasons for which I wanted to do the scene in that way was that the audiences are changing. It seems to me that the straightforward kissing scene would be looked down at by the younger viewers; they'd feel it was silly. . . . Besides, I also wanted to give a visual impression of despair and solitude in that scene.

F.T. Yes, it occurred to me that *Psycho* was oriented toward a new generation of filmgoers. There were many things in that picture that you'd never done in your earlier films.

A.H. Absolutely. In fact, that's also true in a technical sense for *The Birds*.

They proceed to talk about the ways in which Hitchcock's film compares to Robert Bloch's novel, which Truffaut complains about for its tendency to "cheat."[35]

Though Truffaut's readings of Hitchcock are always perceptive, what is interesting is that he demonstrates little interest, here and elsewhere, in his actual *discussions* with Hitchcock about his attempts at emotional realism. Hitchcock speaks with a savvy sense of the shifts in the market to a youth-oriented interest in and demand for less hackneyed, more realistic depictions of sexuality. Why did Hitchcock, however, decide to inject a note of "despair and solitude" in the scene of the lovers in the hotel room? To this personal observation, Truffaut responds, "Yes, there is a new generation of filmgoers, isn't there?" overriding Hitchcock's moral and emotional vision. What I will explore in the following chapters is the legacy of the despair and solitude that informs Hitchcock's sense of a new sexual era.

CHAPTER FOUR

MISFORTUNE AND MEN'S EYES
Three Early De Palma Comedies

F OR MANY YEARS, Brian De Palma's work has been dismissed as misogynistic, on the one hand, and opportunistically derivative, on the other hand. About this latter point, De Palma's astonishingly productive and ongoing intertextual engagement with Hitchcock—commencing with the *Rear Window* homage *Sisters* (1973) and vividly on display in his *Femme Fatale* (2002)—has been viewed by the general run of critics as a plagiaristic and crass appropriation of the "Master of Suspense" by a talented but shallow hack. While critics like Pauline Kael, De Palma's staunchest and most famous champion, Robin Wood, Kenneth MacKinnon, Terence Rafferty, and, most recently, Eyal Peretz, have written thoughtfully and perceptively about De Palma, the majority of treatments of his work have treated it with hostility. In his review of *Femme Fatale*, a deeply surprised Jonathan Rosenbaum admits to "capitulating to" the film's "inspired formalist madness—something I've resisted in [De Palma's] films for the past 30-odd years." Rosenbaum goes on to explain the sources of this resistance:

> I'd always been annoyed by De Palma's intricate borrowings from Alfred Hitchcock, which I've tended to see more as mangled tributes than as perceptive appreciations. My misgivings were only reinforced when his biggest fans, especially Pauline Kael and her most literal followers, implied that Hitchcock was a bit of a hack next to the genius De Palma—suggesting that Hitchcock churned out

dross, which his disciple somehow turned into the pure gold of sublime trash. De Palma's borrowings were all the more irritating when it became clear that much of his supposed fealty to the master came less from his soul than from his big production budgets, which enabled him to hire Bernard Herrmann for *Sisters* and *Obsession*—though all he wanted Herrmann to do was imitate his scores for *Vertigo* and *Psycho*. Say what you will about Hitchcock's calculation, his work displays an almost limitless curiosity about human behavior, whereas De Palma's shows an interest in people (as opposed to types and figures) that approaches zero.[1]

Rosenbaum not only lays out his own experience of De Palma here but indexes recurring themes in the reception of De Palma's work, particularly the films made after his biggest commercial and critical success of the 1970s, *Carrie* (1976). Rosenbaum also provides telling insights into the ongoing views of Hitchcock's work, the way that, on the one hand, he almost always emerges as De Palma's aesthetic and even moral superior, Hitchcock's status as Original Genius intact, and, on the other hand, in the Kael view, the less daring, radical artist. Neither of these critical tendencies tells us much about either filmmaker, each of whose works are important in political as well as aesthetic terms. In the last chapter, I offer a close reading of *Dressed to Kill* (1980); in this chapter, I consider three early, Vietnam War–era De Palma comedies. I challenge the establishment critical position, maintained by critics such as Rosenbaum until his "conversion"(however long it has lasted) through *Femme Fatale*, that De Palma's Hitchcockian thrillers plagiarize the Master without adding anything significant of their own, aesthetically or thematically. (Certainly, Bernard Herrmann was inspired enough by them to compose two of his finest scores.) In my view, De Palma's Hitchcockian thrillers add a great deal to Hitchcock; they extend his aesthetic experiments while expanding and revising his psychosexual politics. Between them, Hitchcock and De Palma submit the masculine subject of Hollywood cinema to a challenging analysis, decentering the male subject while also exposing the perniciousness and hollowness of the structural foundations that support this subjectivity.

Along with Hitchcock's aesthetics, De Palma has inherited many of the Master's ideological problems. Charges of misogyny have dogged Hitchcock, particularly in terms of his films from *Psycho* forward, such as *The Birds* (1963) and *Frenzy* (1972). Critics have also faulted Hitchcock for the implausibility of his plots and for his formal "coldness." In the view of a critic like David Thompson, Hitchcock is a great technician but not a "human" filmmaker, his enclosed, precisely storyboarded worlds devoid of spontaneity and real feeling. De Palma's work has been critiqued along all of these lines as well. But the critiques of De Palma's work, while they echo those of Hitchcock's, reach much more deafening decibel levels.

Indeed, De Palma has effectively taken one for the Hitchcock team, emerging as *the* screen misogynist, *the* implausible plot-*meister*, *the* cold, inhuman filmmaker. The identification with his screen heroines, indeed, his remarkably insistent, urgent, and consistent interest in women characters, which distinguishes him from his New Hollywood peers, save for, possibly, Robert Altman; his radical indifference to conventional narrative, especially the compulsory demand for closure; and the often profound levels of emotional depth in De Palma's films, even at their most extravagantly satirical, are qualities that have escaped his detractors but also many of his admirers. (No soul in De Palma, the most anguished of all filmmakers? Rosenbaum and I have watched different movies.) Most significantly for the present study, critics of either the pro or con positions have generally ignored, overlooked, or simply not understood the crucial theme at the core of De Palma's films, one they share with Hitchcock's: an obsessive interest in the ways in which cultural constructions of gendered identity shape, affect, and most importantly, impede the sexual and social life of individuals.

Kael and Peretz on De Palma

"His new trash heart is the ultimate De Palma joke," the last line of Pauline Kael's review of *Carrie* (1976) affirmed. Kael was a crucial figure in the establishment of De Palma's importance as a filmmaker. Her assessment of his stature as an artist evolved, as her moving reviews of *Blow Out* (1981) and *Casualties of War* (1989), especially, evince. But her early penchant for associating De Palma with the inhuman postmodern glee of endless referentiality had the effect of reinforcing his popular image as little more than an amoral jokester. Throughout, she was perceptive and insightful about De Palma films, and commendable in her commitment to their importance. Yet she also very much used De Palma as a stick with which to beat auteurist critics like her archrival Andrew Sarris—De Palma was her prized bad boy because he seemed to give Sarris's auteur-icon Hitchcock the iconoclastic finger. The early films were much more politically engaged— and emotionally invested—than Kael appeared to realize, despite her perspicuity about De Palma's talent and daring. Given Kael's own frequent disavowal of Hitchcock's stature as an artist—she saw him as a great entertainer, but refused the auteurist view of him as a great director—her appreciation for De Palma's Hitchcockian agon could only stem from her view of him as a brazen raider of pop cultural archetypes. When her view of his work deepened, with *Blow Out*, it was specifically her sense that he'd moved *beyond* genre—i.e., Hitchcock—that enabled Kael to proclaim him a great director.[2]

To give a better understanding of my own sense of De Palma's significance and of what is of significance to him in his films, and of the kinds of critical responses to De Palma that have simultaneously illuminated and obscured his concerns, I want to take a moment to consider an important, frustrating book on De Palma that has, I believe, despite its considerable merits, distorted the central concerns of De Palma's cinema.

In *Becoming Visionary: Brian De Palma's Cinematic Education of the Senses*, Eyal Peretz situates De Palma's importance as a director within a philosophical and psychoanalytic framework of the gaze, arguing that De Palma's cinema allows us to understand the gaze not as mastery of vision but as a blinding rupture within vision itself. Peretz describes De Palma's cinema as "a laboratory attempting to isolate, demonstrate, and give a genetic account, in other words, a historical account, of the emergence of various defensive human gazes."[3] Peretz's book performs an important intervention in the career assessment of De Palma, one of the most critically maligned and, when not maligned, misunderstood of Hollywood directors, even by some of his most fervent supporters, such as Kael. Peretz writes about De Palma in a way that is both stimulating and thoughtful. Both for the insistent force of its belief in De Palma's significance as a great filmmaker and for the acuity of several of its insights, this study is valuable on its own philosophical terms.

For Peretz, De Palma is the "greatest contemporary investigator, at least in American cinema, of the nature and the logic of the cinematic image," which Peretz, following Lacan, describes as a "blankness at the heart of the senses."[4] The three main chapters focus, respectively, on three of De Palma's most significant films: *Carrie* (1976), *The Fury* (1978), and *Blow Out* (1981); the epilogue turns to De Palma's *Femme Fatale* (2002) as a "paradoxical happy ending." The chapter on *The Fury*—one of the very greatest and most difficult, and also, most overlooked (except by Godard) of De Palma films—contains some particularly provocative insights.

Peretz expresses the methodological context of his book this way: "How is one to think through the significance of the art of film for philosophy? What would it mean to introduce film as a question for the philosophical enterprise?" This approach reaps the rewards of some suggestive insights into De Palma's cinema. Peretz provides a bravura reading of the great sequence in *The Fury* in which psychically supergifted Gillian (Amy Irving) has a staircase vision of her psychic twin, Robin (Andrew Stevens); he reads the entire sequence as a meditation on the experience of the cinema itself. Yet, brilliant as this sequence is, it is certainly secondary to the sequence, filmed in disorienting slow motion, in which Gillian, with help from some allies, escapes the imprisoning Paragon Institute. This, to me, is a sequence in which De Palma fully realizes the disparate elements of his sensibility: a penchant for dreamlike lyricism, an appetite for sadistic shock, a prankster wit, and, above all, a rigorously mournful, tragic pessimism. This (too) is De Palma's greatest sequence, and Peretz's lack of attention to it—and to De Palma's staging of the prom sequence in *Carrie*—reveals a certain surprising squeamishness about the director he aims to champion. One almost gets the feeling that Peretz is, on some level, as embarrassed by the director as are many of his detractors; Peretz focuses on the De Palma that can best accommodate a purifyingly intellectualized take on the director. Certainly, one doesn't get a sense here of either the range of De Palma's cinema or—and this is a crucial point that this chapter addresses—its antic, avant-garde comedic origins.

The extent to which De Palma remains a figure of critical opprobrium can be most clearly seen in the enduring ridicule Kael receives for her almost career-long appreciation for De Palma's work. In a *New York Review of Books* account of her career, Louis Menand (with singular obtuseness) cites her highly positive review of De Palma's *Blow Out* as a "shameless rave" that evinced Kael's weakening critical powers.[5] One of the factors in Kael's celebration of this prankster De Palma was her own anti-auteurist dismissal of Hitchcock as primarily "an entertainer" (ironically enough, preeminent auteur-critic Andrew Sarris's own denunciation of Kael). Because Kael did not recognize Hitchcock's greatness as a director, much less the urgency of his directorial obsessions, she remained indifferent to or simply unaware of the extraordinary intertextual dialogue De Palma conducted with an important cinematic predecessor. Although other directors have conducted an agon with a fellow director—Chabrol and Hitchcock, Woody Allen and Ingmar Bergman—no director other than De Palma has more self-consciously inhabited the style and sensibility of another director and yet managed to create a style so distinctly his own. It's not just all of the stylistic devices that are unique to De Palma's cinema—the obsessive use of split-screen; the use of slow motion; the preoccupation with technology—that distinguish him from Hitchcock. In every way, De Palma's cinema, even at its most Hitchcockian, comes up with remarkably distinct effects. Yet the connections between the two directors, who share a predilection for the same thriller genre and the same film grammar, are perhaps more salient.

Salutary though Peretz's book is, it errs in failing properly to draw out the connections and exchanges between Hitchcock's and De Palma's oeuvres. This lapse occurs even though Peretz offers an insightful account of De Palma's relationship to Hitchcock and the critical opprobrium it has generated: Hitchcock as "the ideal model," the "real thing," is precisely what De Palma "seems to obstruct from direct view, which these accusing viewers seem to want; it is the real face of Hitchcock, a face De Palma scars and distorts, that they desire to see."[6] In my view, no critic—including Peretz—has yet written incisively on the precise nature of De Palma's intertextual relationship to Hitchcock's cinema. While other directors, most notably Chabrol and, to a lesser extent, François Truffaut, have also cultivated their Hitchcockian fascinations, De Palma is no mere Hitchcock obsessive but a director unique in the cinema in his sustained, intently focused obsession with the nature and potentialities of *the experience of cinema itself.* De Palma sees Hitchcock's cinema *as* the cinema. Hitchcock is famous for his metatextual cinematic experiments, such as *Rope* (1948) and *Rear Window* (1954), but De Palma goes a step beyond metatextuality. The only way to understand what De Palma does in his Hitchcock homages is to imagine that De Palma immerses himself within the cinematic body of a Hitchcock film and creates a new cinematic life within the Hitchcockian host body. If De Palma's filmmaking is parasitical, the parasite consumes the host and becomes a formidable entity all its own. Quoting Hitchcockian film grammar, De Palma constructs entirely new syntax; extending Hitchcock's faith in pure cinema, De Palma takes Hitchcock's pure cinema to unexpectedly new places.

When De Palma remakes Hitchcock, he uses Hitchcock films generally as a kind of collage of symbols, metaphors, and techniques that he can recombine, with those of other directorial styles and with his own idiosyncratic obsessions, to make altogether new meanings. To give a sense of what I mean, in *Carrie*, De Palma makes one of Stephen King's worst-written yet most suggestive novels an occasion for a vigorous mediation on Hitchcock's cinema that frees Hitchcock's fixations to achieve a radical new vision of both cinema and gender. De Palma recasts Hitchcock's Norman Bates as Carrie White, the excruciatingly shy and awkward—yet secretly and thrillingly powerful—heroine with a living Mrs. Bates for a mother. If Hitchcock's *Psycho* captures feminine anxiety and tormented sexual confusion in black and white, De Palma's *Carrie* transmutes those psychosexual tensions into vividly dramatic color, recombining *Psycho* with Hitchcock's magnificent melodrama *Marnie* (1964), the scarlet suffusions of which now erupt as the palette of the unleashed fury of Carrie's unshackled id. This last is no small point: like Hitchcock, De Palma is a woman's film director who fuses the genres of melodrama and the thriller to create a new genre, the *suspense melodrama.* *Dressed to Kill*, discussed in the last chapter, is exemplary in this regard.

The shower murder sequence from *Psycho* represents the annihilation of a woman's body as the destruction of the cinematic image itself; the shower sequence in the early portion of *Carrie* reassembles Hitchcock's tropes to create a new narrative about female sexuality, conceived not through a threat from the outside but from that within, the undeniable force of nature that erupts in Carrie's first menstrual blood. If this red fluid represents trauma here, in the spellbinding prom sequence it figures female wrath, the explosion of Carrie's no longer pent up force of will. The sequence in which she annihilates her mother with a telekinetically hurled array of kitchen utensils recombines the *Psycho* shower murder with the excessive force of surrealistic cinema, culminating in the religious blasphemy of the mad mother's orgasmic release, a perverse parody of the saintly martyr's ecstatic suffering. And in *Dressed to Kill*, De Palma reimagines his own early shower sequence in *Carrie* as an older woman's fantasy of her sexual awakening, gradually overcome by menace.

To my mind, the deeper problem with *Becoming Visionary* is that the philosophical framework of Peretz's methodology often threatens to subsume the individualistic potency of De Palma's cinema; tellingly, the book's introduction leads with its philosophical agenda rather than its focus on De Palma. One gets the uncomfortable feeling, at times, that De Palma is, while not exactly incidental to the philosophical claims of Peretz's argument, an appropriated vehicle through which Peretz chooses to express them. "De Palma," Peretz writes, is a "philosophical filmmaker in that his cinema involves us in a profound logical investigation of the cinematic ways of producing meaning, or of making sense." Peretz means sense here in a deeply philosophical sense: "De Palma's films call upon us 1) to rethink the major categories of sense that have served, implicitly or explicitly, in all major interpretations of art and film, and 2) to examine the particular significance that the art or medium of film has for the general question of sense."[7]

Peretz's analysis transforms De Palma's deeply corporeal, erotic cinema into philosophical abstraction. In De Palma's depiction of Carrie in the shower—which De Palma, revising Hitchcock, turns into a tableau of sexual metaphors (the phallic shower head spewing water, the steam, the surface of Carrie's skin)—she is a woman in autoerotic plenitude startled into the burdens of gendered identity. Peretz's analysis has a resolute knack for dissolving the sexual specificity of De Palma's cinema into philosophical "rigor": "What Carrie discovers under the shower is precisely that she has a period, that is, that she is a body, and a body as nakedness, that is as something that can bleed and therefore be wounded, a naked body that is not a self-sufficient totality but a vulnerable open surface."[8] But De Palma's fascination with Carrie stems from the fact that hers is a woman's body, not just any, philosophically desexed body. What any analysis of De Palma's cinema needs to address is his fascination and conflictual identification *with* the feminine. If charges of misogyny have been unfairly leveled against De Palma—and I would argue that it is precisely because of his *investment* in femininity that De Palma has been paradoxically branded a misogynist—any serious investigation of his work must address these issues, the gendered specificity of his cinema. Peretz has little to say on the question of misogyny or gender-bending in De Palma's films (he almost entirely leaves out *Dressed to Kill* and *Raising Cain* [1992], welters of these concerns, from his study). *Becoming Visionary* goes a long way toward establishing De Palma as the great director that he is, but the philosophical focus freezes out the erotic body of De Palma's cinema.

Moreover, it freezes out the urgency of De Palma's gendered concerns and his critique of normative constructions of gender and sexuality. The most acutely political point that De Palma makes throughout his films is that even white, heterosexual males who somehow fail to enter or uphold the symbolic order fall into the same kind of socially abnegated position as women, queers, and non-whites in our culture. His films, however, are not sentimental eulogies for this loss of masculine potency and power but rather exposures of the fissures within the model of sexually normative white masculinity, fissures that in turn expose the cracks and the discontinuities in the entire gendered social system. Anyone wanting to break out of, disrupt, or challenge this gendered social system—Kate Miller (Angie Dickinson) in *Dressed to Kill*, Jack Terry (John Travolta) in *Blow Out*—will face serious challenges and pay a terrible price. But to whatever extent Jack Terry is haunted by the memory of the woman, Sally Bedina (Nancy Allen), he failed to save, it is this woman who pays the ultimate price, murdered as a result of Jack's challenge to an indescribably constrictive, annihilating system. That he then dubs her pitiful death-scream into the trashy porno-horror film he works on as a sound man, *Co-Ed Frenzy*, links Jack precisely to the same system that exploits, punishes, and destroys both males who don't fit in (regardless of their sexuality) and, much more destructively, women. Jack may see and hear the horror at the heart of the homosocial social order, yet he, ultimately, not only fails to mitigate these horrors but ends up amplifying them.

Indicative of the ways that he distorts De Palma's politics and his political critique of gender, Peretz's reading of *Blow Out* fails to account for the specific elements in De Palma's treatment of masculinity and sexual politics as well as intertextual aesthetics. Peretz reads the film as the exemplary process of "becoming visionary," of finding ways to transcend the confusion of the senses signified here by the disparity between the eye and the ear. Peretz is at his best in his heady reading of the sequence in which Jack Terry records the sounds from his high perch upon the bridge above the nighttime forest, a natural setting intersected by the man-made: Jack's recording technology, the highway, the bridge. Focusing on one sound that Jack records but cannot make out—which we will discover only later to be the sound of the murderer/assassin's watch from which he pulls out a telltale string, the razory sound of menace and murder—Peretz writes that

> The ear discovers its haunting (in an irregularly rhythmic beat, for example), the
> eye discovers its haunting (in being isolated from the ear as well as through the
> device of the camera movement, for example), and so on. It is as if the relation
> between the cinematic frame and its Other is marked at the very heart of each
> sense, becoming the logic dictating the inner tensions between the senses as well
> as what dictates the modes of their interaction, a disjunctive interaction, with
> each other.[9]

John Travolta and Nancy Allen in De Palma's *Blow Out*. De Palma
extends Hitchcock's deconstruction of the heterosexual couple.

Insofar as it proceeds from such a philosophical position, Peretz's analysis yields
significant insights. And insofar as gender becomes a concern, it continues to
yield insights, such as when Peretz discusses the signature, defining De Palma
technique of the split-screen as, in part, a metaphor for sexual difference.[10] Yet,
ultimately, what Peretz's treatment moves toward and ends with is a view of the
film as chiefly invested in discovering a productive way out of its own inescapable
intellectual maze. The film works toward discovering the "promise for a new
conception of liberty and of the political," which reading Peretz bolsters with
an invocation of Martin Luther King's "Let Freedom Ring" speech.[11] While such
a reparatively hopeful reading of a film such as, say, *Body Double* (1984), which
moves from the traumatic to the exhilarating—but exhilarating as much as anything for its determined shifts in tone—would make a certain sense, it scram-
bles the despairing themes of *Blow Out*, which is De Palma's most unflinching
statement about the precise ways in which individual lives get caught up in and
crushed within the gears of the symbolic order once they threaten to puncture
or disrupt it.[12] Like Linda Williams's reading of pornography, the philosophy of
film approach that Peretz builds on from Stanley Cavell—though without Cavell's
increasingly central interest in such figures as "the unknown woman"—aspires

to the condition of the utopian. Peretz uses philosophy and philosophically re-tooled, Lacanian psychoanalysis to cauterize the unstanchable wound of De Palma's aesthetically charged gender and cultural politics.

DE PALMA'S EARLY FILMS, avant-garde Vietnam War–era comedies, reveal the foundational preoccupations at work throughout his cinema. They foreground the obsessive, maddening theme of surveillance, a theme that powerfully unites his work with Hitchcock's. Just as Hitchcock's films such as *Rear Window* (1954), *Vertigo* (1958), and *Psycho* (1960) all plumb the psychic motivations behind ravenous looking, tied to the desire for domination, so too does De Palma tie scopophilia, an obsessive desire to look in order to gain erotic pleasure and satisfaction, to desires to dominate on the part of his anxious, dubious characters. But even more intensely than in Hitchcock, the scopophilia in De Palma allegorically represents the director's own psychic motivations—namely, his desire to struggle against a powerful predecessor whose cinematic image he fetishizes. In De Palma, the desire to "see" Hitchcock becomes, to lift from Freud, a tormenting compulsion. *Hi, Mom!*, the major film of his early period, clinically examines the figure of voyeurism; it extends *Rear Window*'s critique of heterosexual manhood's desire to subjugate through the gaze to an entire new generation of male scopophiliacs. De Palma associates 1970s manhood with the desire to consume and dominate through the gaze, and it is precisely from this political position that De Palma's cinema will publicly wage its oedipal battle, covert in these early films, with Hitchcock while also commencing a decades-long critique of the codes of American manhood. Taking, then, all of the formal and thematic concerns we have raised thus far into consideration, I turn to an examination of De Palma's early films to establish the grounds for De Palma's political as well as aesthetic sensibility, and to provide a theoretical background for his Hitchcockian cinema. Just as De Palma, far from plagiarizing his predecessor, takes his aesthetic designs further, to unexpected and often radical places, so too does De Palma take Hitchcock's treatment of homo-influenced heterosexual manhood to similarly pointed new levels. Aesthetic and thematic influence, in De Palma's treatment, serves as the occasion for new thinking about sexuality and the construction of American masculinity.

Early De Palma: Oedipal Aesthetics and the Comedy of Manhood

Flagrant imitation of one's aesthetic predecessors is generally considered the early, less confident stage of an artist's career. Copying the Master before they find their own authentic voice, fledgling artists strive to learn through imitation the skills they need to hone their own unique style. De Palma defies this received wisdom of art-making. Rather than slavishly imitating Hitchcock, his early films, such as *Greetings* (1968), *Hi, Mom!* (1970), and *Get to Know Your Rabbit* (1972)—though *thematically* deeply Hitchcockian—stylistically adhere to the avant-garde cinema of the 1960s, especially Godard. There is little in them aesthetically that recalls Hitchcock's precise film grammar or the tendency to swooning romanticism that will later characterize De Palma films. The camera in these early films remains largely stationary, almost stony in its immobility in *Greetings*; in *Hi, Mom!*, the filmmaking bears more resemblance to the documentary genre than to Hitchcockian suspense thrillers; in *Get to Know Your Rabbit*, except for some interesting experimentation with overhead camera shots, the visual quality of the film is shockingly nondescript and impersonal, appositely matching the hollow content, largely provided by the film's curious star, Tom Smothers. The message we should take from the visual and tonal design of these early films is that when De Palma plunged into the aesthetic realm of the Hitchcockian thriller, he did so self-consciously: he undertook an intertextual project that was self-aware, *determined*, not the result of sloppiness or lack of "originality" but, rather, a considered, chosen, and metacinematic aesthetic. In these three early films, De Palma establishes the political concerns that will undergird his oeuvre, informing and illuminating his intertextual Hitchcock project, in which the copy is consistently shown to be distinctive, perhaps even more vital in some ways, than the original—a shocking proposition to an American audience, so deeply primed to extol the artist for his or her exceptionalism.[13]

As I have argued, Eyal Peretz primarily makes De Palma safe for high theory's intellectualizing approach to film—in other words, the approach that has always rendered De Palma a critical pariah—a disposition that De Palma, a somatic filmmaker par excellence, challenges throughout his work. Peretz ignores the function of comedy in De Palma's work, the crude, loose humor that informs it and is a manifestation of the counterculture sensibility most evident in De Palma's Vietnam War draft-dodger comedies but present in his serious Hitchcockian experiments as well.[14]

The director's early films provide invaluable insights into the tensions in the homosocialized white manhood of their era. His critique of the male homosocial—in other words, male group identity—demonstrates that the anxieties that riddle white, straight American manhood exist in a historical continuum. Speaking of Jacksonian manhood in the antebellum period, Dana Nelson writes, "White manhood worked as a transistor for a chain of political, economic, class, and professional displacements between 'white' men. It circuited political and economic inequality as individual failure, and routed frustrations . . . into 'healthy' market and professional aggression."[15] As with Jacksonian manhood, so with De Palma's Vietnam War–era manhood, which, even as it demonstrates racist, misogynistic, and homophobic tendencies, suffers from anxieties so intense that they threaten dissolution, both social and psychic.

The logic of male homosociality is the central thematic of De Palma's films, which entails an understanding of heterosexual relations as an outgrowth, point of exchange within, and battleground for relations between men. In depicting, throughout his films, the heterosexual-homosocial as a sphere of relations between men that are fraught with homosexual panic and internecine cruelty (to get only more fraught, more cruel, with each film), De Palma offers a despairing vision of male friendship and the homosocial as breeding mills for duplicity. In film after film, De Palma treats relations between men as opportunities for betrayal. In *Sisters* (1973), De Palma's first explicitly Hitchcockian film, male rivalry over the contested figure of a woman leads to the murder of both men by the same woman; in *Obsession* (1976), the protagonist's male friend and business partner tricks and cheats him repeatedly; in *The Fury* (1978), two veteran government agents war over the telekinetic son of one of the agents, leading to the deaths of all three—though the two agents are initially presented as old friends, one agent betrays the other, whose son has the power the government wants to harness as an espionage tool; the heroine of the film (Amy Irving's Gillian) dispatches the villain (John Cassavetes's Childress, his dead right arm in a sling) in a bravura montage-sequence finale; in *Dressed to Kill* (1980), a conflict between a psychiatrist and a cross-dressing patient of his turns out to be the madness of one, when it is revealed that the psychiatrist has a dual personality (he betrays himself); in *Blow Out* (1981), the hero, a movie sound man trying to expose an assassination plot, reaches out to a reporter and thereby insures the murder of a woman whom he is trying to protect—the hero's efforts to expose nefarious government secrets are counterbalanced by the hired assassin's to bury them; in *Body Double* (1984), the hero is tricked into being an accomplice to a murder by the murderer himself, who has pretended to be the hero's friend and advocate; in *Casualties of War* (1989), a Vietnam war film based on a true story (and the nightmarish fulfillment of themes of national manhood first developed in *Greetings*), one young man must oppose an entire subset of the homosocial sphere over the contested site of a woman. A group of soldiers kidnap a young Vietnamese woman and brutally rape and beat her. The hero refuses to participate and attempts to free the woman. Not only are his heroic attempts utterly unsuccessful, but he also becomes the target of a murderous plot by the other soldiers. In *Raising Cain* (1992), the protagonist is betrayed by his own father, a psychoanalyst who has performed grisly psychological tests on him since childhood. Like *Dressed to Kill*, *Raising Cain* translates the murderous conflict between the individual male and the homosocial sphere into a psychomachia. In *Snake Eyes* (1998), the protagonist's best friend betrays and attempts to murder him to conceal his role in a treasonous plot. De Palma's 1996 movie version of the 1960s TV show *Mission: Impossible* angered many fans of the original show by having the avuncular Jim Phelps betray his loyal underling Ethan Hunt—a twist entirely consistent, however, with the theme of male relations as a realm of cruelty and betrayal in De Palma's work, as these films evince consistently and constantly. In *The Black Dahlia* (2006), two friends and policemen in the 1940s war over the mystery of the titular female figure, whose hideous murder becomes a maddening, all-consuming mystery (the film and its source material, James Ellroy's novel of the same name, are both based on an infamous real-life murder). If by far the orneriest aspect of De Palma's cinema is his treatment of women, the early films illuminate what is frequently at stake in De Palma's representation of women: they become ensnared within the gears of the competitive, duplicitous, and often quite murderous relations between men in homosocialized patriarchy. An analysis of De Palma's early films makes these thematic preoccupations all the clearer.

The Horror of the Homosocial

In her bracing 1992 study of American horror films, *Men, Women, and Chainsaws*, Carol J. Clover observes that, while studies (such as Tania Modleski's 1988 *The Women Who Knew Too Much*) have been made of Alfred Hitchcock's ambivalence toward his female characters, no such study has been made of De Palma's.[16] Certainly, however, a critical consensus on the misogynistic sensibility of this still-active director (his latest film as of this writing being *Redacted*, his multi-media 2007 film about the current Iraq War) would appear to have been reached. In an essay on *Carrie* (1976), Shelley Stamp Lindsey excoriates the director for his demonization of Carrie's emergent female sexuality: "Carrie presents a masculine fantasy in which the feminine is constituted as horrific. . . . [T]he film presents female sexuality as monstrous and constructs femininity as a subject position impossible to occupy."[17] Though there have been critical women defenders of De Palma—most famously the late Kael, but also the late cultural critic Veronica Geng, the *Village Voice* film critic Amy Taubin, *Movieline* film critic Stephanie Zacharek—most supporters of De Palma have been male critics: Armond White, Robin Wood, Steven Vineberg, Michael Sragow, David Denby, Terence Rafferty, and Kenneth MacKinnon, who wrote an intelligent, nuanced treatment of De Palma in his 1990 *Misogyny in the Movies*.

Robert E. Kapsis persuasively argues that De Palma's reputation as a rip-off artist and a misogynist is as much the result of timing and reception as anything else, noting that De Palma's "reputation history" evinces the difficulty of ensuring artistic credibility while working in the thriller genre. His views have not had a tremendous impact on studies of De Palma, however.[18] The hegemonic critical view of De Palma is best expressed by Robert Philip Kolker:

> Brian De Palma has made a career of the most superficial imitations of the most superficial aspects of Hitchcock's style, worked through a mysogyny [sic] and violence that manifest a contempt for the audience by his films (though in *Scarface* [1983] and *The Untouchables* [1987] he has shown a talent for a somewhat more grandiloquent allusiveness).[19]

Kolker's sensitive work elsewhere is belied by his treatment of De Palma. His view of the director ignores De Palma's self-conscious intertextual project while mildly praising two of De Palma's most mainstream efforts.[20] Tony Williams echoes Kolker's views in his 1997 *Larry Cohen: The Radical Allegories of an Independent Filmmaker*, an otherwise deeply insightful study of another great 1970s auteur.

A strong De Palma supporter, the African American film critic Armond White, who views De Palma as one of the few directors interested in politics and race in the United States, offers an opposing view of De Palma's achievement: "Even though he made *Greetings*, the first (hell, the only) American antidraft movie (in 1968, when the idea was unfashionable—when it counted), he has instead been branded as a misogynist, a pornographer, and a Neanderthal because the erotic themes in his later pictures overshadowed his political themes."[21] The reading of De Palma as a pornographer will be explored later in this chapter. The critical analysis of pornography is one of the central themes in De Palma, and one that has an inchoate life in Hitchcock films, as we discussed in the previous chapter. The political agenda of De Palma's films—which permeate his early work but also inform all of his subsequent films—have been obscured or ignored in most treatments of De Palma, which rely on assumptions about De Palma's apparent misogyny and Hitchcock "obsession."

In her groundbreaking essay "When the Woman Looks," Linda Williams argues that "De Palma's film *Dressed to Kill* extends *Psycho*'s premise by holding the woman [Kate Miller, played by Angie Dickinson] responsible for the horror that destroys her."[22] De Palma extends much more than *Psycho*'s premise in this film, just as all of his other Hitchcock homages extend much more than the premises of their source texts. Without dismissing the work done by Williams, Stamp, and myriad commentators, feminist and otherwise, on the misogynistic propensities of De Palma's oeuvre, I would like to propose a different angle from which to inspect it, one that would allow us to see it organically as an important element in an ongoing critical project: a depiction of male friendship that functions, through studies of betrayal, duplicity, vengeance, greed, and cruelty, as a critique of the organization of the homosocial sphere within capitalist society. Homosocialized male power is the horror that destroys Kate Miller, other heroines, and the hapless male protagonists of many De Palma films. (I treat *Dressed to Kill* at length in the last chapter.) De Palma films interrogate the *necessity* of forming bonds within the homosocial sphere, seeing that necessity as an inevitable burden that must be carried by the American male. The male subject position in De Palma films is as impossible to occupy successfully as the female one.

This new critical perspective on the director brings into sharper focus an anti-patriarchal, pro-woman strain in his work. Despite conventional wisdom, misogyny does not inhere in De Palma films, though they, inevitably, contain some misogynistic elements at times. I argue that De Palma exudes an ambivalence about—and a rivalrous identification with—his female characters rather than a misogynistic hatred. Indeed, with the exception of Robert Altman, De Palma exhibits a far greater and more sustained interest in representing women than many of his fellow New Hollywood peers—Spielberg, Scorsese (with the exception of *Alice Doesn't Live Here Anymore*), Lucas, Coppola, Schraeder, et al. Before De Palma's ambivalence toward his female characters can be measured, we must come to a clearer understanding of his overarching interest in male relations.

RENÉ GIRARD AND EVE KOSOFSKY SEDGWICK privilege the triangle as the graphic schema for erotic competition between men—two men warring over the same woman. Femininity is the economy that allows the men to exchange their desires in whatever forms those desires may take.[23] In relation to the theme of male friendship and male relations, the theme of men's relationship to women emerges as a prominent one in *Greetings* (1968), *Hi, Mom!* (1970), and *Get to Know Your Rabbit* (1972). In them, the figure of Woman functions iconically, as the site of exchange between men, to use Girard's and Sedgwick's formulas of triangulated desire, but also as an impossibly aloof, elusive Ideal around which men revolve and which they must also overmaster and conquer. Though his often essentialist gendered schemas may not endear him to many of his critics, De Palma's treatment of women is inextricably connected to his general critique of the compulsory performance of masculinity and manhood in American life.[24]

An important distinction must be made between De Palma's treatment of women in these early films and in the later, more stylistically cohesive period (his "Red Period") that begins with *Sisters* (1973), which signals both the advent of De Palma's explicitly intertextual relationship with Hitchcock and the persistent, even obsessive interest in the construction of the heroine, and would appear to conclude with *Body Double* (1984). Though these three early films form the foundation for the critique of male relations in De Palma's oeuvre, they should be viewed as initial stages in the evolution of this theme and not as themselves definitive De Palma treatments of either male relations or women in his films. The early films depict male friendship in a more open-ended fashion than the later films (which treat the theme with a nihilistic hopelessness) and conversely depict women in more opaque, less emotionally cathected ways.

In addition to providing crucial insights into De Palma's representation of women and male relations, these early films evince an understanding of the homosocial sphere's reliance upon and abjection of homosexuality. *Greetings* features a sequence in which the heterosexual-homosocial creates a homosexual out of the body of one of its own, a thematic with suggestive implications for the early films, which presage queer theorist Judith Butler's findings in *Gender Trouble* (1990) and *Bodies That Matter* (1993) that gender is a performance, and that heterosexuality depends upon an abjected homosexuality to give it coherence and authority. To wax Butlerian, De Palma's early films figure homosexuality as the excluded domain of normativity, precisely what heterosexuality defines itself against *in order* to define itself. By insisting on heterosexual manhood's thoroughly intimate familiarity with homosexual subculture, they collapse the discrete distinctions between heterosexual normativity and homosexual abjection; they expose normative heterosexual manhood as an impossible, and impossibly maintained, ideal.

As Butler writes, "Heterosexuality is always in the process of imitating and approximating its own phantasmatic idealization of itself—and *failing*."[25] And as she has influentially demonstrated, the body is both a text awaiting inscription from hegemonic power and one that is always already inscribed as gendered and heterosexual.[26] Social construction—the "constitutive constraint"—not only produces the "domain of intelligible bodies" but also "unthinkable, abject, unlivable bodies." These "abject" bodies only serve to haunt the normative domain of intelligible bodies.[27] "There is no power that acts," Butler writes, "but only a reiterated acting that is power in its persistence and instability."[28] Reiterative and citational, gender identity must be perpetually reenacted.

What De Palma's early films allow us to see is that, no less than any other form of identity, white male heterosexuality must be perpetually *reenacted* to be maintained with any coherence at all. The dazzling series of male masquerades in *Greetings* and *Hi, Mom!*—the New Hollywood equivalent of Roger O. Thornhill's costume changes in *North by Northwest*—transgressively threaten to expose the precariousness of male identity they send up. As *Greetings* will amply demonstrate, homosexual identity and the fear of it haunts a heterosexual male identity that is itself under siege, increasingly aware of the burdens of gendered identity.

The early films (among others) deploy homosexuality, an important corollary to the depiction of male friendship and iconic womanhood, both as a field of knowledge that informs and a realm of anxiety that saturates the heterosexualized homosocial sphere. As Sedgwick writes in *Between Men*, "In any male-dominated society, there is a special relationship between male homosocial (*including* homosexual) desire and the structures for maintaining and transmitting patriarchal power: a relationship founded on an inherent and potentially active structural congruence."[29] What is of chief value in De Palma's work is that he exposes the homosocial's incoherence and untenable aims—its ineluctable tendency toward dissolution, a tendency that assimilates all in its path. De Palma's insistent motivation to investigate male friendship, however sullied by betrayal, has queer potentialities that are politically important. Even in his 1969 film *The Wedding Party*, which features the young Robert De Niro and Jill Clayburgh, this critical interest in homosocial relations is the chief interest of the film, as the groom's circle of male friends alternately deter him from marrying and ensure that he does (uncannily recalling bachelor culture in the nineteenth century, which simultaneously shielded men from marriage and prepared them for it[30]).

As Parker Tyler wrote, "While filmdom must have its sentimental charades, must constantly assert its all-too-public discretion, the innocence of really chummy, enduring, and drama-fraught relations between men has to register as a speculative factor, always subject to . . . analysis."[31] The chief object of De Palma's persistent speculation has been the underpinnings of the homosocial sphere itself, presented as hardly innocent, even at its chummiest. Even though these early films bear little seeming relation to the later ones, especially the grandiloquent thrillers, they reveal, upon close analysis, an organic relation in theme and motif to each other and to other films in De Palma's oeuvre—an oeuvre which, I argue, is cohesively bound by an interest in the dynamics of relations between men, which informs the essentialist treatments of women and ongoing interest in queer identity.

Paul's Case: *Greetings*

The hectic *Greetings*, which De Palma edited and also co-wrote, with Charles Hirsch, opens with a metatextual, frame-within-the-frame image of the United States President of the moment, Lyndon Baines Johnson, speaking to us from within a TV set encased by the frame of the film. LBJ calls upon the men of America to assist with the current military crisis and its attendant problems: "I hope you men are determined to help us meet these problems . . . [and] give justice to the people of this nation and the world." As if defensively anticipating rebuttals, LBJ says, "I'm *not* saying you never had it so good—but that *is* a fact, isn't it?"[32] The men of America are addressed as if they were a cohesive group, an imagined community (to use Benedict Anderson's phrase to describe the way citizens of a nation fantasize about and relate to each other) of men.

Greetings's protagonists, three male friends—Paul Shaw (Jonathan Warden), Jon Rubin (Robert De Niro), and Lloyd Clay (Gerrit Graham)—in Vietnam-era

New York City, do not appear to "have it so good." Ironically undercutting LBJ's rhetoric, we abruptly cut to a hand-held view of Paul walking into an African American bar. "Which one of you niggers is man enough to take me on?" hollers Paul inside. In the next scene, set inside a thrift shop, Paul explains what happened ("I got stomped by some spades") and his motives to Jon and Lloyd. "I got to get out of it," he says: Paul has attempted to get beaten up in order to fail his pre-induction physical and thereby avoid being drafted into the Vietnam War.

Despite its freewheeling, Godardian looseness and spontaneity, the film is fraught with wartime anxiety. Its concerns hinge on the pressures to sustain and achieve national manhood, pressures which inspire racism and death-wishes; the mingled racism, desperation, and transgressive humor in Paul's challenge to the blacks in the bar encapsulate the film's obsession with male performance and its attendant anxieties. The scene in the thrift shop, the second in the film, is perhaps the most important one in terms of the film's ribald and anxious negotiation with the pressures of American manhood.

As a transaction occurs between the proprietor and a customer, both Jon and Lloyd mastermind a plot to get Paul "out of it": they devise a foolproof plan for him to fail his pre-induction physical. "We'll do the same thing for you that I did," says Lloyd—and the friends proceed to transform Paul into "a fag" to get him out of military service, in a sequence that plays like a cross between the Pygmalion myth and *The Bride of Frankenstein* (1935). They take off Paul's jacket, roughly tuck his shirt corners in ("Really get them in there"), and hoist up his pants to an absurd height. "I ain't no fag, man," protests Paul. "We're *making* you a fag, man," say his friends.

"Now you got to get some black lace bikini panties," says Lloyd. "Fags, you see," says Lloyd, "fags are really blatant." After instructing Paul to stuff these undergarments with a deceiving sock, Lloyd instructs him to wear a fishnet shirt and to shave his entire body: "Shave your chest, under your arms, your whole body"—and, in a proto-product placement moment, says—"better use Nair." Paul complains about all of this fuss and its effects: "It's rankling me, man." Underscoring this scene is the exchange between the proprietor and his customer, coded, through his flashy garb, as homosexual. Though the camera remains stationary throughout, De Palma flips and intermixes two different versions of the scene as the actors switch roles. In the alternate version, the effeminate customer remains equally so in his new role as the proprietor, while the proprietor-as-customer remains, comparatively, a masculine "rough." The real "fag" and real "man" read coherently as such no matter which role either plays.

It is difficult to judge how much sympathy, beyond his ironic function, the shifting gay man is allowed in this ambivalent scene. What I want to argue for is the queer potentiality of De Palma's overall critique of heterosexual male culture.[33] De Palma suggests that heterosexual men like Jon, Paul, and Lloyd possess an uncanny familiarity with the social and aesthetic capacities of "fagdom." Their ransacking of queer attributes, signs, and emblems signals their own anxious positions as endangered straight men—at odds with straight male culture as a whole—much more powerfully than it signals the homophobia present in the film's culture, to say nothing of our own. There is very little that Jon and Lloyd can do for Paul other than camouflage him; they are themselves victims of the overarching and crushing male system presided over by LBJ, *himself* shown to be worried and anxious about his appeal to fellow "men," as his tergiversations during his broadcast suggests. The general male panic in the air forces the male community to feed off of itself.

The physical intimacy of the men in this scene represents the paralytic bind of average men in a culture of compulsory masculinity that both encourages and agitates against same-sex intimacy while always closing off any erotic potentialities of that intimacy. Only through the construction of an extruded "fagginess" can these men exhibit fidelity and concern. The rough tenderness with which the men turn Paul into a "fag" is itself sexually suspect, emblematizing what Sedgwick describes as the "radically disrupted continuum, in our society, between sexual and nonsexual male bonds."[34] Creating a "fag" out of Paul allows a physical intimacy amongst the men that in other contexts would be suspect; it is only their complementary abuse toward "fag" identity that inoculates them against a similar social contagion.

The following scene's setting—a zoo where the three men stand before a group of caged bears—explicates the homosocial sphere's simultaneous abhorrence of and intimacy with queer sexuality. The juxtaposition of caged animals and the three anxious young men is telling and pointed. Within the larger backdrop of zoological classifications, their interactions in this scene, in which they further appropriate the codes of queer identity, represent their fears of their own endangerment even as they continue to calumniate the "fag." Their simultaneous efforts to mine "fag" identity of its potential benefits and denounce it through ridicule serve as consolatory gestures, attempts to alleviate their own anxieties over participating in a nationalistic program of compulsory masculinity.

Hips swaying widely, wrists limply waving, Lloyd saunters up to Paul and Jon, who improvisationally stand-in for the staunch military personnel who will preside over Paul's actual induction. When asked his name, Lloyd, modeling the "fag"-Paul that the "real" Paul must emulate, responds, "Paul Gerald Shaw; but you can call me 'Geranium,' because the boys say I smell like a flower!" The level of self-consciousness in this series of male performances of the varieties of masculinity is remarkable. Lloyd, ostensibly straight (though Graham's performance has a pansexual floridity), plays a gay man before his straight friends, who are themselves playing specific types of *other* straight men, homophobic militia types. Playing the "fag" functions as a strategy for certain straight men to elude the hegemonic rule of the heterosexual-homosocial sphere. Abject homosexual identity becomes a defiant, oppositional identity for straight men against other, "straighter," men.

As Lloyd sashays up to the "men," he provides asides to complement his performance (an imitation meant to be imitated). "Just walk right up to him . . . and seduce him with your eyeballs," he says, as these organs flutter wildly: being a "fag" involves a training of the viscera. "Get a load of this!" heartily contributes De Niro's Jon, mock-butch in his portrayal of a gruff commando. Again, what makes this scene poignant rather than offensive, or, at least, poignant *while* offensive, is the underlayer of desperation involved in the entire performance. Homosexual identity may be ablated from the larger heterosexual male community, but the young heterosexual men who literally perform modes of masculinity here are themselves ablated from the larger heterosexual male community, which they both satirize and serve. Ultimately, their *own* position within the homosocial sphere bears eerie similarities to that of the homosexual. Paul delivers a line that intensifies these fears: "I can't act like a fag, man. And they're gonna put me on the front lines with the other fags." They are all in this together.

Considering the almost coterminous emergence of the gay liberation movement figured by Stonewall—the landmark riot took place on June 27, 1969, in the same New York City where *Greetings* is set—and the film, the grafting of gay panic onto the performance anxieties of these straight young men suggests a melting of boundaries between sexual and gendered identities. *Greetings* anthropologically surveys the scene of male performativity in the late 1960s. It locates the weirdly touching middle ground between abject and hegemonic identities, one represented by these vagabond goofs' anxious imitation of a gay persona through which they hope to elude their probable deaths on the "front lines."

The political accomplishment of *Greetings* is that it allows for an alienated resistance to the heterosexual-homosocial from those within it. Further helping Paul to evade the draft, his friends next urge him to play an asocial psycho. They tell him what to say in order to traumatize government psychiatrists: "Be real militant!" De Niro's Jon models the psycho-male Paul should portray: "[I want to kill] niggers, spics, and Jews. . . . Ready to kill me a bunch of little commies." De Niro's proto-Travis Bickle impersonation, a model for Paul to emulate, deepens in a subsequent, similar scene: "[I want to kill] Mexicans, niggers, homos, all the undesirable elements. . . . Let my rifle veer to the left, then to the right, to pick off cancerous elements."

These draft-dodgers locate a violently, perhaps even psychotically racist outlook within the persona of the normative American male. Implicitly lauded by

LBJ in his speech, the underlying motivation of ethnic cleansing in the present war explicitly emerges as one of the chief characteristics of the three friends' caricature of a jingoistic American psycho. This improvised psycho-figure exposes the rapacious brutality of the surrounding war simply by revealing the attitudes of rabid jingoism and racism needed to engage in it. Which is to say, the psycho the De Niro character performs is merely a slightly more hyped-up version of the American male LBJ calls to arms and duty. The three friends merely feed back to the nation the bitter meal of masculinity it has served to them.

It should be emphasized, however, that *Greetings* depicts a potential for solidarity between men. Though De Palma will make it his ongoing thematic business to critique the compulsory nature of male friendship, at least at this point in his career, he believes in the powerful potential in male friendship to protect embattled men from the dangers inherent within the homosocial sphere. As in *The Wedding Party*, the male group works together to help one of its own, whether endangered by weddings or war.

Voyeuristic Brotherhood: *Hi, Mom!*

Like a vision that gains clarity through successive lenses, the depiction of the homosocial and its attendant sexual anxieties achieves a sharper focus still in *Hi, Mom!* (1970). As they did in *Greetings*, De Palma and Charles Hirsch conceived the story and the screenplay; De Niro returns as Jon Rubin; Gerrit Graham also returns, albeit as "Gerrit Wood." (Interestingly, there is neither the return of *Greetings*'s Paul nor the actor who played him, Jonathan Warden, as if to suggest that Paul was indeed swallowed up by the war.) The interest in scopophilia that marks *Greetings* becomes an obsession in *Hi, Mom!*, which riffs on Antonioni's 1966 *Blow Up* (obviously an important film to De Palma, who would rework it as *Blow Out*) and exudes a fascination with the Zapruder film and its legendary grassy-knoll perspective of the JFK assassination. *Hi, Mom!* was also known as *Confessions of a Peeping Jon,* an alternate title that riffs on another De Palma touchstone, *Peeping Tom,* the famous 1960 film by Michael Powell, and, implicitly, on Hitchcock's *Rear Window* (1954).

Freud's treatment of the subject of voyeurism is particularly illuminating because of his emphasis on the links between feelings of powerlessness and the sadistic desire to dominate. Freud observes that infantile sexuality "from the very first involves other people as sexual objects." Scopophilia, exhibitionism, and cruelty, linked "instincts," exist somewhat "independently" from erotogenic sexual activity, dominating the early lives of children, who are both free of shame and exhibit a great "satisfaction" in exhibiting their own bodies before others. Onanistic children also develop an interest in the genitals of others, most often developing into "voyeurs, eager spectators of the processes of micturition and defecation,"

129

activities most likely to satisfy eyes hungering for a glimpse of hidden genitals. After repression sets in, this desire to see others' genitals becomes a "tormenting compulsion." Even more independent an impulse than scopophilia, cruelty comes easily to the child, for the affect of pity, like shame, develops late.[35] In his conflation of scopophilia, exhibitionism, and cruelty, Freud appears to suggest that these drives, rather than depending on sexual identity or feeling, manifest themselves as forces with their own agency, onerous demands, power. Moreover, these drives' interrelated qualities hinge on pitilessly attempting to exert dominance over the entire exhibitionistic spectacle.

Freud helps us to contextualize the figure of voyeurism in *Hi, Mom!* Jon's peep-art emerges as an attempt to exert power, an illusory sense of dominance, in a culture in which he has none, a powerlessness specifically represented in the film through his visit to the underworld of a pornographic theater, guided by a highly dubious Virgil figure. Jon's peeping on women emerges as a defense against his own subjugation before the spectacle of the gaze, his abjection as spectator-object.

In *Hi, Mom!*, De Niro's Jon returns to New York City from Vietnam. Rather like a picaresque hero, he becomes entangled in unforeseeably odd adventures: strange political intrigues that involve terrorism and an allegiance with a Black Power theater-of-cruelty troupe. The "Be Black, Baby!" sequence provides some of the most interesting and satirical work on race relations in American film of this era. The black actors who torment the white viewers, who then appreciatively discuss the relevance of their experiences with reporters, appear to enact vengeance for Paul's exploitation of blacks in *Greetings*.

An obvious stand-in for the director, Jon wants to make "peep-art" films. He goes to the office of sleazemeister extraordinaire Joe Banner (the coarse and dislikable Allen Garfield, who anticipates the Dennis Franz of the later films), head of Banner Films, a pornographic movie company that confirms another of the film's alternate titles, *Blue Manhattan*. When Jon—who, as De Niro plays him, is a mixture of jitteriness and confidence—visits Banner's office, the cantankerous Banner yells at him for disrupting his review of a typical Banner offering: "Look what you're disturbing here. Is that gorgeous? You see that cleavage? You don't get that in a Fellini film! You get that in a Banner film!" Garfield, who also appears in *Greetings*, embodies the corrupt depiction of male friendship in these three early films, which may almost be seen as a Garfield triptych: a three-paneled installation of male degradation. Banner's intertextual agon with Fellini presages that which De Palma will have with Hitchcock.

The next scene takes place in a porno theater where a non-Banner film—the competition—is being shown. This scene satirically deepens *Greetings*'s treatment of the invasion of the embattled homosocial sphere by the threat of the

Robert De Niro and the "Be Black, Baby!" performers in *Hi, Mom!*

homosexual. We alternate between shots of the pornographic film on the screen and the two men, Jon and Banner, sitting watching the film. Banner's weirdly utopian class description of the clientele—"This is your public . . . [T]hese guys come from every walk of life: middle-class, rich, poor"—is counterbalanced by the positioning of an elderly, blank-faced patron in the row before Jon and Banner. Jon notices a man going into the bathroom, and prominently turns around to see what the man is doing. Like a grubby Virgil in this flickering inferno, Banner explains, rather thoroughly, the codes of this realm to the smugly cheerful Jon, who is shown to be avidly invested in the activities of the homosexual:

Don't pay any attention. . . . Things go on in there [inside the bathroom]. . . . I shouldn't even tell you what goes on in there. . . . You come into one of these theaters, you do not go into the bathroom. You got that straight? That's one of the laws.

What fascinates, to begin with, about Banner's speech is that it recognizes the role of the homosexual—in fact, enshrines it—within the heterosexual-homosocial. Yet there is an attendant and ultimately fetishized level of "secrecy" surrounding this role, the open secret of homosexuality: "I shouldn't even tell you what goes on in there." The movie makes quite a show of the show Jon makes in curiously fixating on the activities of the homosexual in the straight porno theater. Juxtaposed against Jon and Banner's speech is the film-within-the-film, the porno. We keep cutting back to the representation of the woman in the porno being sexually satiated; her and her male partner's exaggerated heavy breathing diegetically engulfs the scene. There is a pointed contrast made between the colossal energies of porno-cinematic heterosexuality and the puny antics of the homosocial-homosexual.

There is a scuffle in the bathroom and the "pervert" is thrown out. Again, Banner offers commentary: "Don't pay any attention. . . . Pervert—leave him alone. Who knows where he's been?" Banner gets back to the pressing business at hand—pointing out the inadequacies of this particular non–Banner Films work. He points out the lack of satisfaction visibly conveyed by the porno actress's expressions: "She looks inhibited, right? . . . She wants to screw the man of her life. So who do they put her in there with? Some weirdo with gold hair!" As Banner says this, we cut back to the porno—and the "weirdo" with gold hair, like some ersatz Ganymede, seems to stare back at us, as if to suggest his awareness of Banner's derisive appraisal. This moment crucially establishes the nonincidental linkage De Palma makes between the antic events of the porno and the antic events within the porno theater. If porno-cinematic heterosexual relations dwarf the relatively petty scene of male-male relations, the joke here is that the masculinity of the male actor in the porno, the golden-haired weirdo, is no less suspect than that of the pervert skulking around in the theater bathroom.

When we return to the scene of the two "men" speaking, the pervert is sitting next to Jon, and Banner is pontificating about the body. "I believe that people should walk around with a sense of beauty about the body." He presents an interesting case: his daughter is a free spirit comfortable with her nudity, but his six year old son "walks around with a towel around him all the time." Now the pervert begins massaging Jon's thigh. De Niro nervously laughs. Nonchalantly, Banner says, "That's alright, he means well!": a great line, because this pervert "means" all over the place. As the pervert gropes Jon, Jon and Banner exchange glances. Their exchanges are theatrical gestures that appear to acknowledge their awareness that they are playing male roles, that their manhood is a performance. We cut back to the porno. The woman in it bumps her head against a poster on the wall behind her—a poster *of* a woman. Just as the actress bumps up against a representation of a woman, Banner and Jon "bump up against" their own roles as heterosexual men watching a pornographic film that is pitched at them and represents their desires. Their roles, at least ostensibly, contrast with that of the pervert who attempts to manipulate, in pursuit of his own, unclassifiable, unruly desires, the scene of pornographic viewing that includes the spectators almost as the porn film's extruded essence.

Then we see that Garfield and De Niro have switched places, while the pervert has remained in place. The pervert, mechanically, rotely, now begins to massage *Banner's* thigh. Banner pontificates on this point: "This man [the pervert] is obviously somebody who needs a movie. But not this movie. If it were this movie, he wouldn't be doing this to me—he wouldn't be putting his hands on my balls." It is impossible to read Allen Garfield's performance and De Palma's direction of it during the delivery of these lines as arbitrary or accidental. As Garfield says the line, "He wouldn't be doing this to me," he picks up the pervert's hand, and visibly clenches it. "He wouldn't be putting his hands on my balls": with this line, Garfield takes the pervert's hand and deliberately places it on *his*—Garfield's—groin, pressing down as he does this.

This key moment indexes the complex, messy negotiation of forms of male sexuality which occurs throughout De Palma's early films. The pervert becomes a limp, pliable representative of "the perverse," not Poe's antic imp of the perverse, but, rather, perversity's abject form in culture's regime of simultaneous repression and compulsory sexual potency and performance. By physically directing the "perverse" aims of the pervert, Banner signals his own complicity in the fulfillment of these aims. It's almost as if he were enabling or guiding the perversity of the pervert: showing him how it's done. The starkly separate spheres of the homosexual and the homosocial merge and lose distinctiveness.

As Jonathan Dollimore points out, "Freud described homosexuality as the most important perversion of all," "as well as the most repellent in the popular mind," while also being "so pervasive to human psychology" that Freud made it "central to psychoanalytic theory."[36] The pervert's wan, vulnerable embodiment of perversity blurs into his social burden of *also* representing the homosexual. Banner's physical actions here alert us to the homosocial's dependence on the presence of the homosexual, a point insistently made in these three early films. This presence provides a flimsy cover for a deep, despairing absence, the inability of actually representing a queer subject position in this media or, indeed, a perverse one. The pervert-homosexual we see here is a phantom of himself, a shadowy substitute for non-normative sexual desires, a puppet for perversity's masters.

Perversity takes an abject form here: the pervert attempts to make his desire visible, yet primarily signifies the void of signification and would appear to exist largely to be derogated and directed by others. De Palma's representation of the role played by the perverse within the male pornographic sphere corresponds to Freud's theory of psychosexual development and perversity's place both in this development and within culture. As Freud puts it,

> a disposition to perversions is an original and universal disposition of the human sexual instinct. . . . [N]ormal sexual behaviour is developed out of it as a result of organic changes and psychical inhibitions occurring in the course of maturation. . . . Among the forces restricting the direction taken by the sexual instinct we laid emphasis upon shame, disgust, pity, and the structures of morality and authority erected by society.[37]

Socialization buries our polymorphous perversity under repressive decorum, but perversity can only be buried, not eradicated. Repression keeps it buried, and what constitutes repression is an odd assortment of "social dams" such as the curious triumvirate of shame, disgust, and pity. It should be noted, too, that neurotic symptoms are manifestations of the repression of "abnormal sexual impulses": *"neuroses are, so to say, the negative of the perversions."*[38] If the value of psychoanalysis, as Jonathan Dollimore writes, lies in its exposure of the essential instability of identity, "then this is never more so than in Freud's account of perversion. At every stage perversion is what problematizes the psychosexual identities upon which our culture depends."[39]

In Freudian theory, observes Dollimore, "neurosis is understood as a failed suppression of perversion, one which is no less injurious to the individual and to civilization, than perversion in a non- or desublimated form." Freud's view of society is that it actively produces that which "it needs to suppress and sublimate for its own survival."

> [I]n Freud's theory culture develops to a point where it begins to produce, instead of sublimating, perversion; it incites what it should conceal, isolates what it should absorb, pressures into an independent existence what it should transform. And where this results in neurosis rather than sublimation, it is effectively destroying the subjectivity it should be fashioning. We might say in such instances that authority does indeed produce its own subversion, and precisely in the effort to contain it.[40]

Dollimore's analysis of Freud helps us to understand that De Palma creates a scene of "modern nervousness" in *Hi, Mom!*'s pornographic milieu, in which the normative homosocial realm confronts the unreconstructed pervert, with whom it is shown to be not only in league but also in a master/servant power structure. The actual human pervert pales in comparison to the *staging* of perversity, the

134

uses made of the pornographic theater as the architectural and social setting for the unleashing of and indulgence in buried perversions that apparently can take place only through the screening of pornographic film. The pervert merely exists as a skittish sign that a non-normative atmosphere of "perversity"—if the realm of the pornographic theater can be seen as a place where men, awash in perverse impulses they must ordinarily repress, go to escape social inhibitions—has been created. The uses and abuses of the pervert here belie Banner's phantasy of the porno theater as a utopian zone for the access to the perversions for all manner of men. Rather than functioning as a demarcated and special zone for the access to the perversions, the pornographic theater is simply another socially regulated zone where sexual hierarchies, the normal versus the perverse, still apply, hence Banner's derogation of the pervert. As evinced by Banner's simultaneous derogation and sexual exploitation of the pervert (putting the pervert's hand on his groin, using the pervert ambiguously as a prop), however, normativity in its form here as conventionally heterosexual male identity remains hopelessly riddled with perversities and the neuroses their repression generates. Hetero-manhood is always in an irresolvable conflict with itself, simultaneously drawing on and stamping out the perverse energies which must be repressed in order for the normative social order to function as such. This is to say that the scene and the specter of hetero-manhood function as a crucible through which the social order makes sense of itself—at best a paralytic sense. Simultaneously, men must be rapaciously sexualized and sexually constrained, pornographically hyperstimulated and reserved, regulated, and abstemious. I do not offer these observations in anything like a sentimental mode; rather, I am pointing out a series of irresolvable and constitutional discrepancies, which De Palma films illuminate, within normative male identity as it is socially constructed and experientially and publically performed.

The scene of male pornographic spectatorship represents not perversity but neurosis, if we follow Freud, the *negative* of the perversions, the social effect of repressing "abnormal" sexual impulses. The porno theater becomes the place in which normal adult men hoping to access their repressed perversities discover that they are not perverts but, instead, neurotics, alienated from their own sexuality and locked at once into compulsory roles and into the compulsory homosocial order. The pornographic theater is the negative of the perversions.

For a director inextricably linked to misogyny, De Palma demonstrates a remarkable ambivalence toward pornography here, surely the genre of filmmaking most commonly associated with misogyny. An interest in satirizing porn runs throughout De Palma's work, most strikingly in the satirical film-within-the-film opening of 1981 *Blow Out*, which begins with footage from a porny cheapjack horror film, *Co-ed Frenzy*, that concludes with a ludicrously unconvincing woman's scream. (The harrowing aim of the film is to replace that inadequate scream with a wrenchingly authentic one.) Few directors have more resolutely explored the simultaneously joyful sensuality and nihilistic emptiness of the pornographic—not just literally, as in *Hi, Mom!*, but in terms of film texture and themes. If *Carrie's* early girls-in-the shower sequence (which follows the first scene, in which teen misfit Carrie is brutalized by the other girls for her clumsiness during gym class) is a lyrical phantasy of unlimited access to feminine sexuality, *Blow Out* already sees the pornographic film as a site of brutality and spiritual emptiness, whereas *Body Double* alternately views it as a zone for homosocial relations and betrayal while also depicting it as a fiendishly funny, berserk alternative reality that exists primarily for send-up and satirization. Both films tellingly make the pornographic and horror movie industries indistinguishable. De Palma's problematization of the pornographic—an especially striking feature of what so many consider to be a misogynistic filmography—continues to the present day. Some of the most piercing images in his latest film, the flawed but extraordinary *The Black Dahlia*, about one of the grisliest Hollywood murders, are those of the vulnerable, doomed Elizabeth Short (Mia Kershner) either being interviewed by a sleazy, invasive Banner-like movie producer (we only hear his voice; it's provided by De Palma himself) or acting in a pornographic film. The juxtaposition between the intensely graphic sexuality of the pornographic images and Short's suffering, emblematized by her huge, haunted eyes, is truly harrowing.

Though Linda Williams exhibits a striking lack of interest in De Palma's conflation of the horror and pornography genres, her work is quite relevant for De Palma's cinema (which she alternately impugns and dismisses). If, as Williams argues in her well-known essay "Film Bodies," the "body genres" of pornography, horror, comedy, and melodrama function through "seemingly gratuitous excesses," what is most notable about De Palma's depiction of pornography is its *lack* of excess, its barrenness, its abjection.[41] Laura Kipnis's work more directly enriches our understanding of De Palma's depiction of pornography.[42] One of the most important insights of her *Bound and Gagged* is that the pornography that is made for male consumption enables a fantasy that women desire sex in the same impersonal way that men do. If we read *Hi, Mom!* in light of Kipnis's argument, we can theorize that Banner's and Jon's interactions with the homosexual reveal the sad/comic truth that the only people likely to pursue conventionally physically unappealing men such as Banner are other physically unappealing men. The homosexual pervert here facilitates the fantasy-enactment of Banner's desire to be desired, which the pornographic film's action pointedly does not. He substitutes for the fantasy woman to which pornography promises access, an access that will rarely be granted in reality. As such, the pervert bears the burden not only of homophobia but of a misogynistic rage fueled by sexual and emotional deprivation.

Slavoj Žižek theorizes that, unlike the nonpornographic love scene in a "normal" film, which is predicated on the *inability* to "show" us everything, the pornographic one "shows us everything." The effect of this abundance is "extremely vulgar and depressing," for pornography "dispels the charm" of the love scene, leaving us "stuck with vulgar, groaning fornication." Drawing on the essential antinomy—paradox, unresolvability—of the relationship between gaze and eye Lacan articulates in his *Seminar XI*—that "the eye viewing the object is on the side of the subject, while the gaze is on the side of the object"; in other words, the object I look at always already gazes back at me, from a point at which I cannot see it—Žižek theorizes that the problem of pornography is that it *loses* this antinomy.

> This antinomy of gaze and view is lost in pornography. Why? Because pornography is inherently *perverse*. Its perverse character lies not in the obvious fact that it "goes all the way and shows us dirty details"; its perversity is, rather, to be conceived in a strictly formal way. In pornography, the spectator is forced a priori to occupy a perverse position. Instead of being on the side of the viewed object, the gaze falls into ourselves, the spectators, which is why the image we see on the screen contains no spot, no sublime-mysterious point from which it gazes at us. It is only we who gaze stupidly at the image that "reveals all." Contrary to the commonplace, according to which, in pornography, the other (the person on the screen) is degraded to an object of our voyeuristic pleasure, we must stress that it is the spectator himself who effectively occupies the position of the object. The real subjects are the actors on the screen trying to rouse us sexually, while we, the spectators, are reduced to a paralyzed object-gaze.[43]

Žižek's theorization of pornography illuminates a crucial aspect of what De Palma presents to us here, the essentially paralytic, abject position of the male spectators.[44] Just as the draft dodgers of *Greetings* rely upon the derogated, *more* abject figure of the "fag" to maintain a precarious sense of autonomy in the face of crushing national male might, the spectators of pornography in this film use the figure of the pervert to assuage their anxieties, their confrontation with their own revealed vulnerability as spectator-objects. De Palma reveals—in an inchoate manner that will manifest its full acuity in his later, more mature films—the anxieties that undergird the misogyny and homophobia that undergird the homosocial.

Films such as Orson Welles's *The Lady from Shanghai* (1948), with its famous shootout in a hall-of-mirrors climax; Hitchcock's *Rear Window* and *Psycho*; and Powell's *Peeping Tom* critique the film spectator's scopophilic sadism, the ravenous desire to look and to control the spectatorial field and the actors/characters within it.[45] If De Palma's cinema will become a prolonged and productive agon with their work, what De Palma stages in *Hi, Mom!* is an anticipatory allegory of his own forthcoming cinematic project. The scene of beleaguered, anxious male viewers in the porno theater dwarfed by images over which they attempt to exert dominance, intruded upon by a perversity that they then attempt also to dominate and deploy for their own purposes, reflects De Palma's own agon with his corrupt cinematic fathers, whose incorporated visions he will obsessively turn into his own tormenting compulsion to see and see again.[46]

The famous "Be Black, Baby!" sequence further intensifies these thematics, representing one of De Palma's profoundest preoccupations, a deep ambivalence toward theater, theatrical performance, and spectatorship. These attitudes come through strongly in his early *Dionysius in '69*; in the ironic, Mephistophelean menace of the stage performances in *Phantom of the Paradise*; in the staged coronation of the prom king and queen in *Carrie*; and in the extraordinary sequences in *Blow Out* in which Jack Terry frantically races through Philadelphia "Liberty Day" parades (which evoke the 4th of July) in an attempt to save Sally Bedina's life. In the "Be Black, Baby!" sequence, De Palma's ironic and skeptical disposition toward the theatrical fuses with his interest in the politics of race. As an example of De Palma's penchant for inserting these matters into the usually white-washed genre of the Hitchcockian thriller, in *Sisters* he casts a black actor, Lisle Wilson, in the role of leading man—albeit one who will be killed, Marion Crane–fashion, halfway through the film. Wilson's Phillip Woode meets Danielle Breton (Margot Kidder) when he is surreptitiously filmed in a *Candid Camera*–like TV series, *Peeping Toms*, that questions what Phillip will do when the seemingly blind Danielle undresses in front of him. Further satirizing society's unacknowledged racist attitudes, De Palma, who wrote the screenplay, has the TV show producers giving their contestants hilariously and horrifyingly pointed gifts: to Danielle, a collection of steak knives; to Phillip, passes for a date to New York City's famous "African Room," where he ends up bringing Danielle after the show. Within this venue, a huge mask of a surreal-looking gorilla in bluish light hangs from a wall as if presiding over the black waiters in "safari" skirts who attend the patrons. (Later, Danielle, "possessed" by the spirit of her dead twin Dominique, will make use of one of her prize steak knives to dispatch Phillip.) De Palma's interest in race and satire extends to his much-maligned 1990 adaptation of Tom Wolfe's novel *The Bonfire of the Vanities*.

As the liberal white New Yorkers who want firsthand knowledge of the "black experience" are brutalized—assaulted, mugged, humiliated—by the "Be Black, Baby!" performers, *Hi, Mom!* deepens its treatment of the politics of vision with race-related anxieties. The spectators believe that they can experience black life vicariously, from the safe distance of theatrical spectatorship, whereas the performers, most but not all of whom are black (Gerrit Graham is one of the them), aggressively shatter the fourth wall and drag these spectators into the performance, indeed, making the spectators and their suffering *into* the performance.

The sequence challenges the prevailing fantasy of the passivity and safety of the spectator while also obliterating any sense of the racial other's acquiescence to the white gaze. After the spectators stagger out of the theater building, where they were tortured on staircases in the dark, and are interviewed by reporters, they gush about how moving and meaningful the performance was. Daringly, I think, De Palma extends Hitchcock's critique of the spectator's presumed moral as well as physical distance from representation to consider the racist dimensions of this spectatorial hypocrisy.

Corporate Brotherhoods: *Get to Know Your Rabbit*

Allen Garfield's sleazy charms also figure in the depiction of the horror of the homosocial in De Palma's next film, *Get to Know Your Rabbit*. Orson Welles has a small role in this film as a master magician, Mr. Delasandro, who teaches the hero, Donald Beeman (Tom Smothers), magic tricks. In aesthetic terms, the movie is notable only for allowing De Palma the opportunity to practice the overhead shots and the split-screen images that would come to mark his distinctive style; but its themes are an interesting extension of those in the previous films we have discussed. Donald desperately eludes the attentions of his corporate boss, Mr. Turnbull (Jon Astin of the 1960s TV show *The Addams Family*), who insists that he must come back to life as a corporate drudge. Turnbull invades and infiltrates Donald's life, even, at one point, kidnapping and coercing Donald's elderly parents and conscripting them into his cause. Donald just wants to be allowed to become a tap-dancing magician. Like *Greetings* and *Hi, Mom!*, *Get to Know Your Rabbit* (the titular rabbit is a prop Welles's imperious magician wields; at one point, Welles disdainfully informs Smothers: "You're holding your rabbit all wrong.") figures the homosocial sphere as a binding realm the individual male longs to escape. Unlike those films, it depicts the homosocial sphere as corporate, linking it to other regimes of economic and gendered power.

Harassed by his corporate boss, harried by his haughty mentor, and desperate to reimagine his life, Donald goes into the thrift store milieu familiar from *Greetings* and emerges garbed in "something seedy." He then meets the apparitional embodiment of seediness: Allen Garfield, as Vic, a brassiere-shop owner, who coerces Donald into going to an orgiastic, never-ending party. Garfield seems to exist in these films to offer the Faustian bargain of male friendship or complicity in male relations to the protagonist. (The sleazy, pre–*NYPD Blue* Dennis Franz will succeed Garfield in this capacity in later De Palma films.) As in *Hi, Mom!*, Garfield signifies the crudest demands of the homosocial. Yet in that film, De Niro's Peeping Jon sought *him* out. In *Get to Know Your Rabbit*, the specter of Garfield rises up, unbidden. Garfield's appearance here is almost aleatory, the summoned-up manifestation of the repressed homosocial id. Donald, of course, helplessly acquiesces to Vic's desires and goes to the party with him.

This party turns out to be a child's nightmare of an adult party: claustropho-bic, gaudy, packed with people, overladen with a suffocating sensuality, as such the inverse of the unsettling child's party invaded by adults on the lam in Hitch-cock's *Young and Innocent* (1938). A goddessy, aloof, smiling woman who appears to be a model takes a shine to Donald. "Are you with someone?" Donald asks. "Is that type of cheap broad with no brassiere ever with anybody?" retorts Vic, with characteristic derisiveness. "She's the type of cheap broad who knows exactly what to do in the backseat of a car." Vic then drives them to his shop, where the woman tries on and models brassieres. As Vic is driving Donald and the model, who sit in Vic's backseat, Vic encourages their physical expression. "I took the rear-view mirror off! Don't worry!" he cackles. Once in the shop, Vic leaves Don-ald and the model alone together, and the mood turns swooningly romantic. When Vic returns, armed with more brassieres, the model, enchanted by Donald now, tells Vic, "I'm not in the mood anymore." Vic grows monstrously angry, upbraiding them both. "I know what's going on here . . . cheap broad!" he says. After his apoplectic fit, Vic calms down, grows sad and withdrawn, and Donald and the model comfort him.

The scene with Vic is matched by two apposite subsequent ones. After his training of Donald has come to an end, Mr. Delasandro, the magician, asks Don-ald, "Would you like me to look upon you as the son I never had?"—to which question Donald imperturbably responds, "No." "I hope this is not a decision you'll regret," responds the old wizard. Then, later, Donald discovers that his old boss Turnbull has become a shambling, unkempt hobo. (The rejection of Mr. Delasandro—of Orson Welles—is crucial. De Palma foregrounds his own am-bivalence toward the great visual stylists, such as Welles, Hitchcock, Powell, and Pressburger, who he will emulate and reimagine.) Donald's decision to extract himself from the homosocial realm leaves it in chaos. The three emissaries of the homosocial realm—Astin's Turnbull, Welles's Delasandro, Garfield's Vic—all register with alternate amounts of anxiety, disdain, despair, and rage, the ter-rible loss of individual dreamer Donald's decision to break off from the collective male ranks they represent. Yet of all of the loner-drifters in these three films, the Donald of Tom Smothers is surely the least appealing and sympathetic. Blank, blandly self-satisfied, he represents the triumph of the individual will but also the dark side of the individual will-to-power. The callousness and coldness of his self-absorption are evinced by Donald's cruel response to Delasandro's paternalistic plea. The son kills the father with unkindness.

Women and the Homosocial Sphere

In light, then, of De Palma's interest in the cruelty that he sees as inherent in the homosocial sphere, a cruelty exemplified by the failure of male friendship, his treatment of women in films must be given a long overdue reappraisal and revaluation (as should his cinema). Women are the objects of exchange in these worlds dominated and controlled by men. As such, women in many De Palma films become representations of the corrupt interactions between men. This is not to say that women are merely treated as victims (as they are in, say, a film like Neil LaBute's *In the Company of Men* [1997]). If a streak of misogyny informs many of De Palma's films, this misogyny is intimately and inextricably linked to his politically radical deconstruction of relations between men. What I want to argue for is a better understanding of the logic of De Palma's treatment of women, one informed by his depiction of male friendship and relations. Women, whether brutalized or not, are often the central figures of De Palma films: *Sisters* (1973), *Obsession* (1976), *Carrie* (1976), *The Fury* (1978), *Dressed to Kill* (1980), *Blow Out* (1981), *Body Double* (1984), *Raising Cain* (1992), the unfairly maligned *Mission to Mars* (2000), and the sumptuously oneiric *Femme Fatale* all have strong female characters at their centers. *Carrie*, in my opinion De Palma's masterpiece (and a hugely important queer-cult film), is especially provocative in light of De Palma's preoccupation with homosocial relations. Here, De Palma begins to suggest that homosocial spheres of *all* kinds breed cruelty and betrayal. This is a film in which the roles of men are minimized and women take the center stage. In *Carrie*, the major characters are all women; the sympathetic Carrie's betrayal by and cruelty at the hands of her oppressors all involve, chiefly, relations between women. There is no sense of solidarity between the pariah Carrie and her female "friends." For De Palma, sameness (to whatever extent the term is applicable) connotes alienation and promotes cruelty. Carrie is a solitary individual at odds with her *own* homosocial sphere, like many of De Palma's male protagonists.

Briefly to return to *Greetings*, the kind of work I am asking to be done on De Palma should begin here, at least. This film makes starkly apparent the role of Woman in the realm of relations between men. Women become the counterbalance, the leverage, for the stability of male friendship. They do not need to be in the frame to pervade it. In one striking sequence, the three men are crawling around, vertiginously, on the ledge of a tall Manhattan building. As Lloyd, who, as Graham plays him, is by far the most sexually ambiguous of the three men, recounts his tale of sexual escapades with three women—"I was in a bod sandwich"—his two friends are shown to have fallen asleep. Noticing their lack of responsiveness, Lloyd yells at them: "Hey, come on!" His tale of masculine performance fails to signify unless heard by his compatriots.

At one point, Paul goes to the home of a woman with whom he has a computer-dating-arranged assignation. During their conversation, he reveals that he doesn't own a car and that he's already eaten; he makes it clearly obvious that he is only there for sex. Brassy and demanding, she upbraids him for being ill-prepared for their date. Like a general describing the battle-readiness of his troops, she points to specific elements of her romantic-evening-ready attire: "You see these shoes? 'Socialites'!" He wilts visibly under the glare of her scorn. She storms off. Yet when Paul goes to check in on her, she is lying in her bed, silent, naked. He walks off and out of the apartment. More than any other, a profound sense of loneliness, of a lack of connection, permeates this scene. This sense of male indifference and female isolation also tinges the scene in which Lloyd, feverishly pontificating over the JFK assassination and his multiple conspiracy theories, uses the silent, naked body of the woman he is in bed with as a living canvas, turning her over, and back again, drawing strategic sites of the grassy knoll upon her body. Like a cadaver, her body mutely complies with his feverish demands and doodling. The necrophiliac quality of this scene provides further evidence for the lack of relatedness between men and women, even in a scene that establishes physical intimacy between them. (The necrophilia here is too half-hearted to vie for the status of perversity.) On another computer date scene, a kind of Keystone Kops version of a porno, Paul and a woman have wild antic sex. Here, the footage is deliriously sped up, a blur—a fast-paced version of the solemn disconnection in the other versions of man-woman relations. The comical scenes in which De Niro's Jon lures a stiff blonde woman (Rutunya Alda) back to his room, having convinced her he is a successful moviemaker, and takes pornographic pictures of her under false pretenses, adds to the tone of alienation and disconnection.

142

All of the film's themes culminate in the Vietnam jungle-set climax. Despite his ingenious efforts, Jon has been drafted, but seems to be handling his new situation with customary glib aplomb. In his new military garb, he talks to a TV reporter with his characteristic slickness. He and the reporter notice a Vietnamese woman (who anticipates the victimized female figure Oahn in 1989 *Casualties of War*, a film that De Palma wanted to make since Daniel Lang's essay on the subject was published in *The New Yorker* in 1969). After questions of whether or not she is Viet Cong, Jon announces that he will have to shoot her, anyway, even though she waves a white flag. But when he goes up to her, the TV reporter and his crew behind him, he asks her to pose for the cameras and also to disrobe: "take off your shoes—as if you were alone in your room." As she complies and is filmed, De Palma (who edited this film as well) intercuts shots from the previous porno montage Jon had made with the blonde woman (Alda) he tricked. Puerile male fantasies continue unabated: the Vietnam War has become yet another satirical blue movie. De Palma equates the Viet Cong woman's sexual exploitation with the militaristic exploitation of war and carnage, which the film has depicted as the culmination of masculinist cruelty. And by intercutting this scene with shots of the blonde woman who had been tricked into being photographed, De Palma condenses the tendency toward war and the tendency toward the exploitation of women into the same male obsessions.

The approach to sexuality here—and I am making a comparison I have no doubt both filmmakers would reject—is close to Yvonne Rainer's in her 1990 film, *Privilege*. Rainer creates a memorably tortured scene in that film: a young woman's undergarments are pulled down with agonizing, infinite real-time slowness. Rainer has said that she wanted to capture the dehumanization of pornography in that scene.[47] What De Palma achieves in this scene is quite similar—by linking pornography to war, he makes the statement that both are versions of rape. And in a metatextual way, through the stand-in figure of Jon, figured parodistically as the "director" of this scene, he indicts filmmakers as well for their sublimated versions of rape and even murder.

A dizzying collapse of political questions, this scene climaxes, and with it, the film itself, with a reprise of LBJ's speech: "I'm not saying you never had it so good, but that *is* a fact, isn't it?" Now, the LBJ scene takes on a new and deeper resonance: it equates exploitation with the theme of knowledge. The sense that American men never have it so good as when they are playing at war and exploiting women becomes the "fact" of American male life that males must helplessly acknowledge. The autoerotic, homoerotic perversity of male play, even embattled, fraught, endangered male play, cedes to the inevitable entrenchment and enforcement of the national masculinist superego.

In *Greetings*, Allen Garfield, playing the "Smut Peddler," prods De Niro's Jon with his wares: pornos such as *Great Danes* and *The Horny Headmaster*. As they observe women, the Smut Peddler asks Jon, "Do you like girls? Would you like"—in reference to a blonde woman—"to bang her?" The first question is a kind of sexual rebuke. But the second question, fueled by a homoerotic complicity, is an invitation to male bonding. These films are about the underpinnings of male bonding in America—at least, the underpinnings as De Palma depicts them: a shared complicity in the brutalization of women and other men. In depicting, in these three films, the heterosexual-homosocial as a sphere of relations between men that are fraught with homosexual panic and internecine cruelty (the levels of which deepen with each film), De Palma begins to develop his bleak vision of male friendship and the homosocial. In film after film, De Palma treats relations between men as opportunities for betrayal, and this emerges as the crucial framework for his studies of all forms of gendered subjectivity. It seems to me that any discussion of De Palma needs to account for the thoroughgoing and often radical critique of patriarchal power; the unsettling, weirdly sympathetic interest in the endangered woman; the number of female characters who retaliate against oppressive forces, with often greater success than the male protagonists; and the productively paranoid regard for the organization of sexualities and genders through homosocialization that dominate his films. Without a critical, nuanced understanding of these themes, the radicalism of De Palma's films will lie forever buried beneath the heap of conventional assumptions and uncritical commonplaces that bind most treatments of his startlingly anti-patriarchal work.

In the next chapter, I discuss *Taxi Driver*, which adds a tragic realism to De Palma's early comedies. If we see the film as intertextually linked to those earlier works, we can understand the ways in which they anticipate *Taxi Driver*'s themes and the ways in which Scorsese deepens and extends those in the comedies. The key themes in the De Palma comedies—voyeurism; pornography; homosocial worlds; balked heterosexual relations; racism, homophobia, and misogyny as fundamental to normative male identity—also inform *Taxi Driver* and are treated with a new urgency.

CHAPTER FIVE

A SENSE OF *VERTIGO*
Taxi Driver

XEMPLARY OF THE PESSIMISTIC bleakness of the New Hollywood, Martin Scorsese's 1976 film *Taxi Driver* is one of its director's most poetic and disturbing films, awash in a melancholy longing for some unattainable state of transcendence. This longing is unsurprising in a protagonist devised by Paul Schrader, the screenwriter, who wrote, in his prior phase as a film critic, a book about "transcendental style" in the cinema of Ozu, Bresson, and Dreyer. Schrader's titular character, Travis Bickle (Robert De Niro), drives his striking, dingy yellow cab through an Expressionist New York City in which steam rises up malevolently from the streets, giving vent to gathering tensions. From the opening shots of the film, in which Travis's cab juts into view like a mythic barge astride a sea of streets, to the final moments, in which the film speeds up as Travis looks into his rearview mirror and directly at us, as watchful of his unseen cinematic audience as he is of himself, the film alerts us to its own stylized, irreal, metatextual qualities and sensibility. This is not a film set in a real place, though the 1970s Manhattan it evokes is verisimilitudinously grimy and vibrantly raw; not a film about living, breathing, authentic characters, though the characters on display have become part of our pop mythology; not a film that allows us any release or narrative closure, though by the end Travis has been established as a victor over the "excremental city," as Robin Wood describes it.[1] *Taxi Driver* broods over certain key themes, chief among them the contemporary condition of American male identity. It depicts this identity as fundamentally split, essentially multiple and fragmentary. The various untethered parts of the self each actively spy on each other and on themselves as a whole. Travis's subjectivity consists of a number of warring components, each equally paranoid and disconnected. What unites all of the different selves within Travis is a fundamental bewilderment over his own male identity, especially its gendered, sexual, and raced aspects. *Taxi Driver* depicts American manhood as a stranger to itself.

As many critics have noted, this is a film that foregrounds paranoia. As we discussed in Chapter 1, Freud drew illuminating and still controversial connections among jealousy, paranoia, and homosexuality—his tripartite monster. He postulates in his 1922 essay, "Some Neurotic Mechanisms in Jealousy, Paranoia, and Homosexuality," that within the process of jealousy lies a sense of terrible grief.

> It is easy to see that essentially [jealousy] is compounded of grief, the pain caused by the thought of losing the loved object, and of the narcissistic wound; further, of the feelings of enmity against the successful rival, and of a greater or lesser amount of self-criticism which tries to hold the person himself accountable for his loss.

This aspect of Freud's argument—the grief in jealousy—has been greatly deemphasized, the focus most often placed on his linkage between paranoia and homosexuality. This linkage has been the basis for what we can call Paranoia Studies. Paranoia is at the heart of "the culture of surveillance" in Foucauldian theory and also the difficulties inherent in postmodernity, with its collapse of "grand narratives," disorganization of aesthetic hierarchies (high and low forms of art), and endless self-referentiality. While paranoia's importance cannot be overstated, and will be crucial to the argument I make in this chapter, what I want to attempt to recover is the importance of jealousy, which *Taxi Driver* illuminates, in the triad of jealousy, homosexuality, and paranoia. It is misleading to unhook jealousy from Freud's view of the links among the three.

Patrick O'Donnell helpfully summarizes the traditional profile of the paranoiac and his symptoms, which derives from Freud's classic study of the Saxon supreme court judge Daniel Paul Schreber.

> These symptoms include megalomania; a sense of impending, apocalyptic doom; racist, homophobic, or gynophobic fear and hatred of those marked out as other deployed as a means of externalizing certain internal conflicts and desires (the scapegoating of otherness thus is essential to the ongoing work of paranoia); delusions of persecution instigated by these others or their agents; feelings of being under constant observation; an obsession with order; and

fantasizing of the reviled, abjected self as at the center of intersecting social and historical plots. When not limited to the symptoms of individual psychopathology, paranoia is often viewed either as a universal personal condition (one available to individual subjects across history, as much to Julius Caesar as to Lee Harvey Oswald), or a mindset that, like a contagion, can temporarily afflict a nation or a people (the United States during the Salem witch trials; Germany during the Third Reich).[2]

O'Donnell quickly adds that his own treatment will not pursue this Freudian line of inquiry—to do so would be to grant paranoia itself a self-defining legitimacy that forecloses critical analysis of it. The classic psychoanalytic portrait of the paranoid as he summarizes it, however, retains a resonance, and speaks to key aspects of *Taxi Driver*. Though the 1970s films are known for their exquisite bleakness and pessimism, they are not films that represent postmodernity (though filmmakers like De Palma and Kubrick, especially, seem "postmodern" in their active deconstruction of the filmic event, apparatus, and experience) if postmodernity, with its defining suspicion of representation, is taken to be the end of belief in art-making. *Taxi Driver* critiques, rather than collapses into, a culture of disconnection and despair. The film, in other words, isn't merely more evidence of a breakdown in sign, meaning, intersubjectivity, and belief, but a personally made and felt work that attempts to make sense of this breakdown. Travis Bickle's paranoia emerges as an appropriate response to his larger culture, though he is never anything but ironically heroized.

147

Scorsese's film depicts Travis Bickle as the continuation of the kinds of characters De Niro played in Brian De Palma's early comedies, but, crucially, minus the self-knowingness.[3] He is, like them, a voyeur who roams through a pornographic realm—of theaters and his own mind—but unlike them has no ironic detachment or distance. At the same time, he could not be more detached or distant from the world in which he lives or from himself. Many of the themes of those comedies play out darkly but not unhumorously in Scorsese's film. Travis is what his Jon from *Greetings* and *Hi, Mom!* attempted so studiously to avoid becoming: a Vietnam veteran. Recalling Jon's racist tirades in his mock performances as tough old military honchos, Travis exudes racist attitudes, but without Jon's irony. Like Jon as well, his male subjectivity is inextricably caught up in, indeed, constituted by, his visual obsessions, but Travis is left perplexed by them—flaccid—whereas Jon uses his visual mastery cunningly, always attempting to dominate others, particularly women, through it. If Jon's sexuality is a bit nebulous, and in *Hi, Mom!* quite detached from heterosexual pleasure even as the pursuit of it seems to drive its protagonist, Travis's sexuality remains an elusive, maddening blank, one the film offers us very little help in decoding.

Robert De Niro's
Travis Bickle: the
haunted subject
and the blankness
of the gaze.

As in *Hi, Mom!*, the pornographic theater in *Taxi Driver* is the symbol and the site of male visual obsessions and fantasies of sexual potency figured as *visual* dominance. Forever haunting and haunted by the pornographic realm, Travis remains fundamentally cut off from its pleasures and possibilities, cut off, most acutely, from the freedom of fantasy. Always adrift, Travis is also disconnected from the sexual potency associated with pornographic film though not necessarily with spectatorship. Writing of the scene in which, alone in a Times Square porn theater, Travis watches the screen, Amy Taubin remarks, "I think it's safe to say that Travis never comes to orgasm, that, for him, the only possible release is death." As Taubin concludes, the film "will deprive him even of that," and us of closure.[4] Travis's sexual stasis is crucial to a film that treats the increasingly frenzied visibility of sex as an overarchingly oppressive system.

Travis pursues and inhabits scenes of heterosexual intercourse without ever seeming to be directly involved in them. He does not "satisfy" either himself or the normative sexual expectations of audience. In that he never exhibits or fulfils a defined, precise, embodied sexual identity, his persona recalls the sexually inviolate males of nineteenth-century American fiction, especially in the antebellum period, who were coping with increasingly public and heated discussions of and demands for sexual health and morality. As I argue in *Men Beyond Desire*, many fictional nineteenth-century males remain sexually blank and, in their avoidance of any direct sexual involvement, sexually inviolate. Their sexual inviolability signals their inviolability on emotional, psychic, and often physical levels as well. These inviolate males are, however, often the object of male *homosocial* desire, which is not without homoerotic dimensions but principally seeks to assimilate males into the ranks of same-sex group identity and behavior. Inviolate men resolutely avoid both homosocial and homoerotic affiliations as well as heterosexual contact and ties, marriage especially. Fundamentally cut off from both women *and* other men, from both heterosexuality and the homosocial, Travis truly is, in his own words, "God's lonely man," a phrase that Paul Schrader lifted from an essay by Thomas Wolfe. And like the American males of antebellum fiction, such as Natty Bumppo in James Fenimore Cooper's *The Last of the Mohicans* (1826) and the other Leatherstocking novels, Travis openly declares his hatred of racial otherness, a disposition that reaches an apotheosis in his murder of a young black male petty thief in a bodega, aided by the Hispanic store owner. Yet, as I will develop below, Travis's much-discussed racism is a more complicated issue than it appears.

If Travis's hard, isolate, stoic, killer manhood, to evoke the famous paradigms of D. H. Lawrence, is a contemporary version of nineteenth-century American masculinity, what distinguishes the film's version of the isolate, sexually inviolate American male is that he now *openly* expresses his alienation from and contempt for homosexuality, a key component of his litany of hatreds: "All the animals come out at night," Travis famously observes while driving. "Whores, skunk pussies, buggers, queens, fairies, dopers, junkies. Sick, venal. Someday a real rain will come and wash all this scum off the streets. I go all over. I take people to the Bronx, Brooklyn, I take 'em to Harlem. I don't care. Don't make no difference to me. It does to some. Some won't even take spooks. Don't make no difference to me." One wonders if it would make a difference to Travis if he were forced to take "buggers, queens, fairies" to their presumably nefarious destinations. The repetition of like terms (*buggers, queens, fairies*) for one despised minority emphasizes Travis's particular horror and rage at the sexually deviant.

In order to make sense of the film's treatment of homosexuality, however, we must first consider how the film depicts gendered identity. Questions of gendered identity impinge on those related to sexuality. We know very little about Travis's sexuality, but we do learn a great deal about his sense of his own masculine identity. Any study of the representation of homosexuality in Hollywood film must

149

first attend to the representation of gendered identity, rather than simply focusing on explicit or coded representations of queer figures and desire. That is, essentially, the project of this book. In order to discover the ways in which homosexuality and homophobia inform the Hollywood screen, we need to develop a better understanding of how screen gender manifests itself. Any depiction of sexuality and desire flows from the larger depiction of gender. My reasons for placing emphasis on these points, which many will no doubt take as self-explanatory, is that some of the most significant queer theory treatments of film (as well as literature) take almost exclusive interest in sexuality itself and in the representation of queerness, rather than considering the entire, overarching structure of gendered identity, especially in national terms specific to constructions of gendered citizenship, from which any queer theme emerges.[5]

Isolate Manhood vs. the Homosocial

The depths of Travis Bickle's mental illness are revealed by his intensifying isolation, penchant for firearms, attempted assassination of the presidential candidate Charles Palantine (Leonard Harris), and spectacular climactic display of murderous violence. Travis's brooding, disconnected, isolate manhood, his intense loneliness, is repeatedly contrasted against different styles of masculinity: the homosocial world of his fellow cabdrivers; the modishly nerdy, smug, quirky, bespectacled Palantine-campaign worker Tom (Albert Brooks), who attempts to protect Betsy (Cybill Shepherd) from Travis; Sport (Harvey Keitel), the cowboy-hat-wearing white pimp who controls the twelve-year-old prostitute Iris (Jodie Foster); and various other males shown to be quite distinct from Travis in style and outlook, particularly the African American men who elicit the racist Travis's most perplexing glares and, in one grisly instance, his vigilante wrath. By depicting Travis's social estrangement as a specifically gendered one, the film makes a powerful political point about the failures and constrictive demands of male socialization. In this regard, it has a great deal in common with De Palma's oeuvre from his early comedies forward and with Sam Peckinpah's disturbing masterpiece *Straw Dogs* (1971), which portrays its math-professor protagonist David (Dustin Hoffman), an American living in Cornwall with his sexually charged Cornish wife Amy (Susan George), as a weak-willed (though privately sadistic) man cut off from the homosocial realm.[6] The loutish Cornish lads who paint his house and leer at (and eventually rape) his wife treat David like an idiot because his masculine identity, unlike his intellect, appears so much less developed than their own. As in Hitchcock's *Frenzy*, the rape scene in *Straw Dogs*, horrific but also unsettlingly dreamlike and pornographically perverse, involving not one but two rapists and sodomy as well, serves as a microcosmic critique of the film's investigation of the relationship between gender anxiety and sexual violence. *Taxi Driver* also bears a striking resemblance to Herman Melville's famous short story "Bartleby, the Scrivener," another New York City story about the failure of male relations and a sexually inviolate, isolate male protagonist who remains fundamentally cut off from the social order that he famously prefers not to enter.

Like De Palma's early comedies, the film explores individual male relationships to the homosocial, or the same-sex group. Travis hovers around the edges of a male group of fellow cabdrivers. A would-be sage nicknamed Wizard (Peter Boyle) presides over this idiosyncratic cabdriver homosocial, which also consists of "Doughboy" (Harry Northup), so-named because he will "do anything for a buck," and the African American Charlie T. (Norman Matlock), who slyly and knowingly refers to Travis as "Killer." In the first scene in which Travis interacts with this group, we see him outside the storefront window, approaching the diner (the Belmore Cafeteria, no longer extant) from behind the seated men; when he sits, he does so at a table connected to those at which they sit but also separate from them. Travis is always shown making his way towards and then *joining* the group, never already integrated within it as the scene commences. The homosocial is a priori; it exists before Travis attempts, always with great awkwardness, to insert himself within it. Moreover, before he enters the diner, a young, debilitated man tries to reach out to Travis, probably for help—he could be one of George A. Romero's zombies. Travis quietly pushes him aside, in a subtle, easily missed, but significant moment that alerts us to the ways in which the homosocial kills off individual male identity to solder its collective own.

In a scene that follows the opening credits and the first, montage sequence of Travis driving through the Expressionist city, Travis talks to the dispatcher who gives him his cabdriver job. Wizard is first introduced in this scene: we see him in antic but unheard conversation with another cabdriver through the window behind the dispatcher. Given the strained, awkward discussion between Travis and the dispatcher ("You gonna bust my chops?" the dispatcher tells Travis after he makes a feeble joke), Wizard's relative ease of conversation and self-presence, even in unheard conversation, and the way his conversation with a fellow cabdriver is framed in the shot as a mirror reflection of Travis speaking with the dispatcher, conveys a sense of Wizard as Travis's ego ideal, a double who possesses secret, confident male knowledge, access to which Travis is barred. (Again, prolonged exposure to Wizard deeply ironizes this idealization.) In this regard as in so many, the film evokes Hitchcock and his signature use of the male *doppelgänger*.

The first cabdriver homosocial scene opens *in medias res* with the shambling but apparently well liked as well as self-promoting Wizard telling an improbable story to Doughboy and Charlie T. about having his sexual way with a lascivious woman customer as Travis makes his way into the diner. The first words heard as this scene opens are Wizard's as he reads off an itemized list of this woman's arsenal of sexual enhancements: "Eyeliner, rouge . . ." Woman is a construction, a spatialized collection of individual components and a force to be conquered. The upshot of Wizard's anecdote, as he tells it, is that he responds to his female customer's sexual provocations (her make-up, her putting on of her pantyhose as he watches, her "spray-on" perfume), with a resolute sexual dynamism that silences her into submission. "What did you do?" Doughboy eagerly asks, and Wizard explains that he "whips" out his organ, asking her, "Do you know what this is?" "It's love," she responds in his narrative, and afterwards tells him, as he recounts it, that this was the best sexual experience of her life. All of the men sit at the same small adjoining tables, while Travis sits at his own, tentatively. He does, however, shyly and rather sweetly smile as Wizard tells his story of his sexual conquest. But when Doughboy asks Travis, tellingly, "How's it hanging?" Travis looks blank, uncomprehending, as he often does when invited into their coarse, lively banter. At Doughboy's question, Travis looks around, then back at Dough-boy. "What's that?" he responds after a moment, visibly confused. When Travis first arrived, Wizard had remarked, with obvious though not entirely ungenial sarcasm, "Here's Travis, he's a ladies' man." Like Wizard's comment, Dough-boy's question casually mocks Travis precisely for *not* being a smooth, casual la-dies' man or laid-back enough to respond comfortably to questions like "How's it hanging?" The implicit suggestion of Travis's *own* sexual prowess within this colloquial question leaves him both discomfited and bewildered. In a remarkable transition, Travis contributes to the randy conversation with a grisly report of a cabdriver who was brutally assaulted, his ear cut off in the process.[7] Fascinating-ly, Travis's response to heterosexual conquest narratives and homosocial sexual competitiveness is a narrative of urban violence and victimization, articulating what will prove to be the film's central theme: the substitution of violence for sexuality. If, as Peter Krämer observes, sexualized violence defines the New Holly-wood, it is of importance that in so many films of the era, nowhere more sharply than in *Taxi Driver*, violence emerges as the substitute for sex.[8]

Unable to be fully integrated within the one realm that would naturally in-clude him, the male world of cabdrivers—who, after all, seek out other men for comfort, much like Travis and the men who go to porn theaters—Travis looks elsewhere. Through point-of-view shots, his eyes and ours drift over to some flashily dressed black men at an opposite table, whose appearance suggests that they are pimps, then down below to Travis's own glass of water, into which Travis drops antacid tablets (from a private vial). The Godardian close-up of the bub-bling water conveys the intensity of Travis's increasingly agitated mind, his pent-up rage, as well as his onanistic, dreamlike self-fixation. To Travis, the world at large is so much white noise, like the seething antacid water, his authentic and singular world only that of his own thoughts. When he was introduced to Charlie

T., he offered no greeting. The other black men he stares at, given his frequent racist comments, may enflame his anger, but they also seem hardly the only or the clearest trigger for or embodiment of it.

In the next scene between Travis and the cabdriver homosocial, now in a middle position within the more brightly lit diner, Travis once again only edgily integrates himself into the group. Once again, Travis enters the group only after it has already been established as one, always an intruder into this private male realm, never a constitutive component of it. This time, Wizard is telling a story about a "midget" who came into his cab with a tall, attractive woman. "I like to hold a midget," Doughboy smilingly and enigmatically responds. Next, Wizard tells a story about picking up two "fags" in rhinestone T-shirts who not only verbally berate ("Bitch!") but also physically pummel each other. (Violence informs inter-male relationships, whether straight or gay.) This is an "American free country," Wizard remarks. "God love you, do what you want." But he opposes their public fighting in his cab. Interestingly, the discussion takes the direction of "fag rights" in California: Doughboy explains that not only can fags can get married in California but also that if they divorce, one of the pair must pay the other alimony. "They're way ahead in California," one of the group remarks, humorously turning the entire discussion into one that trades in an initial homophobia ("fags") for a general awe at cultural differences between the coasts.

Charlie T. then asks if Travis has the five dollars he owes him, a surprising disclosure that some kind of exchange occurred at one point between these men, given the intense blank stares Travis shoots at Charlie T. As Travis takes out a big wad of cash to count the bills, Charlie T. remarks with an almost taunting merriness, "My man is loaded, loa-*ded*." Again, this remark's obvious sexual connotations seem like a goad of sorts to Travis's sexual prowess ("load" being, to state the obvious, a slang term for male ejaculate): if Travis is, indeed, loaded, it is with murderous violence, not sexual desire.

To take the associations further, Travis is also shown to have amassed quite a "wad" of cash, which, given his austere existence, he has little use for, save to attempt to give it to Iris so that she can flee to a commune in Vermont. Money is male "spend" in this film or, more properly, its substitute or the marker of its absence. Travis remarks earlier, "Every night I have to wipe off the come on the back seat," adding, "some nights I wipe off the blood." He could not be more alienated from his own sexuality. Linda Williams writes of the signature shot of the hard-core narrative film—the "money shot" in which a man orgasmically ejaculates before the camera. "In combining money and sexual pleasure—those simultaneously valuable and dirty things—the money shot most perfectly embodies the profound alienation of contemporary consumer society."[9] But Travis, despite his endless intimacy with the pornographic, appears never to feel sexual

153

pleasure or to experience sexual release at any point throughout the film. Money emerges as a signal of his banked sexuality. At the same time, the film proceeds very much from an awareness of the compulsory aspects of male sexual performance—that sexual potency defines normative manhood as such.

If ejaculate is the visible sign of male sexual potency, as reified by the money shot of the pornographic films Travis so obsessively watches, his menial relationship to its emission, wiping it off the seat of his cab, conveys a sense of his alienation from all the means of its production, somatic, social, and cultural. Moreover, that the waste fluids Travis must confront are, at times, ejaculate mixed with blood extends the metaphor to heterosexual relations generally, blood being most obviously associated with femininity and female sexuality. As he is to male sexuality, Travis is alienated from heterosexual relations. The images of heterosexuality in the film are thoroughly negative—the well-dressed man and the black hooker Travis picks up seem lurid and imbecilic, and another passenger (played by Scorsese) that Travis picks up wants to kill his wife in hideous ways not only for having an affair but for having it with "a nigger." Racism is inextricably enmeshed with heterosexual ambivalence.

Travis then asks Wizard if he can speak to him outside, and as the two walk out, Charlie T., in a separate shot, says to Travis, "Goodbye, *Killer*," pantomiming shooting a gun at Travis as he says it, again sounding as if he is knowingly taunting his deadly serious stooge. For Charlie T. is more than right: Travis *is* a killer, loaded with rage.

Outside, Travis talks to Wizard about feeling like "he wants to do something." This is one of the few moments in the film in which Travis actually seems like he is asking someone for help, and therefore one of the film's most moving scenes. Wizard is not unmoved, attempting to offer what help he can, but his affect mainly suggests befuddlement at Travis's intense but inarticulate, meandering statement-questions. Travis claims he really wants to do something, but it isn't clear what this something *is*, though it is most likely connected to the rage that he feels over Betsy's rejection of him. While Wizard commiserates to a certain extent with Travis's expressions of anomie and "bad" feelings, saying that it happens to all of us at times, his best advice is that Travis should simply go out and get laid, the cure-all solution for whatever ails American manhood. (There is a similar moment in the much later Scorsese 2004 movie *The Aviator* in which Leonardo DiCaprio's Howard Hughes instructs one of his aides, worried over Hughes's errant behavior, to "go home to your *wife*," DiCaprio's intonations similarly suggesting sexual intercourse as remedy.) Disorientingly and disturbingly, Scorsese shoots the scene in which Travis humanly attempts to connect to Wizard through a red filter, charging the whole scene with an apocalyptic menace, one embodied by the exchange of looks between Travis and a young black street tough who, with a younger male, taunts some prostitutes, one of many moments that presage later events in the film. The young black tough anticipates the young black male that Travis shoots in the bodega, and, in his harassment of the prostitutes, Sport and his exploitation of young Iris.

The last scene between Travis and the cabdriver homosocial, one of the last in the film, transforms the pattern of these scenes. Now, the scene begins with Travis *already* integrated into and talking with the group, and seeming much more laid-back, part of things, comfortable within the group identity. And now it is Charlie T. who walks towards and then joins the group, though with none of Travis's former awkwardness. ("Charlie T.," Wizard acknowledges him, with none of the derision with which Travis was usually greeted.) What accounts for the change in Travis's relationship to the homosocial is that he has finally achieved something like a normative male identity. But the grisly kicker is that he has only been able to do so through his acts of murderous violence, his rescue of the adolescent prostitute Iris, and the fifteen minutes of fame that ensue for Travis when he is proclaimed, in one of the film's sharpest ironies, as a hero. The violence and the rescue of Iris, together, symbolically signal Travis's gendered and sexual normalization: *gendered*, in that he demonstrates that he is no longer intimidated by other men; has become someone who "stood up," as he fiercely attested in one of his voice-overs; and has performed an act of male heroism, rescuing the paravirginal female innocent; *sexual*, in that his rescue of Iris functions conventionally as a marker of some kind of heterosexual intimacy, commitment, relationship, and provides a genuine "climax." Far from signaling some kind of satisfying multivalent closure (on narrative, character, and gendered terms), Travis's inclusion into the homosocial order by the end is a harrowing joke.

Male Psychosis and New Hollywood Aesthetics: *Vertigo* and *Taxi Driver*

"Given the central status of deception in relation to the symbolic order," Slavoj Žižek writes, "one has to draw a radical conclusion: the only way *not* to be deceived is to maintain a distance from the symbolic order, i.e., to assume a *psychotic* position. A psychotic is precisely a subject who is *not duped by the symbolic order*."[10] In one of his many memorable voice-overs, Travis exhorts his unseen audience thusly: "Listen, you fuckers, you screwheads. Here is a man who *would not take it anymore*. A man who stood up against the scum, the cunts, the dogs, the filth, the shit. Here is a man who *stood up*." In several respects, Travis is the Lacanian-Žižekian psychotic, the one who is not duped by the symbolic order. Yet, as a prototype of the serial killer who would come to haunt American popular culture so indelibly, Travis may also be said to be someone whose overdetermined identification with his surroundings leads him to "stand up" in the murderous ways that he does. In other words, far from being antagonistic towards the symbolic

155

order and able to see through it, he actually intensely identifies with it, adopting its dictates and its logic as his own. The Symbolic, as Lacan theorized, is the order of the Father's language and law, representative of the Father's desire to dominate. Travis fiercely identifies with the paternal superego and therefore feels acutest horror at those who violate proper paternal law: Palantine, a false father who symbolically pimps out and controls Betsy; Sport, a degenerate father who sexually and emotionally exploits his child prostitute Iris.

Moreover, Travis implicitly views the Father as the *White* Father, and his order as a strictly heterosexual and family-oriented one. Travis is driven by his racism, on the one hand, and his staunch opposition to sexual deviance, on the other hand. In his fierce commitment to restoring Iris to her family—the very people that she attempted to escape—Travis attempts to impose white patriarchal rule on the excremental city. Like Sodom, Gomorrah, and Babylon, New York City needs to be purged of its "filth." Far from not being duped by the symbolic order, Travis is its dutiful, filial embodiment, deploying the Father's wrath—"*true* force"—against the "sick, venal" degenerates who defy the Father's rule. *Taxi Driver* is a poem of force about a desire to deploy the Father's force.

Exemplary of the New Hollywood's agon, or conflict, with the classical Hollywood past, its intertexual engagement with Hitchcock was a furious rejection of this cinematic past as well as a fervent enshrinement of it. If *Taxi Driver* recalls *Vertigo* (1958) and other Hitchcock films at so many points, it does so to express its disengagement with the Hitchcock text as well as its Travis-like overidentification with it. While Brian De Palma has for so long been derided for this trait, such an overidentification is a commonplace of the 1970s cinema, which has been rightly described by Noël Carroll as a cinema of allusions.[11] De Palma's problem, as it were, is simply that he makes this overidentification especially apparent and itself a site of cinematic consideration. If Hitchcock looms as a false father in *Taxi Driver*, *Vertigo* looms as a text that must be reenacted and then destroyed, like Scottie wishes to do with Madeleine Elster's dream. *Vertigo* figures its villain Gavin Elster as a false father whose ingenious narrative ensnares and enslaves another man, the protagonist Scottie Ferguson, who then obsessively overidentifies with this narrative. If *Vertigo* is about a man duped by the false father, *Taxi Driver* is about a man who stands up *to* the false father and his corrupt narrative, rewriting it for his own ends. The quest to embody true force is the quest to embody the true father and gain access to authentic narrative.

THE "WHOLE MOVIE," Pauline Kael wrote of *Taxi Driver*, "has a sense of vertigo."[12] Kael perceptively saw the theme of "no sex" as central to *Taxi Driver*. As she added, though, "no sex can be as disturbing as sex. And that's what it's about: the absence of sex—bottled-up, impacted energy and emotion, with a blood-splattering release."[13] Even though she was, along with Robin Wood, the most acute inter-preter of the New Hollywood, Kael did not recognize Hitchcock's importance as a filmmaker nor the importance of his influence on the young directors of the New Hollywood beyond the fact that they made expedient uses of him. I believe that it is necessary to enlarge Kael's perceptive reading of Scorsese's film with an analysis of the centrality of its agon with Hitchcock, crucial to its themes and to its achievement.

Vertigo is such a familiar film touchstone at this point that its plot scarcely needs description, but we should recall a few of its major themes. John "Scottie" Ferguson (James Stewart) is a retired San Francisco detective who quit the force because of his fear of heights, his titular vertigo. An old college friend, Gavin Elster (Tom Helmore), enlists Scottie to follow his wife, Madeleine (Kim Novak), whom Elster claims to believe is possessed by the spirit of Carlotta Valdes, a nine-teenth-century female ancestor who went mad after she was brutally discarded by her wealthy and powerful married lover, who keeps their child as his own. ("A man could do that in those days," Pop Leibel, the old, urbane Argosy Book-shop owner sadly notes as he recounts the story. "They had the freedom, and the power.") Carlotta eventually took her own life. As it turns out, Elster has created an entire narrative in which to entrap Scottie. Elster devises a plot to kill his wife that will use Scottie's vertigo as an alibi; moreover, the woman Scottie believes that he is following is not Elster's wife at all but a different woman, Judy Barton (also played by Kim Novak), trained by Elster to masquerade as his real wife. This film about the pursuit of an unknown and unknowable woman begins with the pursuit of an unknown, unknowable criminal *man*, chased by the hero, along with a cop, across nighttime San Francisco rooftops. The criminal male and the criminal female—"Madeleine" Elster is really Judy Barton, complicit in the real Mrs. Elster's death—alternately serve as the object Scottie pursues. The artificial Woman, Elster's replica of his wife, stands in for, replaces, the pursued man; an unacknowledged homoerotic desire—pursuit of a man—is replaced by a pursuit of a woman who cannot, on several levels, be acknowledged.

Drenched in a Bernard Herrmann score that is alternately jazzy and melan-cholic and that recalls, repeatedly, his famous work for Hitchcock, *Taxi Driver* is awash in Hitchcockian tropes, themes, cinematic motifs. Like *Vertigo*'s Scottie fol-lowing Madeleine in his car, Travis prowls through the city, relentlessly in pursuit of some imaginary ideal. First he believes this ideal to be Betsy (Cybill Shepherd), who is introduced in idealizing slow motion; with her blonde hair and glassy de-meanor, Shepherd recalls, to a certain extent, the Madeleine Elster of Kim Novak. (Unlike Novak's Madeleine, however, Betsy has a prankster sense of humor, e.g., the scene where she spills water all over her co-worker Tom, giggling as she says, "Nothing," and turns the cup upside down to reveal that it only contained water.

157

Next, she tries to get him, in a decidedly odd moment, to light a match as if some of his fingers had been blown off. All of her behavior in this scene hints at reserves of aggression carefully hidden beneath pastel prettiness.)

In the most lyrical moment of the film, Travis tells us about Betsy for the first time and we are introduced to her character. In hand-held, *cinema verité* shots, we pass through the streets to Palantine's office, which Betsy enters, the film speed switching to slow motion. The De Palmian slow motion italicizes the idealizing, irreal nature of Travis's fixation on her. That Martin Scorsese makes a cameo appearance as a man she passes by, sitting outside the Palantine headquarters, is important. For one thing, Scorsese will play the hideously vengeful man who claims that he will shoot his wife in the face and the vagina with a .44 Magnum. The introduction of Betsy, a dreamlike reverie of an ideal, remote, blonde woman, nods to *Vertigo* as the directorial cameo nods to Hitchcock and his penchant for such.

The lyrical, *cinema verité* style of the sequence is telling in several other ways. As we make our way through the cityscape, we see people of different races walking through the sunshiny streets, Bernard Herrmann's score striking tender harp notes. Then we see Betsy walking into Palantine's office in slow motion, as Travis fixatedly and deliberately writes/speaks: "They . . . cannot . . . *touch* . . . her." If this brief passage is the one really lovely moment in the film, bearing no trace of Travis's hatred towards blacks, shown in the street scenes without animosity, it suggests that what Travis needs is love. His idealizing love of Betsy (never more, of course, than idealization, since he doesn't know her at all) allows him to drift through the streets in his mind with a sense of joy and wonder, embracing the diverse city citizenry, a passage that offers a brief respite from an increasingly horrific vision of the world.

When, much later, Travis in his cab at night almost runs into the teen prostitute Iris (Jodie Foster) and her teen prostitute friend (played by a real-life teen prostitute who was consulted by the filmmakers), the moment jars, not only because of its inherent shock but because Iris now appears to occupy the place of Travis's forever-pursued ideal, a place which can be occupied by no one. (Clearly Iris cannot substitute for the Madeleine-manqué, Betsy, but then again Betsy can never substitute for Madeleine, either.) Through Betsy and Iris, *Taxi Driver* reimagines the split between Madeleine Elster and the tough, coarse, vulnerable Judy Barton, and in so doing reimagines *Vertigo*'s double narrative as well.

Scorsese substitutes Hitchcock's endlessly vertiginous geography—exquisitely provided by San Francisco's incessant hills, which Scottie ascends and descends, repeatedly, in his car—with vertiginous cinematography and editing. The cinematographer Michael Chapman provides surrealistic color schemes: the juxtaposition between the dingy yellow of Travis's Checker cab and the bright, swirling, kaleidoscopic, hallucinatory colors of the endlessly alive city; the ominous treatment of commonplace moments like a child manipulating the water gushing out of a fire hydrant, shot through an intensely dark lens; the desaturated hues of the climactic sequences in which Travis kills Sport and his ilk, a kind of cinematographic exsanguination, draining the image of blood, in ironic contrast to the excessive bloodletting of the climax. (While the color was desaturated in order for the film to avoid an X rating for its graphic violence, it is important to note that the color manipulation has aesthetic purposes as well, adding to the climax's oneiric affect.) The editing by Tom Rolf and Melvin Shapiro disorientingly keeps the mood dreamlike and sustains a momentum of movement and shifting change even within stasis. As Travis's cab barrels through the streets, the camera moves alongside the cab as streetlights above us blur past, one after the other. Trapped in nullity, we yet seem to be headed toward an indefinable *somewhere*. As Travis takes different poses in his narcissistic encounters with his own image in his apartment, the inherently limited apartment space paradoxically becomes a warren of images, an effect enhanced by the use of dissolves and the restless cutting, all of which evoke the simultaneous emptiness and capaciousness of Travis's self-world-making mind, the ways in which he substitutes endless mirror images in conflict with one another—exemplified by the now-legendary "Are you talkin' to me? Well, I'm the only one here" routines in which Travis talks to himself in the mirror—for social contact. Throughout, *Taxi Driver* maintains a constant sense of movement, sensation, and stasis all at once. In its simultaneous progression and regression, the film is one long elaboration of the famous *Vertigo* effect.[14]

What is perhaps most politically radical about Scorsese's evocation of *Vertigo* occurs right at the beginning of the film, and thereby charges the film with its peculiar significance. At one point during the stylized, montage credit sequence, we see Travis driving through the city. In *Vertigo*'s famous credit sequence, designed by the legendary Saul Bass, a woman's face is used as a canvas: we focus on the spatialized components of her visage (her eyes, her mouth, her single eye); these parts of her face become a series of geographical vistas. At one significant moment, the color red suffuses the entire screen. In shots that directly cite the first moments of *Vertigo*'s credit sequence, we see, through a red filter, Travis's eyes moving right and left, taking in the whirling sights of the neon-lit nighttime city. The image of Travis with his eyes moving right and left recalls the image of the woman in *Vertigo*'s credit sequence, whose eyes anxiously dart back and forth at both the start and at the end of the credits. In their palpable distress and apprehension, the woman's eyes embody as they anticipate *Vertigo*'s mood, particularly its thematic of woman's suffering at the hands of obsessively controlling and duplicitous men. The first shot of Travis's moving eyes evokes the voyeuristic frenzy of the film, most explicitly denoted by the all-caps venue sign "FASCINATION," a club that Travis passes by during his nocturnal cabdriving. But in the next shot of those darting, roving eyes, they appear anxious, wary, apprehensive. By having Travis's eyes embody and anticipate *Taxi Driver*'s moods of apprehension in a manner similar to the woman's eyes in *Vertigo*'s opening credits, Scorsese implicitly places Travis/De Niro in the feminine position, helpless in the hands of men and their narrative power.

Deepening the Hitchcockian resonances, the red filter also recalls Hitchcock's extraordinary 1964 film *Marnie*, in some ways his most Expressionistic work, in which the color red suffuses the screen whenever the titular heroine sees this hue and experiences waves of hysteria as a result. In her superb essay on the film, Michele Piso argues that *Marnie* is a deeply despairing film about class differences and their destructive effects: "the world of capital dominates and chills the erotic and creative aspects of life."[15] Piso pays particular attention to the abandoned mother of this film and the significance of Hitchcock's Expressionistic trope of the color red that suffuses the screen when Marnie panics at the sight of the color: this is the "blood of the terrified and violated body, the blood of women, of murder and rape . . . the red of suffering."[16] Though not often discussed in readings of the film, *Taxi Driver* is very much about class as well as gendered abnegation. Travis can in no way fit in with the comparatively normative world that Betsy, Tom, and Palantine inhabit. But at the same time, he can no more successfully enter the underworld of the macho-louche pimp Sport. Travis Bickle has something else in common with Hitchcock's Marnie—a genuine bewilderment if not outright revulsion at the spectacle of heterosexual sex.

Travis's desire for true force is, among other things, a desire for power in a world in which he is, like women, subjugated. This is an example, one of many, of the way that the Hitchcock text could be manipulated for newly radical effects in the New Hollywood cinema. Hitchcock's incipient feminism becomes the template for Scorsese's exploration of the valences between the female subject position and that of isolate, non-normative masculinity. To be sure, this exploration will not be consistently conducted in Scorsese's later cinema—though it does inform his best subsequent films, *The King of Comedy* (1983), *The Last Temptation of Christ* (1988), and *The Age of Innocence* (1993)—and in no way blunts the force of Travis's misogyny and increasingly murderous hatred.[17] Travis's own subaltern gendered position, however, provides us with a basis for reading the film's events and thematic preoccupations as elements of its larger cultural critique. Far from isolate, a special case, Travis embodies the ills of a self-destroying culture at war with itself. The hollowness of romantic ideals—embodied here in the decaying flowers festering in Travis's apartment, sent to and returned to him by Betsy, images of which recall the flower shop of *Vertigo* where Scottie spies on Madeleine and the stench of which leads Travis to speculate matter-of-factly that he now has "stomach cancer"—metaphorizes the barrenness of culture. The later shot of Travis burning the flowers in the sink before he goes to self-declared war with his culture is the ultimate cinematic expression of sexual ambivalence and class rage at once.

Perhaps most poignantly of all, what *Taxi Driver* extends is *Vertigo*'s inextricably linked themes of loneliness and wandering. When Scottie's friend Midge (Barbara Bel Geddes) asks him what he's been doing in the many days in which she hasn't seen him, he responds, wistfully as well as evasively, "Wandering." Scottie and Madeleine have a telling discussion about wandering, a penchant for which they both share. "But only one is a wanderer," Madeleine, both vulnerable and coolly flirtatious, remarks. "Two together are always going somewhere." Scottie responds, "No, I don't think that's necessarily true." This film about the duplicity of appearances and obsessive desire has at its core a theme of endless seeking, endless desiring, endless wandering. Travis is a wanderer as well, through an unloving city that provides all too willingly the labyrinth to match his mazelike mind. The wandering in both films enhances their vertiginous designs.

Rear Window: The Second Scorsese Cameo

After being rejected by Betsy after he takes her to a pornographic film, a scene which I discuss below, Travis picks up a male customer, played by Martin Scorsese, who, after Travis turns off the meter once he brings the customer to his destination, insists that Travis turn the meter back on, and just allow the cab to idle. The customer commands Travis to look up at a window in an adjacent building. "What, are you blind?" the gruffly impatient customer says as we, along with Travis, fumble towards recognition of the correct window. In this nighttime scene, the light within this window, actually two windows bifurcated by a pane, eerily glows. Through curtains, a silhouette of a tall, cigarette-smoking woman appears. This image cites film noir conventions of the cigarette-smoking *femme fatale* and chiaroscuro lighting, noir being the genre that, along with Hitchcock, most powerfully informs this film.

The customer informs Travis that the woman above is his wife. But she is in another man's apartment. "You know who lives there? A nigger lives there," he tells Travis. He proceeds to outline his intentions, which are to shoot his wife in the face with a .44 Magnum, and then to shoot her in the vagina with it as well: "Now *that* you should see," he says, boasting. Interestingly, the cuckold makes no mention of what he will do to his wife's lover. Cynthia Fuchs argues that the film suggests that this customer's extreme rhetoric "coincides with Travis's extreme agitation."[18] I can see why Fuchs reads the scene this way, but I believe that careful scrutiny reveals that, far from sharing in the customer's rage, Travis is horrified—and overpowered—by it. In this coldly terrifying scene, one of the most striking effects is Travis's enforced servitude to another man's gaze. His eyes must do as they are commanded—he *must* look up at the window. Reinforcing his submission, he *must* hear the customer's vile words. Travis is one of the discontents of this man's desire.

The specific film most prominently referenced in the scene is Hitchcock's 1954 film *Rear Window*, not only its themes of voyeuristic looking—L. B. Jeffries, "Jeff," the photographer protagonist with his leg in a cast, played by James Stewart, obsessively spies on the neighbors of his apartment complex, famously using a telephoto lens at one point—but also its central thematic of a murderously unhappy marriage that leads, literally, to murder, Thorwald's (Raymond Burr) murder of his wife, an unhappy, accusing invalid who anticipates *Psycho*'s Mrs. Bates. Jeff identifies the Thorwalds' apartment as "the rear" when he calls the police to rescue his fashion-model girlfriend Lisa (Grace Kelly), who has ventured into the apartment as an attempt to aid Jeff in solving the mystery of Thorwald's wife's disappearance (and to get closer to the diffident Jeff). Lee Edelman has written about the sodomy metaphors of this "rear" window, and Robert Samuels has written about the "bi-textual" visual schemes of the film, and Hitchcock's films generally, that disrupt its heterosexual main plot. What is most interesting about these homoerotic valences is that an unhappily married heterosexual couple can become a kind of queer metaphor for the ostensibly heterosexual protagonist's own sexual anxieties and potential homoerotic desires.

162

The customer Scorsese plays in *Taxi Driver* dominates Travis from the rear; he forces Travis to follow all of his orders, and Travis does so, though not without conveying a sense of real ambivalence. This ambivalence may contain fascination, to be sure, but may also be motivated by disgust at what he hears. Repeatedly, Travis adjusts the rearview mirror to take in what the customer is saying, to see the customer's face properly. Yet what *we* see in the mirror is not the customer's face but Travis's face; and the expression on his face is increasingly one of alarm. In some shots, Travis's reflected, rearview mirror face appears to be staring at Travis's own face: a self-confrontation that obliterates the presence of the customer. Travis is forever the narcissistic voyeur who seeks out only his own image.

This exchange/non-exchange of looks between the men is framed by the overarching visual spectacle of the wife, who takes on a mythic quality by being spectacularly and abstractly visualized above the men, not just a shadow of herself but also a kind of Shadow-Goddess. Nevertheless, the last shot of her silhouette, coming, as it does, after the customer's descriptions of the barbarous violence he intends to enact on her, is poignant. It is almost as if she were silently imploring Travis to help her, though, of course, how could she be? With its depiction of female sexuality and illicit heterosexual sex as a spectacle in which disconnected men together partake, this entire episode functions as a metaphor for Travis's frequent pornographic viewing and for pornography itself.

Pornography plays a much larger role in this film than simply being a fixture of Travis's personal tastes: the cab dispatcher at the start, after Travis tells him about his long nights spent wide awake, instructs him, "They got porno theaters for that." The film diagnoses as a malady the increasingly inescapable cultural associations being made between male desire and pornography, inescapable because of pornography's rise to prominent visibility in the 1970s, with films like *Deep Throat* becoming mainstream hits. Travis's metaphorical pornographic viewing, a voyeurism he must now partake in at *another* man's behest, here corresponds exquisitely to his self-fixated confrontation with his own mirror image, as Scorsese represents his experience of the conversation. As Berkeley Kaite theorizes it, pornography reveals the similarities between narcissism and voyeurism:

> There is a commingling of narcissist and voyeur. . . . With the hard-core pornographic moment, voyeurism and narcissism overlap, the scopic drive being essentially autoerotic: its object is the subject's own body, a guarantor of imaginary self-coherence. Identifications are shifting and mobile, involving narcissistic fantasies and, initially in the development of the subject, a search for autoerotic satisfaction.[19]

163

While the voyeur seems compelled by an aching need to see the other and possess the other by seeing, what the voyeur chiefly longs for is *a sight of the self*. Pornography endows the spectator with the illusion of autoerotic plenitude, yet it proceeds from the logic of prohibition: homoerotic desire is banned, and femininity must conform to the demands of the masculine gaze.

As Laura Kipnis argues in *Bound and Gagged*, pornography that is made for male consumption enables a fantasy that women desire sex in the same impersonal way that men do. Moreover, the scene of pornographic viewing—at least in terms of the pornographic movie theater and its collective male audience of the pre-video, DVD, and Internet eras—allows us to understand the complexities of sexuality in terms of the desires of its presumably heterosexual male viewership. As Kipnis argues, the only people likely to pursue sexual encounters with the abject men who watch porn in porn theaters are the other abject men in the same theater. In much the same way that De Palma depicts an inescapable homosexual undercurrent in male pornographic viewing in *Hi, Mom!*, Scorsese suggests that the sadomasochistic qualities within the scene between Travis and this depraved, cuckolded man lend the scene between them a homoerotic aspect. In a way, the cuckolded customer performs a grisly pornographic film *for* the involuntarily committed viewer Travis: the husband forces Travis to stare at his wife; to *hear* especially graphic details of the hideous violence that will be substituted for sex. He puts Travis in the position of the child in the primal scene, forced to witness and to hear the spectacle of parental sex. The customer's specific descriptions of *where* he will shoot his wife, in the face and in the vagina, evoke fellatio and the penetration of vagina by penis, sexual acts transmuted into murderous violence. In seeing his own wary face instead of the customer's, Travis remains locked within the narcissistic circuit of his own desires. Narcissistic self-fixation, while potentially homoerotic, functions here as homoerotic ban; were Travis able to see the customer's face, the sight of this man's face in the mirror might potentially explode, through explication, the homoerotic complicity between them. When he picks up Betsy at the end, for example, he does at one point see *her* face in the rearview mirror. The film evokes, however, the Hitchcockian homoerotics of doubling, especially Hitchcock's efforts to collapse homo/hetero gendered and sexual polarities.

Seeing himself in the mirror reinforces the idea that, instead of seeing an object of desire, Travis sees himself only. But does Travis actually experience autoerotic fascination within the narcissistic self-desire he inhabits? Given the ways in which he appears bewildered by the sexual in any capacity, it makes sense to consider if Travis can even experience sexual desire within or for himself. Travis is the Male Medusa, a male staring at his own sexuality and gendered identity with horror, as his reflection stares back at him with a similar reaction. The Male Medusa theme reaches greatest intensity near the end of the film, in the shot of Travis looking at himself in the rearview mirror as Betsy gets out of his cab. Though there are shots of Betsy captured in the rearview mirror during this final encounter between them, now Travis is neither seen by her nor sees her. He sees only himself in the rearview mirror. The image of himself in the mirror strikingly recalls Caravaggio's self-portrait as the Medusa (circa 1597).

AS DISCUSSED IN CHAPTER 3, one of the key moments in Hitchcock's *Psycho* vividly evokes the scene of pornographic viewing: in his darkened office alone after Marion Crane (Janet Leigh) leaves it, Norman Bates (Anthony Perkins) takes down a painting of the biblical story of "Susanna and the Elders" and stares through a peephole into Cabin 1. He voyeuristically observes Marion as she undresses down to her black undergarments, a marker of sin that will be shed when Marion attempts to take a purifying, healing shower. This representation of Norman's voyeurism evokes the solitary male viewer of early peep shows and anticipates the later porn-arcade viewer who pops quarters into the machine to get the porn film running.[20]

While it is entirely possible that Norman is, as the psychiatrist puts it in his infamous denouement speech, "touched by her, aroused by her," entirely possible that Norman "wants" Marion sexually, it is also entirely possible that he does not, that he feels no desire for her, indeed, feels nothing at all. It is this potential "nothing" within the heart of *Psycho's* pornographic gaze that, I believe, Scorsese takes to its breaking point in *Taxi Driver*, in which Travis stares and stares, at pornography, at the city, and at its pageant of people. He transforms the city and its citizenry alike *into* pornography, collapsing all he sees into this mode of viewing. But he does so without pronounced erotic stimulation or even an attempt at sadistic mastery. Despite his all-the-animals-come-out-at-night retributive scorn, his look primarily projects a blank nothingness.

Laura Mulvey famously argued in her seminal 1975 *Screen* essay, "Visual Pleasure and Narrative Cinema," that Hollywood movies are organized around the patriarchal heterosexual male gaze, which objectifies women by transforming them into the object of this gaze.[21] In a sexually imbalanced world, writes Mulvey, "pleasure in looking has been split between active/male and passive/female." The male protagonist/spectator's scopophilic pleasure (a ravenous desire to look) arises from "using another person as an object of sexual stimulation through sight"; the woman is "coded for strong visual and erotic impact" so that she may "connote *to-be-looked-at-ness*."[22] The spectator, also gendered male and heterosexual, joins in a shared state of narcissistic omnipotence with the onscreen protagonist. Mulvey argued, as we have noted, that the male spectator-protagonist has two strategies for dealing with the castration anxieties provoked by the spectacularized woman: voyeuristically investigating or fetishizing the woman. In the wake of the vast influence of Mulvey's theory, many critics, Gaylyn Studlar, in her study *In the Realm of Pleasure*, in particular, have found masochism a useful counterargument.[23] While the masochistic gaze would be one way to theorize Travis's ambivalent and conflicted looking, I believe that in *Taxi Driver* the problems with vision and the gaze run far deeper.[24]

Like the pornographic gaze of the film, Travis's looking is a staring into nothingness, a looking that reveals the limitations of the gaze itself, the paradoxical ways in which, in Lacanian terms, the gaze revolves around our *inability* to see, the void at the heart of the senses.[25] But whereas in Lacan this is an ontological state of affairs that reflects a schism between human mind and human sense, in *Taxi Driver* this schism is grounded in the process and the effects of male socialization, especially in terms of sexuality as it is tied to gendered visual mastery. It is tied as well to an aggrieved view of the social decay of modern urban life. Being raised as male and being forced to embody conventional standards of masculinity entails certain traumatic experiences for Travis that are reflective of his particular cultural and social moment, and some of which are also consistent with the kinds of constrictive pressures that have historically been placed on American masculinity: enduring the effects of having been a soldier of war with no support whatsoever upon his return; being forced to be a social agent in a city as famous for its isolation and loneliness as for its diverse populace and cultural fascinations; having to make sense of contemporary, evolving sexual mores and gender roles. He must accomplish all of this even as sex, in the form of pornography, is being rendered a modernist, urban spectacle before which Travis can remain a passive, non-active spectator, not even masturbating before the pornographic spectacles he unceasingly watches. These personal, cultural, and social contexts together lend meaning to the blankness, the nothingness, of the film's pornographic gaze. The blankness—the essential inscrutability—of the pornographic gaze of *Psycho* evolves into the death-gaze that will in turn dominate Scorsese's film. The apocalyptic image of death culture in the spellbinding shot in the coda of Norman's face, on which Mother's skull-face is superimposed, dissolving into the shot of Marion's car being pulled out of the chthonic swamp, transforms in *Taxi Driver* into a movie-length shot of a man, whether in his car or in a porn theater, two modern coffins, staring at his world with the eyes of death.

My focus here, as it is throughout this book, is not on the merits or ills of pornography but on the unremittingly negative view taken of pornography by Hitchcock and the New Hollywood. For Hitchcock, pornography is clearly the result of voyeuristic attempts at sadistic visual mastery. Jeff in *Rear Window* avails himself of all of the goings-on in his apartment complex as if everyone from athletic Miss Torso to abject Miss Lonelyhearts—the Adam of a postlapsarian urban world, he names these creatures himself—and all of the messy complexities of their lives were simply being put on display for his delectation. That he uncovers and solves a murder mystery is actually quite incidental to the larger ethical question of his own smug, contemptuous disregard for his fellow human beings, as conveyed by his strangely self-satisfied grin at the spectacle of Miss Lonelyhearts, alone in her apartment, pantomiming a romantic evening with an imaginary gentleman caller before collapsing into sobs as she recognizes her loneliness and the hollowness of her fantasy performance. Ravenously regarding his neighbors and their lives as action to be contemplated at will, Jeff turns them into the fodder of pornographic fantasy, popping them into his eyes the way we pop a porn video or DVD into the machine, or log in to a porn website, except that, at least in diegetic terms, Jeff uses real people as his pleasure. Exposing Thorwald gives Jeff an easy, though literally quite painful (his other leg is broken in the process), "out" for his scopophilic indulgences.

In many ways, the story that Gavin Elster devises to ensnare Scottie in *Vertigo*, and Scottie's voyeuristic surveillance of Madeleine, also anticipates pornographic viewing. The heartbreaking story of Madeleine's ancestor Carlotta Valdes—a mixture of authentic and fake elements, as Judy Barton later informs us—evokes sadomasochistic pornography through its narrative of the humiliation and enslavement of a woman. "Men could do that in those days," the Argosy Bookshop owner and amateur historian Pop Leibel (Konstantin Shayne) sadly observes as he tells the story of a rich married man of the nineteenth century and his sexual exploitation, abuse, and discarding of his mistress, the beautiful Carlotta. After he takes their illegitimate child for himself, the rich man cruelly discards her, turning her into the "sad" and then the "mad" Carlotta, who haggardly wanders the streets and stops passersby to ask, "Where is my child? Have you seen my child?" What is pornographic about this narrative is specifically that it is a story of a woman's humiliation devised by one man both to torment *and* to incite pleasure in another man. More oddly still, the Carlotta Valdes backstory actually anticipates what Gavin will do to *Scottie*—put him in the feminine position of being seduced and abandoned, made sad, then mad.

Horrified, but also engrossed, riveted, and seduced by Elster's story, Scottie takes on the assignment of following Elster's wife, falling into the evil Elster's duplicitous designs. Elster presents his "wife" Madeleine to Scottie at the fashionable restaurant Ernie's, further evoking the pornographic display of woman as sexual spectacle. Scottie's gaze at Madeleine, a contorted look backwards that allows him impossible visual access to Madeleine, is an instance, characteristic of Hitchcock's films with Stewart, of what I call rear viewing, a kind of backward-looking, aversive looking that deconstructs male visual mastery and as such has queer implications.[26] As I will develop, Travis Bickle's frequent bouts with his own rearview image extend Hitchcock's queer trope of rear viewing in complex and highly significant ways that relate to the deconstructive readings of Travis's gendered and sexual identity both.

With mordant humor, Hitchcock wordlessly and implicitly acknowledges in *Vertigo* that Scottie has taken the assignment by quietly cutting to the scene, presumably the next morning, of Scottie in his car, waiting to follow Madeleine. Scottie follows Madeleine around as she drives in her car, both winding up and down the vertiginous streets of San Francisco. What is especially interesting to our present concerns is the way in which Hitchcock represents Scottie and Madeleine in these haunting, languorous car-on-car sequences. Madeleine, as we will learn, does not exist at all, being the product of Elster's fantasy, and also of Scottie's; she is Stanley Cavell's model of the unknown woman par excellence. Scottie is, in narrative terms, the "real" person, grounded in his investigative techniques and affiliation with the law and with the social order. Yet, as the scenes of Scottie in vehicular pursuit of this unknown and unknowable woman are filmed, Madeleine driving in her car appears in shots of actual location footage (though we almost never see Kim Novak as Madeleine in her car, only the figure of a woman driving), shots of someone *actually* driving through San Francisco. Scottie, when shown in medium shots driving behind her that allow us to see, through James Stewart's immensely fluid and vivid ability to convey a range of feelings, his varying reactions to her destinations, is always filmed through rear projection, a process, often callously mocked today for its artificiality, in which an actor is filmed in a studio against a backdrop of previously shot footage in motion behind the actor. Madeleine, at least through our post-studio-era view, comes to seem much more of a real cinema subject than Scottie, shot in the artifice-heavy, unrealistic, and, in Hitchcock's use of it, quite poetic device of rear projection. If the males of Hitchcock and the New Hollywood engage in "rear viewing" and "rear projection," a multivalent phrase for our purposes that conveys, along with the tropes of cinematic technique, both anal fixation and a disavowal of one's own desires, putting them *behind you*, Scottie may be said to serve as Madeleine's rear projection, the embodiment or the reflecting screen for whatever may be her own elusive and enigmatic desires. More pointedly, the voyeuristic viewer of the spectacle of woman—here a voyeur only to himself, since his object knows she is being watched, and since another man has created the entire voyeuristic scenario *for* Scottie—who believes that he can simply indulge in languorously prolonged, masturbatory viewing, is himself the true object of the gaze, the true sexual spectacle, rendered as illusory, as artificial, as the mysterious non-woman he pursues and observes.

In a fine reading of *Taxi Driver* as a modernist rather than a postmodern work, Martin Weinreich observes that the film is "cyclical. The protagonist ends up where he started, in a taxi making its way through the city, and any belief in personal development of Travis is illusory. In the rear view mirror all his enemies and problems still lurk. . . . [We are left with] a feeling of Travis walking and walking without ever getting anywhere."[27] Though he doesn't evoke Hitchcock's *Vertigo* in his reading, Weinreich could just as easily be describing Hitchcock's film. Wandering and movement in both works amount to cyclical stasis. Like Scottie once again looking down at someone whose death he has inadvertently caused at the end of *Vertigo*, Travis, in another film of ceaseless wandering and social and individual disconnection, moves towards non-movement, once again alone in his car, wary of his adversaries, none more threatening than himself.

The Scene of Pornography: Travis Takes Betsy to the Movies

If *Taxi Driver* makes clear that the male homosocial group defines itself by defining itself against homosexuality, the film also registers a profound ambivalence towards normative sexuality, which is to say, institutionalized and compulsory heterosexuality. While Travis idealizes and rhapsodizes over Betsy, his choice of film when he takes her out on a date—*Swedish Marriage Manual*, the second half of a pornographic double feature headlined by *Sometime Sweet Susan*—reveals his ignorance about several aspects of heterosexual romance: dating etiquette, choice of entertainment, and, principally, what constitutes heterosexual sex. For Travis, despite his Midwestern courteousness (asking Betsy out initially for "coffee and pie"), heterosexuality is indistinguishable from pornography. The film articulates more clearly than any other the cultural equivalence of male sexuality and pornography from the 1970s forward. Travis only understands heterosexual romance through pornography, the lens through which he appears to view everything that occurs between adult men and women. Women are either the inspirations for dreamlike reveries or the body around which orgiastic sex revolves, as revealed by the clip from *Swedish Marriage Manual*. Travis, for his part, seems as bewildered by as he is dependent upon the pornographic. In the shots of him sitting alone in the porn theater at two different points in the film, his expression conveys befuddlement or a kind of blank worry, not sexual excitation or any other form of pleasure. And in the latter scene of him as a spectator in the porn theater, he pantomimes shooting a gun at the screen, just as Charlie T. did in the diner when he pantomimed shooting at Travis, and just as Travis will literally do to Sport and his affiliates at the climax. The pornographic screen becomes a screen for institutionalized, compulsory heterosexuality in its overarching cultural, social, and mythic contexts: both a surface on which images of man-woman sexual relations play, a surface upon which Travis projects whatever may be his own fantasies, and a way to screen *out*—efface—any aspect of the real that obtrudes into his fantasy images. Taking *Psycho*'s prognostications to a diagnostic level, *Taxi Driver* foregrounds what I have termed *pornographication*: the compulsory submission to pornographic sexuality that defines our cultural moment.

169

Amy Taubin diagnoses Travis's decision to take Betsy to a pornographic film as his unconscious self-sabotaging, revealing not only his own self-hatred but his general anger towards women.[28] Taubin, a critic I greatly admire, provides many fine insights into the film. Overall, she views the film as a conservative work that exhibits racist, sexist, and also opportunistic attitudes (the latter stemming from Schrader's uses of a real-life case in his depiction of Travis). Given that I run occasionally hot but mainly cold on Scorsese's films, finding just about all of his films after *The Age of Innocence* as empty and self-serving as they are flashy, and am skeptical of Schrader's work before he came into his own as an auteur in the 1990s, I have a lot of sympathy for Taubin's view. I do believe, however, that the unlikely duo of Scorsese and Schrader make a provocative team here and in *The Last Temptation of Christ*. Fusing Scorsese's baroque Catholic sensibility to Schrader's depraved-Calvinist austerity, *Taxi Driver* remains the greatest film of the New Hollywood precisely because of its series of refusals, chief amongst them a refusal of male heterosexual mastery. Travis's fumbling, feeble attempts at dating Betsy—and while it is clear that he wants to date her, there is no sure, clear sense of what he wants from her *beyond* dating her—reveal a masculinity left unmoored by and within the larger culture. Far from exerting his sexual will on her, he invites her to share in his own bewilderment before the sexual. Embodied in a vast, looming screen on which bodies writhe in a manner disassociated from any emotional or romantic register, all sexuality in this film proceeds from a pornographic basis. Far from experiencing pornography as the domain of male sexual privilege in which women's bodies, to say nothing of desires, are subservient to male will, Travis inhabits pornographic spaces—the screen, the theater, the concession stand at which an unyieldingly unresponsive female employee refuses to give him the time of day, shouting for the manager when Travis persists in chatting with her—much as he inhabits the rest of his world, with befuddlement and repeated failures of connection.

Taubin skeptically regards *Taxi Driver* as "the star vehicle," built around Robert De Niro. One of Taubin's criticisms is that the film doesn't invest its other characters, especially the women characters and also the blacks so denigrated in Travis's voice-overs, with enough agency, with independent life.[29] In that De Niro gives his most acutely observed, touching, and frightening performance in this film, calling the film a star vehicle need not disqualify it from greatness. (I would also note that De Niro's performances would become as varied in quality as Scorsese's films over the years.) But more importantly, this film obsessed with an individual psyche does, at key moments, explore the psyches of others in depth, and Betsy's own spectatorial involvement in the pornographic scene is one of these. She and Travis do speak for a certain amount of time before walking into the porn theater. She registers her surprise and confusion over his choice of cinematic entertainment for their date. Though much more aware than he of the implications of their seeing a pornographic film, she nevertheless walks into the theater with Travis and sits down with him to see the film.

Swedish Marriage Manual, which is often said to be the 1969 Swedish pornographic film *The Language of Love* but may really be one of its many sequels, is what is referred to in the porn industry as a "white-coater," a porn film that uses the mock-educational format of the medical documentary as a covert means of depicting graphic sexual acts. In the clip we see, a rather drab housewife in a frock explains her lifelong sexual ignorance to a man in a white coat, presumably the family doctor. As they speak, the film intercuts their conversation with images of an orgy, the action of which all seems to revolve around one woman. Of interest here, lesbian as well as interracial sex is represented within these orgiastic scenes, as women kiss other women and black and white bodies cavort and intertwine.[30] Travis and Betsy, a postlapsarian Adam and Eve looking at the degradation of the sexual into impersonal arrangements in which all intimacy and emotional connection has been discarded in favor of carnal contact, *together* stare at this mock-medical pornographic spectacle.

One of the central topics of inquiry in the work of the French poststructuralist historian Michel Foucault is the medicalization of sex from the late nineteenth century to the present and its numerous ill effects, chiefly the equivalence between psychic health and sexual morality, i.e., properly marital sexuality. Inciting sexual preoccupations of all kinds while then pathologizing almost all kinds, save the marital heterosexual version, would be, for Foucault, the chief aim of the juridico-medico discourse of sex. Foucault would readily concur, I think, with the reading that "juridico-medico discourse" promotes a sense of sex as both compulsory *and* as pornographically "depraved." The film is taking a different stance here, however, in my view. The logic of the white-coater is the logic of pornography *generally*, a genre that educates the viewer not only about the compulsory nature of sexuality but also about the division, newly enforced within 1970s culture, between emotions and sex. If the 1970s was the era of an apparent sexual freedom but also *Looking for Mr. Goodbar* (1977), in which the sexually promiscuous woman is murdered by her one-night stand, *Taxi Driver* would appear to be saying that sexual freedom more often took the form of sexual and emotional deadening—of disassociation and disconnectivity. Pornography, with its impersonal sexual situations and its emotionally blank, affectless depiction of sexual acts, became figured in the 1970s as the logic, narrative, meaning, and the representation of *all* forms of sexuality, leading to the phenomenon that I have called *pornographication*. Betsy is initially at least curious to see this film that Travis reassures her is a typical date movie. Her subsequently horrified reaction suggests more than discomfort with pornography—it suggests her own ambivalence towards sexuality. The entire scene is also an exquisite meditation on class. Betsy's rejection of Travis as well as the crude pornographic spectacle seems to come from a place of middlebrow disdain for his tacky ideas about entertainment— "This is a film that many couples go to see," he attempts to reassure her as she hesitates before the box office—and from a sudden and undeniable realization that they come from different worlds.

171

Perhaps Betsy, intrigued by what *Travis* experiences sexually, is trying to access her own experience of sexuality by entering the pornographic theater with him. Clearly, something about him speaks to her. Far from being repelled by his ridiculous but, then again, probably emotionally accurate come-on line earlier, "I think that you're a lonely person," it seems to incite her interest in him. When Betsy gets up in a huff and storms out of the theater, much to Travis's surprise, she may be aghast not just at the stupid porn film but at the naked revelation of the levels of bewilderment and ambivalence both she *and* Travis experience before the scene of sexuality. Perhaps Betsy realizes that to watch this porn film with Travis is to share in his loneliness—and *that* would be too much for anyone to bear. What's most pornographic about *Taxi Driver* is its naked depiction of the utter isolation and loneliness of its male protagonist. Somehow D. H. Lawrence's model of hard, isolate, stoic, killer manhood as essential American manhood is easier to bear if associated with and relegated to the confines of the nineteenth-century American literary past.

Man's Favorite Sport

While most critics have cited John Ford's great, troubling western *The Searchers* (1956) as the chief intertext for *Taxi Driver*, I have attempted to show in this chapter that Scorsese's agon with Hitchcock is also a central intertextual issue. The film redeploys the Hitchcockian triad of voyeurism-pornography-homosexuality to critique American masculinity. Still, it is helpful to recall John Wayne's Ethan Edwards at the end of Ford's film, famously detached from family and future in the memorable closing shot of Ethan walking away from the reunited family and heterosexual coupledom. "Schrader's Travis Bickle is Ethan Edwards split open," Amy Taubin suggestively writes.[31] A former Confederate soldier, Ethan searches, along with young, mixed-race Martin Pawley (Jeffrey Hunter), for his niece Debbie (Natalie Wood), abducted as a child by Comanche Indians, who kill most of her family. Motivated by race hatred, Ethan's goal is not to rescue Debbie but to kill her because he fears that she has been defiled by having been forced to become a Comanche squaw to the villainous Scar. It is easy to see a reworking of the plot of *The Searchers* in Travis's attempt to rescue the thirteen-year-old prostitute Iris, played indelibly by the young Jodie Foster in a wide sunhat, big eccentric sunglasses, floral-print top, red short-shorts, and red platform shoes.

Her pimp, Sport, played by Harvey Keitel, recalls Scar, the Comanche chief who embodies the threat of otherness and incites Ethan's race hatred. More deeply, Sport embodies and brings to a head the film's obsession with the psychosexual logic and emotional turmoil of white masculinity. In the original script, Sport and the other men Travis climactically kills were supposed to be African American, but Scorsese and Schrader, fearing the potential for violence in theaters showing the film, both decided to change Sport and the other men into whites.[32] In some ways, the filmmakers evinced a lack of courage in their convictions by turning Sport into a white man—the themes of racism saturating the film demand some form of resolution or confrontation that never really comes through. As I discuss below, however, I do believe that the film actually critiques racism rather than simply exudes racist attitudes, as some have accused it of doing. In another and perhaps more significant way, turning Sport into a double, racially and in gendered terms, for Travis allows the film to provide its most penetrating analysis of one of its central preoccupations: the substitution of violence for sexuality that defines Travis's version of masculinity.

In his well-known essay "The Incoherent Text," Robin Wood writes of the scene in which Sport and Iris dance together, Sport holding her whisperingly close to his body in a gesture that combines the paternal with the pedophilic, as the "Scar" scene.

> The relationship of *Taxi Driver* (and [Schrader's film] *Hard Core*) to *The Searchers* has been widely recognized. Scorsese and Schrader were fully aware of it and refer to the brief scene between Iris and her pimp/lover Sport (Harvey Keitel) in the "Scar" scene—the equivalent of a "missing" (and arguably essential) scene in *The Searchers* defining Debbie's relationship to Scar and Comanche life. It is a scene that Ford could not conceivably have filmed, and Scorsese and Schrader are quite right in implying (I presume) that its absence definitively highlights the cheating, evasion, and confusion that characterize the last third of his film (itself an archetypal incoherent text). It is certainly to their credit that the "Scar" scene exists in *Taxi Driver* (significantly, it is the only substantial sequence that takes place beyond Travis's consciousness); it is less certain that it presents any sort of valid equivalent (to equate life with the Comanches to life in a brothel may strike one as dubious on several counts) or that its existence helps clarify what the film is saying.[33]

Wood goes on to describe the scene as the film's one moment of genuine tenderness; moreover, in his view the film calls into question the easy assumption that *anything* would be preferable to prostitution: with Sport, Iris may have found something preferable to home and family, since she attempted to escape her personal versions of both.

This scene does much more, however, than fill in a lacuna in Ford's film. It is the closest approximation of fulfilling heterosexual love and sexuality in the film. As such, at least insofar as I read it, its purpose is less relevant to showing us what Iris might find appealing or seductive in Sport/Scar (i.e., the complexities of interracial attraction that Ford found it so difficult to explore, allegorized in the disproportionate power relations of the warped white couple of Sport/Iris), than it is to diagnosing a general disturbance within white male sexuality.[34] For, if the scene ironizes Travis's failed attempts at heterosexual intimacy, at intimacy of any kind, by demonstrating that the morally repugnant Sport has more of a way, more charm and appeal, and more physical and emotional closeness with a woman than Travis, it also ironizes Sport by making the object of his desires and the "woman" whose body he exploits and spirit he dominates a girl. The girl stands in here, in a poignant and grotesque fashion, for the woman whose own sexuality is either balked or opaquely unimaginable and whose love or even companionship is unattainable. In this manner, it ironizes Betsy, shown to be blocked in her desires as well. It also ironizes Tom, her hapless colleague who randomly remarks "I love you" to Betsy and receives not even the slightest flicker of recognition from her. A parody of normal heterosexual love and romance, the image of Scar and Iris dancing intimately embodies the gendered and sexual failure at the heart of the modern, urban world critiqued by the film. In this regard, Hitchcock once again hovers over the film's thematic project. Films such as *Vertigo*, *Psycho*, and the neglected masterpiece *Frenzy* (1972) provide similar diagnoses of what Henry James observed in the latter nineteenth century: "a decline in the sentiment of sex." But Hitchcock and certain New Hollywood directors go much further, diagnosing not just a decline but a fatal impasse in relationships between men and women, an impasse the logic and causes of which lie deeply rooted in the general failures, terrors, and propensities for sadism within the male psyche. The impossibility of sex in Hitchcock and his tradition in the New Hollywood share Lacan's radical position towards institutionalized heterosexuality. For Lacan, heterosexuality is not the natural given of human life. As he once wrote of man-woman relations, *"Il n'y a pas de rapport sexuel"*: there's no such thing as a sexual relationship, nothing inherently *natural* about heterosexuality.[35] Hitchcock and the New Hollywood directors who follow him, such as Scorsese (here and in *The Age of Innocence*), Friedkin (in *Cruising*), Spielberg (in the opening scenes of *Jaws* and in *Close Encounters of the Third Kind*), Jonathan Demme (in the post–New Hollywood *Something Wild* and *The Silence of the Lambs*), and De Palma generally not only refuse any stable, coherent, "natural" version of heterosexual relations, they blow the concept itself to smithereens.

Hitchcock's acidly comic, frightening doubling of Norman and Sam in the climactic section of *Psycho*, which as I argued in Chapter 2 has homoerotic undertones, plays on the physical similarities between the actors, Anthony Perkins as Norman, John Gavin as Sam, as an allegory for the correspondences or complicities between "sick," queer masculinity and apparently normal, heterosexual masculinity. Scorsese takes this straight/queer doubling further in *Taxi Driver*. With his black cowboy hat, long dark hair, white necklace, tank-top T-shirt, gaudy rings, and bulging-arm musculature, Sport presents an image of hypermasculinity paradoxically adorned with feminine and gay signifiers or resonances. His hipster dandyism italicizes his very masculinity to the point that it comes to seem parodistic, a kind of male drag. Sport represents the blur of styles of heterosexual and homosexual masculinity in the disco 1970s most exquisitely displayed by John Travolta as the dancing icon Tony Manero in John Badham's 1977 film *Saturday Night Fever*. Travis, in contrast, looks plain and Midwestern, though also urban-haggard and existentially beleaguered. When Travis narcissistically displays and interacts with his own image in those famous scenes in his apartment, what is striking is how lean, bare, and barren his body is; he's so pared down that, despite his martial armaments, he seems as vulnerable and pitiable as he does terrifying. Sport's masculinity is riper, more palpable, fleshier—in a word, queerer. (The serial killer Jame Gumb, played by Ted Levine, is analogously and much more excessively depicted as a collage of straight and queer masculine styles in *The Silence of the Lambs*.) As Keitel plays him, Sport is also theatrical and playful in manner, in a way that Pauline Kael found oddly winning. His swagger and machismo are mock-swaggering, mock-machismo performances of masculinity. Travis's rendering of himself into a tougher, leaner, meaner version—exemplified by his Mohawk haircut—is also an ironic mock-masculinity that calls attention to gender/masculinity as a performance. (His final-act transformation plays out like a grotesque parody of gay coming out, complete with change of appearance and pursuit of illicit desires.) To echo Judith Butler, masculinity is a copy for which there is no original.

While both Travis and Sport play Indian and extend Ford's racial/racist politics, what is significant about this racial as well as gendered play is that all forms of it occur within white male identity. It's almost as if white masculinity had absorbed all of its outside threats: femininity, homosexuality, and racial difference. Travis at the climax, adorned in Mohawk and guns, presents himself to Sport as his fiercer, tougher double—more Indian, more masculine, and also, at last, *more* playful. "Suck on this," Travis tells Sport as he shoots him in the stomach. Travis's punning line accomplishes several things at once. It demonstrates that the man who didn't know what "moonlighting" meant at the start of the film (the taxi dispatcher mentions the word, and Travis is bewildered by it) has become a talented punster, comfortable with manipulating language, which depends on ease with it. It also openly declares that the violence of the confrontation between the men is a substitution for sexual contact between them, synthesizing both the homoerotic-homophobic themes of the film and its general preoccupation with the substitution of violence for sexuality.

175

The extraordinary climax, in which Travis kills Sport, his henchman who monitors Iris's sexual sessions and collects the money from the customers, and the mafioso customer who's having sex (or about to do so) with Iris, returns us boldly to explicit evocations and homage to Hitchcock. After Travis decimates his foes, becoming badly injured himself in the process, the police come in as poor Iris screams and sobs. (Far from reveling in Travis's rescue of her, she registers the hideousness of the violence within his efforts on her behalf, a point that Cynthia Fuchs makes as well.) In slow motion, evoking Charlie T.'s similar gesture earlier, Travis pantomimes shooting himself in the head, raising a bloody finger to his temple and "pulling the trigger" as he makes the sounds of a gun firing. The desaturated colors and stylized camera work of the climax return us to the Expressionist boldness of the credits sequence, alerting us that this is an aesthetic climax as well as a plot-related one, the culmination of Scorsese's agon with the cinematic past, Hitchcock especially. Evoking the moment in *Psycho* when Norman, as seen in a dramatic overhead shot, takes Mother down to the fruit cellar ("You think I'm fruity, do you?" she caustically asks him), Scorsese uses an overhead shot to show us the police in the doorway, which has the effect of transforming the entire scene into a still life, a frieze of masculine excess and failure. From the overhead perspective, the scene of violent, bloody struggle and death looks puny and sad, the police officers toy soldiers. Evoking *Frenzy*'s famous backward-gliding camera movement in its representation of the second murder in the film, of the protagonist's loyal girlfriend Babs, the camera tracks backwards, down the stairs it had ascended, past Sport's dead body and the mysterious ring with an eye on it on one of his fingers, into the street and through the crowds and police cars. We are pulled out of the abyss, yet pulled into a deeper one—the social order that created not only Travis but also the men he killed—and left there unmoored.

"The hallucination that Travis enacts in [the climactic] scene—and which results in real death—is the hallucination of masculinity," writes Amy Taubin. "It's the search for that ideal image of masculine wholeness that subtends the entire history of the movies. It's also what makes Scorsese's raids on the cinematic image bank not merely an aesthetic exercise in reflexivity, but also an expression of a dilemma that's both personal to Travis and bigger than Travis himself."[36] This dilemma lies in the "heroic" nature of masculinity, an ideal already shown to be fissured in Ford's and John Wayne's Ethan Edwards, and now demonstrated in Travis to be "broken into bits under the pressure of the feminist and civil rights movements," and, I would add, Stonewall and gay rights as well. Scorsese's "raids on the cinematic image bank" would prove to be showily hollow in many of his subsequent films, but in no way here. His use of Hitchcock's backward-tracking shot to bring the climactic shootout to a conclusion takes Hitchcock's aesthetics and themes to a new level of social critique. In *Frenzy*, we follow the serial killer John Rusk (ginger-blond Barry Foster, a ringer for Michael Caine, who Hitchcock wanted for the part) taking Babs (Anna Massey), the indefatigably loyal girlfriend of the wrongly accused man, to his apartment, where we know he will kill her. As the camera follows Rusk and Babs up to his apartment, Rusk closes the door behind them as he says to her, "You know, Babs, you're really my kind of woman," precisely what he said to his previous victim, who he raped and then murdered. Then the camera moves backward, down the stairs we had just scaled, through the hallway of the building, and back out into the street, with its sounds and sights. We are forced back into the social order, reminded of and punished for our powerlessness as we merge into the relentless activity of the endlessly chaotic social world. This backward direction returns us to the living world, but it is a movement that refuses all of the Hegelian imperatives of Western culture and the social order, with its mythologies of endless movement forward and towards greater and greater progress. It is the aesthetic equivalent of Freud's death-drive, the movement towards stasis, inorganic nothingness, death. It is the "rear" view of the social order and what it produces (pimps and other exploiters of women and girls, serial killers) and obscures (suffering and our complicity in its production). In *Taxi Driver*, Hitchcock's rear view gains a wider and more comprehensive scope. The street brims with police officers and rubberneckers converging outside of the prostitution-ring building in which Travis, the murdered men, and the weeping, traumatized Iris wait for justice. Those on the street are *aware* of the mayhem going on within the building, but the same sense of profound powerlessness dominates. Unlike those on the street in *Frenzy* who have no idea that Babs, like the other women, is being hideously killed, those outside in *Taxi Driver* know what's going on inside of dark buildings, or will soon be told, but remain helpless. We are able only to gawk with the statuary spectators, fixed in their frieze-like positions. There is no movement forward, only backwards, to death and inescapable despair.

Racism and *American Bandstand*

Many critics have impugned *Taxi Driver* for its racism. Certainly, *Travis* is racist. Yet I would argue that, on balance, the *film* is not racist. Instead, it is a critique of racism—not only that of its protagonist but also that of the culture that produced him and which is the object of the film's most stringent critique. I believe that *Taxi Driver* is the classic example of another D. H. Lawrence maxim: "Never trust the artist, trust the tale." From everything that the screenwriter Paul Schrader has said about the process of writing this screenplay—"Travis Bickle is me"—and from attitudes exhibited in his other work of the period, I believe that it's fair to say that he had racist attitudes at that time, and I'm not prepared to say that Scorsese was devoid of them, either. Yet a work of art must be judged on its own terms, and not on the failures, limitations, or dubious questions hovering over its creators, unless those extraneous factors prove so overwhelmingly negative that the work of art becomes fatally compromised by them, as is the case with the works of Nazi filmmaker Leni Riefenstahl, important though they are in aesthetic terms.

It is also important to reexamine the depictions of Travis's racism. The film actually makes the question of Travis's racism much fuzzier than critical accounts have suggested. Travis refers to blacks as "spooks," but the person who uses the word "nigger" is the grotesquely racist and misogynistic cuckolded customer who claims he is about to shoot his wife in the face and in the vagina. ("Do you know who lives there? A nigger lives there, and that isn't my apartment. My wife is in there, and . . . I'm gonna kill her.") It is the customer, much more than Travis, who inhabits the racist elements in De Niro's proto-Travis Bickle impersonation in De Palma's *Greetings*: "[I want to kill] Mexicans, niggers, homos, all the undesirable elements. . . . Let my rifle veer to the left, then to the right, to pick off cancerous elements." That the customer's hideous racism is tied to his hideous misogyny is not at all accidental or incidental, for there is a consistent discourse in the film linking attitudes, generally but not always phobic, toward race and sexuality. Moreover, when Travis uses the term "spooks," it is to note that whereas some cabdrivers won't pick up black customers—"spooks"—"it makes no difference" to Travis, who does pick them up.

As discussed earlier, when Travis rhapsodically fantasizes about Betsy, the images of blacks we see, images that would appear to be floating through his mind, are noticeably devoid of phobia. Fulfillment in his desire—at least in terms of this brief reverie—appears to quiet his racist demons. The indifferent young woman (played by the woman who would become De Niro's real-life wife, Diahnne Abbott) behind the concession stand whom Travis hits on in the porn theater, is African American, suggesting that her race is not in any way a deal-breaker. When Travis sits in the Belmore Cafeteria in the first cabdriver homosocial scene and his eyes wander over to the black male pimps at the table across from him, his expression is wary, but also largely enigmatic, as is his regard of Charlie T. In the second cabdriver homosocial scene, when Travis follows Wizard out of the cafeteria to ask him for advice, he stares at a young black male, who is accompanied by a younger black male. Travis stares fixatedly at the former, who also stares backs at him. The young black males then harass some prostitutes, who fight back. I want to suggest that we don't know with entire certainty what Travis is thinking and feeling in any of these gaze-encounters with black males. While, given his phobic attitudes, he's *probably* thinking racist thoughts, it's also possible that he may be having other reactions. It is worth noting that Travis stares in the same manner at *Sport*, whose ironic verbal banter matches the ambiguities of Travis's gaze. Given the manner in which the images of black masculinity are tied specifically to male sexual dispositions towards women—the pimps, the guys who taunt the prostitutes—is it possible that what arrests Travis about these males is their apparent mastery over women? If so, this would clarify his extermination of Sport and his own homosocial realm as motivated by jealousy—crucial to Freud and to this film as part of the complex triad of paranoia, jealousy, and homosexuality—over Sport's masculine power and control over women rather than simply a retributive purge.

Travis's look turns everything into pornography, contributing greatly to the pornographic gaze of the film, by which phrase I mean a gaze that is as critical of pornography as it is itself pornographic. While we are allowed to inhabit Travis's perspective on the world, the *film's* perspective far exceeds that of Travis, and it is the critical distance between Travis's look and the film's gaze wherein we can locate its political critique. We are made to understand Travis's palpable racism, sexism, homophobia—his phobic attitudes generally—but we are also made to understand, on the one hand, that the larger culture has produced these attitudes in him, or at least offers little in the way of their amelioration, and, on the other hand, the unspeakably intense loneliness of Travis's life, which makes him pitiable as well as monstrous. For a film and a protagonist obsessed with masculinity, the encounters with other forms of masculinity take on a particularly urgent life. Travis stares at Sport and at black men with revulsion but also with "something else," an affect that exceeds our powers of comprehension and which our interpretive efforts are invited to decode. This something else could be bafflement, envy, or, possibly, desire. This desire may be sexual desire, but could also be desire for some kind of achieved gendered authenticity, a confidence or purposefulness the black males embody in Travis's mind. In any event, simply categorizing Travis's apprehensions of black masculinity as racist misses out on a great many of the film's pointed ambiguities.

Amy Taubin writes,

> Travis's racism is evident to anyone who looks at the film carefully. It's there in his body language when he's hanging out with a group of cab drivers, one of whom is black; it's there in his eyes when he's looking through the window of his cab at the action on the street. It is there, most overtly, when he shoots a skinny black junkie who's trying to hold-up a neighborhood deli. It is not merely that Travis shoots to kill; it's the way he looks down at the dying man—as if the guy were not even human.[37]

Again in respectful disagreement with Taubin, I would argue that there is an ambiguity, a puzzlement, over race rather than simply "racism" here. This ambiguity greatly complicates both Travis's and the film's attitudes. A character tormented over his own masculinity, Travis would appear to regard black males as males who are not tormented over *their* masculinity, who embody a coherent version of gendered identity. Charlie T. suggests that not only is he "on" to Travis's psychosis but that Charlie T. can have fun with this knowledge. That Charlie T. can be so playful—"Goodbye, Killer!"—provokes in Travis not violent retribution but a blank, mystified reaction that may evince wonder and envy at Charlie T.'s confidence as much as racial hatred. As mentioned earlier, his triumphant attack against Sport also includes a comfort with verbal play that suggests a newfound confidence—however horrifyingly won.

Moreover, while Travis's killing of the junkie is indeed a jarring and deeply disturbing scene, to say the least, I'm not convinced that the character's race motivates Travis's shooting of him. He may shoot to kill, but *he* doesn't actually kill the junkie. It is the Hispanic bodega store owner who clubs the junkie to death. Again, Travis's gaze at the suffering junkie is consistent with the ways that he has looked at black men throughout the film. While he may indeed be looking at the young black man with the indifferent disregard of someone who does not find him human, his intent blankness may also be an expression of bewilderment, fascination, or both. I do not in any way want to lessen the horrific violence and impact of this scene, but I do want to contextualize it as an aspect of Travis's obsession with potency—as the scene with Andy, the Gun Salesman (Stephen Prince, whom Scorsese would make the 1978 documentary *American Boy* about), exemplifies. The junkie represents not just a raced masculinity that Travis abhors but another mirror image, a man with a gun confronting Travis, recalling the mirror image of Travis whom he challenged in his apartment. ("You talkin' to me? Well, I'm the only one here.") In shooting the junkie, Travis is fulfilling his fantasy of masculine potency, or, better yet, anticipating its fulfillment, which will occur in the climax. This film is not, finally, about sexual performance but about the performance of masculinity, which holds the promise of access to male potency. Travis's most ardent fantasies revolve around becoming an invincible, hypermasculine man, and this is a fantasy that, far from harmless, has real effects, produces real deaths, while becoming more fulfilling, more authentic, more satisfying, than any other experience, certainly including, it is suggested, sexual intercourse. In the end, the (nightmarish) fulfillment of gender trumps the pursuit of sexual fulfillment. The ominous joke here is that if, as Laura Kipnis has eloquently argued, pornography serves as a free space for male fantasy, pornography-obsessed Travis's fantasy is not for sex but for the reclamation of his own lost, violated, embattled manhood.

180

In my view, the film suggests that what motivates Travis's apprehension of black masculinity is envy for black male potency, which he then attempts to emulate. Perhaps, then, this is what is truly racist about Travis, though also a racist disposition that the film illuminates rather than indulges in: for Travis, black males, as they have been made to do in centuries of racist iconography and mythologies, embody an ideal of masculine potency that reduces black masculinity to that presumed, mythologized attribute. The Freudian view of jealousy and grief's importance within his tripartite schema of jealousy-paranoia-homosexuality finds an analogous urgency in Scorsese's film. Travis's envy for black male potency—his fantasies of it—stem from his larger disconnection from the world of other men; indeed, his racism is a paranoid defense against this disconnection.

In one of the many poignant moments in which Travis watches television alone while eating poison food (white bread with sugar and booze poured over it), he watches, in the scene that *immediately follows* the one in which he shoots the junkie, the iconic 1970s program *American Bandstand*, hosted by Dick Clark. In a frame-within-the-frame close-up of an image from the show also in close-up, we see a young African American male and female couple dancing closely. The film expresses the same ambivalence over television as a national screen that we saw in De Palma's early comedies and will see in his later films. We see the smiling, gentle face of the young black male behind the woman, embracing her. This young man's face so closely recalls the face of the thin young man who held up the deli—both young, lithe men with similar delicate features—that the similarities cannot be, I believe, accidental. The sweetness and gentleness of the young black man on *American Bandstand* reminds us of the tragic waste of the young man in the deli while also memorializing him. But something more is going on here, and it relates to the film's general critique of compulsory, institutionalized heterosexuality, the spectacle that looms above and crushes Travis, who can only stare at it in blank befuddlement. The young African American couple dancing, and all of the other couples dancing along with them, are, of course all heterosexual couples, swirling in a pageant of romantic ardor that reminds the audience of their romantic experiences, potential for romance, or need to develop one. The *American Bandstand* broadcast represents the institutionalization of normative gendered, sexual, and romantic aspirations, much as the prom sequence does in De Palma's *Carrie*. Dancing with a woman in a national broadcast version of idealized romantic love, the young black man is the fulfillment of Travis's unrealizable dreams. In shooting the junkie, he is not only killing off black masculinity but youthful male promise, a grisly memorial to the destruction of his own.

181

Given the ambivalence over visual technologies—televisions, movies, cameras, pornography—in 1970s cinema, it comes as little surprise that Travis not only rejects but actually destroys the screen. He points a finger as if it were a gun at the screen in the porn theater, and in a later scene he tips over the television set with his boot-clad foot. The television set explodes thunderously as it hits the ground, a mini-apocalypse. The spectatorial ambivalence thematized in *Psycho* reaches deeper levels in the New Hollywood, as this moment evinces—what comes to the forefront is the drive to destroy the screen itself and its endless play of compulsory images. Television images become a parodistic taunt, signifying and extending the cinema screen's invasion of private, self-oriented spaces. The soap opera, its didactic function analogous to the white-coat porn film, enacts the scene of heterosexual romance for the viewer but also prescribes how to desire. In destroying the TV, Travis wages war on the passivity its images instill. That what plays on the screen at the moment that Travis tips the TV over is a scene on a soap opera between a male and female couple, who appear to be having some disagreement that they resolve with a kiss, extends the thematic concerns of the film—Travis's rejection of the normative sexual order.

This rejection is linked to the film's adamant refusal to grant its protagonist or its own narrative heterosexual closure. In one of the harrowing ironies of the film, Travis is extolled as a hero for having "rescued" Iris, complete with a halting, hypersincere voice-over letter from Iris's father thanking him for what he did for their daughter. As her father talks about Iris's being happily ensconced in schoolwork, we think back to Iris's adamant refusals to return home. Has Travis secured not her freedom but an imprisonment that, hard though it is to imagine, is even worse than her sexual enslavement by Sport? Fully integrated, at last, into the male homosocial realm of his fellow cabdrivers, Travis now finds that a customer awaits him: Betsy. He takes her to her destination, seeing her idealized yet also ghostly image in the rearview mirror. We expect that, just as Travis has now been successfully homosocialized, he will be properly heterosexualized as well. But after a taciturn goodbye on his part (he doesn't let her pay the fare) and a befuddled one from Betsy, Travis drives off, alone. Or is he alone? The film speed accelerates as Travis stares at himself in the mirror, and his reflection seems to be staring back at him, with an expression that fuses the paranoid with the accusatory. The mutually paranoid and accusatory looks between Travis and his own reflection are held in suspension, achieving an equilibrium of inescapable despair. Travis can never break out of the circuit of his own egotism, can never catch a true glimpse of himself, and therefore can never really see or acknowledge anyone else. I can think of few American films that provide so consistent and unflinching a critique of not only the construct of traditional masculinity but also of the normative social and sexual order that produces and upholds it.

CHAPTER SIX

MIRROR SHADES
Cruising

S THE NEW HOLLYWOOD was drawing to a close, the year 1980 brought us two films in the acutest Hitchcockian New Hollywood tradition: Brian De Palma's *Dressed to Kill* and William Friedkin's *Cruising*. Both of these films made at the end of the 1970s brought the decade to a head and to a close. Though rarely discussed in the same context, these masterpieces of the psychosexual thriller have much in common, generated, as they are, from an engagement with the same intertext, Hitchcock's 1960 *Psycho*. *Dressed to Kill* employs *Psycho*'s "double" narrative, similarly killing off its star halfway through the picture, while *Cruising* takes to a delirious degree the doubling of straight and queer masculinities in Hitchcock's film. At the center of all three films is a male writhing in the agonies of his gendered and sexual confusion. De Palma had also set his sights on adapting Gerald Walker's 1970 novel *Cruising* and wrote a screenplay adaptation of it before Friedkin took over the project. *Dressed to Kill*—for which De Palma wrote the original screenplay—plays out as a much more heterosexually oriented story, yet it bears some elements of *Cruising*'s plot and is not without a few queer elements of its own. Though not a typical pairing, *Dressed to Kill* and *Cruising* should be read together as meditations on the phenomenon of cruising, as a sexual practice but also in social and cultural terms. Gay cruising haunts De Palma's treatment of straight cruising; in turn, Friedkin uses gay male cruising as an allegory for straight male masculinity and sexuality.

Each notable for having generated fairly unprecedented activist controversy, both of these difficult and brilliant works demand careful analysis. Each became instantly infamous, though whereas *Dressed to Kill* did garner some lavish critical praise, *Cruising* was largely reviled. Feminist protesters lined up outside of theaters showing *Dressed to Kill*, reading excerpts from reviews by prominent critics, such as Pauline Kael and David Denby, who praised the film despite its purported misogyny in the form of violence against sexually active women. Even more dramatically, legions of gay activists not only protested *Cruising* but disrupted the process of making the film.

One of the tactics of the protesters of *Cruising* remains especially suggestive: shining mirrors down on the production from rooftops so that the glare would impede photography of the film. This was an oddly appropriate tactic against a film obsessed with mirrors and self-recognition. As a feminist and queer critic who loves both of these movies, my task in this chapter and the next is to make my admiration for them consistent with my theoretical and political positions. When even a critic I respect such as Thomas Waugh notes that he protested against *Cruising* before its release, I am forced to acknowledge that intelligent people can participate in a movement that I find censorious and short-sighted.[1]

The protests for both *Dressed to Kill* and *Cruising* presciently signaled the rise of identity politics in American life, which would greatly inform the culture wars of the 1980s forward. The backlash against them, despite the box-office success of De Palma's film, also ushered in a new era of Hollywood conservatism, one of the reasons why we can view them as the death knell of the New Hollywood, known for its often pessimistic content and themes.[2] A great deal of ideological blood was spilled on both sides of these debates, with art emerging as the victim of each position. Something strange began to happen in the early 1980s: art ceased to be art and became *representation*, and representation became directly related to identity, on both individual and group levels. The great messy complicated films of the New Hollywood were often what I have called elsewhere "ideological gumbos," complex mixtures of different ideological stances that cannot be reduced to one political statement or sensibility. Yet from the 1980s on, film and other forms of art became reduced to just such singular identities. Representation of any one "group" no longer related to the complex of themes in the work itself or to the filmmaker's sensibility; now, any individual from a group identity or any group's identity, once depicted, had to conform to some imagined sense of responsibility to that group identity and put forth the "positive portrayal" of it.[3] The negative images of queerness in *Cruising* as well *Dressed to Kill* are not inert, but dynamic: they solicit the viewer's response and challenge it.[4] The vitality, boldness, and inconclusiveness with which *Dressed to Kill* and *Cruising* treat issues of sexuality and desire as well as gendered identity make them as riveting to watch today as when they were released. Reclaiming their audacity, I make the case in this book that each film builds on Hitchcock's most radical effects to explore the politics of gender and sexuality in American culture.

The collapse of heterosexual and homosexual masculinities in Hitchcock's films such as *Rope*, *Strangers on a Train*, and, especially *Psycho*, most vividly thematized and staged in its climactic face-off between mirror men, Sam Loomis interrogating Norman Bates in the office, becomes a template, psychological, aesthetic, or both at once, for many significant New Hollywood works. Coming at the end of this heady period of 1970s moviemaking, *Cruising* takes the ample bleakness of the 1970s to a new level of pessimism as it dazzlingly reassembles *Psycho's* visual and thematic preoccupations. There is a famous moment in *Psycho* in which a highway cop with black sunglasses taps on the window of Marion Crane's car in the morning after she has pulled over to the side of the road to get some sleep. This moment becomes a trope on which Friedkin's film endlessly riffs. Like the first half of *Psycho*, Friedkin's film is about a descent into the underworld on the part of a "normal" protagonist. The opacity of the cop's intimidating gaze behind his black sunglasses and the inscrutable authoritarian masculinity he embodies in *Psycho* become a model of maleness subjected to endless appropriation, fetishization, and parody in *Cruising*, as the "Precinct Night" scene emblematizes. The mirror shades and leather jackets worn by the nighttime denizens of the sadomasochism (SM) clubs in which most of the film takes place are male drag regalia, parodies of standard masculinity that take on a fevered, fetishistic life of their own. The film's plot—a heterosexual cop assigned to investigate a series of murders in the SM underworld becomes more and more involved in this underworld over the course of his undercover assignment within it, to the point where his own sexuality becomes questionable—elaborately thematizes Sam and Norman's confrontation, the curious and surprising hetero-male fascination with homo-male identity. At the same time, the film explores the varieties of homosexual male fascination with the codes, appurtenances, surfaces, and textures of hetero-masculinity. Evoking the "FASCINATION" sign from *Taxi Driver*, the film's credits open with the hugely all-caps letters of the title, as we stare at the word, each letter a blinding white tower against a black backdrop: "CRUISING." The title inevitably evokes the first shot of Hitchcock's classic 1935 film *The 39 Steps* as well, in which Hitchcock pans to the right over the blinking, all-caps letters of the phrase MUSIC HALL. Like *The 39 Steps* and several other key Hitchcock films, *Cruising* thematizes theatricality, the duplicitous masquerades of identity. So denatured, the title and the practice it denotes will be the subject of our endless fascination as well as bewilderment.

As I have noted throughout, the "positive images" argument that has, one way or another, dominated academic treatments of film since the 1980s is a limited and limiting way to experience and think through movies. Negative images of homosexuality can indeed be indefensibly pernicious. But they can also be

185

indistinguishable from attempts to get at something in the nature of homoerotic-identity and experience. Mart Crowley's surprise hit play *The Boys in the Band*, the off-Broadway production of which, directed by Robert Moore, premiered in April of 1968, teems with negative images of homosexuality, particularly in the nightmarish climactic section in which the party-throwing protagonist forces all of his guests to confront their own self-hatred, before descending into a heap of his own. Though Friedkin's impressive and interesting 1970 film version of the play requires much more elaborate treatment than I can give it here, what is worth noting about it for our present purposes is the early indication it gives of the director's interest not only in homosexual identity but also in its contours, "weird" psychology, unpleasant aspects, in a phrase, its negative images. More-over, the film, as does the play, makes its central themes the nature of closeted gay identity and the effects of internalized homophobia, and in this manner serves as an important precursor to *Cruising*, which elaborates greatly upon both themes.

Friedkin's work can be described generally as an investigation of the ugly sides of everything: bodies, identities, desires, law enforcers, religion, cities, relation-ships, houses, natural settings. The ugliness of his films has led some critics to impugn him as an ideologically suspect filmmaker. Just as many critics have not only classified but dismissed his greatest film, *The Exorcist* (1973) as misogynistic for its representation of the gruesome ravages inflicted on its pubescent young heroine (Linda Blair), so too have critics over the years denounced and dismissed *Cruising* as homophobic. What I want to suggest here, as I have in regards to other works, is that at times the works or instances of representation which seem most offensive are actually those which are most acutely attempting to get at the heart of desire, identity, prejudice, and phobia. To my mind, the oddly sympathetic as well as frightening *Cruising* is just such a film. In Friedkin, ugliness becomes a means of stopping the endless motion of the social order in its tracks and forcing us to acknowledge the sheer weirdness of our social behaviors and interactions. The world isn't pretty, but it is more interesting in its variegated and discordant weirdness than we often give it credit for.

Mirror Shades and Black Tank Tops

As we discussed in Chapter 2, Hitchcock stages a confrontation in *Psycho* between Norman Bates (Anthony Perkins), the mother-obsessed, cross-dressing titular fig-ure, and Sam Loomis (John Gavin), the presumably heterosexual boyfriend of the murdered Marion Crane (Janet Leigh), as her sister Lila (Vera Miles) searches the Bates house for Mother. Hitchcock seizes upon the confrontation between Sam and Norman as an opportunity for a study in straight and queer masculinities. By pairing them visually in the same frame as they face off, Hitchcock emphasizes the physical similarities between both men (tall, lanky, dark-haired, dark-eyed), while noting the contrasts (one somewhat vulnerable and feminized, the other more conventionally masculine and, it would appear, physically stronger). By making the Norman-Sam scene and Lila's investigation of the house parallel lines of action, Hitchcock draws further striking contrasts. We are made to question which is the real drama, the more heightened suspense: the woman's investigation of the Terrible House, or this male-male confrontation-encounter. Demonstrating the same darkly playful distortion and manipulation of straight and queer masculinities he demonstrated in the 1951 *Strangers on a Train*, in which he cast gay actor Farley Granger in the straight role, straight actor Robert Walker in the queer villain one, Hitchcock has Gavin's Sam say the more sexually suggestive—the cruiser—line to Perkins's Norman: "You are alone here, aren't you? Would drive me crazy." It's not just these lines in Joseph Stefano's superbly nuanced script but also Gavin's surprisingly insinuating delivery of them that startles, as does, in its own way, Perkins's pointedly clueless, or anything but, response, "Now, that would be rather an extreme reaction, wouldn't you say?"

Cruising is a world of men wearing mirror shades and black tank-tops, leather and metal spurs. Its SM realm of narcissistic fetishism, full of clones and other doubles, extends the final section of Hitchcock's *Psycho* and its doubles into an entire feverish film. Friedkin takes Hitchcock's physical doubling of the actors to a luridly emphatic degree in *Cruising*, in which similarly garbed and physically similar men throng the protagonist, who in turn resembles them. Especially when wearing a black tank-top while surrounded by other dark-haired, dark-eyed men, the protagonist as played by Al Pacino looks like one in a series of men manufactured by the same factory. Masculinity itself will come to seem the product of this queer factory assembly line, the domain and the creation of a queer aesthetic. A riff on the highway cop's dark, impenetrable sunglasses in *Psycho*, the mirror shades worn by the killer signify this film's narcissistic gaze, in which every look and every image conforms to male vision, always figured as a vision of *other* men.

187

A reporter for *The New York Times*, Gerald Walker based his 1970 novel on a series of real-life killings in the gay community related to the blackmailing of the closeted victims. By placing the action of the story in the SM subculture of the gay world, William Friedkin, the director and the screenwriter, added a significant new element to Walker's plot. The film's depiction of SM subculture has been recuperated by some contemporary viewers and critics as a valuable documentary portrait of pre-AIDS gay culture, a record of a vanished moment in gay history. Beyond this, SM culture serves as an allegorical realm which Friedkin uses to explore issues of male sexuality generally. A perfervid counterworld, SM here is the "under-nature," to lift from A. P. Rossiter's study of Shakespeare, *Angel with Horns*, to straight masculinity and to the normative social order.[5]

In his invaluable guide to status quo movie opinion, Leonard Maltin observes, with characteristic incisiveness, that in *Cruising*, the "gay world [is] presented as sick, degrading, and ritualistic."[6] (He gives the film a rating of one-and-a-half out of four stars.) While some will no doubt continue to find Maltin's view accurate, the film depicts its SM world as ritualistic but never as "sick," and, if "degrading," never degrading in a way not actively solicited by the various denizens of the SM bar that the protagonist Steve Burns (Al Pacino), an ostensibly straight New York City detective working undercover to investigate the gay murders, visits. Ritualistic this world certainly is, however, and it is precisely the SM world's ceremonial qualities, its customs reaching the formal, structured gravity of religious ritual, that heighten its character as an allegorical universe. Thronging Burns in close quarters as he inches his way within the club, the cavorting, sweaty, leathered-up, mustachioed, blissed-out SM men perform like worshippers in a ceremony commemorating an unseen, or only subliminally seen, god.

Is this god the phallus god of queer masculinity? Yes, but also no. There is a wide *range* of pleasures on display, and within this range numerous possibilities for sexual fascination and experience. If the phallus would appear to dominate the gay male imaginary, this film—with its daring, indeed, shocking, depiction of fisting within the public space of the private world of the SM club—makes the anus an equally reverenced site of queer male desire. The spectacle of fisting is counterbalanced by the frequent depictions of men performing or experiencing fellatio, frequently on long, phallic nightsticks. By mounting, as it were, a world informed by phallic *and* anal preoccupations at once, the film explores the varieties of male sexuality—the possibilities of the male body as a site of worship and a geography of distinct pleasures. The principle binarism of phallus/anus organizes a series of binarisms—penetrator/penetrated, active/passive, butch/femme, powerful/powerless, sadism/masochism—that all work to allegorize the major dichotomy at the film's center, straight/gay masculinity. Moreover, the range of sexual pleasures here transcend the phallus/anus dichotomy, such as in the shots of men reaching upwards to squeeze nipples jutting from hairy chests or, in the pornographic film-within-the-film during the third murder, sniffing each other's leather jackets, olfactory fetishism at its height. Erotogenic zones abound.

Dazzlingly shot by James A. Contner in dark blue tones that give a ghostly yet vivid intensity to the actors and sets, *Cruising* is a phatasmagorical *tableaux vivant*, a film noir in color, but a denatured, death-in-life color. Jack Nitzsche's eerie, snakelike score coils around the bodies, adding to the film's sense of increasing constriction. The strange, special SM world of the film dominates its aesthetic as well as thematic ambitions. Irreal and hyperstylized, SM here functions as theater, ritual, pageant, performance. It provides a serviceable metaphor for the film's obsession with the chimerical nature of reality. *Cruising* constantly undermines the sense of realism it also stringently seeks to produce. Friedkin's investment in ugly reality—the shots of body parts and cadavers in pitilessly lit morgues—contrasts against the dreamlike atmosphere that finally engulfs the protagonist and viewer.

What we see may or may not be actually occurring, may or may not be meant to be taken seriously: everything in the movie is suspect. Burns descends into the maelstrom of desire, the unconscious of gender; his descent into these depths is figured as a literal descent, down into the dark chthonic spaces of the SM clubs. The constant play between the symbolic and literal in the film is a crucial one. Though it has documentary value, the film is as determinedly non-mimetic—non-realistic—as it is self-consciously verisimilitudinous. To take it literally as an attempt at a realistic representation of gay life is to ignore its self-conscious, de-naturing stylistics. Moreover, it is to ignore the film's much broader concern: the psychosexual dimensions and foundations of American masculinity. None of this is to say that *Cruising* presents an attractive or nuanced vision of gay life. But within its often negative portrayal lies something more challenging: a provocation to contemplate queer male desire in unfettered forms within a larger homophobic culture.

Like other challenging films discussed in this book, *Cruising* offers a critique of homophobia by demonstrating the depth of straight culture's attraction-repulsion to queer life and desire, and straight masculinity's crisis over its own identity, which hinges on misogyny as well as homophobia. The film presents the protagonist's relationship with his girlfriend Nancy (Karen Allen) as balked, with Burns unable to discuss anything about his work or his confusions about it with her. Bland pseudo-classical music (Barre Phillips's "Three Day Moon") plays over their stilted scenes in bed in which they are physically close but emotionally remote. In the first scene between them, Nancy's head is shown on Burns's chest, and then his face is seen in close-up. These independent shots, the initial choice not to photograph them in the same frame, emphasize their distinction and separateness rather than proximity and intimacy. When their faces do occupy the same frame, Nancy's head remains on Burns's chest, and as they speak they never look at each other. Through such choices of shots and his physical blocking of the actors, Friedkin conveys the sense of characters at an impasse: Burns's relationship to Nancy is never a respite from the baroque intensity of his undercover assignment. Their scenes are parodistic variations on the scenes from *The Godfather* films in which Kay (Diane Keaton) asks Michael Corleone, famously played by Pacino, about his business, usually being rebuffed or told, "This one time, you can ask me about my business," only to be flagrantly deceived yet again. Friedkin draws on the polarities of Pacino's established star image—his icy, deadened stoicism in *The Godfather* films, especially the second, as well as his manic, feverish intensity in Sidney Lumet's 1975 *Dog Day Afternoon*, in which he played a real-life gay bank robber trying to get money for his boyfriend's sex-change operation—to problematize Burns's sexual identity, shown to be in defensive flux. Pacino's performance in *Cruising* has often been criticized, but, in my view, he effectively

189

plays the role as blank, somnolent, vacant, yet wired and tense, too. Half-awake, half-dead, yet animated by his own increasingly urgent curiosity, Burns floats in and out of multiple worlds and hovers between sexual polarities.

The film depicts the ostensibly straight Burns as increasingly sexually suspect. In some scenes, the film suggests that he is about to have a sexual encounter with one of the males who cruise him, in the club or in the park. In one dazzling SM club scene, a man comes up to him, flirts with him, and draws him to the floor to dance. Burns dances with this man, snorting his cocaine-soaked handkerchief along with him. As Burns gets high, the dance extends into a frenzied group event, Burns, in black tank top, in the gyrating center. As the men dance, another man is being fisted by a scrupulously methodical pro, who greases up his hand and forearm with Vaseline. (It's like watching a reality-TV medical show.) The energetic cutting combines the actions, the dancing and the snorting and the fisting, into one continuous stream of frenzied motion, as if all of the men were sharing one body that moved in tandem.

In one of Friedkin's many inspired and thematically rich effects, this scene begins with a close-up of the blinking-light sign of the American flag hanging on the wall of the club. The way Friedkin shoots the sign in the first shot in the sequence, it looks stadium-sized, nothing like a sign hanging on a wall; strangely, though, it also looks like it has been shot in black and white. When Burns dances with the SM men, we cut to another shot of the blinking-light flag, yet now it flares into bright color. The same effect occurs within the shots of the men dancing. As if the flag were igniting their flesh tones with dynamic color once their dancing reaches a particular height of intensity, the cinematography shifts from dark blue-black tones to brighter ones, the dancing (and the fisting, and the snorting) transforming the stylized, mimelike SM world into raw, animal life. This is the film at its most Melvillean and Whitmanian: a dream of brotherly American love suffused with the raw possibilities of the erotic. (The Vaseline on the fisting-pro's hand and arm, and the entire, public ritual of fisting, which involves numerous spectators all participating in the event, provides something like the sperm-squeezing motif in Melville's *Moby-Dick*, in which the sailors squeeze each other's hands and the "milk and sperm of human kindness" at once.)

The film vividly registers here Burns's attraction to the strange underworld he covertly investigates. Within the sequence of Burns dancing, we cut to medium close-ups of two significant characters: the soulfully dark and beautiful Skip (Jay Acovone), and the leather-cap-with-eagle-insignia-wearing Stuart Richards (Richard Cox), who, it will be strongly suggested (though only suggested), is the killer. Both stare at Burns, with alternate longing (Skip) and erotically taut menace (Richards). He also stares back at them, forming a circuit of desiring possibilities. Burns's incipient queer desire—defended against by increasingly violent and

Al Pacino at the center of Dionysian queer ritual in *Cruising*.

then strikingly passive bouts of lovemaking with Nancy—deepens the insistent suggestions made by the film that it is Burns himself who is either the killer or who kills in emulation of the killer he has sought and, perhaps, found. If Burns does really kill Ted Bailey (Don Scardino), the affable, sunny, ginger-haired gay neighbor that the undercover detective may love, at the end, the film makes it clear that he would have done so out of conflict over his own homo-desires. Once again, violence will emerge as the substitution for sex and desire, as it did in the fatal economies of *Psycho* and *Taxi Driver*.

While many critics have discussed the significance of the Ted character as a "positive portrayal" of homosexuality, some of the most poignant and important moments in *Cruising* involve Skip, a character who has not been mentioned in the critical essays on the film that I have read. Certainly, Skip, as played by Acovone, is a much more erotic presence than the sweet but sexless neighbor Ted. A melancholy, beautiful, dark-haired, dark-eyed young man, Skip imbues the dark male doubling trope of this film to a level of erotic depth.[7] His physical appearance and affect recalls the suffering homoerotic icon Saint Sebastian (a martyr pierced by arrows) as well as the brooding, sensitive young men of 1950s Hollywood (Sal Mineo, especially) and in Hitchcock films. He represents idealized queer desire and stands in for a tradition of male suffering associated with the homoerotic and, as we shall see, with homophobia.

In the striking scene that introduces Skip, Burns walks into the SM club and is startled to find it inhabited by . . . cops and detectives! It's "Precinct Night," a perfect masquerade for this film fetishistically obsessed with the codes and surface appurtenances of normative masculinity. The SM world, a funhouse mirror, inverts and parodies Burns's own undercover, drag-civilian role, reflecting his own masquerade back to him. Thrown out for being in civilian garb, Burns, as Pacino plays him, looks comically nonplussed. As Burns stares in befuddlement at the SM players in their cop-drag, languorously writhing in each others' hairy arms and fellating each other's prop nightsticks, Skip looks at Burns from across the crowded room. His dark eyes seem to rise up from the swirling SM sea and fix upon Burns, who stares back at him. Skip walks up to Burns, and the men walk out of the club together. On the street, Skip tries to negotiate a sexual encounter with Burns, but the undercover detective says, "Not tonight," and walks away. This scene, more than any other, evokes a similar one of rejection in John Rechy's 1963 gay classic, *City of Night*, a novel that presages the atmosphere of sexual panic and excitement in *Cruising*. (Indeed, Rechy was brought in by Friedkin as a consultant for the film.) In Rechy's novel, the protagonist, a hustler who inhabits the underground gay world of cities like New York and San Francisco, spurns the advances of a young man who wants to have sex with him, not as a customer but as a lover, telling his rejected suitor with a "gentleness" that surprises the narrator, "You've got me all wrong."[8] In Rechy's novel, it is strongly implied that the hustler-narrator's rejection of the "youngman," as he terms such characters, is a self-rejection, a refusal to acknowledge his own same-sex desires, which he keeps at bay by turning all sexual encounters with other men into monetary transactions. I would argue that Burns is drawn to Skip, and rejects his sexual advance, not only because he does not suspect that he is the killer but also because Skip touches him. Had he proceeded with the sexual encounter, Burns would have been doing so because he suspects Skip. But in a later scene, we see Skip, in a tussle with a fellow SM patron at a jukebox, wearing the same leather outfit, including eagle-insignia cap, that the killer wears. The film repeatedly sandbags us in terms of the murderer's true identity, especially by strongly suggesting, in the end, that it is Burns himself who is the killer, or another one.[9]

Despite the deliberately conflicting evidence the film keeps offering, I do not believe that the scene of Skip brawling with a fellow patron is meant to establish that Skip is the killer. Rather, the film appears to be suggesting that even soulful, beautiful young men can be troubled, potentially violent—don't assume anything about gay men, one way or another. In any event, Skip is also shown to be a friend to the victim who will be killed in the peep show, a man who works in the fashion industry. Skip visits him in the glossy boutique where he works. As this future victim warmly ruffles Skip's hair in the store, Skip's affect is warm and winning. The implication made is that it's the sexual feverishness and enclosed intensity of the SM world that turns the mournful, soulful Skip into a pugnacious hothead. The film explores the dark aspects of enclosure and sexual ghettoization. While opposed to the hetero-homosocial realm of normative masculinity—here figured as the world of law and order, cops and detectives—the gay SM world runs a similar risk of stagnation and stifling conformity that leads to competitiveness and, potentially, to violence, as it does in the straight male world. Inescapably, it is the homosocial itself, whatever its desiring cast, that leads to discord and despair, one of the most consistent themes of the New Hollywood.[10] That Burns does, indeed, lead the detectives to investigate Skip would appear to be a defensive maneuver against the feelings Skip awakens in him. During the sting operation in which the police burst in on Burns and Skip in a cheap hotel room, Burns, as we can hear over the wire, instructs Skip about what to do to him. The killer tied up one of his victims (the first murder in the film) face-down on the bed, and then stabbed him in the back. Confused by Burns's instructions, Skip asks hesitantly, "You want me to tie you up?" The most telling detail is that we hear, as the detectives rush up the stairs to "save" Burns from this decidedly non-killer tryst, Burns saying some of the words of the maddening, nursery-rhyme ditty the killer says before *he* murders his victims: "Who's here? *I'm* here. You're here." It's not clear whether or not Burns is goading Skip into revealing his identity as killer, himself playing the killer role, or himself the killer.

193

The man who is most strongly suggested to be the killer, Stuart Richards, will be shown to be obsessed with his dead father. Adrian Martin observes that "Friedkin makes it emphatically clear that Richards is—like Norman Bates in *Psycho* (1960)—literally not himself when he kills: he speaks with his father's voice, becoming the possessed vessel of an aggressive Other."[11] By having Burns utter the killer's mantra, here and in the climactic park scene in which he propositions Richards in order to expose him as the murderer, Friedkin not only associates Burns with Richards, collapsing their identities as the killer, but also links Burns to Richards's agon with the Father. Burns's contact, the older Captain Edelson, played with weary, melancholy gravitas by Paul Sorvino, is clearly a father-figure as well, one who will, by the end, suspect *his* symbolic son of murderous violence. Stuart kills as a result of his father-complex; Burns kills, if he does indeed do so, within the same paradigm. (There is an unexplored hint that he himself avoids his father's literal and symbolic "call"—he winces a bit when Nancy mentions, "Your father called.") What *Cruising* diagnoses is the repetition-compulsion of homophobia—the endlessly cyclical nature of denial and disavowal that leads to hatred of sexual otherness.

The image of Burns tied up on the bed reverses the power dynamics of the murders. Here, it is the ostensible victim who commands the would-be murderer's actions. No murderer, Skip is doubly victimized, by Burns's betrayal and the detectives' cruel treatment of him once they burst in on the pair in the hotel room. A harrowing scene follows in which the detectives interrogate Skip at the police station, harassing him mercilessly until they discover that his fingerprints don't match up with the killer's. A police tactic used to unsettle the suspect here involves the appearance of a seeming denizen of the gay underworld: an enormously tall and powerful black man in a thong periodically appears, first slapping Burns (still undercover), then Skip, more forcefully, all part of the series of masquerades in the film, the cops now performing SM roles just as the SM revelers played cops. (By making this decoy a black male, Friedkin evokes the history of white male exploitation of black male physicality, recalling the horrific violence of the enforced boxing matches between slaves in Richard Fleischer's 1975 film *Mandingo*. Less admirably, he deploys black male physicality for comedic and shock effect.) After physically abusing him, the detectives tell the whimpering Skip that he will have to masturbate and then take the "floating ball" test—if his balls don't float in the water, they will know that he's the killer. This could be the seventeenth-century witch trials. The scene ends with one of the detectives tapping a knife—a steak knife, from the restaurant where Skip works—ritualistically against a table. This gesture recalls the images of the detectives cutting steaks—made to look as menacing as possible—in the restaurant where Skip works as a waiter, while it also links the detectives to the murders. Friedkin collapses all male worlds into one—the detectives become indistinguishable in their ritualized violence from the SM world and from the killer.

Murder Most Strange

Unsettlingly but also undeniably, the murders in *Cruising* are amongst the most arresting set pieces in the film, each a microcosmic meditation on the film's themes. Alerting us to the aesthetic as well as thematic importance of the murders, Friedkin turns the second one, set in the park, into a Stan Brakhage set piece, the nighttime frame awash in strange and vivid colors. Most strikingly, the killer speaks in a post-looped voice (provided by the actor James Sutorius) that gives his character an otherworldly, vaguely seductive menace. Complementing this bodiless voice are clinking sounds of metal (spurs, keys) that accompany the images of the killer, his back to us, his face unseen, only the dark-haired back of his head visible, walking into the SM bar at start and close of the film. Friedkin anticipates Michel Chion's concept of *la voix acousmatique*, the voice without bearer, most famously figured in *Psycho*'s Mrs. Bates, whose voice we hear but which is never associated with her body.[12]

As Slavoj Žižek elaborates on Chion, the voice without bearer "cannot be attributed to any subject and thus hovers in some indefinite innerspace," functioning as a sexual "threat that lurks everywhere."[13] Friedkin, I argue, delays, defers, delimits *désacousmatisation*, "the moment when the voice finally finds its bearer."[14] One of the ways that he does so is to have the killer played by different actors in all of his appearances, some of whom will also play the victims in different scenes. Indeed, the only constants are the killer's outfit and props: leather cap with eagle insignia; leather jacket and dark pants; boots; a large knife that looks like a steak knife, hidden in a boot; mirror shades that obscure his eyes but capture, much like the phallus-knife-camera of *Peeping Tom*, images of his victims; and that hypnotic, post-looped voice.

Désacousmatisation "equals subjectivization": the moment in which the object "begins to speak, subjectivizes itself."[15] There is no proper moment of *désacousmatisation* here, no moment when the disembodied voice unites with the body from which it issues. The killer remains, always, a collection of components, all surfaces and objects, clothing and props: apparel not only stands in for subjectivity but also constitutes it. The killer's voice always maintains a distinct distance from the body it appears to inhabit. Bizarrely, the most authentic aspect of the killer's persona is, in fact, the most artificial one of all, that uncanny post-looped voice, recalling the equally irreal effect of the demon's voice, post-looped and provided by husky-voiced Mercedes McCambridge, in Friedkin's earlier film *The Exorcist*. The queer *voix acousmatique* of *Cruising* embodies, as it were, the film's ethics of sexual indeterminacy. Hovering between ghost and presence, indeterminacy and embodiment, the killer's out-of-body voice is the voice of queer desire and homophobia at once.

In the first murder scene, the killer and his victim—a hunky, muscular, dark-haired, Italian-American-looking man who affably introduces himself as an actor and who picks up the killer in one of the SM bars—go to a hotel room. The victim stands before a mirror; across from him, the killer stands in his SM leather get-up, captured at a canted angle in the mirror image. The actor then walks over to the killer. They begin kissing, and it is strongly implied that they have sex. The mirror that captures both killer and victim establishes a trope of narcissism as an important element of gay interaction, identities, and the intersubjectivity of cruising. Some critics fault the film for such references, finding them stereotypical, conventional, and phobic. If ever there were a plausible stereotype, I might suggest, gay male narcissism is certainly one.[16] But less polemically, I believe that the film generally depicts gay male sexuality through citation. The varieties of gay male sexuality on display, in a way analogous to the film's portrait of the killer as a collection of signs, coalesce into a catalogue of cultural constructions of gay male sexuality rather than anything like an attempt at an authentic, verisimilitudinous portrait. In other words, the film is interested in surface and style rather than depth, and in its citation of gay male narcissism, the film presents narcissism as one among the many items in the image repertoire of gay male stereotypes. The film obsesses over this repertoire, contemplating the various iconic cultural images of homosexuality while attempting to decode its desiring logic.

In one of the most homoerotic shots of the film, we see the killer and the hotel-room victim's hairy legs side by side, as well as their boots. The fetish objects, such as leather boots and leather jackets, in the film reinforce the obsessive trope of narcissistic doubling, as do the paired hairy legs and the shot of the actor staring at both his own muscle-bound upper torso in the mirror and the image of his pickup, who turns out to be the killer, also in the mirror. The film deepens its themes of doubling through its uses of stereotypes—identity becomes uniform. *Cruising* frequently cites fetishism, narcissism, SM, leather, the "clone," and other prominent articles within the arsenal of stereotypical attributes and images of queerness. While some might argue that Friedkin's use of homophobic cliché is itself redolent of his own homophobia, his obsessive brooding over the very nature of the cliché relates to one of the most non-clichéd aspects of his work in the commercial thriller-blockbuster genre: his films' consistent effort to denature reality. In *Cruising*, we are made to stare at these stereotypical images long enough that they come to seem newly strange. If we recall, from Chapter 4, our discussion of Judith Butler's theory of gender, *Cruising* comes to seem, very much like De Palma's early films, a textbook case of her view of gender performance as reiterative and citational. If gender identity must be perpetually reenacted, *Cruising* makes it clear that this applies no less to homosexual gender identity. Like the religious garb worn by high priests, the stereotypical appurtenances of gay male identity in the film are aspects of its ritualistic and perpetually reenacted ceremonies of community building.

Post-coitally, the actor wakes up to find his pickup rifling through his belongings. The actor looks frightened, which the killer picks up on: is the actor afraid of being robbed, or of something else? Most interestingly, though the actor is muscular and apparently strong—the shot of him before the mirror looking at the killer earlier invited us to appreciate his Atlas-like physique—the killer reduces him to a state of childlike helplessness and obeisance. Perhaps this response stems from the SM nature of the milieu in which they met, presumably seeking dominant/submissive role-play. But as the scene plays out, the actor seems truly frightened, beyond the extent of sexual fantasy. ("You look frightened," Sam Loomis says to Norman Bates in the office. "Have I been saying something frightening?" "I don't know what you've been saying," Norman responds.) Turning him over on his stomach, the killer ties the actor's hands, saying he wants to make sure the cords are not bound too tightly. "What are you going to do?" the actor whimpers. The film refuses conventional notions of gay masculinity by making the actor strong and buff rather than pitiably weak-looking, as so many gay males in film have been depicted, particularly in this period (think of John Hurt in the *Cruising* parody, the 1982 film *Partners*). But then this masculine, able-bodied man cannot resist the killer's commands—he acquiesces to his own destruction. Of the numerous ways to read the depiction of male identity here (one of which would be to see the film as homophobically emphasizing, in the end, an essential gay "weakness"), I will offer this one: the film refuses any correlation between physical appearance and personal identity. In this manner, surface does not dictate depth. The muscular actor's vulnerability contrasts poignantly against his hyper-masculine physicality. "I know what I have to do," the killer responds, and then stabs the actor repeatedly in the back. This action, like my phrasing of it, has an obvious metaphorical purpose: the killer who had sex with the actor stabs him in the back, betraying him in the most violent manner for his complicity in the killer's own sexual desire. "You made me do that," the killer says afterward. Fried-kin, as he did at certain moments in *The Exorcist*, adds subliminal imagery here. Subliminal shots of male-male anal penetration punctuate the murder scenes in the hotel room and in the porno peep show. While one could quite easily read these subliminal shots as homophobic—as Friedkin equating male-male sodomy with murderous violence—I read them differently. They serve as evidence of the associations in the killer's mind between the two acts, rather than as the film's own equivalence between the two.

197

Despite the strenuous efforts on the film's part to confuse the identity of the killer, such as the use of different actors to play him, the film also seems to reveal that the character Stuart Richards, a Columbia University graduate student who is studying the American musical theater (one should be permitted to groan at this detail, but again, those stereotypes . . .), is the killer. Richards, played with taut intensity by the dark-haired, dark-eyed, tall, lean, cryptic Richard Cox, is tormented by oedipal conflicts. These oedipal conflicts contextualize the internal homophobia that, as the film suggests, motivates the killer's violence. In an unsettling flashback/dream sequence, Richards meets and talks with his dead father in the park. His dead father, in that haunting post-looped voice, tells him, "You know what you must do."[17]

Pornographic Manhood

What is interesting about the murder of the fashion-industry victim is that, in the shot of him driving his car at night and headed to a peep show, he looks like an average urban male; there is no typing of him as wildly effeminate, as there might have been in a film with a different sensibility. The film doesn't go to great lengths to do so, but, to a certain extent, it attempts to make us perceive him as a person before he is killed. In the previous scene that introduced the character and in which he interacts with Skip, he seemed mainly concerned with appeasing his fashion-photographer diva boss. In the private peep show room with a man whom he has successfully cruised—sadly for him, the killer—the soon-to-be victim assumes a different, more vulnerable aspect. As the coin-operated pornographic film flickers before (or behind) them, the man crouches before the killer, signaling that he is about to perform oral sex. His expression in the crouching position, however, is neither leering nor detached, but one of longing, an impression deepened by the killer's oddly, surprisingly tender gesture of taking his victim's head in his hands and caressing his hair. Before these positions are taken, Friedkin shows us a close-up of the hands of the men as they sit side by side: one man places his hand over the other's, another surprisingly tender gesture.

The horrific murder that follows violates not only the body but also the soul— it obliterates the shared connection, the intimacy between the men along with the victim's life. Many gay men have reported feeling such intimacy with the men they have cruised and hooked up with. The "gay male arena of sexual sport," writes Judith Stacey, "also spawns less obvious, more productive effects on intimacy and kinship. Sexual cruising, as we have seen, initiates lasting familial ties."[18] Certainly, of such ardent potential affiliations, *Cruising* provides the merest whiff, unlike the actor in the gay porn film playing over the murder scene who generously offers his leather jacket for his admirer to inhale. Cruising in Friedkin's film leads to violence, suffering, murder. What the film attempts to convey, however, is that, on the one hand, the potential for violence that inheres in cruising has to be at least part of its illicit thrill—though to say this in no way suggests that such an illicit thrill parallels or is tantamount to an actual desire to be injured, however much such a desire may inhere in the intersubjective erotics and psychology of cruising—and, on the other hand, that the murders document the fatal ruptures between queer desire and normative masculine identity in our culture. (I return to this point in the Coda.) To whatever extent the killer can connect to his victims, and they to him, *they* will have to bear, most onerously, the burden for whatever desiring, sexual, and emotional traumas that lead him to seek out gay sex and then kill his sexual hook-ups.

During the murder in the porn-theater booth, the victim's blood splatters against the screen, a touch that can hardly be considered arbitrary. Blood drips from the symbolic screen phallus as it pours out of the innocent gay victim. The point of such associations reinforces the symbolic significance of the murders: they represent the crisis in normative masculinity brought on by the increasing visibility of gay life as well as the killer's own torment over his desires. The spectatorial ambivalence thematized in *Psycho* reaches a grim level of murderous intensity in the New Hollywood, a period of filmmaking in its last phase here.

The pornographic screen once again emerges as a symbol for emotional conflicts between men. We can say, further, that *Cruising* horrifyingly literalizes the New Hollywood disposition towards pornography, its searing sense of pornography as a form of social death. In the New Hollywood cinema, pornography emerges as an allegory for the deadening of all emotions related to sexuality, and, at the same time, as one of the forces behind this deadening. The shot of the killer's bloody hands—like those of Lady Macbeth, but without her wrenching guilt—wiping off the victim's blood on one of the sex-code handkerchiefs (the film is preoccupied with what these handkerchiefs and their placements in pockets signify in terms of sexual predilections), and slipping a bloodied coin into the coin-operated porn-machine is an apt summarization of these attitudes toward the deadening effect of pornography. The peep show has become the private realm of death within a public space of secret sex. In many ways, this moment confirms what *Psycho* prognosticated: the pornographication of the human subject, reduced to the unceasingly alienated labor of the pornographic image, and endlessly tethered to currency and its blood-drenched allure.

Cinematic Fascisms

In his famous essay "Is the Rectum a Grave?" Leo Bersani writes that

> It has frequently been suggested in recent years that such things as the gay-macho style, the butch-fem couple, and gay and lesbian sado-masochism, far from expressing unqualified and uncontrollable complicities with a brutal and misogynous ideal of masculinity, or with the heterosexual couple permanently locked into a power structure of male sexual and social mastery over female sexual and social passivity, or, finally, with fascism, are in fact subversive parodies of the very formations and behaviors they appear to ape. Such claims, which have been the subject of lively and intelligent debate, are, it seems to me, totally aberrant.[19]

As Andrew Hewitt has shown, the equivalence between homosexuality and fascism, centered in certain scandalous aspects of the Nazi party in World War II Germany, is a homophobic cultural construction deployed by straight culture as one version of queer "essence." As Hewitt reminds us, German fascism *used* homosexuals as objects and victims.[20] Still, Bersani is quite right to point out that certain quarters of gay male culture have appropriated fascist imagery, and that this appropriation, far from transcending or providing a utopian alternative to its source material, reveals that queer desire runs the risk "of idealizing" the very forms of gendered identity that condemns queer desire in the first place. As Bersani continues, the "logic of homosexual desire includes the potential for a loving identification with the gay man's enemies."[21]

The apotheosis of this identification in *Cruising* is the "Precinct Night" scene. Cops are shown to be not just symbolically but also quite literally the gay man's enemies in the film, which begins with two especially odious policemen patrolling the streets, hunting for gays, and includes scenes of intense police brutality against gay suspects. Throughout *Cruising*, which as even some of its staunchest critics point out has a documentary value, the SM world reveals a disturbing allegiance to and fetishistic preoccupation with the codes of fascism, particularly its established ideals of hypermasculinism, ritualized behavior, ritualized dress, and homosociality, which the Nazi party attempted to promulgate as an ideal without any taint of homosexuality. To whatever extent the gay male world of the film indulges in fascistic fetishization, using this register as the source material of baroque fantasy, it also parodies it. This parody, moreover, is a way of negotiating the experience of social powerlessness—fetishizing one's enemies is a way of keeping them at bay.[22]

Laura Frost compares the transgressive French writer Jean Genet's eroticization of Nazi masculinity in his novel *Funeral Rites* to the theories of Klaus Theweleit's studies of the men in the Freikorps, the paramilitary forerunners of the Nazi movement, and Wilhelm Reich's *The Mass Psychological Structure of Fascism*. Arguing that Genet exemplifies their treatments of the subject only up to a certain point, Frost writes that, "Genet represents the fascist psyche in the same terms, but then complicates it by revealing how it disintegrates—and, moreover, by bringing about that disintegration in the service of pleasure. According to Reich and Theweleit, military 'phallic' display is, ironically, an attempt to extinguish, not establish, sexuality . . . Genet's eroticization of the fascist soldier body in *Funeral Rites* relies on and redeploys fascist aesthetics for ends quite antithetical to fascist ideology. Genet 'disarms' his SS soldiers and militiamen by inscribing them in scenes of impending sexual pleasure, a most frightening position for the fascist subject."[23] While the sagging, sallow bodies of the actual cops in *Cruising* could not be further from the chiseled and ramrod Nazi male bodies fetishized by Genet, the film shares with his work an understanding of the hypernormative male body—tautly held to masculinist perfection—as a site of transgressive worship. If, as Theweleit maintains in *Male Fantasies*, the male subjectivity of German fascism was held together, almost literally, by its misogynistic abhorrence of feminine fluidity, *Cruising* everywhere depicts the authoritarian-male-worshipping men of its SM underworld as bodies that are simultaneously parodies of hypermasculinity—mustachioed, hairy-chested, adorned with boots, spurs, studs—and bodies melting into a collective, sweat-drenched pool of wet male flesh. Indeed, the one body in the film that truly evokes the hard, chiseled masculinities Theweleit and Genet evoke in very different registers is the looming, cowboy-hat-wearing black man, a cop masquerading as a denizen of the SM underworld, brought in to scare

Skip into confessional submission—and as an African American man, he defies even as he embodies a hard-body Nazi ideal. Moreover, Burns's vulnerability—his threatened submission to the corrupt seductions of the gay SM world, in a word, his penetrability—further disrupts any notion of an impregnable straight masculine psyche and perhaps even body. In these ways, *Cruising* takes similar themes in Hitchcock's *Rope*, equally obsessed with homoerotic obsessions with fascism, to the *nth* degree.

Cruising inherits and circulates homoerotic fascist imagery not just from the Nazi era but also from the avant-garde films of the 1960s that drew upon it, such as Kenneth Anger's extraordinary 1964 leather-biker epic *Scorpio Rising*. In this film as in those of the post-studio era, spectatorial ambivalence intersects with volatile cultural and identity politics. As Juan A. Suárez writes of the climactic portions of Anger's film,

> The cyclists' antics become progressively more dangerous until one of them loses control of the machine and crashes . . . As an outcome of the erotic tensions built up through contemplation of the bikers' bodies and of ritualized violence, the crash almost has the character of sexual release. These last scenes also desublimate the violence that remained latent throughout the film, yet ready to burst to the surface. Ominous lines in [popular songs quoted in the film] . . . together with the skulls that recur throughout the movie, spell a vague menace that takes concrete shape first in the gang's Nazism and sadism, and, subsequently, in masochism and self-destruction. The shifts from the masochistic imitation of television images, to the sadistic desecration, and then to final self-annihilation suggest that sadism and masochism are inextricably entangled in the subject's relations with the culture industry and its products. [24]

Recalling the ambivalence towards television—embodiment of the culture industry—in De Palma's early comedies and *Sisters* and in Scorsese's *Taxi Driver*, Friedkin has Burns watching a raucously loud TV set (its back to us) in an attempt to drown out the rancorous argument between Ted and his apoplectic lover (James Remar, who would go on to play Harry, serial-killer Dexter's adoptive father on the Showtime series). Like Travis Bickle, the agitated Burns finds that mass media only adds to his sense of the world as a deafening inferno. While the SM world of *Cruising* provides alternatives for heady pleasure, those alternatives present themselves as inextricably linked to atmospheres of enclosure, exclusivity (the whole point of cruising being to distinguish one prospect from a pool of others), stagnation, and the threat of various levels of violence, including murder. While these levels of violence explored by the film may amount to nothing more than a filmmaker's perfervid fantasy—though the novel and its film were, after all, based

201

on real-life cases—they nevertheless allegorize, in the hyperbolic manner of the psychosexual thriller, the inherent tensions in the act of cruising in a homophobic culture and the ineluctably constrictive nature of enclosed worlds such as SM. The fascistic valences of this world serve as an especially dark reminder of the ways in which all forms of fantasy, homosexual or otherwise, depend on normative structures of power.

Cruising begins with a sequence that evokes Luchino Visconti's 1969 film *The Damned* and evokes the film at several points. Visconti, a gay filmmaker, treats German Nazism as an increasingly perverse orgy of decadent homosexuality and pornographic violence. *The Damned*'s initially scandalous, indelible image of Helmut Berger's drag performance as Marlene Dietrich in *The Blue Angel*, at a birthday bash for his character's grandfather, and depiction of the apocalyptic massacre of the Brownshirt officers by the SS during The Night of the Long Knives as a gay orgy remain touchstones of cinematic Nazi depravity. *Cruising* evokes Berger's drag-performance by having not one but two rather buff guys in drag, one in a blonde wig that evokes Dietrich-Berger, the other a brunette. As these men in drag saunter through the streets, they are preyed on by corrupt cops. The cops pick them up and force them to come inside their squad car, ostensibly to be questioned for whatever offense they have purportedly committed, but actually so that the cops can sexually abuse them. "Come up here, I want to show you my nightstick," says Desher (Mike Starr), the cop in the front seat. The cop in the back seat, DiSimonne (Joe Spinell, who also plays the dispatcher who gives Travis Bickle a job in *Taxi Driver*), will also be shown cruising in the SM bar. The point made by showing us the secret homo-desires of the cops is, as in *The Damned*, to collapse worlds of law and order, of masculine rectitude, with homoerotic decadence.

As the late, great Robin Wood writes in his insightful and brave early defense of the film (especially noteworthy considering how very long it would take the film to get anything like a serious critical appraisal, much less a sympathetic one),

> The near-beginning of *Cruising* (after a prologue showing the finding of a half-decomposed arm in the river) succinctly takes up the excremental city theme of *Taxi Driver* and seems to apply it specifically to the homosexual subculture. "They're all scumbags," says a cop in a patrol car [Desher], introducing a point-of-view shot of a nocturnal street populated exclusively by cruising gays. This simple vision, which presumably typifies the kind of thing against which gay activists were protesting, is very strongly qualified by three facts. First, the cop in question is given unmistakable signifiers (physical appearance, expression, body language, intonation) indicating, "This is a very unpleasant, uptight, potentially violent person." Second, a couple of screen minutes later he is compelling a male transvestite to suck him off. Third, his fellow patrolman [DiSimone] has been

indulging in a diatribe against his wife to the tune of "I'll get that bitch"—the film's first intimation of violence is established within the context of "normal" heterosexual relationships, with strong connotations of patriarchal domination and brutality, before any gays have appeared.[25]

When DiSimone claims that his wife has left him, and vows revenge, it is in the course of lamenting that "kids used to to play stickball" on the streets. Friedkin cuts to traveling shots from the cop's point of view of gay nightcrawlers swarming the streets, looking very much like hordes of George A. Romero's zombies. To add to Wood's point, it is important to note that the image of these gay zombies proceeds from DiSimone's line of vision, rather than, necessarily, from the film's. Moreover, his misogyny as well as authoritarian role alert us to the instabilities of normative masculinity, a point greatly amplified by the revelation that the apparently homophobic DiSimone gets blow-jobs from transvestite-hookers, visits SM clubs, and cruises Burns twice, first in the SM club and then in the park. The film comes extremely close to collapsing heterosexual and homosexual worlds into one world of queer desire. Save for the presence of Karen Allen's Nancy, this world could be described, as Eve Kosofsky Sedgwick did Melville's 1891 *Billy Budd, Sailor*, as one in which "every impulse of every person . . . that could at all be called desire could be called homosexual desire, being directed by men exclusively toward men."[26]

203

This collapse of straight/gay worlds, then, is the chief justification for the rampant fetishistic fascisms in the film, its languorous and obsessive fixation with leather jackets, leather caps with eagle insignias, jackboots, ritualized masculinities, and diverse images of male power. Masculinity in whatever desiring context here emerges as a self-fixated world compelled only by a worshipfully narcissistic-fetishistic reverence for itself. The killer rises up as the embodiment of the essential split between straight and gay male worlds, but the murders and the economy of violence horrifyingly establish the connections between them.

These attitudes inform the extraordinary, deliberately frustrating climax. After searching through Stuart Richards's apartment and discovering a closet—natch—full of his SM regalia and, more tellingly, a box full of unsent letters to his father, whom we learn from Stuart's friend died ten years ago, Burns becomes convinced that Richards is the killer. The film corroborates this conclusion—before it then quite actively undermines it—by showing us Richards speaking with his dead father in the park. Through its dreamlike atmosphere, heightened by having the killer's disembodied voice coming out of the father's mouth, the scene demonstrates Richards's madness and seems designed to establish his killer-identity. In some striking touches, however, we see Burns spying on Richards in such a manner that Richards must *notice* Burns spying. Richards looks up from his newspaper—blaring a headline about the "Gay Killer"—on the bus to see Burns staring intensely at him from among the other passengers; looks out of his window to see Burns staring up at him from below, returning Richards's look with an eerie, knowing smile. These shots play with Hitchcock's tropes, evoking Bruno Anthony's tormenting and teasing hounding of the "straight" Guy Haines in *Strangers on a Train*, except reversing the identities and having Burns, the straight investigator, seeming the eerie, bedeviling presence. Indeed, the shot of Burns staring, from among a crowd of other passengers not staring, at Richards on the bus very deliberately, it seems to me, evokes the humorous, tense shot of Bruno Anthony staring transfixed and in one direction at Guy, from within a crowd of spectators whose heads constantly move from left to right, as Guy practices tennis on the court.

When Burns does confront Richards, it is in the park at night, on a bench surrounded by trees in a wide expanse of darkness eerily bright with a mysterious, chill blue light that bounces off the black trees and black leather ensembles of the men. This is the moment the entire film has built toward, in which Burns finally performs the titular act, coming on to Richards on the bench. Of course, his come-on is fraught with menace—he repeats the childish, sing-songy ditty "Who's here, *I'm* here, you're here," which Burns also quoted in the sting-operation scene with Skip, and which the film gives no evidence that anyone else but the killer, knows in its proper form (therefore suggesting once again that Burns, who does seem to know the complete ditty, may be the killer, or one of them). And Richards knows that Burns has been following him and invading his apartment. So, the entire cruising scene between them is also a violent confrontation between two wary mirror men who are "onto" each other. When they find a secluded spot to have sex—or anything but—Richards's first comment is, "How big are you?" to which Burns memorably responds, "Party size." Then Burns instructs Richards to pull down his pants, explaining, "I want to see the world." What happens next is, in my view, rendered deliberately confusing in terms of Richards and quite explanatory in terms of Burns. After Richards pulls his pants down, we cut to a shot of his boots; the killer, we have seen, keeps the knife in his boot. Richards pulls his knife out—but it is impossible to tell if he pulls his knife out of his boot before or after Burns's foot stomps on his own. We do very clearly get a shot of Burns pulling *his* knife from his boot, and then stabbing Richards with it. The matching gestures and props reinforce, once again, the idea of men as pairs of murderous doubles.

Later, in the hospital where he is being treated, the wounded but still living Richards is told by Edelstein, the police captain, and Burns that the fingerprints on the bloody coin from the peep-show murder match his, and that if Richards confesses to the murders, he will only get eight years of jail time. Richards protests that he didn't attack Burns, but that Burns attacked him. The scene ends with Richards saying—but now in the disembodied killer's voice—"I didn't kill

Al Pacino confronting Richard Cox, who may be the killer, at the climax of *Cruising*. Hitchcock's male doubles in *Psycho* take on a sinister queer explicitness in Friedkin's film.

anyone." Much like Friedkin's earlier, Oscar-winning hit *The French Connection*, *Cruising* leaves the detective-protagonist unsuccessful in his quest to capture the criminal. (In the closing moments of *French Connection*, the criminal mastermind famously waves good-bye, while on a departing train, to Gene Hackman's Pop-eye Doyle, standing furiously and impotently on the train platform.) But *Cruising* goes much further, strongly suggesting that it is Burns himself who is the real killer.

After the hospital scene, we learn that Burns's neighbor Ted has been murdered. The subsequent scenes showing us the gentle, ginger-haired Ted's bloody body—and Edelstein's horror once he discovers that Burns, as "John Forbes," was Ted's neighbor—and of the killer-figure walking into the bar once again, keys and spurs jangling, his black leather-jacketed back to us, strongly suggest that not only does the killer continue to roam free but also that the killer is Burns. Either he has begun to kill, or he has been the killer all along—or, at the very least, he has in no way apprehended the killer or stopped the wave of killings. At the very least, the film concludes with a sense of the utter futility of Burns's efforts.

In the final images, Burns cuts himself shaving, looks at his cut in the mirror, and then looks at us. His expression as he looks out at us is almost plaintive, as if he were silently asking us for help. Or, as if he knows that we know he is the killer. We then cut to Nancy as she discovers the SM leather regalia that Burns wore during his undercover investigation. She dons it herself. As we cut back to Burns looking at us, we now hear the same clinking sounds of metal (spurs, keys) that accompanied the shots of the mysterious man who enters the SM bar before and after the murders. We do not see Nancy again, but we hear her approach as Burns stares at us.[27] Queer identity can be donned at will, regardless of sexuality or gender, but no utopian possibilities spring from this apparent freedom. Dressed to kill, Nancy has become an unseen but horrifyingly audible queer monster: auditory senses now remain the only witness to and the only warning of an impending queer apocalypse.[28] We cut to the river, where another boat makes its way across the water. In the opening shots, the boat was a striking blood-red, but now it is yellow. This color's more hopeful register is belied by the overall grim tone. More dismembered remains may await discovery. The shards of identity and the remnants of once living bodies are all that remains.

NO CHILD WAS LEFT BEHIND in the making of *Cruising*—no child left before the camera, to be sure. This is one of the most childless films ever made, and certainly on the face of it would seem an achingly coeval fulfillment of Lee Edelman's thesis in *No Future: Queer Theory and the Death Drive* that queers, denounced by society and associated with death, should, instead of fighting for a place at the table of hopeful liberal politics which never included them in the first place, assume our death-drive status and present back to society the very images with which we have been homophobically associated: nullity, anti-life, and death. In doing so, we position ourselves "against life"—we reject the binding reproductive logic of heteronormativity and, especially, its focus on the figure of the "Child." Fighting against the "fascism of the baby's face," we should join, instead, with Leonard (Martin Landau) in *North by Northwest*, stomping on Cary Grant's hand, desperately clutching a crag on Mount Rushmore, as Grant says, "Help me."

For all of *Cruising*'s grimness, however—its apocalyptic tone, especially in conclusion—there is a vitality that comes through in the filmmaking, especially in that galvanizing sequence in which Steve Burns joins the dance. Moreover, what is bracing about the film is that it uses the power of art to disturb sexual assumptions and hierarchies and, more importantly, to critique a culture of homophobia.[29] By showing us a breakdown in firm distinctions between straight and gay masculinities, and the reciprocal fascinations maintained by each, it organizes a dialogue between the two—a disruptive, menacing, coy, hypocritical, and violently explosive dialogue, to be sure, but one as riveting as the film's surfaces and as hypnotic as the killer's disembodied voice. *Cruising* may diagnose the end of culture, but as a work of art, it is a sign of life.

CHAPTER SEVEN

THE GENDER MUSEUM
Dressed to Kill

De Palma's Obsession

T HE SERIES OF HITCHCOCKIAN thrillers directed by Brian De Palma from the early seventies to the mid-eighties, followed by intermittent returns to the genre, constitutes one of the most remarkable projects in the American cinema: an intertextual engagement with the work of one powerful director by another whose own cinematic sensibility emerges through imitation, parody, agonistic competition, and authorial empathy. De Palma's intertextual relationship to Hitchcock's films is in deep need of revaluation. Long dismissed as derivative, schlocky, and opportunistic, or hailed as heartless postmodern riffs on cinematic tradition, De Palma's Hitchcockian thrillers are precisely calibrated and scrupulous critiques of Hitchcock's key films, extensions of both their own formal innovations and thematic preoccupations. De Palma's Hitchcockian thrillers use imitation as a way of reconsidering Hitchcock and the nature of the cinematic medium at once; Hitchcock becomes a sign for cinema, a system that De Palma ruthlessly interrogates and takes to its most excessive formal and thematic levels. De Palma's Hitchcock-centered films turn film viewing itself into the subject of filmmaking. A deconstructionist ahead of his time, De Palma focuses from his early films forward on the very nature of film aesthetics. But he brings a rapturous sensibility to his deconstructionist techniques; he makes deconstruction disorientingly, disturbingly sensual. Little wonder he has been such a difficult filmmaker to peg, or, for many, to like, even though he is, in my view, the greatest director to have emerged from the riveting group of visionaries associated with the New Hollywood.

De Palma's relationship to Hitchcock, derided for so long, has longstanding precedents. Structurally and stylistically, his engagement with the genre of Hitchcockian suspense is analogous to the classical Roman tragedian Seneca's revisionary reimagining of Greek tragedy. Seneca's elaborate variations on Greek tragedy foreground and intensify the physical and emotional violence of the genre. New rivers of blood gush through Seneca's revisionary tragedies, adding a corporeal intensity to their austerity that is analogous to De Palma's blood-thriller versions of Hitchcock. Hitchcock has often, and rightly, been called the cinematic Shakespeare. In almost every one of De Palma's thrillers, an image of a bloody hand—in torment, in protest, in suffering—rises up, a figure from tragedy in its Shakespearean as well as classical form. De Palma's revisionary Hitchcock recalls as well the agon that antebellum American authors such as Edgar Allan Poe and Herman Melville had with Nathaniel Hawthorne, the Apollonian counterpoint to their Dionysian excessiveness. De Palma is an artist whose Dionysian sensibility—evident from *Dionysius in '69* (1970), his underground film version of *The Bacchae*, to his 2002 Hitchcockian thriller, *Femme Fatale*—combines the comic and the tragic, the controlled and the excessive.

In the cinema, there are no equivalents for De Palma's intertextual Hitchcock project, though Hitchcock has been endlessly imitated (by Chabrol, Truffaut, Chris Marker, many other New Hollywood directors such as Spielberg, John Carpenter, and others). No other director has ever been so committed to reproducing not only the thematic and generic but also the formal qualities of another director, and no other director has so nakedly exposed the inherently imitative and dependent process of art-making. De Palma's imitation of Hitchcock, however, allows him to *reimagine* both the suspense genre and filmmaking technique. His use of the split-screen is unprecedented and unmatched in the American cinema, and represents most acutely the ways in which his own formal innovativeness makes him a singularly important director beyond his Hitchcock agon.[1]

De Palma reassembles Hitchcock tropes into new designs; he critiques them while repurposing them for new visions of the cinema and of genre. His technique, as Terence Rafferty once observed, resembles collage. De Palma's collage cinema takes disparate strands from the works of other directors and weaves them into new patterns. He seeks to defy, parody, exceed, and radically re-envision the texts he repurposes. The point of the films, in my view, is not to pay homage to directors like Hitchcock, or to the numerous other directors De Palma cites, such as Orson Welles, Michael Powell, Howard Hawks, Billy Wilder, Godard, and even

De Palma's own contemporary, Roman Polanski, only seven years his senior. He is not interested in simple appropriation of available cinematic goods. His cinema, while rigorously controlled even at its most excessive, is chiefly experimental, an ongoing exploration of the nature and most importantly the *experience* of the cinema. His films foreground critical distance from their source materials, giving them a notably cool, analytical tone, yet they also whip audiences up into states of bewilderment, terror, and ecstasy through their perfervid twists of plot, effect, and form. His favored technique of the split-screen emerges as the aesthetic as well as political code of his films. Fundamentally split off at their cores from their own identities *as* films, De Palma films look at themselves looking at the cinematic medium while also directing their gaze upon the audience. Self-regarding, metatextual, intertextual, and defiantly poststructuralist, De Palma's films keep one eye on the cinematic past and one on the shifting, transforming nature of the film medium.

I reclaim De Palma's explicitly Hitchcockian texts as particularly powerful allegorical treatments of the experience of watching films. Their chief subject is cinema-viewing as a heightened form of voyeurism. While my focus here is on De Palma's agon with Hitchcock, which defines the better part of his career, it is also true that De Palma, as do many other New Hollywood filmmakers, takes classic Hollywood as his parodistic and satirical subject. (Think of not only the parodic recreation of the "Odessa Steps" sequence from *Battleship Potemkin* in *The Untouchables*, but also the critique of *Citizen Kane* in *Phantom of the Paradise*; the opening citation of *Double Indemnity* in *Femme Fatale* and the further noir elaborations of *The Black Dahlia*.) As Steve Neale and Frank Krutnik define it, satire "is often confused with parody, but the two are quite different. Where parody . . . draws on—and highlights—aesthetic conventions, satire draws on—and highlights—social ones." De Palma films make it clear that parody and satire can function together. They simultaneously parody older aesthetics and satirically draw our attention to their social implications.[2]

While De Palma's representation of women is indeed a vexed issue in any appraisal of his work, it needs to be considered from a number of perspectives rarely included in critical discussions, none of which I offer as exculpatory, but which are nevertheless a necessary counterbalance to the often simplistic charges of misogyny leveled against the director. First, De Palma's woman problem is perhaps his most visible inheritance from Hitchcock; critics who accuse De Palma of misogyny often fail to consider what factor his intertextual relationship with Hitchcock might play in his representation of women. Hitchcock has been accused of the same offenses, of course, yet is always reinstalled as the Master of Suspense, and, quite simply, the Master, in critiques of De Palma. The conservative and stately role into which Hitchcock is inserted in these critiques works to confirm De Palma as inferior and misogynistic upstart while alleviating Hitchcock of his own ideological disturbances, although it is also true that Hitchcock has been frequently—and unfairly, to my mind—denounced as misogynistic as well, albeit preponderantly within the realm of academic feminist film theory. De Palma's prevailing interest in critiquing normative masculinity and male relations, especially within male groups, also gets overlooked, which is a serious obfuscation of the political work of his cinema.

De Palma's output is so varied at this point that to focus on his Hitchcock agon runs the risk of missing out on a great deal of his achievement. Yet the importance of reconsidering De Palma's Hitchcockian project lies in the blunt fact that it has never been properly considered in and of itself. Critics who have denigrated De Palma have been content to dismiss him as derivative. Moreover, when they have praised him, it has been for the films that signal an apparent *break* with Hitchcock, such as *The Untouchables* (1987), *Mission: Impossible* (1996), and, later, *Scarface* (1983), now hailed as a fan-culture breakthrough, especially in the African American community, though it was critically drubbed at the time of its release. While these and other De Palma films certainly have their dazzling strengths, they are not, in my view, nearly as interesting as De Palma's Hitchcockian efforts.

De Palma's Hitchcock films replicate many surface elements of Hitchcock's oeuvre, principally plot structures and suspense set pieces. Yet De Palma uses these more obvious borrowings as a point of departure for the more serious business of investigating and reimagining Hitchcock's formal and thematic concerns. If Hitchcock often seems to hang his most obsessive personal fixations on thin and often nonsensical plots (*Vertigo* being the chief example), De Palma makes these plots even thinner and more nonsensical. As with Hitchcock, plot becomes a means to an end, a track on which to move along formal, symbolic, and emotional preoccupations. Given the wobbliness of Hitchcock's own plotting—which is not a criticism of Hitchcock, a director whose brilliance makes such literal-minded questions seem especially puny, fodder for types Hitchcock dismissed as "The Plausibles"—it seems particularly simplistic to fault De Palma for availing himself of them. The question of De Palma's copying of Hitchcock's suspense techniques, penchant for set pieces, and means of constructing those set pieces presents more of a legitimate challenge. As I will show, while De Palma does indeed quote liberally from Hitchcockian texts, he submits these quotations to close readings. De Palma never cites Hitchcock for his own sake but only in order to consider Hitchcockian effects from a range of new perspectives.

Some of Hitchcock's most perceptive critics give De Palma's work short shrift. I greatly admire John Orr's wonderfully fresh readings in *Hitchcock and Twentieth-Century Cinema*, but he writes casually and disappointingly of De Palma as "sensationalist" and "lurid."[3] Slavoj Žižek only glancingly mentions De Palma in his essay "Is There a Proper Way to Remake a Hitchcock Film?" De Palma's must be the least proper way, since his work remains largely ignored by Žižek and others who frequently discuss Hitchcock. No one would discuss Nathaniel Hawthorne at length without bringing up those he influenced, such as Herman Melville and Henry James, yet Hitchcock's great author cult—however richly deserved—proceeds unimpeded by any consideration of De Palma's aesthetics.

"Perhaps," writes Žižek, "more than the direct 'homages' to Hitchcock of De Palma and others, the scenes that announce such a proper remake are to be found in unexpected places, like the one in the hotel room, the place of crime, in Francis Ford Coppola's *The Conversation*: Coppola is certainly not a Hitchcockian, yet the investigator inspects the room with a Hitchcockian gaze, like Lila and Sam do with Marion's room, moving from the main bedroom to the bathroom and focusing there on the toilet and the shower." As he continues, "What makes this mini-remake of a scene so effective is that Coppola suspends the prohibition operative in *Psycho*: the threat *does* explode; the camera *does* show the danger hanging in the air in *Psycho*, the chaotic bloody mess erupting from the toilet."[4] Without knocking Coppola's 1974 film, let me say that I do not believe that the most ingenious or resonant way of remaking Hitchcock is necessarily to keep one's borrowings skillfully hidden, in the "unexpected" places of the films of a director who is "certainly not a Hitchcockian." Yet at the same time, what Žižek seems to praise is the explicitness that Coppola brings to the Hitchcockian template: the disgorging of the Real, the toilet's outpouring of the blood, gore, and mayhem kept simmering beneath the hygienic sheen of Hitchcock's bathroom surfaces.

One might ask, how is the making explicit of tensions beneath, though just barely, the Hitchcockian surface different from what De Palma does in his films, which are certainly "explosive," as the bravura climax of *The Fury* evinces? At the end of this 1978 gothic-espionage-telekinetic-teen thriller, the heroine, Gillian (Amy Irving) annihilates, finally, the horrible, cold, manipulative, dead-armed villain Childress (John Cassavetes). She does not simply kill him; through the force of her psychokinetic wrath, she literally blows his body to smithereens. To the rousing sounds of John Williams's perversely celebratory, Herrmann-esque score, Childress's decapitated head careens to one side of the screen and his dismembered limbs to the other as apocalyptic clouds of blood, gore, and smoke engulf the screen itself. De Palma reveals his fearless and fecund relationship to the cinematic past, making mincemeat of his predecessors and of oedipal fears at once. To return to Žižek, it's as if this truly supreme explosiveness is invisible to the theorist, who can only perceive a lesser, if undeniably, chilling explosiveness that is still very much embedded within the fabric of the diegesis. De Palma's explosiveness explodes the diegesis, whereas Coppola's, while heightening and intensifying it, firmly preserves it.

De Palma's in-your-face Hitchcockianism is one aspect of his style. Often, though, his Hitchcock references are rearticulated and reordered to the extent that they are unrecognizable as such. Hitchcock's jokes become De Palma tragedies, his tragedies De Palma jokes. Hitchcock's playful fireworks scene in the delicious *To Catch a Thief* (1955) ironizes Grace Kelly's ostensible display of her jewels, glittering on her far more lusciously displayed breasts, to the titular cat thief played by Cary Grant. The metaphorical display of orgasmic, explosive sexuality in the fireworks both intensifies and parodies the sexual tension in Kelly and Grant's banter. Fireworks in De Palma's 1981 *Blow Out* provide the backdrop for Jack Terry's (John Travolta) harrowing inability to rescue Sally Bedina (Nancy Allen), a woman he has put into peril in the first place. As the Liberty Day fireworks explode behind them in nighttime Philadelphia, Jack holds murdered Sally's lifeless body against his own. Conversely, the wrenching scene in *Rear Window* in which James Stewart's Jeff watches, in helpless panic from across the courtyard, the murderer Thorwald's discovery of Lisa Fremont (Grace Kelly again) in his apartment (he threatens her, knocking the lights out and plunging the whole scene into terrifying darkness), becomes in De Palma's *Body Double* a harrowing but also perversely humorous murder scene (the infamous power drill one) that the hapless hero (Craig Wasson) can do little to circumvent. The constant relay between terror and humor in De Palma refracts that in Hitchcock and takes the relay to a new level of postmodern play. But it does more than that—whereas in Hitchcock the humor very strategically alleviates the terror, it is the very relationship between terror and humor that becomes the drama of the De Palma film. The tension between the two modes is never more fully sustained or thematized than in *Dressed to Kill* (1980), a film that also draws out another underlying tension in Hitchcock, adumbrated in *Psycho*: the emergence of pornography within the form of mainstream cinematic narrative.

De Palma was one of the first film directors to treat Hitchcock as an established film grammar, a genre unto himself. By treating Hitchcock as a school rather than merely as a predecessor or competitor whose works could provide an example for commercial success, De Palma forced audiences to reconsider and relive the traumas and implications of Hitchcock's cinema. The "proper" way to use a predecessor is, apparently, to evoke certain effects and instances of technique, but not to dwell on them. Steven Spielberg's *Jaws* (1975) famously opens with a highly effective and disturbing variation on *Psycho*'s shower-murder sequence—the skinny-dipping girl's nighttime swim and murderous attack from the shark—but then proceeds to camouflage all of its borrowings from Hitchcock. If Spielberg makes use of Hitchcock, he does so only sparingly, such as, to give another example, his evocation of the Mount Rushmore sequence in *North by Northwest* in his *Close Encounters of the Third Kind* (1977), when the hero and his female ally try to scale Devil's Mountain surreptitiously. De Palma's use of

Hitchcock certainly isn't sparing; it's the whole meal. He recreates Hitchcock's major effects and then languorously, disturbingly distends them. In so doing, De Palma solicits criticism, but he also forces us to rethink Hitchcock and the work of the cinematic past generally. De Palma's metatextual meditations are not ends to themselves but, instead, tethered to much larger political and social concerns. And these concerns are with the gendered and sexual logic of patriarchy and what happens to individuals when they attempt to challenge and, much more threateningly, break free of the social order.

Psycho-sexual: De Palma and the Hitchcockian Thriller

Any one of De Palma's Hitchcockian thrillers—particularly from what is referred to as his Red Period, beginning with *Sisters* (1973), which signals both the advent of an explicitly intertextual relationship with the Hitchcock suspense genre and the persistent, even obsessive interest in the construction of the heroine, and concluding with *Body Double* (1984), though *Raising Cain, Snake Eyes, Femme Fatale*, and other works also obviously revisit Hitchcock thriller themes—can be taken as representative of his intertextual project and his aesthetic-political concerns. *Snake Eyes* is a kind of sequel to De Palma's early comedies and a culminating statement of his disposition towards normative masculinity. This is not to suggest that De Palma would not continue to offer such statements. The brilliant, largely misunderstood *Redacted* (2007) (which I am relieved to see justly valued in Robert Kolker's 2011 edition of *A Cinema of Loneliness*, even though Kolker's position towards De Palma's Hitchcockian films remains sadly unchanged), about a rape-murder during the current Iraq War, is in my view a much more incisive film about the gendered politics of war and imperialism than Kathryn Bigelow's 2009 *The Hurt Locker*, despite my admiration for Bigelow's previous work. (Indeed, I am left wondering what political value Bigelow's subsequent films will retain.)

What I will offer now is a treatment of what arguably remains De Palma's most controversial film, *Dressed to Kill*. It remains controversial primarily for the scene in which its seeming protagonist, Kate Miller (Angie Dickinson), is killed, like the heroine in *Psycho*, halfway through the picture. In a variation of the shower where Marion Crane (Janet Leigh) is murdered, *Dressed to Kill* contains a particularly savage murder scene set in an elevator, an appositely closed space. Reviled by feminist critics, this film, though a critical and commercial success in its day, has been largely ignored in most assessments of De Palma's career—left largely unmentioned, for example, by Eyal Peretz in *Becoming Visionary*. While I do not view it as the equal of De Palma's Hitchcockian thrillers of the 1970s, each of which I find to be a more successful work, *Dressed to Kill* is nevertheless a great if flawed film, and worthy of serious treatment. It is certainly worthy of much more scrupulous treatment for its representation of female sexuality than it has yet, for the most part, received.

De Palma is a 1960s counterculture believer in the myth of sex as liberation. He's also a tormented Catholic who struggles with the sense of sex as sin, a view that he defends against through the alternate strategies of idealization and coarse humor.[5] In my view, De Palma's depiction of women has often been misunderstood. Where others see a misogynistic hatred at work in his films, I view his position towards women as one of rivalrous and ambivalent identification. De Palma empathizes with women's position in patriarchy, affirms and identifies with their desire to transgress against its strictures, especially in matters of sexuality. Admittedly, he will then often—for the mingled reasons of his pessimism and his profound ambivalence—pull back to watch as the often dire if not utterly fatal ramifications of their intransigence unfold. In his great Hitchcockian films *Sisters*, *Obsession*, *Carrie*, *The Fury*, *Dressed to Kill*, and several films afterwards, women dominate the action and defy male power, even if the penalty is sometimes death.

Dressed to Kill's Kate Miller, played by Angie Dickinson, is a classic figure of ambivalent female identification for De Palma. It should be remembered that not only did De Palma write the original screenplay for this film but also wrote it after writing one for his own film version of Gerald Walker's 1970 novel *Cruising*. William Friedkin eventually made an equally brilliant and controversial film from this source material (discussed in the previous chapter). De Palma's script for *Cruising* has not been made available, but I find it hard to believe that a great deal of it didn't get repurposed in his original screenplay for *Dressed to Kill*. De Palma uses, I argue, gay male cruising as a template for heterosexual cruising in his film. Insofar as gay cruising haunts the heterosexual sexual gamesmanship and conquests of De Palma's film, gayness or gendered and sexual "deviance" as a generalized threat invades the realm of this apparently heterosexual thriller. It is revealed that Kate Miller's killer is Dr. Robert Elliott (Michael Caine), or, more properly, his psychotic alter ego "Bobbi." The post-looped voice of Bobbi—reminiscent of the killer's voice in *Cruising*—is provided by De Palma stalwart William Finley. Recalling the psychosexual and gendered confusions of Norman Bates, Bobbi wants to become a woman, and blames Dr. Elliott for circumventing his desires. "I'm a girl trapped in this man's body . . . and you're not helping me to get *out*." As Finley plays Bobbi, such lines begin at a falsetto pitch and end with a more masculinized growl, a microcosm of Bobbi's conflicts.

Kate Miller is presented sympathetically as a bored, restless, and deeply sexually unfulfilled housewife whose husband makes perfunctory love to her and dismounts her as soon as he has had an orgasm, ignoring her moans and obvious lack of sexual fulfillment. He kisses her and pats her on the cheek, a gesture that conveys his obtuseness about the force of her sexual needs. Her indifferent husband doesn't in any way seem to understand her need, deprivation, or her rage against him. She's left in her position on her back on their bed, still desperately hoping to achieve some satisfaction after pantomiming sexual ecstasy. De Palma aligns himself with those who are culturally silenced, here the sexual woman, inprisoned in her social roles. De Palma identifies with Kate's urgent need for affection, tenderness, and, most importantly, sexual release.

Known for his dream sequences and plot-bending narratives, De Palma teasingly begins *Dressed to Kill* with a sequence that would appear to be Kate's own masturbation dream-fantasy. It is also a set piece that establishes, much like the opening sequence of Hitchcock's *Vertigo*, the general preoccupations of the film. If Scottie's chase of the criminal over San Francisco rooftops, subsequent helpless position as he hangs suspended from the ledge of a building, and inadvertent causing of the death of a policeman who tries to help him all signal what is to follow—the pursuit of an inaccessible, elusive ideal; the suffering caused to others because of this pursuit; a state of helplessness on physical and metaphysical levels at once—Kate's shower scene appositely condenses *Dressed to Kill's* major themes: a woman's yearning for sexual excitement and release; a commitment to erotic, bodily, sensual pleasures; the ineluctable failure of men either to protect women or to treat them well; the threat of violence that inheres and terrifyingly manifests itself within scenes of sexual pleasure.

A great deal can be said about Hitchcock's, De Palma's, and Scorsese's Catholicism as illuminating explanations for their shared themes of sexual guilt. Beyond its Catholic themes, De Palma's work is a critique of the social order from which they emerge. The menace that interrupts erotic pleasure and ends Kate's life has, in my view, a different purpose from that commonly assigned to it in readings that take the elevator murder as evidence of De Palma's misogyny. This grisly murder represents—as do the killings in *Cruising*—an anticipatory sense on the part of a New Hollywood filmmaker that the permissiveness—cultural, social, sexual, aesthetic—of the 1960s and the 1970s was coming to an abrupt and jarring end with the birth of the reactionary 1980s.

Kate will successfully cruise and be cruised by a thirtysomething stud, Warren Lockman (Ken Baker), in the Metropolitan Museum of Art (actually filmed in its Philadelphia equivalent). Later that night in his apartment, Kate gets up to leave while he is sleeping. Before leaving, she stops at his desk to write him a note, variations of the message "I loved the afternoon. Maybe we'll meet again." On the desk as Kate writes her note (crumpling the first attempt, writing a new one in which she replaces "the" with "our") lies an issue of *Newsweek*, the cover of which reports Ted Kennedy's challenge to Jimmy Carter for the Democratic presidential nomination. One immediately registers the sexual scandal of Chappaquiddick from 1969, which De Palma will evoke in his next film *Blow Out*. If anything, though, Ted Kennedy was to the left of Jimmy Carter's liberal politics, and was one of the few Democratic challengers to a sitting president who had a real chance of winning. Whatever the specific import of this cover, in political terms, it alerts us to impending waves of change that affect even this post-coital scene presumably distant from changes in the national and political life. Far from evincing a reactionary, anti-woman sensibility, the menace and the murders in *Dressed to Kill* represent, in part, forces of cultural change that threaten to police against and otherwise circumvent sexual freedom. With uncanny precision, *Dressed to Kill* anticipates the sexual panic and moral condemnations—largely directed towards gays—of the imminent AIDS era. Indeed, Kate Miller is a martyr for sexual freedom. It is the post-1970s culture that surrounds her, rather than the film, that victimizes her because she seeks out this freedom. She is also, of course, a victim of a sexually tormented man's envy and retribution, a point to which we will return.

When Kate opens Lockman's drawer—a metaphor for sexual contact, clearly—and discovers an official document alerting Lockman to the fact that he has contracted a venereal disease, the linkage between sex and illness is jarring and also perversely funny. While it is predictable that many would read this touch as yet another misogynistic one, Kate being punished for her sexual adventurousness, in my view something other than misogyny is at work here. First, De Palma's perverse humor frequently links sexuality to humiliation and even bodily harm (*Carrie*, of course, but also Jake in *Body Double*). Further, innocent and sympathetic characters often encounter terrible, undeserved violent fates (Lisle Wilson in *Sisters*, Carrie Snodgrass in *The Fury*). Second, with uncanny prescience the film anticipates a new culture of morality and condemnation about matters of sex. In the pre-AIDS era, VD was as ominous a repercussion for sexual trysts as was imaginable. The possibility that Kate has contracted it suggests her fall into a culture of repressiveness and judgment about sexuality. At the same time, it shows that she continues to be victimized by the varieties of male arrogance and indifference to women's well-being.

De Palma's views of sexuality are deeply complex, and critics who would want to pigeonhole him as either sex-positive or -phobic will encounter difficulties with his work. Throughout a De Palma film, sex is presented at once as beguiling and menacing, irresistible and murderous. While De Palma, as I have established, is a 1960s counterculture champion of sex as liberation, he is also someone interested in extreme states of experience—sexual ecstasy and also the worst violence inflicted on the vulnerable human body imaginable. Perhaps most of all, he is fascinated by the emotional experiences of such extreme states. De Palma's films are deeply personal perhaps especially because they invite the audience to imagine, along with the director and his characters, the worst possibilities imaginable. But this dire fantasy is not a gratuitous one—it is tied to De Palma's political vision, consistently leftist throughout his career from the early anti-Vietnam comedies to the anti–Iraq War *Redacted*, of a society that crushes dissent and controls through

216

conformity. Breaking out of her pastel plastic world of conformity and sexual deprivation, Kate challenges the status quo of female sexuality. The problem is that, in doing so, she becomes enmeshed in a much larger, and, indeed, incomprehensible, network of transgression, prohibition, and rage-fueled, retaliatory violence.

A New Pornography: When the Woman Showers

The shower sexual fantasy at the start of the film alerts us to its irreality through its stylized, dreamlike atmosphere. This is a prime example of the way in which De Palma cites Hitchcock only to stretch out the quote to its delirious lengths while adding new thematic elements that revise and challenge Hitchcock's effects, themes, and aesthetics. Engulfing steam; Kate's pouting, Marilyn Monroe–like sexual performance—ostensibly for her husband Mike, shaving in the over-the-sink mirror, but really for the camera, for us—as she touches herself; the obvious use of a body double for Kate/Dickinson; and an overall pornographic ambience all add to the dreamy, sensual state into which the film plunges us right from the start. De Palma innovates not only the New Hollywood but also his own treatment of pornography in this sequence, which attempts to imagine a pornographic narrative cinema that emphasizes the pleasurable potentialities, rather than despair, of hard-core. De Palma's pornographic sensibility rejects the crudeness of hard-core while exploring its unprecedented, singular access to the body and to sexual experiences. *Dressed to Kill* is essentially an experimental film in its exploration of the possibilities of mainstream narrative film for the representation of sex, bodies, pleasure. De Palma's pornographic tableaux, however, is inescapably linked to violence and laced with menace.

We must first *enter* the steamy bathroom before we can see this scene of the sexual: the first shot of the film tracks towards the bathroom from within the Millers' bedroom, passing the unmade bed; the softened, bright light of the bathroom, streaming in from a yonic oval window that almost subliminally recalls the porthole window in the ship cabin in Hitchcock's *Marnie*—another film of fraught male-female relations—invitingly contrasts against the darkened aspect of the bedroom. This movement, investigating the bedroom, seeking out the marital couple in their nude luxuriance in the bathroom, accomplishes several thematic goals at once. *Obsession*, early on, puts us in the position of a young girl watching—looking up at—her parents as they dance at a lavish and celebratory party, a public scene of heterosexual, adult, and parental romance and sexuality that this girl witnesses with awe. *Dressed to Kill* reaches deeper into the viewer's unconscious, plunging us into the primal scene, forcing us to glimpse our symbolic screen parents having sexual intercourse, which image will be pointedly deferred. Kate will, among other things, be represented as a mother as well as a wife, her son Peter (Keith Gordon) a whiz-kid computer science geek (obviously a stand-in for the science-fair-winning geeky young De Palma) being one of the significant characters in the film. (*Unlike* Orestes in the *Oresteia*, he *avenges* rather than murders his adulterous, murdered mother.)

The image of Mike shaving in the mirror, a towel around his waist, is an iconic image of normative, paternal masculinity—a stoically expressionless face, a muscular upper body, no genital nudity—with two exceptions: he is Peter's adoptive father or stepfather ("My father died in the Vietnam War," Peter pointedly informs Dr. Elliott later, a telling echo of De Palma's early films), and the razor he wields looks exactly like that which Bobbi will sport when she/he slices up her/his victims. Indeed, in De Palma's original script for *Cruising*, that film would have opened with a man shaving more than his face; as his razor moves downward, each shot in extreme close-up, he also shaves his stomach. Then we see an extreme close-up of his razor "trembling over his pubic area." As the man closes his eyes, the razor "jerks below the frame," the man's "eyes snap with shocked pain," and then blood "streams down hairless thighs."[6] These queer psychosexual anxieties spill over into *Dressed to Kill*'s scenes of heterosexual eros. De Palma uses them to intensify those within male-female relations. Hetero-oedipal masculinity's claims to authority will be modified, linked to the queer, psychotic masculine. Moreover, Mike's shaving in the mirror reminds us that the scene of male narcissism is not the domain of queer masculinity alone. His indifference to Kate in the shower, in her autoerotic and beckoningly sexual poses or in her sudden peril, signals not only his lack of concern for her but also to his own indifference to his masculine roles as heterosexual seducer/seduced and father-husband-protector.

As a gay viewer, I feel that I should share something about my experience of De Palma's representations of femininity, Kate Miller in the shower in particular. I can imagine—and have experienced—several moments throughout my ardent moviegoing life in which such scenes of sexualized femininity have alienated me not only with their sexist, objectifying coarseness but also with their implicit (at their mildest) appeal to my presumed heterosexual desiring response. I can think of no other filmmaker who so thoroughly immerses me in the carnal beauty of women, no filmmaker who makes the sensual and erotic appeal of women's bodies more palpable, heady, and deliriously stimulating. Watching Kate in the shower, caressing herself, the idealized rosaceous soapy body-self of her fantasy, as the steam and the sounds of showering water visually and aurally intensify her ardent autoerotic spectacle, I feel myself at one with her desire and her body and with the spectacle overall.

I offer this especially personal response as a counterargument to the treatment of the film by theorists like Linda Williams.[7] Though throughout her important work Williams has striven to problematize the dismissals and cries for censorship of pornography from feminist critics in particular, Williams's treatment of De

Palma's pornography-minded cinema—a simultaneous evocation and critique of the genre—has been consistently and thoroughly unsympathetic. Williams does not take into account in her reading of *Dressed to Kill* that its images are presented for more than one kind of viewer, for more than the eyes of that hegemonic screen spectator the white heterosexual male.[8] More than many films do, *Dressed to Kill* works to solicit the queer gaze—the gay male gaze, the transgender gaze, and, I would argue, the lesbian gaze as well. Indeed, one of the odd effects of the body double in the shower is to create the impression that Kate/Dickinson is not merely caressing and stimulating herself but also a younger, *different* woman whose body she explores. In some shots, the middle-aged Kate's hands appear to be roaming over the breasts, stomach, belly button, and luxuriantly bushy vagina of a lushly young female body. Pino Donaggio, whose scores for De Palma's Hitchcockian thrillers enact the same kind of intertextual agon with Bernard Herrmann, Hitchcock's greatest composer-collaborator, that De Palma films do with Hitchcock, provides music that teasingly, obsessively intensifies the atmosphere of sexual abandon.

When the hunky, threatening young male figure appears and grabs Kate from behind—overpowering her, seeming to rape her, with a suggestion that he does so sodomitically, adding a queer valence—the violence is the climax to her masturbatory scenario. Of the many ways one could interpret this resolution to the scene, the one I offer is that Kate has, on some level, internalized the misogynistic messages of both her culture and of her relationship to her indifferent husband. Mike coldly looks over at Kate and at us. Along with her, we are violated, overpowered, rendered helpless. As we look at Mike for help along with Kate—the shot is from her point-of-view—the steam overpowers the image, so that not only is Mike obscured before the glass shower door but so are we, as well, from *his* view. There is no one to protect us, no father, no husband, as we yield to the rapist threat behind us. What makes this entire sequence so powerful is that not only are we invited to gaze with longing on Kate as the woman to be looked at, but we also look *through* her eyes, feeling what she feels, feeling, in the end, her powerlessness and her yearning for help. De Palma inhabits all of the contours of woman's experience—her desire, her sexuality, her cold treatment by indifferent patriarchy, her violation from the sudden appearance of a dangerous man—and puts us in her place.

By the time we get to the scene of actual lovemaking, which leaves Kate miserably unsatisfied, and which seems hardly terribly rousing to her husband, either, the trauma of the primal scene has been considerably diminished, parental sex rendered routine. Actual, rote couple sex can in no way match the intensity and danger of fantasy. In this manner, De Palma continues the Hitchcockian exploration of pornography that runs throughout his own work as well as the

New Hollywood. Pornography emerges here as a special realm through which desires and fears—on the part of a sexual and sexually unfulfilled woman—can be explored.

Read Her Desire: The Museum Sequence

Kate's relationship to her psychiatrist Dr. Elliott (Michael Caine) provides an ironic contrast to that with Mike. De Palma's original screenplays contain nearly as many facets as his visual schemes. When Elliott greets Kate for her appointment, he performs as his own receptionist, since Mary is out for the day. "I hope you're not going to keep me waiting long, I want to get to the museum early," Kate says, and he playfully reassures her with, "The doctor will see you now." These few brief lines establish that Kate is a bored but also pampered woman used to getting her own way (though not sexually) and subtly begins to suggest the feminine split in Elliott's personality. The all-white suit Kate wears, which Angie Dickinson's golden-blonde hair contrasts against so strikingly, suggests a Kubrickian Hitchcock aesthetic—an almost antiseptic, abstracted version of the Hitchcock fixation, the cool blonde. The aesthetic of the cool blonde's cool whiteness pointedly contrasts against her sexual passion and then, horrifyingly, her spilled blood.

In her session with the psychiatrist, Kate veers from expressions of a wearied, resigned loneliness to a testiness that stems from her deep sexual frustration with her husband. Elliott encourages her to "think about where your anger is going," which immediately triggers an "I'm sorry" from Kate, reaffirming her internalized sense of "maybe there's something wrong with me." "Stop apologizing," Dr. Elliott commands, "and tell Mike he makes you mad." "Tell him that he stinks in bed?" she responds, somewhat incredulously. Kate claims that she "moan[s] with pleasure at his touch," asking, quite rhetorically, "Isn't that what every man wants?" Dr. Elliott appears to be a sensitive psychiatrist, and an honorable man, who gives Kate good advice, telling her to communicate her sexual frustrations to her husband, and patiently explaining to Kate why he, Elliott, cannot sleep with her despite finding her attractive. ("Because I love my wife, and sleeping with you isn't worth jeopardizing my marriage. Is it worth it to you, to jeopardize yours?" Poignantly, Kate responds, simply, "I don't know." We never see Elliott's wife, though he mentions her again towards the end, when even more provocatively sexually solicited by Liz.) Yet Elliott is also the ultimate embodiment of the consistent De Palma trope of betrayal. In his alter ego guise as Bobbi, Elliott will annihilate Kate, precisely for having aroused him.

In the famous sequence set in the Metropolitan Museum of Art, Kate is cruised by a man, Warren Lockman, as she sits on a bench looking at art. Before he makes his appearance, she observes her fellow museum-goers. As she does so, she writes down items she should buy (eggnog, nuts, a turkey). Like that of

Angie Dickinson and Michael Caine in De Palma's *Dressed to Kill*: the psychiatrist is
both ally and menace; the woman is betrayed by males in positions of authority.

numerous characters in Hitchcock films, her life is a vacant one, all too brightly
lit up by the action she perceives in other people's lives. Kate appears to see her
lack of sexual fulfillment as the cause of her malaise, but De Palma, through that
deadeningly routine shopping list, alerts us to her socialization as a capitalist consumer as well.

221

The other people in the museum comprise a kind of disordered, bored-house-
wife version of *A Christmas Carol*. From Kate's point-of-view, we first see (all from
a distance) a young, blond heterosexual couple, arms around each other, looking at art work; a rather stiff youngish blonde woman looking up at a piece of
art who is then engaged in conversation by a guy who asks, "Do you come here
often?"; and an Asian family, the parent figures of which stare intently at a museum plan while their young daughter first pesters her mother ("Mommy!") and
then runs off transgressively by herself after being chastised and then ignored.
As Kate somewhat voyeuristically observes the ambient populace, she also alternately gazes at two paintings, one, by Alex Katz, of a woman, her head in her
hand, staring at the viewer; the other of a gorilla on a carpet (by an artist unknown to me). This palpably visual figure on the carpet is a particularly arresting
image: tightly clenching its body to fit into the constrictive spaces of the carpet
and the canvas, the simian beast looks absurd, confused, perhaps even mournful.
The woman in the Katz painting, with her quizzically challenging expression, appears to embody Kate's own restlessness, her will-I-or-won't-I indecision but also
her daring. Condignly, the gorilla represents aspects of Kate's own predicament,
the constrictiveness of her marriage and her own feelings of entrapment. Just as

Kate's sexual yearnings are too big for her confined, predictable life, the gorilla's girth exceeds the space allotted it.

The smiling, sexy young couple suggest the youthful promise of Kate's life, now spent. That the young man keeps transgressively squeezing his girlfriend's butt, and she keeps removing his hand for propriety's sake (a man, perhaps a guard, passes by and monitors them, though not in an unfriendly way) while also laughing, charmed as well as annoyed by the attentions, conveys a sense of playful male sexual interest in a woman, all of which are shown to be devoid from Kate's life. The guy hitting on the woman in the next metaphorical "panel" connotes this same sense of deprivation; the woman's initial lack of interest, however, suggests female sexual ambivalence. (Later, they will be seen walking together as Kate makes her disoriented, urgent way through the museum-maze.) The little girl breaking away from the disciplinary sternness of her mother—as well as the total indifference of her father—and running off on her own suggests Kate's own desire to break free. This girl also anticipates the eerie, silent girl, holding her mother's hand, who stares intensely at Kate in the elevator before she is murdered. All of these figures, flesh and blood, paint and canvas, form a pageant of possibilities lost and available to Kate, presented with great subtlety, not just by De Palma but also Angie Dickinson in her controlled yet richly felt, palpably emotional performance.

When the mid-thirtyish stud sits next to Kate, she immediately registers his erotic possibility, abetted by the way he places a pen against his lips. With his dark hair and tinted glasses, sport jacket and two-toned shoes, this man strikingly contrasts against Kate, with her stylish blond hair and white coat, blouse, and pants, gold bracelets and necklace, two-toned leather gloves, and taut, tan high heels. As Pauline Kael observed of the shot of their feet in their sleek shoes alongside each other, commodity fetishism dominates their interaction.[9] Gay male cruising— the background for De Palma's writing of his script for this film, given that he had previously attempted to make *Cruising*—provides the template for this very prolonged heterosexual pickup. The shot of Kate's and the man's paired shoes reminds us of the complementary shots of the shoes worn in Hitchcock's 1951 *Strangers on a Train* by Guy Haines (Farley Granger) and Bruno Anthony (Robert Walker)—straight Guy's monochromatically solid and sensible, queer Bruno's as two-toned and flashy as he is—and especially of the cruisy moment when the men's shoes tap against each other as they meet for the first time on the train (and it is Guy's shoe that does the initial tapping, significantly).

For whatever reason, exactly, Kate takes her left glove off, pretending to be nonchalant as she reveals her bare hand to the stud, unaware that her wedding ring now glints on one of her fingers. The stud immediately gets up and walks away, to Kate's left. Startled, Kate gets up to walk away in the opposite direction.

De Palma gives us a floor-level shot of her shoes turning precisely to the right, as if they had a militaristic life and precision of their own, adding to the ritualized aspect of this sexual game and each of its gestures. As she walks to her right, she passes by a Philip Pearlstein painting of a female nude, the figure's lower body and hairy vagina visible, contrasting against the precisely clothed Kate. Like the other paintings, the Pearlstein image pointedly comments on the action, recalling the image of the naked Kate in the shower, and once again substituting—as did the body double—for Kate's own body.

De Palma's camera glides before, alongside, behind, and around Kate as she makes her way through museum corridors and the paintings hanging on the walls, alternately in flight from and in pursuit of the stud, which suggests the competing desires of the female hysteric, simultaneously pulling up and pulling down her dress in the classical psychoanalytic image of the figure. The sequence works on many levels at once. It is a melodramatic exercise in female desire, with Donaggio's score recalling the emotionalism of classical Hollywood women's films.[10] The sequence is a precise allegory of female sexual desire's fate in male-dominated culture—the mazy routes and myriad obstructive walls contribute to a sense of entrapment. Like labyrinths, culture and desire, inescapable and un-navigable, entrap the woman.

The sequence is also a simultaneously harrowing and darkly humorous meditation on cruising. Cruising for sex isn't as easy as it seems. Odious Detective Marino (Dennis Franz, long before his NYPD *Blue* glory days) may believe that "there are a million ways to get killed in this city," but a considerably smaller number of ways to find sexual fulfillment exist. Far from ridiculing Kate's attempts at achieving sexual pleasure here, De Palma shares in it to a certain extent but also sees in it more philosophical, social implications—her pursuit of the erotic allegorizes her gendered social position as well as the elusiveness of sexual satisfaction.

In one of the strangest touches, the stud taps Kate's shoulder, and now *he* is wearing the glove that she dropped on the floor. As the entire sequence has suggested, his interest in her has a fetishistic quality. Indeed, *Dressed to Kill* may be said to be particularly concerned with the varieties of fetishism: straight, queer, and transgendered. Seemingly in defeat, Kate exits the museum and stands outside. The camera pans grandly to the left—from where Kate now stands on the front steps of the museum and throws away her *other* glove, to where the stud awaits in a Checker cab, waving Kate's glove at her as an invitation to join him. As the camera pans, it takes in the image of Bobbi—tall, blond, in black sunglasses, and long black leather coat, looking very similar to Karen Black in disguise in Hitchcock's 1976 black comedy *Family Plot*, Hitchcock's final film. (The first time one sees the film, the image of Bobbi will be registered on a subliminal level only, since we are not introduced to the character until later.) Like Hitchcock's last film, *Dressed to Kill* is particularly interested in the crisscrossing narratives of seemingly unrelated characters. It shares *Family Plot*'s vital fascination with the infinite variety of female identity. The various costumes (designed by Hitchcock's frequent collaborator, the famous Edith Head) donned by the criminal woman played by Karen Black—at one point, she wears a cream suit that Angie Dickinson's outfit in De Palma's film will evoke—send up the idea of femininity as a masquerade.[11]

In her blonde wig and in her fearless ability to coordinate kidnappings and other crimes, Black's character represents Hitchcock's self-conscious send-up of his legendary obsession with cool blondes. De Palma similarly takes the idea of the cool blonde to its breaking point—in both horrific and satirical terms—here. Moreover, the valences between *Family Plot* and *Dressed to Kill*, which I believe have been largely unnoticed, demonstrate that De Palma's films are in engagement with late Hitchcock as well as "classic" Hitchcock.

In another visual statement that links straight masculinity and queer and deviant forms of it, we see Bobbi, peripherally, picking up Kate's other glove. Trophies of femininity for both the straight and queer/transvestite/transgendered male, Kate's gloves materially embody classical tropes of heterosexual male fetishism, which, as Freud theorized, is a psychic technique on the male's part to overcome the trauma of his childhood realization that his mother was "castrated." Phallic attributes associated with women—noses, shoes, and here, textured, tactile gloves—restore the mother's phallus. The fullness of an inhabited female identity will become an increasingly significant idea in this film obsessed with gender and envy.

Once in the cab with the stranger, who pulls her in, Kate experiences what is, in my view, the most exhilarating orgasm in the cinema. Because she has been so very unsatisfied, her orgasmic release is especially transcendent. The stud does everything for her that her cold, stoic husband cannot or will not do. Kate's new lover lavishes attention on *her*. He nuzzles her nipples; he massages her legs and buttocks; he pulls off her panties, taking them past her legs and over her exquisitely arched high heels. And in a sublime moment, he reaches his hand between her legs, past her skirt, and presumably to her sex. In response, Kate cries out in ecstasy, a joyously exultant cry to which the city responds with the barbaric yawp of its blaring car horns. De Palma matches the anguished release of Jo Conway's/Doris Day's scream at the climax of the Albert Hall sequence in *The Man Who Knew Too Much* (1956) with the orgasmic release of Kate's transcendent cry of pleasure in the cab. This scene completely revises the nightmare nighttime world of "blood and come on the backseat" in *Taxi Driver* with a celebration of the carnal and the corporeal right in the sunlit center of the antic brazen hubbub of urban life. Adding to the transgressive thrills here, the cabdriver adjusts his

Karen Black in Hitchcock's *Family Plot*: delirious female masquerades and an undiscussed intertext for *Dressed to Kill*.

rearview mirror to take this sexual spectacle in; though conscious of the cab-driver's probably moralistic as well as prurient gaze, Kate achieves her orgasm undeterred. It is the last moment of genuine release and abandon in the film.

Institutional Power and Other Systems of Betrayal

When the stud takes Kate back to his apartment, De Palma cryptically pulls back the camera so that we can see the sleek, modernist building in which he lives, and as the camera pans vertically to the upper level at which his apartment is located, we shift from day to night. The whole effect is an ominous one: architecture has a foreboding, obdurate, unyielding relationship to scenes of the sexual, as it will again, and more elaborately, in De Palma's *Body Double*. This building seems to exist in a time and space entirely of its own; like the museum, it is a laboratory for experiments in modern sexualities, cold and pitiless. With the shift from day to night, we move from sexual joy to terror, violence, and death, all of which nega-tive forces are organized around the theme of betrayal.

As I argued earlier, the theme of betrayal in De Palma's work runs deep. Clear-ly, it stems in De Palma from two major intertexts: Christianity and Hitchcock's oeuvre. What De Palma and Hitchcock share, perhaps above all else, is a Catholic sensibility, which they intermesh with their Freudian understandings of sex, gen-der, and the body. Judas's betrayal of Jesus to the Jewish and Roman authorities—sealed with a kiss—informs all of the discursive histories of Christian thought. It is also a theme that informs American culture generally, especially the "oxymoronic oppressor," whose personal behavior belies his public role (historical examples include the religious leader who supported slavery) and who represent our social and moral paradoxes.[12] In De Palma films, the oxymoronic oppressor is usually someone in a position of authority who betrays the protagonist's trust, usually father figures who behave in anything but paternal ways, while also, for a great deal of the narrative, masquerading as the kindly, nurturing father, husband, doc-tor, or similar roles. Dr. Elliott is the ultimate oxymoronic oppressor in De Palma, recalling charming, murderous Dr. Murchison (Leo G. Carroll) in Hitchcock's 1945 film *Spellbound* (one of his least appreciated great films, driven, as is *Dressed to Kill*, by a woman's desire). What interests De Palma, I think, is the way in which Elliott can be so warm, suave, dashing, and intimately generous with Kate while also being the agent of her destruction. In *Spellbound*, Dr. Murchison mentors his young protégé psychiatrist Dr. Constance Petersen (Ingrid Bergman), align-ing himself with her against the crude sexism of their fellow psychiatrists at the mental asylum Green Manors. In the climax, he calls her a gifted psychiatrist but a "rather stupid woman," and attempts to kill her, before finally deciding to shoot himself.

Dr. Elliott's therapeutic nurturing of Kate recalls those scenes from the historical origins of classical psychoanalysis in which Freud counseled hysterical women, whose maladies and Freud's diagnosis of them provided the foundational beliefs of the emergent science, famously described by Freud's patient Anna O. as the "talking cure." His nurturing manner hideously contrasts against his murder of her. Elliott's hypocrisy would appear to be firmly locked within the paradigms of the Hitchcock gothic, yet it is one tile in a far larger mosaic. De Palma envisions America as an intricate web of lies and deceptions. This web is woven by the architects of the nation—like the figure of the President in his early *Greetings* who conscripts young American men into war while telling them "they never had it so good"—and then successively spun by all the nation's citizens.

More generally, the duplicity and hypocrisy of corrupt father figures stems from the tendencies toward these qualities inherent in the homosocial sphere and in the forms of institutionalized masculine power. The homosocial and patriarchy work as one—they are interlocking systems. Dr. Elliott's psychiatric power and the power of the police, embodied by the tacky, coarse Detective Marino—who casually sends the prostitute Liz Blake (Nancy Allen) into peril in order to solve the murder case—function together as the forms of irresponsible, untrustworthy institutionalized power, cultural and social systems in which individual lives flounder and the enterprising often meet untimely deaths. De Palma's next film, the starkly despairing *Blow Out* (1981), will make all of these themes especially salient and vivid. Jack Terry (John Travolta), a sound man for cheapjack, soft-core-porn horror movies like *Co-Ed Frenzy*, records the sounds of an accident in which a presidential candidate, McRyan, is killed. Jack saves the prostitute, Sally Bedina (Nancy Allen), who was in McRyan's car as it careened off a nighttime bridge into a lake. When he discovers that McRyan's accidental death was anything but, and that he was murdered by a rival candidate and his ring of conspirators, Jack attempts to expose the conspiracy, wiring Sally, before she meets with a TV reporter to give him all of his evidence, so that he can make sure that the reporter doesn't distort or misuse his evidence. But it turns out that Sally isn't meeting with the reporter at all, but with Burke (John Lithgow), the trained and sociopathic assassin who arranged McRyan's death, shooting out the tire of his car as it sped across a bridge, recalling the infamous Chappaquiddick scandal.

In the extraordinary sequence set during a nighttime fireworks display during Philadelphia's Liberty Day celebrations, which involve extensive parades, Jack attempts to save Sally, who desperately cries out from a rooftop, extending her hand outward in a gesture of indelible poignancy, but he gets there too late. (This shot of Sally crying out on the rooftop against the backdrop of a jingoistic flag is one of the signature images from De Palma's career.) Sally has already been murdered by Burke, and Jack can only kill Burke with his own knife. Jack's assignment at the start of the film was to find and record a better scream for *Co-Ed Frenzy*; by the end, he has found one, using Sally's piercing scream, which he recorded and still has on tape, for the horror movie. As Sally's horrifyingly authentic scream now pours out of the mouth of the actress in the cheesy horror flick, Jack attempts to drown out the sound, putting his hands over his ears, shutting his eyes tightly. This is a deeply anguishing aural assault and indelible image, but it is also an infuriating one—it is Jack who has supplied Sally's voice, his actions that have led, in part, to her death. What could be a greater violation of someone's integrity, spirit, personhood, and memory than to have their final moments of life before they are murdered transformed into a mass-market product, into schlock anonymity? De Palma makes us understand the full implications of his sympathetic hero's narcissism and moral callowness, but also makes sure that we understand that his failings only dimly mirror the far larger failings of the culture whose insidious corruption he attempted to expose. Murderous misogyny emerges as the culmination of this culture's levels of greed, corruption, and dehumanization, as the technological and commercial exploitation of Sally's suffering and screams harrowingly evince.

While these themes of betrayal and insidious corruption would not appear to be at work in the more playful *Dressed to Kill*, this film prefigures the nightmarish, paranoid, pessimistic world of *Blow Out*. And in this film, it is the women who must make their way through it. Outliers, renegades, wrenches in the system, enterprising, desiring women like Kate Miller and like Liz Blake (Nancy Allen), who witnesses Kate's final living moments in the elevator and, more or less, sets out to avenge her, find themselves attempting to navigate treacherous social worlds that open up to greater and greater levels of treachery, intrigue, betrayal, danger, and violence. Exposed, the social order in De Palma films proceeds to unmask itself perpetually, as new levels of hypocrisy and murderous danger widen before his resilient but often hopelessly outmatched protagonists.

For these reasons, the depictions of institutionalized spaces in De Palma films take on an especially charged, ominous relevance. The museum through which Kate attempts to bend the limits of the closed social order to fit her own desires; Warren Lockman's officious building within which women meet horrible deaths; the psychiatric office, tellingly placed at the basement level, where Dr. Elliott nurtures women he kills; the police station where suspects spy on each other and innocent bystanders are conscripted into their own possible deaths; the vast, winding, ghostly, blue-black darkness of the mental asylum where Dr. Elliott has been sentenced, its location in a dream sequence in no way mitigating its adherence to the overall themes of institutionalized corruption; the suburban house, a model of plush conformity and comfort always shown in darkened and foreboding aspect; and the bathroom, that site of purification, ritual, and familial intimacy, in De Palma as it was in Hitchcock a zone of despair, depravity, and violence: all of these spaces ultimately connote danger and death. Recall as well the institutional spaces of the asylum in *Sisters*, the Church of San Miniato in Florence in *Obsession*, the gym where the prom is held in *Carrie*, the Paragon Institute in *The Fury*, but also the apartments, family homes, bathrooms, kitchens, bedrooms, and other domestic, intimate spaces in each of these films as realms that promise one thing—security, protection, solace—and deliver something else. That something else is the perpetual revelation of the social order as a death-face, the grinning skull of social knowledge. That image leads us back to *Psycho*.

Psycho Revisited: Murder as a Crisis in Gender, Sexuality, and Form

With *Dressed to Kill*, De Palma set up the challenge for himself of reproducing the plot and several of the major themes of Hitchcock's *Psycho*: the criminal woman; the sexually conflicted male; the double narrative, split between two protagonists; murder as an act that bifurcates narrative as it brings all of these simmering elements to a head; a psychiatric "resolution"; and a final refusal of this resolution with a sequence that affirms the narrative's commitment to an essential bafflement over its own chief preoccupations. In terms of the last point, the final scene of Norman in the cell obliterates the psychiatrist's explanation of the film's events. Hollow in and of itself, the psychiatrist's explanation is no match for the harrowing images and words of the coda, which exceed all rational explanation. We see Norman, but only hear Mother's voice. Is Norman possessed by the ghost of his dead mother? Is he hiding behind her voice, or is her voice all that is left of him? Has he ever existed at all? Mother's duplicitous, self-serving voice represents the triumph of indifference. Norman's pinched and increasingly ghoulish face is consumed by another visage, his mother's grinning, skull-face, superimposed upon Norman's. This image is itself consumed by another, of the car being dragged out of the swamp. The car's appearance, the grillwork on the trunk, oddly evokes a face itself, grinning at mayhem and death. The bleakness of these images and of the terrible scenes of violence that preceded them suggest the end of the world, not the anodyne rational "closure" ostensibly offered by the psychiatrist.

Analogously, De Palma reproduces almost exactly the denouement scene in the police station with the psychiatrist explaining "what happened": Elliott's male side, his sexual arousal at women, blocked the female side of him, Bobbi, who wants to become a woman. And whenever this happened, "Bobbi got even," killing the women, like Kate, who aroused Elliott. But then the film sandbags us with an elaborate nightmare dream sequence, presumably from Liz's point of view since she wakes up screaming from it, in which Elliott, in an asylum, kills a nurse, the homicidal inmates cheering him on as he does so, and then proceeds to disrobe her and don her outfit. He then invades Peter Miller's house while Liz takes a shower. As Liz showers, she notices the pair of white sensible shoes Elliott wears in his nurse drag. As she vainly seeks a way to defend herself and emerges with great trepidation from the shower, she looks into the mirrored bathroom cabinet above the sink. Suddenly, Bobbi appears, in her customary long blonde wig, black sunglasses, and black jacket, and slices Liz's neck with Elliott's scalpel. Liz has become Kate Miller, the woman in the elevator whose murder she witnessed. At this point, Liz wakes up, screaming, and Peter rushes into the darkened bedroom to comfort her. She initially repels him in terror, then collapses in his arms, weeping, as the film ends. This final image reimagines the final one of Sue Snell (Amy Irving) waking up screaming in her mother's arms from the dream in which Carrie White's (Sissy Spacek's) bloody hand pulls Sue into Carrie's grave.

De Palma's reworking of the resolution-reversing coda from *Psycho* much more elaborately imagines the coda as a woman's nightmare. Though successfully emerging from her inevitable second confrontation with the killer at the climax, when Dr. Elliott, now in drag and wielding his razor, reveals himself to be Bobbi but is shot by the female detective, Ms. Luce, before he can dispatch Liz, Liz remains haunted, traumatized, by what she has lived through. If part of the point of the grisly asylum sequence in which Elliott murders the nurse and escapes is to establish that the psychiatrist is, far from a figure of persuasive authority, one of the legions of the homicidally mad, it places far less emphasis on Elliott's story than it does on Liz's continuing trauma. (The nurse-asylum scene is cited by Quentin Tarantino, a De Palma aficianado, in an early scene of *Kill Bill: Volume 1*. Dressed as a nurse in order to kill Uma Thurman, eye-patch-wearing Daryl Hannah saunters down the hospital aisle, improbably humming Bernard Herrmann's title track from *Twisted Nerve*.)

However profoundly affecting Hitchcock's coda is, it also erases the plight of the women victimized by the narrative, including Mrs. Bates, figured here as her terrifying, heartless "self," self-justifying, self-exonerating to the point of pitiless indifference. Unlike the novel by Robert Bloch, Hitchcock gives us no scene between Lila and Sam after they have learned what really happened; without this scene, Lila's grief is rendered only mutely and ambivalently in her reaction to the psychiatrist's maddeningly playful account of Norman's, or Mother's, story. In De Palma, the focus remains on the woman's experience. Liz is the heroine who survives, much like Carol Clover's famous horror film figure of the Final Girl; yet she continues to be assaulted by inescapable terrors, no less onerous for being psychic now rather than physical.

Indeed, by making his villain the psychiatrist, the figure who provided *resolution* in the Hitchcock film (though a resolution mocked by the coda), De Palma goes much further than Hitchcock in establishing the forms of institutionalized power as the real villains of the piece.[13] To clarify, I believe that in Hitchcock the psychiatrist's explanation is put there for those who might demand a rational explanation, for that class of moviegoers, the bane of Hitchcock's as well as De Palma's existence, who demand literal-minded logic and which Hitchcock named "The Plausibles." The genuine sensibility of the film lies not in the psychiatrist's jejeune explanation but in that overwhelmingly negative, imprisoning coda in which we witness Norman's final dissolution into Mother. Yet, though Hitchcock did indeed make the psychiatrist the villain in *Spellbound*, the shocking subject matter of *Psycho* makes the psychiatric explanation, however shallowly presented, on some level necessary: it's an out, a way for this subversive film to distance itself from the gendered and sexual torment it exposed within the heart of American life, in its most innocuous, rural settings. Not so in De Palma—there is no escape, no out, no sense of a larger authority providing moral and social justice, balance, relief, or escape. Unmoored, we cling to flailing Liz and Peter, far from the image of the typical woman or man, or of the normative heterosexual couple. Liz is a prostitute, and Peter is a highly idiosyncratic, ambiguous male figure whose own sexuality as well as gendered identity remains enigmatic.

One of *Dressed to Kill*'s major innovations of *Psycho* is that the real Norman Bates figure is not Dr. Elliott—or at least not him alone—but Kate Miller's computer-whiz kid, Peter. Like Norman in Anthony Perkins's superlatively nuanced interpretation, Peter, deftly played by Keith Gordon (who would go on to become a film and TV director, most notably on the Showtime series *Dexter*), is a shy, but charming, young man, who exists outside of normative male typing. Nerdy, childlike, with his massy, tousled hair and big eyeglasses, Peter seems barely a teenager. (His dark hair and eyebrows and pale skin associate him, however distantly, with the dark-haired young men in Hitchcock.) He shows, however, surprising pluck when he rescues Liz on the train from the stalking Bobbi, spraying him with a blinding white fluid.[14] The color and texture of this fluid cannot be overlooked; suggestive of semen and therefore of maleness, it functions here as the economy of masculinity, which Peter can bottle up and dispense at will as a technological product rather as something produced by his own body. Little wonder, then, that Bobbi, who despises masculinity, runs away from it, blinded and screaming. In the climax in which Liz attempts to gain access to Elliott's patient files in order to expose the killer, whom Liz and Peter believe to be one of Elliott's analysands, it is not Peter but Ms. Luce (Susannah Clemm), the female detective Marino has assigned to tail Liz, who saves her life. Most tellingly, in the scene between the denouement and the dream sequence in which Liz and Peter talk over the events in an upscale restaurant, Peter expresses avid interest in Liz's account of what will happen to Elliott, specifically of what Bobbi has longed for, sexual reassignment surgery. Gently, almost coyly urging her to tell him all the details of sex change surgery—which involves, as Liz describes it, a "vaginoplasty, to those in the know"—Peter grows more and more intrigued, finally saying that he's come up with a great new science project: "I can make a woman—out of me." Peter's gender fluidity is in no way questioned or challenged or patholo-gized by the film. Indeed, he offers an appealingly levelheaded contrast to the torment of the other characters, Elliott/Bobbi in particular.

That a man can envy a woman for her femininity and her sexuality was lost on the architect of the analytic system of which Dr. Elliott is the modern-day repre-sentative. For all of what I continue to feel is the considerable radicalism of his theories of sexuality, Freud relied on traditional and sexist models when it came to women and female sexuality, and his thinking on femininity, while much more complex than is usually allowed, suffered for it. Jacques Lacan, his French follower and reinterpreter, allowed us to make use of Freud's theory of penis envy—what the girl immediately feels when she sees the anatomical organ that endows the boy with his social privileges—as a general desire for power in culture, which always takes the form of the phallus, the abstracted form of male sexuality.

In his study *Symbolic Wounds: Puberty Rites and the Envious Male*, Bruno Bet-telheim provocatively explores the idea of "male envy" for certain (essentialist) qualities of womanhood, namely, its magical reproductive power. "If we could give greater recognition to boys' desires to bear children," he writes, " . . . our boys and men might feel less envy and anxious hostility towards girls and women . . . . The freer men are to acknowledge their positive wish to create life, and to emphasize their contribution to it, the less will they have to assert power through destructive inventions."[15] In his 1962 revision, Bettelheim adds that "It is exactly because that wish is so deeply repressed in modern man . . . that so many men escape into overt or unconscious homosexuality."[16] By emphasizing the gendered dissatisfaction in both sexes, Bettelheim anticipates Judith Butler's understanding of both sex and gender as cultural constructions. If both boys and girls chafe at their gendered assignments, the envious desire they feel for the other sex could be sublimated rage at being trapped within a defining and defined sex in the first place. At its most progressive, *Symbolic Wounds* does away with the misogynis-tic adherence to the phallogocentric ideology of penis envy, thereby displacing masculinity as the *sine qua non* of gendered life. Parsing what Freud referred to as the "great antithesis of the sexes," "the great enigma of the biological fact of the duality of the sexes," Bettelheim writes of becoming more and more convinced that *"one sex* [always] *feels envy in regard to the sexual organs and functions of the other."*[17] By making the phallus only *one* site of envy, and women's reproductive organs (and nurturing breasts) another, Bettelheim at least begins to allow us the opportunity to view envy as a shared predicament of gendered subjects.

Much more emphatically than *Psycho*—given its considerably distinct cultural context as well as De Palma's sensibility—*Dressed to Kill* makes the sexually conflicted psychotic male's violence against women much more clearly the result of his profound envy for her femininity. While Dr. Levy (David Margulies) explains that Bobbi killed in retaliation against Elliott's male side—the hardening of his penis in sexual arousal over women—another motivation presents itself: Bobbi's jealousy over Kate's comparative social and gendered and sexual freedoms. In her essay on Jonathan Demme's *The Silence of the Lambs* (1991), "The Transvestite as Monster," Julie Tharp, drawing on Daniel A. Harris's work on effeminacy, suggests that "it is far easier for women to cross gender boundaries than for men. Whereas women are perceived to be exercising their assertiveness, men who behave in an effeminate manner are thought to be imitating women."[18] Far more opprobrium logically extends to a male who actually wants to *be* a woman. This opprobrium and the monster's rage are in direct proportion. As is the horror movie's wont, the transgendered monster expresses his or her needs in the vilest ways possible, the killings foremost, but also in the hate-filled messages that Bobbi leaves on Dr. Elliott's answering machine, which De Palma brilliantly substitutes for *la voix acousmatique* of *Psycho*, the voice without a body, like Mrs. Bates, which we hear but is not shown to be issuing forth from her body. "Some blonde bitch saw me but I'll get her," Bobbi vows. "I'll cut those spying eyes out." As Demme's *Silence of the Lambs* will, and with equal controversy, also explore, transsexuals, in order to be approved for the sexual reassignment surgery, must undergo extensive psychological screenings. Part of what makes Bobbi so angry is not only that Elliott blocks his attempts to become a woman but that Bobbi must also submit himself to Dr. Levy's scrutiny; without Levy's approval, there will be no operation, and in effect, Bobbi's hideous violence is an attempt to blackmail Dr. Elliott into agreeing to undergo the surgery that will release Bobbi from her corporeal and gendered imprisonment. Both *Dressed to Kill* and *The Silence of the Lambs* appear to argue that the man who wishes to have a sex-change operation but is too violent to be approved for the surgery will retaliate against women, who comparatively seem to have it all. These fantasies of women's luxuriant power within and over social and sexual realms only fuel the killer's misogynistic and self-hating rage.

Bobbi's capture of Kate's glove is extraneous to the plot. But the detail is important thematically: it serves to alert us to Bobbi's fascination with Kate's femininity and also with her abilities to be a sexual woman. After all, Bobbi witnesses Kate getting into the cab with the stud and follows them up to his apartment, lying in wait for Kate. With harrowing irony, Bobbi envies the sexual freedom that Kate longs for herself on a daily basis and that she can only wield through great consternation. Does the rage that Bobbi unleashes on Kate stem from anti-woman bias or from unspeakably deep levels of longing and frustration? Certainly, films such as *Psycho*, *Dressed to Kill*, and *The Silence of the Lambs* present us with negative images of those on the outside of the normative: the desiring woman, the sexual free agent (Liz), the queer/transgendered male. But horror specializes in negative images, exploring human subjectivity at its worst, its most frightening. As Robin Wood wrote, in the context of De Palma's *Sisters*, what is significant in the horror film is its "time-honored tradition of making the monster emerge as the most sympathetic character and its emotional center."[19] While Bobbi is neither sympathetic nor the emotional center of the film, Dr. Elliott certainly is both sympathetic and a figure of audience identification, and in empathizing with him, we empathize with Bobbi as well.

The negative portrayal of queer masculinity here, as it is in *The Silence of the Lambs* as well as *Psycho* before it, reflects the social opprobrium such subjectivities endure rather than—I would say much more emphatically than—the phobic sensibilities of the filmmakers. Whatever phobic elements inhere in De Palma's construction of the monstrous Bobbi, his or her monstrousness and, most importantly, venomous rage also conveys decades—centuries, perhaps—of unheard queer rage.[20] To read the murder of Kate in the elevator, then, as the *sine qua non* of screen misogyny is seriously to distort the numerous levels of thematic and formal exploration at work in the film.

I believe that one rebuttal will be granted me at least a provisional legitimacy, though probably, and rightly, not an exculpatory one. In a metatextual, intertextual engagement with *Psycho* such as *Dressed to Kill*, the ambitious De Palma must find a way not only to match but to outmatch the Master in his most famous sequence. The enclosed space of the elevator appositely matches that of the shower in which Marion Crane is killed, although in De Palma the characters are not physically naked but clothed, and their apparel carries symbolic weight: Kate in her all-white outfit is all too obviously the sacrificial victim to Bobbi's confusions, represented by her exaggeratedly long blonde wig in particular. But what are we to make of the black sunglasses and leather jacket? Again, I would argue that these touches nod to *Cruising*, further enlarging the intertextual valences between both works, and corroborate gay male cruising as the suggestive backdrop for this scenario of illicit heterosexual relations and violence. Much like the killer in Friedkin's film, Bobbi later speaks in a voice that doesn't come out of his own body.

I would argue that the least defensible part of the murder scene is actually the Hitchcock agon dimension. Simply topping the Master with bloodier and grislier excessiveness seems a poor reason—an ideologically indefensible and suspect one—to create such a sequence. In my view, what justifies the sequence is its precise, terrifying articulation of the major themes of the film. The social order is governed by systems of masculine rationality, but such systems leave those deprived of power scrambling for recognition and pursuing compensatory fulfill- ments of myriad kinds. The horrible murder of Kate is not simply the gratuitous murder of a woman, and not some kind of retribution for her sexual lawlessness, but, rather, a crisis in the desiring motivations that impel the characters. Bobbi's unfulfilled desire to become a woman fatally intersects with Kate's attempts to feel like a natural woman again, a fulfilled, sexual woman. Annihilating Kate is also Bobbi's attempt to force her to recognize Bobbi's own quest for legitimacy. Wielding Dr. Elliott's phallic scalpel, Bobbi holds it up to Kate, forcing her to look at it before he slices her throat with it. This hideous moment goes far beyond simple ravenous bloodletting. It is a pointed gesture, in every way, forcing Kate to withstand the brute force of the phallic power that has oppressed Bobbi—a horrific version of Elliott's hardening penis, which obliterates Bobbi's existence. The murder can be understood as a disorganized expression, perhaps, of Bobbi's own fantasies and, possibly, fears of being under the knife during the sex-change operation for which she yearns. Nothing arbitrary or gratuitous characterizes this scene of excessive, excruciating, but symbolically freighted onscreen violence. Adding to the bewildering complexities of all of this, De Palma had the actress Susannah Clemm, who plays Ms. Luce, the detective assigned to protect Liz Blake, playing Bobbi in all scenes save the climactic one in Dr. Elliott's office. Subliminally, De Palma stages this murder scene as a battle to the death between rival femininities, the masculine woman cop and the sexually adventurous heterosexual woman. The murder, like the film, is lab work, a dissection of the conflicts in American models of gendered and sexual life.[21]

Three Women and a Girl

I would argue that *Dressed to Kill* is thematically very similar to Robert Altman's 1977 film *3 Women*, in my view one of the greatest films of the '70s. Overall, with the possible exception of Larry Cohen, De Palma and Altman are the only major directors of the '70s who consistently demonstrate an investment in strong women characters. Where De Palma differs from Altman, however, is in his delirious fascination with the erotic, which charges his representation of female sexuality.

In Altman's film, two young women, Millie (Shelley Duval, indelible here) and Pinky (Sissy Spacek) who work at a spa for elderly people form a friendship and become roommates; another woman, Willie (Janice Rule), an artist, draws odd, eerie, increasingly violent murals at the bottom of a swimming pool. The murals depict a race of animal-like humans or aliens in various contortions and attitudes of rage and coupling. The savage female figures all gather around an oppressive male figure who looms above them with an engorged phallus. Gradually, the women protagonists' identities appear to switch and then to merge. Particularly poignant is the characterization of Millie, as lonely and disconnected as Travis Bickle, yet who inspires Pinky's fervent efforts to win Millie's friendship. While most people ignore Millie, she initially ignores Pinky. Initially wan and winsome, Pinky, however, goes through a remarkable transformation, emerging from it a bawdy, selfish, fearsome woman who ignores the now desperately needy and attentive Millie. All the while, the pregnant artist Willie keeps drawing the increasingly ominous murals. By the end of this obsessively dreamlike film, the women have all transformed into a new kind of family in which Willie is a grandmotherly figure, protective of her symbolic granddaughter Pinky, whom the mother-like Millie chastises and disciplines. A summary cannot do justice to the unnerving power of this languid, chilling film.

The mother-daughter thematic of *3 Women* evokes psychoanalysis, the woman's film, and the horror film at once. While not a horror film per se, *3 Women* repeatedly references or pays homage to this genre, through stylized eerie set pieces, a dreamlike tonal atmosphere, and its theme of psychic dissolution and exchange. Evoking the tropes of psychoanalysis, Altman, who said he based his oneiric film on one of his own dreams, crafts a new-style woman's film that dramatically foregrounds Freudian themes. It demonstrates that "femininity" is a twentieth-century male fantasy from Freud forward as it shows how deep the investment in this fantasy runs.

Altman and De Palma are rarely discussed in the same context, but their preoccupations are quite coeval. Certainly, if *3 Women* is any indication, both Altman and De Palma share a fascination with strong women and pairs or groups of women. A pair of uncanny twins highlights *3 Women*, the central preoccupation of De Palma's *Sisters*. The directors would also seem to share an interest in violence and misogyny. While blood is not spilled on camera (except perhaps in the scene in which the artist Wille gives birth to a stillborn infant as Millie desperately attempts to help her, while Pinky simply stares implacably and also helplessly from a distance, even though Millie instructed her to go and get help), in every way *3 Women* is as brutal and violent a film as it is a hypnotic and moving one. In this tonal intermixture, it prefigures *Dressed to Kill*.

A satirical disposition is another commonality between the films—Altman's send-up of consumerism, embodied in Millie and her obsession with commercial products, catalogues, magazines, and trends, matches up against De Palma's depiction of Kate Miller as someone who leads an empty, commodity-focused life. ("Pick up turkey!" she pens in dramatic ink in her day planner as she sits in the museum; significantly, she jots no reactions down to any of the art works she beholds.) De Palma's critique of consumerism comes through in the comparison he makes—evoking in heterosexual terms the similar comparison Hitchcock draws in the opening scenes of *Strangers on a Train*—between Kate's and the museum stranger's shoes. Fetishized commodities fuel fantasy and function as the economy that binds human relationships. One also recalls how easily the vulnerable, sheltered Carrie is beguiled by the prom and its decorations ("So beautiful," she almost moans as she looks up at the gaily colored streamers on the rafters), as if it were itself the shimmering adult world of all possibilities.

I mention Altman here because I believe that throughout *Dressed to Kill*, but microcosmically in the elevator sequence, De Palma remakes, or, more appropriately, reinvents *3 Women*. De Palma has taken numerous lumps for his borrowings from other directors, but what critics continually misunderstand is that he is an intertextual filmmaker who makes films about the experience of the cinema and moviegoing. In many important respects, the museum, elevator, climactic, and denouement sequences all function as metacommentaries on the nature of the cinematic. In the museum, Kate is a spectator who gets drawn into someone else's movie, led inexorably into the passageways of another's desires, even as these desires mirror, reinforce, and trigger her own. The cabdriver watches the "movie" of Kate having sex with the museum stranger in the cab's rear-view mirror. Liz witnesses the spectacle of Kate's murder in the elevator as if Liz were watching a film; Peter and Ms. Luce watch, through a basement-level window, Bobbi making her reappearance and attempting to attack Liz during the highly cinematic rain-soaked, thunderstorm-laden climax; the inmates cheer Elliott's killing of the nurse in the asylum in the denouement as if they were watching an action sequence on a big screen; and so forth.

In the elevator sequence, De Palma fuses expressionist, surrealist, and Soviet montage techniques. In the manner of expressionism and especially surrealism, he distorts the images themselves and the film stock. At the same time, he manipulates the possibilities of Eisensteinian montage, subjecting it to his technique of slow motion, which is, along with the split-screen, a signature De Palma device. De Palma's slow motion montage allows us to take in each image and ponder its significance. It also demands that we ponder the significance of each image *in relation* to another image, and then to yet another. If Eisenstein, in the famous Odessa Steps sequence in *Battleship Potemkin*, rams contrapuntal images against one another to produce a startling effect through this juxtaposition, De Palma, instead, transmutes the Eisensteinian ferocity into languor, a distended, dreamlike disorientation.[22]

In the famous shower-murder sequence in *Psycho*, Hitchcock plays around with the nature of the film image, seducing us into believing that we see Marion Crane's body being cut and penetrated by Mother's long phallic knife. De Palma, especially in the unrated version of *Dressed to Kill* (which played in Europe, though not in the U.S., much to De Palma's chagrin) actually and very deliberately shows you Kate being cut, savagely, by her assailant in the elevator. De Palma replaces

Hitchcock's black and white color scheme with a vivid, *Marnie*-like red. He does what modern horror movies do, only more so: he takes implicit or muted effects in classical Hollywood to extremes of representation. If Hitchcock will not show us wounds, De Palma will show wounds in the process of being made; if Hitchcockian blood could only be shown in black and white, De Palma will make the blood on display shockingly vivid and red. (Of course, Hitchcock was himself working around, sending up, and challenging the Production Code and the conventions of propriety in his extremely stylized construction of the shower-murder. I am in no way suggesting that De Palma is exceeding Hitchcock in terms of the possibilities of stylization; rather, I am saying that, from the basis of Hitchcock's experiments with and innovations of style, De Palma is coming up with his own.)

Liz, in slow-motion montage, stares down at the crumpled, blood-on-white-garments body of Kate Miller lying on the floor of the elevator. But Kate also stares back at Liz and at us. De Palma's array and succession of close-ups—the close-up being a device that he uses quite sparingly, for the most dramatic effect—are expressionistically and surreally distorted. These unexpectedly extreme close-up images of not just faces but eyes, eyelashes, nostrils, mouths, and chins force us to rethink our way through the maze-like plan of images. The presentation of Kate's face—grimly bloodied, but in a theatrical, stylized manner that vaguely suggests a Kabuki mask—lends the entire moment a level of artifice and even camp.[23] Yet the haunting expression in Kate's eyes, especially in the sense that it conveys of some inscrutable and urgent message being transmitted to Liz, who takes up Kate's story, makes the moment poetic and poignant as well as unnerving. By giving the victimized woman a witness, and a witness who is another woman and will take up this dead woman's cause, De Palma pursues a feminist revision of Hitchcock. To be sure, Hitchcock also provides this feminist angle through the character of Lila Crane, Marion's sister, played by Vera Miles. Lila emerges as the female investigator who helps to solve the mystery of her sister's murder. But in De Palma, the exchange, the witnessing, and the avenging take place between women who share no biological ties.

Moreover, Liz is right there, with Kate, as she dies. De Palma's version of Sisterhood is Powerful occurs between women who are connected to each other not only because they are fellow women but simply because they are human beings who feel pain. The matching, eerie, dreamlike extreme close-ups of the women—Kate's imploring eyes, Liz's horrified and stunned expression—radically revises Hitchcock's shower sequence. In *Psycho*, what deepens the horror and terror is that Marion is completely alone save for her killer. In *Dressed to Kill*, what deepens the terribleness of Kate's murder is that it is witnessed by someone who can do nothing to stop it. Further, it is witnessed by a man who is indifferent to it. Liz, a high-class prostitute, waits for the elevator with a john. An enterprising businesswoman, Liz speaks to the john about Wall Street trading. Very much returning us to the early shower-fantasy sequence, the john is a middle-aged businessman type who physically as well as behaviorally recalls the indifferent Mike, unresponsive to Kate's screams of rape. The john takes one look at the scene of carnage in the elevator and runs away, down the same stairs from which Bobbi had spied on Kate getting into the elevator. Straight white men have little interest in helping or saving women in this film; the john not only does nothing to save Kate, but leaves defenseless Liz to confront the killer all by herself.

Liz's act of witnessing and the dangers it exposes to her throughout the remainder of the narrative suggest that the violence perpetrated against Kate is the violence perpetrated against all women, on some level, within the misogynistic, claustrophobic confines of patriarchy. The distortions and manipulations of cinematic technique serve the purpose here of creating an emotional and psychic sense of unity as well as division between the women, one dying and violated, one living and imperiled. If the cinematic technique alarmingly cuts up the represented bodies of the women, form matching content, it more resonantly works to unite these bodies and identities into one. Kate and Liz become mother and daughter, on a surface level, sisters on a deeper level, friends for a fleeting second, and most importantly women with a common enemy, the men in positions of power who betray them.

Adding to this feminist discourse, the apparently extraneous detail of the little girl in the elevator who stares at Kate is quite a telling one. Having fled Warren Lockman's apartment once she discovers that he has recently received a notice telling him that he has a venereal disease (again, I won't attempt to exculpate De Palma for his sick sense of humor, but as I have suggested, this touch has some political dimensions that should be considered), Kate rides the elevator down to the ground floor. (The killer watches her getting into the elevator from a fire exit door that glows an infernal red.) But then she remembers that she left her wedding ring in Lockman's seventh-floor apartment, and goes back up to retrieve it. The door opens on another floor before she can get back up to the apartment, and in walks a woman with her young, dark-haired daughter. Almost instantly, the little girl stares at Kate, in a deeply unnerving manner that makes Kate, already upset, visibly uncomfortable. More than this, it seems to make her deeply sad. The mother bends down and tells the little girl that it isn't polite to stare, but the girl, hesitant only for a second, cannot—or will not—stop staring at Kate. That this is a mother-daughter pair, literally, is significant to the connection that will develop between Kate and Liz, even if this connection is most significant for not being biological, and also significant when we think of the crucial importance of mother-daughter relationships in previous De Palma films, symbolic in *Sisters*, ghostly in *Obsession*, profoundly familial and central in *Carrie*.

Feelings of guilt and shame seem to suffuse Kate as the little girl stares at her, staring at her even as her mother leads her out of the elevator and the building, chastising her once more. Peeping Toms come in all shapes, sizes, and genders. But the import of the little girl relates to the allegorical design of the film. As I suggested of the museum sequence, the various personae Kate observes in the museum seem like allegorical representations of her past, present, and future selves. They also represent her desires, fulfilled or balked. So, too, does this little, scopophilic girl suggest a stage in Kate's life, her own girlhood perhaps. Perhaps the little girl is an eerie, uncanny figure of warning and prophecy, impelling Kate not to go to the seventh floor. Or, the little girl is the face of social shame, her eyes communicating judgment and even disgust. In any event, the moment with the girl deepens the film's themes of female desire and entrapment and female-female relationships. It should also be noted that the staring girl has a precedent in the little Asian girl, also disciplined by her mother, in the museum. Between them, these distinct yet similar girls signify a female intransigence: a willfulness, a refusal to play by the rules that may get them into trouble but that they maintain anyway. And, even more eerily, both of these girls seem to be messengers of chaos and death. Uncannily, the misbehaving, running girl in the museum, once she runs past Kate and to the right of the screen, her footsteps reverberating (and vaguely echoing the children running from the schoolhouse in *The Birds*), seems to bring the museum stranger with her, depositing him on the bench next to Kate. In a way, the elevator girl similarly seems to "bring" the killer into contact with Kate, or vice versa. Either way, the girl figure signifies unity and division at once, embodying the woman's desire and functioning as a harbinger of the woman's fall into danger and encounter with doom.

And then we have the "third woman," the killer, the blond in the leather jacket, Bobbi, who here is played by Susannah Clemm, who also plays the female detective Ms. Luce. In De Palma's original (unrated) version, Bobbi holds the razor up to Kate's face, forcing her to look at it, before slashing her face with it. The entire murder is a horrific evocation of gendered envy but also retribution—Bobbi taunts Kate with a phallic power that the hyperfeminine Kate does not possess. Or perhaps her gesture is meant to expose Kate to the horror and ugliness of the phallus itself before inflicting these directly upon her. Bobbi holds a funhouse mirror up to both Kate and Liz. She is a nightmarish image of female power and desire run amok who represents the dark side of their own desires, on the one hand, and attempts to exert and maintain agency, on the other hand. Of course, Bobbi is also an image of the monstrousness of the gender-ambiguous male, although on the first viewing of the film, this aspect of the character does not register immediately.

While homophobic as well as misogynistic aspects in the representation cannot be simply dismissed, I believe that overall De Palma's vision, however horrifying, is one of anguish and bewilderment. Gender and sexuality, which become hopelessly enmeshed with violence, are themselves dreamlike, uncanny mysteries that defy logic. The techniques of slow motion montage and distorted images serve to link not only Kate and Liz but also both women to the image of the killer/Bobbi. These women are like the tripartite image of women as mother, wife, and death in Freud's 1913 essay "The Theme of the Three Caskets." Bobbi also emerges as the "death-mother" who brings not the male but the *female* subject to her end. (Of course, looked at another way, she desires nothing more than the death of her own masculinity, embodied in Dr. Elliott, Bobbi's "masculine side," whose sexual potency sends Bobbi into vengeful fury.)[24]

This aspect of Bobbi's role comes through most vividly in the denouement, when dreaming Liz, in the steamy shower as Kate had been at the start, sees Bobbi in full blond wig and leather regalia in the mirror before Bobbi slits Liz's throat. As Liz stands alone in the tub, resourceful but outmatched, she evokes an Expressionist nude, heartbreakingly vulnerable, exposed, and defenseless. Bobbi, "feminine" yet driven by phallic rage, represents some unknowable, unthinkable disturbance in feminine identity. She, or he, or some entity between these gendered polarities, represents the full range of identity's pleasures and terrors— masks, masquerades, cross-dressing, drag, despair, violence, death. The modern, independent woman who exerts her own agency remains haunted by the nightmarish image of feminine power and gender ambiguity at once. To my mind, these are astonishingly resonant riffs on the feminine-versus-the-queer thematic that I argue is central to Hitchcock films. It seems to me that De Palma comes up with, if not the "proper" way to remake Hitchcock, certainly a dynamic one. In radically enlarging even as he preserves the cell-like enclosure of the physical and emotional spaces of Hitchcock's shower-murder scene in his scenes in the elevator and the bathroom (and the museum and the cab and the doctor's office), De Palma enlarges and revises the gendered commentary in Hitchcock to include a wider range of intersubjective possibilities, desires, and political implications.

Female Narcissism and Transgendered Desire

In conclusion, I wish to draw our attention to perhaps the most important sequence in *Dressed to Kill*, though one easily overlooked. (Robin Wood also discusses it in his treatment of De Palma in *Hollywood from Vietnam to Reagan*.) In De Palma's characteristic use of the split-screen—the device, along with his use of slow motion, through which he most forcefully establishes his directorial sensibility as distinct from Hitchcock—we see, on the right side of the screen, Nancy

241

Allen's Liz, the business-savvy hooker, engaging in two conversations at once, one with her art broker, from whom she gets advice on which art works to invest in, and the other with her high-priced call-girl madam, as Dr. Elliott listens, on the left side of the screen, to one of Bobbi's messages. Both Liz and Elliott have their televisions on; the same program, an episode of the *Phil Donahue Show* in which Donahue interviews Nancy Hunt, née Ridgely Hunt, a male-to-female transsexual, plays on both of their television screens. This extraordinarily subtle sequence provides, much like the elevator murder, a microcosmic meditation on the film's themes.

Liz, a marvellously distinct characterization from De Palma and Allen, juggles roles with an aplomb that illuminates some of the film's gendered concerns. On the phone with her art broker, she is tough, taut, direct, in a word, masculine. With her madam, she is soft, giggly, enthusiastic, almost girlish, especially in that she manipulates this mother figure of sorts into giving her additional call-girl assignments by saying that she needs "$1000 for my mother's operation." Unlike the mother-obsessed (literally and symbolically) psychos of the slasher horror film, Liz manipulates the fiction of an unseen mother with pressing needs without any emotional investment in the fiction. She is able to use the iconic image of Mother for her own advantage, and to *manipulate* Mother in the guise of the madam, a symbolic mother who "feeds" Liz, for her own ends. In terms of gender fluidity, Liz's effortless ability to oscillate between the sweet daughterly voice and the tough, masculine businesswoman's voice is especially striking; she can move between gendered identities with ease, unlike Elliott/Bobbi. In contrast, Elliott silently listens to Bobbi's—his own—venomous rantings and then also silently listens to and watches the television program with Nancy Hunt. As Elliott listens to and watches the show, he does so intently, paying it close attention; Liz doesn't pay attention to the show at all, treating it as background noise.

As the show plays out in Liz's apartment, she looks at herself in a three-piece tabletop mirror, applying her make-up. This is a classic representation of female narcissism, one with deep roots in the Western tradition, which has historically represented Woman as vain and shallow, easily seduced by surfaces (think of Milton's Eve, falling in love with her own reflection before being socialized into proper submission to Adam by him and by God). Like the split-screen, the three-piece mirror splits Liz's image; indeed, it trifurcates it, suggesting the depth of her self-fascination.

Of all of Freud's theories about femininity, perhaps the one that has inspired the most positive feminist recuperation has been his theory of female narcissism. Women, Freud notes in his famous 1914 essay "On Narcissism: An Introduction," "especially if they grow up with good looks, develop a certain self-contentment which compensates them for the social restrictions that are imposed upon them in their choice of object. Strictly speaking," Freud continues, "it is only themselves that such women love with an intensity comparable to that of the man's love for them. Nor does their need lie in the direction of loving, but of being loved; and the man who fulfils this condition is the one who finds favour with them."[25] Several of Freud's insights illuminate this sequence: female narcissism is a defense against and a means of negotiating at least a partial satisfaction from a social order founded on gender hierarchies; and narcissism in others is attractive.[26]

Freud's narcissistic woman may be arming herself with the attributes of the very phallocratic order that imprisons her within its gender hierarchies, but she nevertheless fights toward something like a personal, self-determined version of gendered subjectivity in her narcissistic project. Liz, who applies make-up with practiced skill, transforming herself into a sexual commodity, takes charge of her own sexuality, using male desire as the currency through which she pursues her real objects of desire, art works or, more properly, the financial rewards they will return as investments. No indication is made in the film that she sexually desires men, or women, for that matter; unlike Kate, Liz longs for capital, not sexual fulfillment, seeing sex as a means to this end. She channels her sexual energies into her image of herself as a successful art-collector, a player in the fields of ac-quisition and investments. Liz's character recalls the "fast-talking dames" of '30s Hollywood, but she also represents, in her own way, a different version of Marion Crane while being placed in the structural position of her Lila Crane, who investi-gates her sister's disappearance in *Psycho*.[27] Kate Miller and Marion Crane share a desire for romantic-sexual fulfillment, romantic in Marion's case (it doesn't appear that she and Sam have difficulty having sex), sexual in Kate's. Their foray into the criminal and the sexually illicit, respectively, is motivated by the urgency of their desire for men, for marriage to a man in Marion's case, for respite from her pas-sionless marriage in Kate's. Liz, however, wants neither marriage nor sex. Arming herself with make-up before she goes out to have sex with men who pay her for the privilege, Liz manipulates the social order's own construction of womanhood and femininity, turning herself into an image-icon of femininity with the most market appeal, deploying femininity to gain the most profit. In this regard, she recalls Hitchcock's Marnie (Tippi Hedren), who similarly constructs an appealing image of herself in order to get money from beguiled businessmen. Yet Marnie really *is* getting money for her mother. And whereas Marnie's responses to men and to heterosexuality are shown to be balked as a result of childhood trauma, Liz doesn't seem to see sex as a big deal one way or another; for her, it's simply a job.

All of this makes her performance for Dr. Elliott in his office in the climax especially interesting. Faking a need to see him for therapeutic reasons, she con-cocts an extremely pornographic dream-narrative about being raped by a "big" man with appositely large genitalia; she then proceeds to strip down and present herself in fetishistic sexual regalia to Elliott, all in an effort to distract him from her real purpose, getting at his patient files. For his part, despite initial conscientious objections, Dr. Elliott is easily seduced, looking at himself in the mirror with an enigmatic and erotic smile as Liz claims to be further undressing. The gothic thunderstorm outside, the lightning that glints against the desktop mirror in which Elliott looks at himself, lends the moment an eerie perversity. Male sexuality in this film, Elliott's in particular, strikes discordant, ominous notes: there's something wrong with it. The apparitional but thoroughly menacing man in the shower at the start, the intensity of the stud's appearance on the bench beside Kate in the museum, and now Elliott's participation in heterosexual sex and seduction all convey a sense of male sexuality as disruptive, intrusive, overwhelming, or just plain weird.

De Palma's distinctive split-screen technique takes on an especially charged metaphorical relevance in *Dressed to Kill*. He counterbalances Liz's scene of female narcissistic desire against Dr. Elliott's immersion in the program they both watch about the transsexual woman. De Palma used the split-screen in *Sisters* (1973), his first great film, to contrast the two styles of femininity on display here, Grace Collier (Jennifer Salt), the modern, feminist, independent woman newspaper reporter, and Danielle Breton (Margot Kidder), the essentialist siren, an actress who seduces men with conventional artful female wiles. In a striking contrast effected by the split-screen, Grace tangles with two skeptical police detectives about the murder she has just seen in Danielle's apartment while Danielle carefully applies makeup to her face in a mirror: the contemporary professional woman's struggles with male sexism is juxtaposed against the traditionally sexy woman's *ars erotica*, her manipulation of the surfaces of femininity for seductive sexual ends. In the famous split-screen prom-destruction sequence in *Carrie*, the film makes the daring decision to employ a split-screen just at the moment of greatest narrative tension and release, dissociating us from the horror that ensues as its heroine unleashes her apocalyptic wrath. Yet the prom sequence is only the most explicit and well-known manifestation of the theme of splitting in *Carrie*. Throughout the film—as he does throughout his career—De Palma creates images that split themselves, bifurcated views in which one or several characters are cut off from, in opposition to, or in a mirroring relationship to the others, often through his use of the split-screen but through other methods as well, such as the split-diopter lens.

Both Liz's and Elliott's respective quests—if we can see Bobbi's quest to become a woman as also paradoxically Elliott's quest, even though he resists it—are symbolized by the transsexual Nancy Hunt's story insofar as it is related to us by the *Phil Donahue Show* episode. Donahue, classic sensitive liberal that he is, interrupts himself as he says to Nancy that she led a "normal—I guess that's a prejudicial way to put it—traditional heterosexual lifestyle." Nancy responds, laughing, "Oh, I've always been a devout heterosexual." The transsexual woman's heroic efforts to live her life as the person she is, to transcend the impositions of her anatomy, mirrors the efforts made by Kate, Bobbi, and Liz, and perhaps Elliott and Peter as well, to free themselves from the social and cultural constrictions that impose themselves upon, indeed, imprison, the sexual and gendered lives of social subjectivities. Unlike Marion Crane or Kate Miller, or Bobbi/Elliott, Liz Blake manages, more or less, to enjoy an existence in which she pursues her own ends, makes up her own rules, and manipulates the social/cultural constrictions on sex and gender for her own purposes. Yet what is poignant in this sequence, and in the film as a whole, is the sense of the cost and the dangers of seeking out one's own desiring pleasure in a culture in which such pursuits and pleasure itself are so narrowly constricted.

A great deal more needs to be said about this film and about De Palma as a whole. I would compare *Dressed to Kill* favorably to Luis Buñuel's astonishingly overvalued *Belle de Jour* (1967), another film about a bored and sexually adventurous housewife, but one made without the emotional plangency that De Palma brings to his vision. Catherine Deneuve's transformation into a prostitute at a local brothel in *Belle de Jour* is a cinematic enactment of the male fantasy that women's secret desire is to get down and dirty. In *Dressed to Kill*, Kate Miller's desire for sexual pleasure has little to do with male fantasy, and everything to do with her own desires for pleasure, connection, and attention. Her plight speaks to the discontentment with male desire that runs throughout the films we have discussed, a discontentment that takes many and varied forms and that, overall, challenges the notion that Hollywood films chiefly support the needs and demands of hegemonic manhood.

IDEOLOGY AT AN IMPASSE

HROUGHOUT THIS BOOK, I have attempted to demonstrate the possibilities of aesthetic and emotional engagement with movies while also demonstrating why I find critical approaches that proceed from identity politics frustrating and delimiting. As a gay man with a multiracial, immigrant, and working-class background, I am particularly bewildered, at times, by the number of earnest critics who have told me what kind of art and popular culture I should love. At the same time, however, I believe that I speak from queer theory and feminist perspectives. It is important to consider ideological and political matters in any critique of representation. To fail to do so is to ignore, obfuscate, diminish, blunt, and otherwise denature the importance of representation to human life and understanding. To fail to do so is to enter into the kind of aggressive and willfully insensitive traps of critics like Camille Paglia, who take an understandable opposition to leftist academic dogma to such a thoughtless degree of rhetorical extremism as to be largely useless as an oppositional voice. In other words, Paglia isn't the answer, and I say this despite my love for her early work. It is important, I feel, to establish why I wouldn't want criticism to embrace her principles, such as they are, while also taking another opportunity, for the sake of clarity, to articulate my positions in this book.

Paglia announces in her collection of occasional pieces *Vamps & Tramps* that she wants "a revamped feminism." She's not thrilled with queer theory, either.

I also want a revamped feminism and queer theory. I don't, however, want the same versions of either that Paglia does. Her 1990 book *Sexual Personae* continues to thrill me in its range and daring. Paglia's subsequent work, however, especially in a popular vein, has been notable chiefly for its brazen incoherence but, more frustratingly, its irresponsible politics, a lurid blend of the perverse and the reactionary that isn't always as much fun as it sounds. Take, for example, Paglia on the murdered young gay man Matthew Shepard and the significance of cruising, which seems particularly relevant to this book:

> Cruising isn't love; it's hunting—where the stalker can suddenly become the prey. This game is sensationally exciting, but it comes with heavy risks, including death. As a lesbian with a male brain, I see the hypnotic allure of cruising and have indeed celebrated it as gay men's heroic act of defiance against (as D. H. Lawrence would put it) home and mother and everything in morality and custom that enslaves the sex impulse.
>
> But let's get real. On the biological level, constant cruising illustrates Mother Nature's profound sex differences: Men do it, and women don't. On the psychological level, cruising shows that gay men are perpetually hungry for a masculinity that should reside confidently within them but clearly does not. What exactly was Matthew Shepard looking for when, after living in Europe and on the East Coast, he returned to his father's macho alma mater at the University of Wyoming? What symbolic family drama of reconciliation or profanation was at work? Until gay activism gets some psychological depth (available to us through great literature and art), it will have nothing persuasive to say about gay life.[1]

While I agree with Paglia about the importance of art to understanding human experience, and while I also agree with her that bland liberal pieties often blunt the vitality of art as well as sexuality, her politics seem driven by an incessant need to shock her presumably complacent audience. Moreover, she exhibits so little compassion for the subjects she speaks of that she ends up brutalizing them anew. The murdered Matthew Shepard neither needs nor deserves Paglia's attempt to enthrone him as a Genet-like sexual outlaw.

This seems to me an entirely obvious point to make, but one that seems lost on the increasingly erratic Paglia: an enormous distinction exists between art and life. Life isn't a movie—thank God. I may feel enraptured by the darkly, disturbingly sensual allure of a work like *Cruising*, but I wouldn't want what it has to "say" about sexuality, gay men, or its titular activity to legislate the human experience of these realities. We go to movies to experience states of play and siege unavailable to us in life, often for good reason. When Northrup Frye was describing the power of Shakespeare's valedictory play *The Tempest*, he was describing the power and the allure of all art: "The play is an illusion like the dream, and yet a focus of reality more intense than life affords." At its most evocative, the dream-world of film paradoxically makes life more real, more palpable, more intense. Yet to confuse the movies, with their brazen access to the unconscious, with real life is a very great mistake. There's a world of difference between submitting to the pull of a film like *Cruising* and believing that someone who goes out cruising for sex gets what they were looking for if the rough trade they pick up savagely murders them.

In championing the power of great art to illuminate the shadowy recesses of what motivates our desires, as I have tried to do in this book, I have been making the case that art promiscuously fails to heed the strictures that academic criticism—which is to say, ideological criticism—has chosen to impose on it. Unfortunately, the academic criticism that does not impose these strictures—which extend into orthodoxy the necessary demands for ethically responsible representation of historically oppressed groups like women and racial and sexual minorities—often maintains a dismissive or blithely ignorant attitude towards the questions raised by ideologically minded, theoretically inflected criticism. The rejection of ideology for the sake of aesthetics, philosophical ruminations, and the like has not been an entirely satisfactory alternative, either. So we find ourselves at a maddening impasse: either we perpetuate the PC approach to film art that has been so onerously constrictive for anyone with a passion for movies, or we pursue the route, increasingly attractive to some, of aesthetics without ideology or theory, without a concern for the ethics of representation, though these ethics have a very deep impact on the lives of actual living, breathing, feeling subjects. Let me quickly add that, writing self-consciously in a polemical vein here, I am quite aware that I am failing to do justice to the nuanced, idiosyncratic, and often quite vital work done in both of these critical schools.

In my experience, academics tend to take one of two approaches to film, especially in its Hollywood context: either regarding all films made within the industry with suspicion, or treating all Hollywood films like barbarously lively spectacles in which one can be happily freed from all thought. Certainly, many Hollywood films deserve the former attitude and openly solicit the latter. Yet time and again throughout the decades, there have been works of Hollywood film that achieve the highest level of art and sophistication, *and* present us with provocative political challenges as they offer penetrating—though also often disorganized—political critique. Ideological criticism, with its focus on positive images (but only positive images of the oppressed; one assumes that positive images of rich, happy white people would be its own form of blatant oppression), has presented film, especially in its mainstream form, as an endless train of grotesquely offensive images. It's almost as if the mere act of photographing someone, to wax Sontagian, is a violation so deep that only a committed and pervasive ideological defense against such images can withstand their assault.

It remains vitally important to question the ethics of film representation, to critique the means whereby film, our national mirror, especially in its Hollywood form, chooses to construct identity. But as a mirror, Hollywood films only provide a reflection—a very alluring and sometimes irresistible reflection—of its audiences and their concerns; they are not themselves actual life. And as a reflection, a dreamworld, films function according to their own logic, indifferent to the demand we place on them for responsible representation. We should try to resist repeating the mirror stage with every film we see—of identifying too completely with the image of ourselves as we are or would like to be on the screen. We should recognize these cinematic personages *as* images, as reflections, as mirrors, and stop mistaking them for real life.

Films such as those discussed in this study will repay the literal-minded approach inherent in ideological criticism by confirming this criticism's central tenets. Read literally, these films do indeed reflect misogynistic, racist, and homophobic attitudes; they often present women as victims, and indulge in racial and sexual caricatures. But I have been arguing that many works cannot be understood if read literally. This is not to suggest that literal-minded films aren't made by Hollywood—indeed, it is fair to say that most Hollywood works, especially of the present, are deeply literal-minded—only that the works I discuss here are not among them.

Perhaps it's perverse, but directors like Hitchcock and De Palma who put female characters in perilous situations often exhibit—to my mind at least—much more concern for and, even more importantly, interest in female subjectivity than many other directors do. Analogously, few films have captured the heat, danger, and excitement of gay male sexuality in the way that Friedkin's *Cruising* does, especially significant considering that it was made on the cusp of the Reagan revolution's extraordinarily successful conservative makeover of the United States. *Taxi Driver* is a vision of paranoia, loneliness, and deeply held phobic attitudes, but it is not itself an expression of these attitudes. If I have succeeded at doing anything in this book, I hope it is that I have made a legitimate case for the power of popular art and its potential capacity for political resistance.

INTRODUCTION

1. See the new afterword in the second edition of Modleski's study of Hitchcock, *The Women Who Knew Too Much*, 2005.
2. Sigmund Freud, "Three Essays on the Theory of Sexuality," which is included in *The Standard Edition*, vol. 7.
3. Modleski, *The Women Who Knew Too Much*, 114.
4. For fine readings of *Frenzy* that recognize its importance not only as a film but also to Hitchcock's career, see Orr; Lowenstein.
5. For more on this theme, see Modleski's treatment of the film and its "rituals of defilement" related to cannibalistic drives and to devouring the bodies of women in *The Women Who Knew Too Much*.
6. Kael famously praised Arthur Penn's *Bonnie and Clyde* (1967) for revealing the "dirty reality" of death, but when Hitchcock did so his work apparently turned "rancid." (The "whole point of *Bonnie and Clyde* is to rub our noses in it . . . The dirty reality of death—not suggestions but blood and holes—is necessary.") See Kael, *Kiss Kiss*, 69.
7. See Dixon, *It Looks at You*, 2.
8. Ibid., 14.
9. See Halberstam, *Female Masculinity*, in particular the chapter "A Rough Guide to Butches on Film," 175–231; Barton, "Your Self Storage"; Richard Dyer, "Gays in Film"; and Ellis Hanson's introductory essay to the volume he edited, *Out Takes*, 1–15.

My understanding of Halberstam's critical position has changed, however, in light of her heated opposition to Hanson's work on gay male pornography and race collected in the reader *Gay Shame*, edited by David Halperin and Valerie Traub. Her opposition to Hanson's work is made clear in an issue of *Social Text* 23, nos. 3–4 (Fall–Winter 2005), and in several discussions in *Gay Shame*. Halberstam's more recent stances place her very much in the "positive images" tradition—in my view, a disappointing development.

10. Among the best feminist reevaluations of Mulvey are Susan White, *"Vertigo* and Problems of Knowledge in Feminist Film Theory," in *Hitchcock: Centenary Essays*, eds. Richard Allen and Sam Ichii-Gonzales, 279–307; Marian E. Keane, "A Closer Look at Scopophilia: Mulvey, Hitchcock, and *Vertigo*," in *A Hitchcock Reader*, eds. Marshall Deutelbaum and Leland Poague, 231–249; Ann M. Kibbey, *Theory of the Image: Capitalism, Contemporary Film, and Women*, 38–44. More problematically, see Edelman, *"Rear Window's* Glasshole," in *Out Takes*, ed. Ellis Hanson, 72–97, which does not so much critique and enlarge Mulvey as it replaces her limitations with its own.

Patricia White has valuably called our attention to the strangely unselfconscious ease with which several prominent gay male critics, such as D. A. Miller and Edelman, discuss Hitchcock films with an exclusive emphasis on issues of queer male sexuality, ignoring the roles of women in the films and larger feminist issues. "Miller is not obliged," writes Patricia White, "to offer a feminist analysis of Hitchcock's film [in this case *Rope*]."

> Yet Miller's metaphor of (male) anus as cut cuts feminist film theory and its considerable insights out of the picture as well. Homosexuality is reserved for the same sex, the male. Implicitly, the woman can represent only difference, that is, heterosexuality. The anus deconstructs sexual difference (the opposition phallus/lack), but access to this supplement is reserved for male members. . . . [Comparing Lacanian queer theorist Lee Edelman's similar arguments to Miller's, we can deduce that the] two theorists have found the ultimate master of "anality" in Hitchcock himself.

See White, "Hitchcock and Hom(m)osexuality," 215, 217.

As the title of D. A. Miller's groundbreaking essay "Anal *Rope*" suggests, the particular concern of his essay is the anus. Miller theorizes that in *Rope* the anus functions as a zone of phobic repression. Hitchcock's refusal to make a film with any cuts (though of course several exist) expresses, in Miller's view, the director's fused fears of castration and sodomy, figured as the core, defining practice of gay male sexuality. Both Miller and Edelman's work invaluably frame Hitchcock films as key sites for queer theoretical engagement. At the same time, both theorists reify the notion of the indispensability of the anus to gay male sexuality in a manner that produces a series of distortions of Hitchcock's work and its value. They distort the importance of female characters in Hitchcock while maintaining a view of Hitchcock's films as sadistic, homophobic, and also resolutely impersonal.

In her afterword to *The Women Who Knew Too Much*, "Resurrection of a Hitchcock Daughter" (123–161), Modleski takes Edelman to task for failing to consider the importance of misogyny in Hitchcock, especially the theme of domestic violence. While I agree with Modleski, I also take issue with her own polemical treatment of the importance of homophobia as opposed to misogyny in American culture—as if the two evils didn't flow from similar vile sources: a hatred of feminine "weakness" and profound but unacknowledgeable male sexual anxiety. Modleski does not treat the issue of homophobia, or homophobic violence, with much sensitivity here, which I find disappointing. The two critics, in a way, end up cancelling one another out.

11. To my mind, Mulvey's biggest critical failing has been her inattention to queer issues. And this is a problem that persists well into her most recent work; it is astonishing, given the range of queer theory engagements with classical Hollywood, that Mulvey has never, as far as I know, incorporated these queer perspectives into a badly needed updating of her revolutionary early essays.

12. Žižek offers the beginnings of a mordant counter-response to the post-theory position in his essay "Is there a proper way to remake a Hitchcock film?"

13. See especially Krämer, *The New Hollywood*, 72: "breakaway hits from 1967 to 1976 tended to be narrowly focused on male protagonists, marginalizing women in the process." I see what he means, but I would argue that the 1970s were rife with unusual and arresting female presences, such as Shelley Duvall, Genevieve Bujold, Karen Black, Jane Fonda, Diane Keaton, Sissy Spacek, Cicely Tyson, Liv Ullmann, Tyne Daly in *The Enforcer*, and many others in supporting roles, such as Lee Grant, Talia Shire, Maureen Stapleton, Piper Laurie, et al., who lent a distinctive shine to New Hollywood movies.

14. Numerous highly important directors whose work is very meaningful to me—such as Larry Cohen, John Carpenter, George A. Romero, and David Cronenberg—and who reimagined and revised the Hitchcock canon are not discussed in this book. Their omission reflects only the constraints of appropriate manuscript length.

15. Nystrom, *Hard Hats, Rednecks, and Macho Men: Class in 1970s American Cinema*, 3.

16. Kolker, *A Cinema of Loneliness: Penn, Kubrick, Scorsese, Spielberg, Altman*, 49. If Penn's *Bonnie and Clyde* "opened the bloodgates," surely this effect was one that had happened earlier with *Psycho*. David Thompson has recently argued that *Psycho* radically altered American culture, as the subtitle to his book on the film evinces: *The Moment of Psycho: How Alfred Hitchcock Taught America to Love Murder* (New York: Basic Books, 2010).

17. Lowenstein, "The Master, The Maniac, and *Frenzy*," in *Hitchcock: Past and Future*, eds. Richard Allen and Sam Ishii-Gonzales, 184. Tom Gunning quoted from *The Films of Fritz Lang: Allegories of Vision and Modernity*, 5.

CHAPTER ONE

1. While this book focuses on his homosexual males, it should be noted that lesbian figures are also important to Hitchcock's work—in *Rebecca* (1940), especially, but also in *Suspicion* (1941), *Stage Fright* (1950), and in his unmade film *The Short Night*, which was in the planning stages when he died—and that any study of issues of gender and sexuality in Hitchcock that does not consider the full range of sexual identities depicted in them can only be a partial one.

2. Allen skillfully unpacks similar "cruising" scenes in *Man '56*, *North by Northwest*, and *Torn Curtain*. These scenes are also cited as a homoerotic triptych in the 1999 Hitchcock art installation *Phoenix Tapes*. See Allen, *Hitchcock's Romantic Irony*, 147–153.

253

3. Edelman, *No Future: Queer Theory and the Death Drive*, 86.

4. We can add some other examples to the list: *The Man Who Knew Too Much*'s "good" mother Jo and vaguely sapphic "bad" mother Mrs. Drayton; *Vertigo*'s sensible Midge and queer-metaphor Madeleine (here the pattern emerges unusually as a battle between Midge, the normative coded as sapphic, and Madeleine, the heterosexual uncanny). What is especially interesting is the dialectic that Hitchcock develops between the pattern of the feminine versus the queer and his ongoing theme of mother-child relationships, as I discuss in relation to *Man '56*.

5. Eric Rohmer and Claude Chabrol, *Hitchcock: The First Forty-four Films*, 27–28.

6. Spoto, *The Art of Alfred Hitchcock*, 242.

7. Horrigan, *Widescreen Dreams*, 118.

8. Mark Shoffman, "Half a Century of Gay Progress."

9. Barry Werth discusses the Newton Arvin case in his book *The Scarlet Professor*.

10. Ina Rae Hark, in her critique of the film as a re-entrenchment of patriarchal values that, as such, rejects the feminist touches of the 1934 version, notes that there is no "hint, as in the earlier version, that the mother resents her child. Indeed, directly before the kidnapping, Jo asks Ben when they are going to have another baby. Her interactions with Hank are never other than those of a devoted mother." See Hark, "Revalidating Patriarchy," 218. I appreciate Hark's nuanced reading of *Man '34*, but I do not agree with her about *Man '56*—it's a much bumpier, more inconsistent film than her reading, which smoothes out its complexities, allows. Moments such as the scene in which Jo turns to her scared son and says "Hank?" rather than immediately coming to his defense or apologizing for him complicate Hark's view, in my opinion.

11. See in particular Sedgwick's *Epistemology of the Closet*.

12. Just about the only scenes of interest in Ron Howard's Oscar-winning *A Beautiful Mind* (2001) are Ed Harris's, as an apparitional Cold War contact (other scenes of interest include the alternative family Russell Crowe—as the brilliant, schizophrenic mathematician John Nash—envisions, his male college roommate and his daughter, an apparitional queer family). Crowe's scenes with Harris are deliberately opposed to the normal world of his marriage and family, happening almost always at night, in secret secluded places; these scenes symbolize the lead character's homosexuality, which the film controversially occluded (for predictable commercial reasons).

13. Bogle, *Cold War Espionage and Spying*, 128–129.

14. Mack, *Running a Ring of Spies*, 41.

15. Kalugin, *Spymaster*, 223.

16. D'Emilio, *Sexual Politics*, 42–43. See also Corber's *Homosexuality in Cold War America*.

17. Bernard's position within the frame is the structural equivalent to the skull in Holbein's famous 1533 painting *The Ambassadors*, which the viewer can only make it out from an anamorphic perspective. Anamorphosis and the Holbein painting are key components in Lacanian theory. What Slavoj Žižek, drawing on Lacan, has famously called the Hitchcockian blot is this detail of the invisible Real that, like Holbein's skull, sticks out. (Or think of a piece of fabric, the point of a shirt collar, perhaps, that sticks out of a firmly clasped suitcase.) As Žižek explains, "the Hitchcockian 'blot' or 'stain'" in terms

of "the signifying dimension of the blot, its effect of double meaning, of conferring on every element of the image a supplementary meaning that makes the interpretative movement work. None of this should blind us to its other aspect, however, that of an inert, opaque object that must drop or sink for any symbolic reality to emerge." In Žižek's Lacanian terms, reality is constructed by the extraction of the key element that frames it, the *object a* that goads us into desire. For Žižek, the formal Hitchcockian device for isolating and representing this stain is the tracking shot. But as this moment from *Man* makes clear, other formal devices, such as the pan, can do the similar aesthetic and thematic work of capturing or framing the blot. See Žižek, *Looking Awry*, 94.

For Žižek, the blot, though its appearance has a phallic aspect, manifests the unconscious presence of the maternal superego. But as I read Hitchcock's films, the blot can also signal unrepresentable queer desire.

18. Though I don't have the space to delve into this aspect of the film's cultural associations here, Morocco's fame as a place for homosexual tourism was always focused on the Arab "boy." Is it possible that the kidnapping of the little American boy is some kind of equivalent to these touristic predilections?

19. O'Donnell, *Latent Destinies*, 9. O'Donnell is discussing pleasurable paranoia as a postmodern possibility, but I believe it has a relevance to Jo's motivations and strategies here.

20. I also discuss this scene in an essay on eating as a sexual metaphor in Hitchcock films, "Engorged with Desire: Alfred Hitchcock Films and the Gendered Politics of Eating," in *Reel Food*.

21. Corber, *In the Name of National Security*, 146. All further references will be noted parenthetically in the text.

22. Rather than conforming to the Freudian formulation of a woman's desire to bear a child as her attempt to overcome an essential lack through the creation of a substitute phallus / infant, Jo's desire for a child is, in my view, competitively heterosexual. She inserts a reminder of her reproductive powers as a direct countermeasure against Bernard's hypnotizing homoeroticism in an effort to jolt Ben out from his spell. Jo does not, therefore, so much express a desire for maternity as she asserts her own right to Ben's body and the potentialities of her own. Of course, I have been arguing, Jo's competitiveness with Ben stems from her frustrations with his success at boxing her in and enforcing societal, gendered constraints on her.

23. During filming, Hitchcock insisted on showing the transfer of make-up between the men; considerable trouble was taken to effect the shot, which proved troublesome, since the make-up wouldn't "come off" properly. Finally, Gélin brilliantly suggested the use of white powder on Stewart's hands to produce the desired effect. Reported in the "Making of *The Man Who Knew Too Much*" documentary on the 2001 DVD edition of the film from Universal Studios.

24. Jensen, *Hitchcock Becomes Hitchcock*, 113–114.

25. Freud, "Some Neurotic Mechanisms," in *The Standard Edition*, vol. 18, 223.

26. Contiguously, the casting of the oddly wooden, stiff, and somewhat masculine Ruth Roman in the role of the "normal" Guy Haines's love interest in *Strangers* opens up

the possibility of both as a strangely queer or, anachronistically put, "ex-gay" couple, especially when Granger's own ambiguous screen sexuality is considered.

27. Discussing Hitchcock's 1963 film *The Birds*, and challenging Raymond Bellour's extensive readings of Hitchcock films as male-oriented texts that produce the normative oedipalization of the male subject, Rose focuses on the shot/reverse shot visual structure of the film and its relationship to the female protagonist, Melanie Daniels (Tippi Hedren). Rose argues that the shot/reverse shot structure privileged in the film mirrors the Imaginary relationship between emergent subject and reflected image in the Lacanian mirror stage, in which the subject first sees and becomes captivated with its own image, and, crucially, mistakes this illusory image of wholeness for an authentic image of a whole, coherent self, the upshot being that subjectivity is based on identification with an illusion. For Rose, the daughter's stronger pre-oedipal bond with the mother makes the Imaginary and the mirror stage especially charged developmental stages for femininity. Lacan further posited that the mirror stage was fraught with aggressivity, potentially suicidal feelings, and, crucially, paranoia. Rose argues that the paranoia latent within the classical Hollywood film system itself is drawn out by the female paranoia thematized and evoked by the shot/reverse shot structure of *The Birds*, which returns the woman and the viewer to the Imaginary and mirror stage phases it evokes. She argues that the woman's position within the film system is *structurally* one of paranoia specifically because her position most strongly evokes the mirror-stage and its attendant emotional conflicts, of which paranoia is one. Moreover, because "passive homosexuality" characterizes paranoia, paranoia, whether in men or in women, is an inherently feminine position.

28. Halberstam, *Skin Shows*, 107–137.

29. If it is indeed true that, as Halberstam puts it, Freud "refuses to acknowledge the specificities of the female case of paranoia, indeed the local, political, and cultural specificities of female fear in patriarchy," I believe that in his 1922 essay "Certain Mechanisms" he nevertheless gives us an indelible account of the interlocking emotional dynamics in the figures of jealousy, paranoia, and homosexuality that illuminate Hitchcock's films and their representation of gender, sexuality, and the fear of queer desire. See Halberstam, *Skin Shows*, 136.

30. If I were to locate the chief difference in emphasis between Rose's essay and my argument here, it is that, following Freud, I emphasize the grief within the woman's narcissistic desire. If Lacan privileges the paranoia within narcissistic looking, Freud reminds us of the gendered grief at the core of narcissism, jealousy, paranoia, and homosexuality. (This is a topic that I will take up at length in my reading of *Taxi Driver*.) On some level, Jo's paranoid knowledge is an act of defensive mourning for her own lost possibilities.

31. Barton, "'Crisscross': Paranoia and Projection," 226.

32. "The hystericization of women, which involved a thorough medicalization of their bodies and their sex, was carried out in the name of the responsibility they owed to the health of the children, the solidity of the family institution, and the safeguarding of society." See Foucault, *The History of Sexuality*, 147. Recently, however, Juliet

Mitchell has offered a striking critique of the dismissal of hysteria as a psychological phenomenon. See her *Mad Men and Medusas*. One of the crucial elements of Mitchell's argument is the overlooked importance of sibling relationships in Freud and classical psychoanalysis.

33. Mitchell, *Mad Men*, 45.

34. Ibid., 49.

35. Pauline Kael once noted that one doesn't often think of acting in Hitchcock's films (she was singling out Robert Walker's performance in *Strangers* as a rare example of notable acting in his films). Of all of the inaccurate treatments of Hitchcock films, surely this is amongst the most easily refutable. To take one example, Hitchcock's multiple use of certain actors—Cary Grant, James Stewart, Grace Kelly, Ingrid Bergman, Tippi Hedren—is striking in that very different, distinct elements of each star's persona appears to be tapped in each film. For instance, Ingrid Bergman's warmly maternal psychiatrist Dr. Constance Petersen in the criminally undervalued *Spellbound* is a wholly different creation from her sad, wan, yet overwhelmingly sensual Alicia Huberman in *Notorious*—and her vacant, haunted, lonely wife in *Under Capricorn* is more distinct still. Often, too, many actors not thought of as particularly adept—Kim Novak, Hedren— give superb performances in Hitchcock's films.

36. Lawrence, "American Shame," 70.

37. Houlbrook, *Queer London*, 209–210.

38. For more about the trendiness of this appropriation of the region for homoerotic pleasure in the 1950s, see Aldrich, *The Seduction of the Mediterranean*, 187–188 in particular, but it's a topic that runs throughout his study; for discussions of the specific 1950s homosexual appropriation of Morocco, see Waitt and Markwell, *Gay Tourism*, 51.

39. Appropriate to its status as remake, *Man* deploys a motif of mirroring to register its concerns and fears. The shadow couple, to use Bellour's term, the Draytons strikingly mirror the McKennas. In Ben's case, Mr. Drayton mirrors him by extruding the darkness always threatening to dominate Ben. In Jo's case, Mrs. Drayton seems much *less* ambivalent about rearing Hank than Jo does. This mirroring, I would argue, intensifies the film's queer implications and the queer implicatedness of the characters. This is a film where mirrors have mirrors. Mrs. Drayton, one of Hitchcock's most gloriously complex characters, while being more maternal than Jo, has a kind of lacquered hardness that anxiously mirrors the unsettling suggestions of a hardness in Jo. But the frowzy, ill-tempered woman accomplice who plays checkers with Hank is much harder—and more sexually ambiguous—still, suggesting that she embodies Mrs. Drayton's own fears about the masculine hardening of her identity by the assassination plot and this world of intrigue. Bernard represents, as I have argued, queer seduction; but Rien suggests the frightening aspect of cadaverous decay within these seductions; Ambrose Chappell reinforces this note of decay; and Mr. Drayton himself seems increasingly shriveled as well as sexually indeterminate. Interestingly, two of these all but explicitly queer characters die at the hands of other men.

40. Santopietro, *Considering Doris Day*, 123.

41. Ibid., 332.

42. Pauline Kael called her "cold," "butch"; one sides, Kael disturbingly argues, with "the scummy little guy beating her up" in the 1955 Ruth Etting/domestic violence biopic *Love Me or Leave Me.* This comment says more about Kael's internalized misogyny than about Day's performance in the film. Kael, *5001 Nights at the Movies,* 439.

43. Again, though I respect Ina Rae Hark's feminist critique of *Man '56,* I believe that she misreads the film as an attempt at masculinist re-entrenchment that successfully restores patriarchal values at the expense of the woman's autonomy and agency. Specifically, Hark does not address the uncertainty and ambivalence in the film as deliberate choices on the part of the filmmakers and actors, as opposed to characteristic parts of the Hitchcockian atmosphere. While they are these as well, the uncertainty and ambivalence in the film are consistently thematized as reactions to conformist gender standards.

44. See Spoto, *The Dark Side of Genius,* 365.

45. Corber, *In the Name of National Security,* 152.

46. Ibid., 152–153.

47. We should keep in mind Hitchcock's relationship with his own wife, Alma Reville, a frequent and important collaborator on many of his projects. While one could argue that her career was subsumed by his, it is also important to note that she was hardly a stay-at-home, domestic prisoner, either. Her simultaneously crucial/occluded role as his collaborator figures the divided manner in which Hitchcock constructs femininity in his films, with empathy and ambivalence mixed. See Pat Hitchcock's *Alma Hitchcock* for a long overdue appraisal of Reville's own life and role in her husband's moviemaking.

48. Spoto, *The Art of Alfred Hitchcock,* 245.

49. Wood, *Hitchcock's Films Revisited,* 361.

50. Ibid., 369–370. Wood argues that the film turns the supremacy of privileged male rationality on its head by showing everywhere that Jo is smarter and shrewder though more "intuitive" than Ben.

51. In fact, Bettelheim, a concentration camp survivor, likened autistic children to concentration-camp prisoners and their mothers to the gestapo who brutalized them. For Bettelheim, autistic children closed off all human emotion the way the prisoners did—in response to their total brutalization by, respectively, the Mother and the guards. The controversial issue of "refrigerator mothers" is explored by the 2002 PBS POV documentary by that name, directed by David E. Simpson, J. J. Hanley, and Gordon Quinn. Once Bettelheim collected his findings in a book, *The Empty Fortress,* he appeared to have tempered his rhetoric somewhat. See Bettelheim, *The Empty Fortress,* 69–70. The pain Bettelheim caused families and especially mothers with autistic children is, as the documentary demonstrates, inexpressibly deep.

52. McLaughlin proceeds to make the point that it is the woman's desires that trigger this process and for which she must be punished. Overall, he both grants Hitchcock a critical disposition towards normativity and views Hitchcock's films as essentially disciplinary. See his essay "All in the Family: Hitchcock's Shadow of a Doubt," in *A Hitchcock Reader,* 149–150.

53. Bonitzer, "The Skin and the Straw," 179.

1. Expressionism was deeply influential on the young Hitchcock of the 1920s, especially through the opportunity he had to observe, when Hitchcock was doing apprentice work in Germany, the great homosexual director F. W. Murnau at work. While he moved beyond such Expressionistic techniques as the distortion of the film image itself, which can be found in his early work, and adopted, instead, the editing techniques of Soviet montage, Hitchcock's continued use of the double confirms his lasting identification with Expressionist aesthetics and philosophy. For an extensive study of Hitchcock's use of the double from German Expressionism and its literary forebears, see Rosenbladt, "Doubles and Doubts in Hitchcock."

2. It is probably inaccurate to call the late Farley Granger "gay." In his lively autobiography *Include Me Out*, Granger discusses the several romantic and sexual experiences he had with women over the years, though in his later years he seems to have been exclusively homosexual.

3. Otto Rank, *The Double: A Psychoanalytic Study*, 74, 85.

4. Allen, *Hitchcock's Romantic Irony*, 10.

5. Ibid., 11.

6. Ibid., 12.

7. Ibid., 65.

8. Ibid., 128.

9. Ibid., 131.

10. Ibid., 154.

11. James offered this observation as his motivation for writing his 1886 novel *The Bostonians*. The novel concerns a battle for the soul of a young woman between a New England lesbian and a reactionary male Southerner.

12. Allen Tate, "Our Cousin, Mr. Poe," *Essays of Four Decades*, 390.

13. I would argue that, far from being a homophobic work, as D. A. Miller famously framed it, *Rope* is a profound critique of homophobia. I make a similar case in my chapter on *Cruising*.

14. This argument about the core dynamics of the woman's film and this genre's transition into the horror film is the central topic of my book *Representations of Femininity in American Genre Cinema*.

15. See Chapter 5 of *Representations of Femininity in American Genre Cinema* for an elaboration of this theme.

16. Naremore, *Filmguide to Psycho*, 66.

17. The physical qualities of the actor cast in the role and the endless permutations of splitting in the character carry on the Hitchcockian aesthetic of split masculinity so powerfully realized in *Psycho*. Jason Miller in William Friedkin's *The Exorcist* (1973), a boxer-psychiatrist-priest, the younger man to the older priest (Max von Sydow), is finally the ultimate split figure, both possessed and resisting the demon, who can only resolve his conflict by killing himself. Al Pacino's Michael Corleone in *The Godfather* films, his dark hair and white skin a striking symbolic contrast of the numerous splits within him (conscientious versus pitiless feelings, patriotism versus family, desire to be

259

respectable versus criminality), is another dark, troubled young man, now deployed for a much broader cultural narrative. John Travolta's disco-dancing Tony Manero in John Badham's superlative *Saturday Night Fever* (1977) extends the theme of the dark, troubled young man into the turbulent, cross-fertilized cultural shifts of the late 1970s (black and gay culture merge through disco, which then becomes a broader cultural phenomenon). Dark, troubled young men will be central to films such as *Marathon Man* (John Schlesinger, 1976), *Taxi Driver, Cruising,* and *Blow Out.*

18. See my essay "Rereading Narcissism."

19. See in particular John Hepworth's impassioned, strained, and ultimately incoherent essay "Hitchcock's Homophobia" collected in *Out in Culture,* eds. Creekmur and Doty, 186–197. Hepworth actually starts off with some poignantly insightful readings of Hitchcock only to descend into enraged histrionics that seem to have more to do with the climate of homophobia in the United States than they do with Hitchcock's cinema, even though I do well understand rage at the former. *Out in Culture* includes both Robin Wood's response to Hepworth (Hepworth takes Wood to task in this essay), and Hepworth's rebuttal to Wood's own.

20. Samuels writes of *Psycho* that "the female body is presented in a more explicit way than in most of his other films. Rarely in a Hitchcock picture, do we see a female character so undressed and perhaps the most revealing scene in all of his work up to this point is the shower scene[.]" Yet rarely do we see a male character this undressed, either. See Samuels, *Hitchcock's Bitextuality,* 140.

21. In Van Sant's version of *Psycho,* he shows us Viggo Mortensen's Sam as a naked body, his muscular buttocks flexed in one shot. Yet here, too, Sam is conventionally represented with no full frontal nudity.

22. Richard Allen has also commented on Novak's gendered ambiguity in *Vertigo* in his *Hitchcock's Romantic Irony.*

23. Durgnat, *Long Hard Look at Psycho,* 31.

24. In other words, Hitchcock used Perkins for the qualities already inherent in his star image, just as he had used other gay/bisexual actors such as Granger and Clift, in roles significant for their panic over *secrets.* Foucauldian queer theory has made every effort to disabuse us of our associations of homosexuality with such secrets of the text; but in the simultaneously closeted and gay-baiting 1950s, what could have been more secretive than homosexuality?

25. There is a remarkably similar precedent for this scene and its visual composition in *The Paradine Case.* In this film, the defense counselor played by Gregory Peck is in love with the *femme fatale* played by Alida Valli. Louis Jourdan has an affair with Valli, kills her husband for her, but seems to love her husband, who had been his superior in the war, most of all. When Peck meets the queer-typed Jourdan for the first time, it is Jourdan who blocks Peck's path in the doorway. *Psycho* reverses matters by having Sam, from the outside, block Norman from *leaving* the office; but these moments, in their surprising intimacy and aching hostility, have greater emotional and tonal similarities.

26. Bellour, "Psychosis, Neurosis, Perversion," *The Analysis of Film.*

27. Just as Hitchcock did in *Rope,* the straight, ostensibly morally superior male investigator hounds a criminal much more poignantly vulnerable than he, in a manner that

makes us question the interpreter's putative general superiority, undergirded by the demands of normative sexuality. This is true not just of *Rope*'s Phillip but also of the supercilious, pompous Brandon. Brandon says to Rupert Cadell before Cadell opens the chest in which David Kentley's body lies, "I hope you like what you see!" The desperation and pain in Brandon's voice belie the apparent triumphalism of the neo-Nazi rhetoric he invoked to justify the murder; it also exposes the depth and urgency behind the lovers' desire not only to impress but also to connect to Rupert.

28. The gesture is performed "straight" by *Rear Window*'s initially randy newlywed couple, who pull the shades down once they first arrive at their apartment after their wedding but whose relationship eventually turns ominously rancorous. The gesture is also evoked in the climactic images of *North by Northwest* in which Roger O. Thornhill pulls Eve Kendall up from imminent death on Mount Rushmore into the upper berth of his rail-car cabin, now calling her Mrs. Thornhill. This extraordinarily concise courtship-marriage scene is infused, as are all scenes of heterosexual eros in Hitchcock, with the threat and thrill of death. Moreover, Hitchcock makes sure that we understand that it is enabled by the destruction of the homosexual, the killing of the villain's queer henchman Leonard, who also, of course, tried to kill Thornhill, memorably stepping on his fingers as he hangs precariously from Mount Rushmore with one hand, holding Eve with the other.

29. I discuss my alternative reading of Clover's theory of the Final Girl and of the slasher horror genre in Chapter 5 of *Representations of Femininity in American Genre Cinema*.

30. Donald Spoto, *The Art of Alfred Hitchcock: Fifty Years of His Motion Pictures* (Garden City, NY: Doubleday, 1976).

31. Doty, *Flaming Classics*, 180.

32. Doty, *Flaming Classics*, 180.

33. Naremore, *Filmguide to Psycho*, 66.

34. Žižek, "Is there a proper way to remake a Hitchcock film?," 258.

35. Similarly reading her character as an early spokeswoman for the Moral Majority, *Psycho II* (1983), a surprisingly interesting sequel directed by Richard Franklin, casts the much later Lila as a fiery, unappeasable right-wing agitator against the release of Norman Bates from a mental asylum.

36. I consider Lila's role in the film, especially her confrontation with Mrs. Bates, at greater length elsewhere. See my essay "The Maternal Necropolis: Femininity, Mothers, and Death in *Psycho*" (in process).

CHAPTER THREE

1. Truffaut, *Hitchcock*, 268.

2. Orr, *Hitchcock and Twentieth-Century Cinema*, 14.

3. I am not the first critic to link *Psycho* to postmodernity—Linda Williams has influentially done so in her essay "Discipline and Fun: *Psycho* and Postmodern Cinema," for example—and many critics have discussed the influence of *Psycho* on not only horror film but also postmodernity generally. Numerous definitions of postmodernism and of postmodern masculinity also abound. The general understanding of postmodernity is that it constitutionally maintains an attitude of suspicion towards "Grand

Narratives" and that it reflects a crisis in representation, the idea that only the shards, the simulacra, of previous forms and beliefs in these forms remain. For my cinema-focused purposes, I use the term postmodern manhood to describe American masculinity after the collapse of the classical Hollywood studio era. A postmodern masculinity would be one that reflected the rejection of any belief in a stable or continuous masculine identity. From a postmodern view (and as an indication of the looseness of such a term, we could say postidentity, postgay, postfeminist, even post-postmodernist), masculinity can only be seen as an image repertoire of available poses, attitudes, and configurations that are specific to a particular historical era. For an especially incisive analysis of the subject, see Linda S. Kauffman, *Bad Girls and Sick Boys: Fantasies in Contemporary Art and Culture*, 1998.

4. Toles, "If Thine Eye Offend Thee . . . ," 173. Toles captures something about the film in a way that no one else ever quite has—the weirdly, almost ferociously animated quality of its utter blankness.

5. Ibid., 150.

6. Norman's queerness emerges from the play of several different characteristics and qualities that work to undermine a stable and coherent male sexuality. If he isn't gay or the "homosexual," exactly, he certainly is the queer, as Alexander Doty argued in his important essay "How Queer is My *Psycho.*"

7. Gilbert, *Men in the Middle*, 77.

8. For further discussions of the importance of *Playboy* to 1950s masculinity, and the ways in which it synthesized male discontent with patterns of middle-class, suburban conformity, see K. A. Cuordileone, *Manhood and American Political Culture in the Cold War*, 194–198.

9. Perhaps the chief valence between *The Heiress* and *Psycho* is that both texts are haunted by a powerful dead mother who threatens to obliterate the living child. Dr. Sloper incessantly compares the shy, awkward Catherine to his beautiful dead wife. At one point, Catherine wears a dress once worn by her mother. Her father compliments her, but just as quickly diminishes her: "Ah, but your mother was fair—she *dominated* the color."

10. Williams, *Screening Sex*, 73.

11. "Regarding the scene in Norman's bedroom, probably the item most frequently discussed is the book Lila picks up and opens. Though Hitchcock's camera resolutely refuses to show us what's in it, all the evidence points to pornography. In the first place, this scene in Robert Bloch's original novel tells us that upon opening the book, Lila sees an illustration that is almost 'pathologically pornographic.' Furthermore, Joseph Stefano's script stipulates that 'her eyes go wide in shock. And then there is disgust. She slams the book closed, drops it.' Raymond Durgnat also points out that she's clearly looking at an image, rather than reading text, because her eyes don't travel across the page. And finally, script supervisor Marshall Schlom insisted that 'Hitchcock wanted to suggest it was a *pornographic* book with a slight raise of the eyebrow. It was so important to him, we shot maybe sixteen takes of Vera, which was unusual for him.'"

Moreover, Hitchcock only used close-ups strategically, when he wanted the audience to be aware of something significant. The close-up of Lila's face registers alarm and surprise; given that this scene extends her investigation of the Bates mystery—which involves both her psychosexual complicity in and moral judgment of the sexual and social mayhem within the Bates house—Lila's response to the volume registers her own possible conflicted sexual responses as well as her stringent judgmental ones towards Norman's perversity, as I discussed in the previous chapter. See Smith, *The Psycho File*, 125.

12. Schaefer, "Gauging a Revolution," 372.

13. Ibid., 394.

14. I don't mean this in a utopian sense, given the kinds of compulsory confessions the social order demands of the sexual lives of individuals, as Foucault astutely observed; but I also can see that such a visibility and articulation of the queer elements in American culture had a potentially positive side in that they indicated increasing visibility on the part of homosexuals who refused to remain invisible.

15. Condemned by the Catholic Legion of Decency, *Baby Doll* was controversial in ways specifically related to its sexual content. The controversy over *Baby Doll* suggests an awareness that mainstream film was verging on something frighteningly new: the representation of the sexual themes and situations the Production Code had made it nearly illegal to show in film.

16. In his essay "Is There a Proper Way to Remake a Hitchcock Film?" Slavoj Žižek writes of Vaughn's masturbation scene that "if he were able to arrive at this kind of sexual satisfaction, there would have been no need for him to accomplish the violent *passage à l'acte* and slaughter Marion!" Žižek calls this a "rather obvious point"; I would call it a heterosexualizing maneuver that matches that in Van Sant's film, an interpretation of Hitchcock's original that assumes a heterosexual subjectivity at work in Norman Bates's viewing (like, for that matter, Žižek's reading). As I suggest in this chapter, we don't know what actually constitutes Norman's desiring experience of watching Marion undress in Hitchcock's film. See Žižek, "Is There a Proper Way," 268.

17. For an incisive reading of the implications of pornographic "rear viewing," see Berkeley Kaite, *Pornography and Difference*, 82–83.

18. See Edelman, "Seeing Things: Representation, the Scene of Surveillance, and the Spectacle of Gay Male Sex," *Homographesis*, 173–192.

19. Ullén, "Pornography and Its Critical Reception."

20. These patterns have a precedent in classic American literature. The first-person narrator and consummate voyeur Miles Coverdale may also be said to turn living people into pornographic objects in Hawthorne's prescient 1852 novel *The Blithedale Romance*, one of the first American works to foreground and critique the male pornographic gaze. In his "inviolate bower" up in a tree, Miles Coverdale watches and eavesdrops on his fellow Blithedalers, believing he eludes the gaze as he wields visual mastery over them. Hawthorne shows this very belief to be an indication of the fragility of Coverdale's psychic character. Moreover, he makes it clear that Coverdale's pornographic gaze derives pleasure from voyeuristically consuming both female and male bodies, a pleasure that is also fraught with homophobic and misogynistic anger and anxieties. For a fuller treatment of Hawthorne's novel, see my essay "In a Pig's Eye: Masculinity, Mastery, and the Returned Gaze of *The Blithedale Romance*."

263

21. Ullén, "Pornography and Its Critical Reception."

22. Waugh, "Homosociality in the Classical American Stag Film: Off-Screen, On-Screen," *Porn Studies*, 127–141.

23. As Herzog continues, "In 1967 Martin Hodas, the 'King of the Peeps,' installed his first set of coin-operated film machines in Carpel Books at 259 West 42nd St. . . . Other forms of peep machines existed in numerous amusement arcades throughout the country, and references to police raids on arcades with 'obscene' peep shows date to at least the early 1950s. . . . Reuben Sturman is credited with mass marketing the privatized peep booth through his Cleveland-based company, Automated Vending. . . . Such innovations in privacy and selectability held an obvious appeal for most users." Herzog, "In the Flesh," 31–33.

24. Ibid., 32

25. If Marion is an allegory for the cinema, and for the death of the classical Hollywood cinema, she also allegorizes the reification of the porn-cinema subject, whose avid performance of and participation in scenes of sexual intercourse is not only a very modern form of alienated labor both also a new form of reification: the endlessly performed, endlessly open-ended labor of providing sexual stimulation through mass-circulated pornographic moving images. What pornographic cinema memorializes more than any other form of narrative cinematic representation, though all forms to some extent do this, is the alienated labor of the cinema actor-subject.

26. For an excellent discussion of voyeurism in *Rear Window*, see Robert Stam and Roberta Pearson's essay "Hitchcock's *Rear Window*: Reflexivity and the Critique of Voyeurism," *Hitchcock Reader*, 199–212. Of particular significance to this reading is their discussion of social isolation in terms of voyeurism. The mastery of the individual voyeuristic will is juxtaposed against the social isolation of the modern, urban space, which has great relevance for *Taxi Driver* as well; the pornographic emerges, I would argue, in Jeff's use of his neighbors as objects of desire without their awareness. If so, one could say that the pornographic gaze, which subsumes the voyeuristic, attempts to transform social isolation and decay into individual *jouissance*.

27. I do not in any way mean to suggest that while heterosexual male eye cult is pornographic, homosexual eye cult is not. Rather, I mean to suggest that, in its conventional form, male sexual desire, always already constructed as heterosexual, of course, takes a visual form that is most often represented as pornographic (leering, appetitive, consuming the visual object). We could posit that—with all due consideration for the extensive historical evidence of homosexual pornography—in the latter twentieth century gay male desire becomes subject to the same pornographication of the heterosexual male subject.

28. In *Manhood in Hollywood from Bush to Bush*, I theorize such looking at the masochistic gaze.

29. Naremore, *Filmguide to Psycho*, 53–54.

30. Ibid., 54.

31. Another set of possibilities would require further elaboration, but let me outline them here, anyway. *Mother* could be looking at Marion. Norman is doing the looking, but

he could be seeing through Mother's eyes. *Her* desiring perspective or lack thereof is a point that I have yet to come across in *Psycho* criticism. It is no more outlandish to consider that Mother is staring at Marion here than it is to accept, during the coda, that Mother has taken possession of Norman, or, for that matter, that this "sick old woman" murdered "all those girls, and that man" (Arbogast). If we accept Mother as a distinct character, her venomous hatred of young, ripe, carnal women who want to appease their "ugly" sexual appetites with her son (echoes of the "ugly" homoerotic murder in *Rope*) may be an expression of her own desire for women, transformed into monstrous self-loathing projected outward. Of course, such desires would emanate from Norman's own unconscious understanding or fantasy of *her* unconscious desires. Is Norman's knife an unacknowledgeable lesbian phallus, directed against the object of desire in order to repudiate this desire? Again, this would signify Norman's internalized sense of his mother's underlying motivations for loathing such women.

32. I discuss the sexually inviolate male at length in my study of nineteenth-century American literature, *Men Beyond Desire*.
33. Melendez, "Video Pornography," 403.
34. Hitchcock's films synthesize, in the view taken by Lee Edelman in *No Future*, cultural associations between homosexuals and images of nullity and death. As I established in *Manhood in Hollywood from Bush to Bush*, I disagree with Edelman's thesis that homosexuals should actually embrace this cultural mythology and, along with that, embrace as well as embody the death-drive. For our purposes, I do not believe that Hitchcock's films synthesize and promote these homophobic associations; rather, they evoke them in order to subject them to a critique that is one aspect of Hitchcock's larger critical deconstruction of the heterosexual couple and heterosexism and, especially, normative models of American masculinity. Queerness in Hitchcock, associated with unruly and maddening desire, exists as a means of further establishing the costs of a cultural narrative of heterosexual normativity; his queers embody the breaking point of sexual norms, the coming apart of stringent standards of sexual order. Clearly, more elaboration of these critical conflicts is needed.
35. Truffaut, *Hitchcock*, 268.

CHAPTER FOUR

1. Jonathan Rosenbaum, "Master Thief."
2. Kael's views of De Palma went through interesting shifts. Though an early De Palma admirer—she voted to give a short film of his a prize in the 1960s, and praised *Greetings* and *Hi, Mom!*—her review of *Sisters* was quite contemptuous. (Characteristically, Peter Biskind entirely misrepresents her review of *Sisters* as a rave in his *Easy Riders, Raging Bulls*.) De Palma's horror rock opera *Phantom of the Paradise* was the turning point in Kael's view of De Palma as a powerful new cinematic voice. It is unsurprising that Kael dismissed *Obsession*, as she did *Sisters*. Both of these films are stringent formal mediations on Hitchcockian themes that take genre seriously. While her reviews of *Carrie*, *The Fury*, and *Dressed to Kill* remain bracing analyses, they nevertheless consistently overlook De Palma's investment in grappling with the Hitchcock legacy. De Palma

265

shares with Hitchcock an interest in the embattled woman's position in patriarchy, and, as did Hitchcock's, his films expose the ways that male anxieties manifest themselves in the form of misogyny. De Palma's Hitchcockian agon (or conflict) is more than delirious cinematic riffing.

3. Peretz, *Becoming Visionary*, 38.

4. Ibid., 18.

5. Menand, "Finding It at the Movies."

6. Peretz, *Becoming Visionary*, 19.

7. Ibid., 49.

8. Ibid., 32.

9. Ibid., 98.

10. Ibid., 118–125.

11. Ibid., 154, 155.

12. For an important and nuanced reading of *Body Double*, see Cvetkovich, "Postmodern Vertigo."

13. As Robert E. Kapsis, drawing on the theories of George Kubler's 1962 work *The Shape of Time*, demonstrates, an individual artist's lifework can be most tellingly appraised "in terms of the position that the artist occupies within an artistic tradition or genre"—in De Palma's case, the Hitchcockian suspense thriller. "According to Kubler," writes Kapsis in his treatment of De Palma's reputation history, "the moment of the artist's entrance in that tradition—early, middle, or late—is crucial to how the artist will be judged by the art world." As Kapsis persuasively argues, De Palma's reputation difficulties emerged, in part, from his timing. "Hitchcock had for decades been the acknowledged master of the form" of the suspense thriller. "The danger of working in a genre at such a late stage in its development [as De Palma did in the seventies and eighties] . . . is that critics will tend to view the recent entrant's work as imitative and unoriginal." See Kapsis, *Hitchcock*, 188–189.

14. An important future study would be a sustained comparison between modes of humor in Hitchcock and De Palma—humor being important to each filmmaker, but very differently deployed in their films. I return to the issue of humor in De Palma in the last chapter.

15. Nelson, *National Manhood*, 132.

16. Clover, *Men, Women, and Chainsaws*, 61, n60.

17. Shelley Stamp Lindsey, "Horror, Femininity, and Carrie's Monstrous Puberty," in *The Dread of Difference*, ed. Barry Keith Grant, 281. In my book, *Representations of Femininity in American Genre Cinema*, I devote a chapter to *Carrie* and offer a reading that is quite antithetical to Stamp Lindsey's.

18. Kapsis, *Hitchcock*, 214–215.

19. Kolker, *A Cinema of Loneliness*, 177. Kolker is a critic I respect, but how Kolker can denigrate De Palma's extraordinary revisions of Hitchcock while praising Scorsese's excruciatingly misogynistic and hateful 1991 Hitchcock-riff *Cape Fear* simply astounds me. In the next chapter, I discuss *Taxi Driver*, which Kolker treats with great insight in this book. *Cape Fear*, however, reveals just how wayward, bombastic, and empty

Scorsese's work has generally become, well into his films of the twenty-first century. The critical indifference to the misogyny of works like *Cape Fear*, in which, with entirely gratuitous violence, the villain bites off the cheek of the protagonist's mistress, and the insipid, misogynistic, and thoroughly racist oeuvre of ardent De Palma–wannabe Quentin Tarantino reveals the entrenched biases in film criticism that have almost entirely forestalled a careful, sensitive treatment of De Palma's work.

20. In the most recent edition of his book, Kolker maintains his view of De Palma as a "bad imitator" of Hitchcock, but now adds an appreciative reading of *Redacted*.

21. Armond White, *Resistance*, 177.

22. Linda Williams, "When the Woman Looks."

23. See Girard, *Deceit, Desire, and the Novel*, 1–52, for his elaboration of "triangulated desire"; for Sedgwick's version, which builds on and yet reformulates Girard's theory into a model for understanding male-male relations in a homophobic culture, see her *Between Men*, particularly 1–27.

24. The theme of triangulated desire is crucial to De Palma's work, especially as it illuminates his view of male-male relations as murderous and misogynistic. It allows us to reconsider the political messages of flawed, difficult, but also brilliant works such as *Body Double* (1984). In this film, the killer hires a porn star, Holly Body (memorably played by Melanie Griffith), to perform nightly erotic dances for the titillation of the claustrophobic actor Jake (Craig Wasson), who the killer embroils in a murder plot to kill his wife. Unbeknownst to Jake, the killer is his friend, Sam. Sam, like Dunne, is initially depicted as the protagonist's only "real" friend, but this friendship is only a ruse to ensnare Jake in the killer's plot. The film inverts its own graphic exploitation of woman as the object of a male's scopophilic gaze by revealing Holly Body's sexual performance as the centerpiece of the killer's plot. In this way, heterosexual relations are subsumed by the larger, consuming narrative of male rivalry. And there is no more homoerotic moment in De Palma than the scene in which Sam tempts Jake to view Holly Body (whom Jake believes is the endangered woman, Gloria Revelle) through a telescope; with a master sadist's precision, Sam leeringly elicits Jake's sexual responses to the woman whose orgiastic dance he views. *Body Double*, like *Snake Eyes* (1998), figures male friendship—shared power between men predicated on the exploitation of women—as a hollow construct, reliant on duplicity and betrayal, preventing any form of desire, heterosexual or homosexual, from achieving realization. *Snake Eyes* goes further and deeper than *Body Double* in suggestively figuring the doomed male friendship as a doomed romance.

25. Butler, "Imitation," 21.

26. Butler, *Bodies That Matter*. Citations from this book will be noted parenthetically.

27. If biological sex confers gendered identity, for Butler, even the term "sex"—as the sign of gender—is normative: regulatory and privileged. The source of the regulation is heterosexual hegemony. "Sex" is a performative ideal, and actively monitored by regulatory power. "Performativity must be understood not as a singular or deliberate 'act'," though, "but as the reiterative and citational practice by which discourse produces the effects it names" (2). The "heterosexual imperative" demands that its subject identify

267

with "the normative phantasm of 'sex,' and *this* identification takes place through a repudiation which produces a domain of abjection," a repudiation which is essential for the subject's emergence as a subject. Another constructive trope, "gender," which Butler distinguishes from "sex," operates "[as] the social construction of sex . . .[which is] absorbed by gender, [becoming] something like a fiction [that is] . . . installed at a prelinguistic site to which there is no direct access" (5). The "heterosexual imperative" is synonymous with "compulsory heterosexuality." "Construction is neither a subject nor its act, but a process of reiteration by which both 'subjects' and 'acts' come to appear at all" (9). "The latter domain of [those abjected bodies] is not the opposite of the former, for oppositions are, after all, part of intelligibility; the latter is the excluded and illegible domain that haunts the former domain as the spectre of its own impossibility, the very limit to intelligibility, its constitutive outside" (xi).

28. Butler, *Bodies*, 9.

29. See Sedgwick, *Between Men*, 25.

30. I discuss the dual nature of nineteenth-century bachelor culture in the introduction to my book *Men Beyond Desire*.

31. Tyler, *Screening the Sexes*, 71–72.

32. As Dana Nelson puts it, the discord and disruption inherent in any democratic model are "soothingly covered over by national self-sameness and unity, and embodied by the national executive. This a virtual (abstracted, imagined) fraternity, where the discomfiting actuality of fraternal disagreement disappears in the singular body of the President" (34). But in De Palma's *Greetings*, the president's body—literally shown decapitated, divorced from the floating, sad, hectoring head we see on the TV screen, symbolically lifeless—signifies the decohesion of American fraternity.

33. I do not want to make the potentially naïve reading that De Palma is a transgressor who privileges the gay outcast as social provocateur and glorious rebel. De Palma is not Genet. Yet is he a straight Genet? That would be my reading; like Genet, De Palma foregrounds the difficulties of relation. Indeed, his works share Genet's anti-relational thesis, but, as De Palma's work matures, he explores this thesis with a great deal more anguish. The early films keep their emotions locked down.

34. See Sedgwick, *Between Men*, 23.

35. Freud wrote *Three Essays on the Theory of Sexuality* in 1905 but kept adding to it until 1924. See *Three Essays*, vol. 7, 191–192.

36. Dollimore, *Sexual Dissidence*, 174.

37. Freud, *Three Essays*, vol. 7, 231.

38. Freud, *Three Essays*, 31.

39. Dollimore, *Sexual Dissidence*, 181.

40. Dollimore, *Sexual Dissidence*, 188. Dollimore is also discussing Freud's 1908 essay "'Civilized' Sexual Morality and Modern Nervousness," which he argues makes, as "a fascinating commentary on the authority/subversion/containment process," a good point of comparison rather than contrast to Freud's seeming ideological opponent Foucault.

41. Williams, "Film Bodies: Gender, Genre, and Excess."

42. Kipnis, *Bound and Gagged*.

43. Žižek, *Looking Awry*, 109–110.

44. It seems to me that the problem of pornography is that it is never perverse *enough*. It's the *illusion* of a total immersion in an ever-undulating perversity, the promise it holds out of a return to polymorphous perversity and an access to a range of pleasures, that pornography offers but never fulfills or realizes that makes pornography so vexing.

45. Another important study might explore just how much Welles's depiction of cinematic violence influences De Palma's own, beyond the more obvious intertexts of Eisenstein and Hitchcock, who De Palma himself frequently cites in interviews as inspirations. Seeing *The Lady from Shanghai* again, one is especially dazzled by its climactic screen violence, balletic and jarring at once, very much recalled within De Palma's technique.

46. As Kenneth MacKinnon writes, these early films "are the most overt statement" in De Palma's canon "of the intimacy between personal and social voyeurism. When ordinary individuals are not appearing on television they can make their own movies, do their own prying, or feature themselves as spectacle." MacKinnon wrote this in the period before De Palma's extraordinary expansion of these themes in his 1990s and twenty-first century films, but the basic point holds true. MacKinnon also reminds us of the film De Palma made before *Greetings*, *Dionysus in '69*, based on Euripides's play, which foregrounds the hazards of the male gaze, since it climaxes in the beheading of Pentheus, who, refusing to believe in Dionysus, spies on the wine god's group of nocturnal female worshippers, the Maenads, one of whom is Pentheus's mother. These bacchantes rend apart animals' flesh in the nighttime forest. When the Maenads discover Pentheus voyeuristically gazing upon them, they rip off his head; his mother, before she regains her daytime senses, carries his head on a stick. See MacKinnon, *Misogyny in the Movies: The De Palma Question*, 186–187. Relevant to any discussion of homosexuality in these early films is the startling moment when Dionysius kisses Pentheus on the mouth in *Dionysius in '69*.

De Palma's career-long concern with the pornographic needs more study, but Eyal Peretz provides insightful commentary on the role pornography plays in *Blow Out*. See Peretz, *Becoming Visionary*, chapter three generally, and especially 198, n54.

47. Personal conversation with Yvonne Rainer.

CHAPTER FIVE

1. Wood, "The Incoherent Text: Narrative in the '70s," in *Hollywood from Vietnam to Reagan . . . and Beyond*.

2. O'Donnell, *Latent Destinies*, 13–14.

3. De Palma was initially offered *Taxi Driver* but encouraged Scorsese to direct it instead. While it would have been fascinating to see what De Palma would have done with this film, Scorsese was the right choice as the director, as De Palma astutely realized, in part because Scorsese's films focus on character psychology more intently than De Palma's whirring cinema-meditative experiments do. This is not to suggest that De Palma's characters lack depth or feeling, or that probing their inner life is not his concern; but in *Taxi Driver*, Travis's psychology is the entire film.

4. Taubin, *Taxi Driver*, 55.

5. I am thinking of the film writing of D. A. Miller, Lee Edelman, and Diana Fuss, in particular.

6. Examples of the apparent milquetoast David's private sadism include his torturing of the housecat and his increasingly brutal treatment of his wife.

7. This Vincent van Gogh touch, the cabdriver's cut-off ear, corresponds, I believe, to Scorsese's evocation of van Gogh's *The Starry Night* in the opening montage sequence, in which the nighttime urban colors bleed into a blurry, uncannily vivid palette. Like the van Gogh of cultural myth, who cut off his own ear, Travis is a visionary artist who lives a resolutely, fiercely solitary life, cut off from the social order. Scorsese, in his relentlessly intertextual way, evokes Vincente Minnelli's 1956 van Gogh biopic *Lust for Life* in the later shot of Travis, preparing for urban combat, pushing the limits of his endurance by holding his arm above a flame for a grotesquely long duration, just as Kirk Douglas's van Gogh holds his hand above a flame to prove his romantic constancy in one scene of Minnelli's film.

8. This is a point that Peter Krämer makes generally throughout his important study *The New Hollywood*.

9. Williams, *Hard Core* (1989), 107.

10. Žižek, *Looking Awry*, 79.

11. See Noël Carroll's "The Future of an Allusion," in which he coins this phrase. See also Noel King's essay "The Last Good Time We Ever Had: Remembering the New Hollywood Cinema."

12. Kael, "Underground Man," 132.

13. Ibid., 134.

14. When Scottie looks down and experiences vertigo, he both appears to fear that he will fall and desires to fall. Hitchcock, with the help of Paramount second-unit cameraman Irmin Roberts, created a particular effects-shot to convey Scottie's fearful/desiring vertiginous gaze: the *"Vertigo* shot" was created through a technique thereafter called a "dolly zoom"—the camera simultaneously zooms in and tracks backward, which keeps the foreground stable as the background extends infinitely backwards.

15. Piso, "Mark's Marnie," in *A Hitchcock Reader*, 290.

16. Ibid., 299.

17. Indeed, I would say that Scorsese's career is increasingly marked by an unforgivable misogyny, especially apparent in terrible films such as his remake of *Cape Fear* (1991) and *Casino* (1995).

18. Fuchs, "*Taxi Driver*," 710.

19. Kaite, *Pornography and Difference*, 81–82.

20. A suggestive line can be drawn from Hitchcock's *Rear Window*, *Psycho* (1960) and *Frenzy* (1972) to the pornographic preoccupations of the New Hollywood cinema. Michael Powell's famous 1960 film *Peeping Tom* is also a key text in terms of the prefiguring of these pornographic themes, but I remain much less convinced than many other critics are of this film's radicalism. I believe that a strong case can be made for the political value of Hitchcock's work, chiefly in terms of his representation of non-normative male sexuality and in what I call his incipient feminism, which takes the form of his

exploration of how misogyny is developed and its grisly effects. If Hitchcock's films are, indeed, full of what Tania Modleski calls "lethal misogyny," I believe that the misogyny on display in the films is subjected to rigorous analysis, whereas, in my view, Powell's film is much more invested in its own misogyny. Linda Williams, in her famous article "When the Woman Looks," argued the reverse—that *Psycho* was misogynistic, and *Peeping Tom* much closer to being a feminist work.

21. Mulvey, "Visual Pleasure and Narrative Cinema," 63–64.

22. Ibid., 62–63.

23. In her study, Studlar revisits the von Sternberg-Dietrich films that embody fetishistic scopophilia, the second of the two Mulveyan avenues available to the male spectator-protagonist for the negotiation of the castration fears represented by the spectacularized female body. Studlar positively employs Deleuze's utopian study of masochism in the works of the nineteenth-century Austrian author Sacher-Masoch, *Coldness and Cruelty*, as a means of establishing an economy of masochism as a radical alternative to Mulvey's view of male sadistic visual reign over the spectacularized woman. Studlar argues that the pre-oedipal relationship between the son and the mother provides a powerful alternative to the post-oedipal, symbolic mode of male domination from which both Mulvey and Freud position male sexuality in relation to femininity. From a neo-Deleuzian position, Studlar champions masochism as a means of understanding the male relationship to femininity as a position of awe that recalls the infant male's subservience to the looming, powerful pre-oedipal mother.

24. I discuss the masochistic gaze in chapter four of my book *Manhood in Hollywood from Bush to Bush*. I argue that in the period I study here (roughly 1989 to 2008), the masochistic male gaze works in relation to the narcissistic gaze of the main protagonist, the homoerotic object of desire for the alternate, masochistic protagonist.

25. Eyal Peretz summarizes these terms thusly in *Becoming Visionary*: the Lacanian gaze is "that concept signifying the moment of the field of vision opening up as an image, that is, in relation to an internal closure, the inscription of a beyond, a blinding that is the 'place,' says Lacan, from which we are seen, and, as we can add, from which our eyes *open as sense*, as a relation to a closure that continues to haunt them. . . . The gaze is also, says Lacan, the place of the inscription of the 'subject,' in the field of vision, a place that is a blind spot in the field of perception; as such, we can say that the 'subject' is that openness to an excessive and blinding beyond that is always more than it and more than the world it inhabits; the 'human subject' is thus the one 'seen' by a beyond, a blind and blinding blank gaze of time, that opens its (the human) eyes" (15).

26. To represent Scottie's desire, Hitchcock shows us Scottie, seated at the bar, trying to get a surreptitious glimpse at Madeleine behind him, as the camera sweepingly pulls back, its gaze far more expansive than Scottie's strained point-of-view. This is truly a rear projection: Madeleine is a spectacle Scottie projects backwards. Gliding into the dining area from behind, the camera then tracks in on Madeleine and Elster, seated at a table having dinner, none of whose views or movements could be elements of Scottie's look. When Madeleine and Elster rise from the table and move forward out of the dining room, and toward Scottie, Elster stops to speak with a waiter, while Madeleine

walks forward, presenting herself, as we come to understand later, for Scottie's appraisal. In a complex series of shots, Scottie awkwardly stares at her from an averted, surreptitious position while she both pretends not to notice and makes sure that he is indeed staring at her. This kind of strained, backward looking is characteristic of Hitchcock's representation of the male gaze in his films with Jimmy Stewart. Recall, for example, as discussed in Chapter 1, the agonized attempt to look the Draytons in the face as Ben McKenna speaks to them while seated in the opposite direction in the Moroccan restaurant in *The Man Who Knew Too Much*. We can establish that Hitchcock deploys Stewart, as body and screen presence, in schemes of what Lee Edelman calls "behindsight" in his essay "Seeing Things: Representation, the Scene of Surveillance, and the Spectacle of Gay Male Sex," in *Homographesis*, the "disturbance of positionality" in representations of male-male sexual contact (173–192).

27. Weinreich, "The Urban Inferno," 14.
28. Taubin, *Taxi Driver*, 48–9.
29. Ibid.
30. Harry M. Benshoff and Sean Griffin ask, in their study *Queer Images*, what label we should "put on group sex? If the group comprises only one sex, then one might still describe this arrangement as homosexual. But what about a group-sex scene comprising men and women together? Are the participants still heterosexual, or are they now something else?" As they continue, the "term 'heterosexual orgy' is something of an oxymoron, as it is part of the design of such an arrangement for sexual desire and pleasure to flow from person to person without regard to gender. Group sex is queer sex" (6).
31. Taubin, *Taxi Driver*, 20.
32. See the "Making *Taxi Driver*" feature on the DVD of the film, directed by Laurent Bouzereau, Sony Pictures, 1999.
33. Wood, "The Incoherent Text," in *Hollywood from Vietnam to Reagan*, 47.
34. Ethan feels she has been defiled by having been forced to become a Comanche squaw. The film is full of grotesque conflations of Native Americans and savagism, and overall is reactionary. And yet, it undeniably depicts Ethan, in his single-minded obsession, as a cold, pitiless, terrible force of blind hatred, on the one hand, and, on the other hand, as a man imploding from his own hate, as his inability to express his grief in anything but rage-filled rhetoric reveals. In other words, the film is as much a critique of Ethan's murderous manhood as it is an endorsement of his attitudes. His younger companion on the trip, Martin Pawley (Jeffrey Hunter), himself half-Cherokee, serves the purpose of pointing out Ethan's murderous rage for what it is (though Martin's concern for white womanhood is also clearly just that, since he himself pitilessly abuses his own, unwanted Indian wife, "Look" [Beulah Archuletta]).
35. Quoted in Bruce Fink's *The Lacanian Subject*, 104.
36. Taubin, *Taxi Driver*, 21.
37. Ibid., 17.

1. I was in much the same position as a college student just on the verge of coming out when, having seen and loved Jonathan Demme's *The Silence of the Lambs* (1991), I witnessed the massive gay protest against that film, including efforts to out its star, Jodie Foster, as "Absolutely Queer."

2. For a thoughtful and nuanced discussion of the public reactions to *Cruising* and *Dressed to Kill*, see Kendrick, *Hollywood Bloodshed*.

3. Ergo, the serial killer Jame Gumb in *The Silence of the Lambs* came to be seen as offensive because he was such a "negative portrayal" of the "gay man." What gay activists refused to acknowledge, did not understand, or were unable to anticipate was just how many gay men loved Demme's film and how—quite disquietingly, I will add—rapidly the Jame Gumb character became a cult icon, along with the film, often lovingly enshrined in drag performances and even a queer musical (2003's *Silence! The Silence of the Lambs Musical*, with lyrics by Jon and Al Kaplan). Much the same phenomenon occurred with the similarly protest-incurring *Basic Instinct* (1992), a psychosexual thriller directed by Paul Verhoeven with lesbian themes. While I intensely dislike Verhoeven's film, save for Sharon Stone's marvelously witty and sexy performance, I have to acknowledge that it spoke to some lesbian audiences, though presumably not those who were standing outside theaters protesting the film. When a marginalized, persecuted group vehemently protests a work before they have either even seen or read it, they engage in their own form of cultural oppression and constrictive thinking. While I can understand the pain and the rage of gay activists sick to death of yet another offensive portrayal of gay people, and feminist activists infuriated at the brutal violence against women promoted by our culture, I nevertheless feel that the activists protesting *Cruising* and *Dressed to Kill* missed the point of both films, which most of them probably never saw, anyway. Both films are pointed critiques of the overall social structures that produce homophobia, misogyny, gay-bashing, and violence against women. Both films evoke 1960s and 70s sexual liberation; at the same time, they prophetically warn against the reactionary lockdown of sexual expressiveness that would characterize the 1980s and beyond. Sadly, the liberal/leftist activists who clamored for the positive portrayal ended up contributing to the same reactionary, constrictive programs they ostensibly railed against. Making for leaders as convincing as Regan and Goneril, the self-serving daughters of King Lear, the traditionalists and the politically correct liberals of the culture wars both insisted on and succeeded in promoting rigid standards for what should and should not constitute art. In film terms, austerity, antiseptic blandness, and predictability replaced the New Hollywood vitality, boldness, and weird inconclusiveness. (The enormous conglomerates that turned Hollywood into a theme park version of itself didn't help much, either.)

4. D. A. Miller provides a more appreciative, though still quite critical, analysis of the film, perhaps because he discovers that "Friedkin grasps the originality of the scene quite as much as did Michel Foucault, who saw in these 'laboratories of sexual experimentation,' as he called the SM backrooms of New York and San Francisco, a

reinvention of sex, where 'the idea is to make use of every part of the body as a sexual instrument'" (71).

5. Rossiter, *Angel with Horns*.

6. Entry for *Cruising* in *Leonard Maltin's Movie Guide* (New York: Plume, 2004).

7. He evokes the iconic queer figure of the "sad young man," as discussed by Richard Dyer, *The Matter of Images*, 42.

8. Rechy, *City of Night*, 56.

9. Adding some evidence to the idea that there is only one killer, during the murder of the fashion-industry victim in the peep show, there is a shot of the first victim, the actor, being murdered in the hotel room. The presence of this shot establishes continuity between the two murders in the mind of the killer. This is not definitive evidence, of course, but it is suggestive.

The murder of Ted at the end is, in my view, meant to indicate two possibilities: first, that, rather than confront his own awakened homo-desires, Burns has killed someone who either incited them or, more plausibly I think, represents his human link to the gay world he inhabited; second, that violence can occur between gay men (if Ted's angry lover is the one who kills him) just as savagely and unremarkably as it can between straight men or between sexually tormented, self-denying men and their victims. In any event, Paul Sorvino's cop seems to think, with horror, that Burns has killed Ted; moreover, Ted's lover accuses Burns of being in love with Ted.

10. This thematic is one consistent with nineteenth-century American literature, which similarly critiques the necessity of male homosociality in American culture, the inescapable conformity to group identity and gendered standards that informs American masculinity.

11. Adrian Martin, "*Cruising*: The Sound of Violence."

12. Chion, *The Voice in Cinema*.

13. Žižek, *Looking Awry*, 127.

14. Ibid., 126.

15. Ibid., 127, 128.

16. For a decidedly nonpsychoanalytic reading of *Cruising*, particularly its themes of voyeurism, doubling, mirroring, and the term he prefers, cloning, see Guy Davidson's argument "Contagious Relations," in which his focus is on "contagion" as "an apposite figure for the relations between not only identity and milieu but also acts and images (i.e., the relations between sexualized acts and pornographic images)" as well as "the contagious relations between representations and actions that we observe in the film" (49).

17. Ingeniously, Friedkin cast Leland Starnes in the role of Stuart Richards's father. Starnes was Richard Cox's own acting teacher at NYU. As Cox reports on the DVD documentary on the making of the film, he and Starnes had a combative relationship.

18. Stacey, "Cruising to Familyland: Gay Hypergamy and Rainbow Kinship," in *Men's Lives*, 427.

19. Bersani, *Homos*, 207.

20. I am greatly oversimplifying Hewitt's much more nuanced argument, but this is its gist. Hewitt, *Political Inversions*.

21. Bersani, *Homos*, 208.

22. The film suggests, in my view, that the gay male fixation with cop masculinity and authority so spectacularly represented by "Precinct Night" must be, on some level, a means of exploring exactly what it is about gay male desire that might lead it to become erotically enflamed by its very persecutors. I don't mean to be high-minded about the raunchy antics on display here, or to argue that the film is high-minded. It is, however, interested in plumbing the depths of desire in its least culturally sanctioned forms.

23. Frost, *Sex Drives*, 112.

24. Suárez, *Bike Boys*, 171.

25. Wood, "The Incoherent Text: Narrative in the '70s," *Hollywood from Vietnam to Reagan . . . and Beyond*, 57.

26. Sedgwick, *Epistemology*, 92.

27. Mysteriously, the sound effects of Nancy's jangling walk towards Burns are audible on neither the video nor the DVD editions of the film.

28. Alexander Doty uses the phrase "queer apocalypse" to describe the final moments of *Psycho* in his essay on the film in *Flaming Classics*. Certainly, *Cruising* would appear to be reworking *Psycho*'s voice without a body in its representation of Nancy's unseen but noisy approach. Friedkin's use of the close-up of Burns's face in the mirror parallels Hitchcock's shot of Norman's face with Mother's skull-face superimposed upon it.

29. For an interesting and welcome discussion of the film's class politics, the role that fantasy plays in its depictions of masculine identities, and also of the numerous positions for spectatorial experience it makes possible, see Derek Nystrom, *Hard Hats, Rednecks, and Macho Men: Class in 1970s American Cinema*, 129–157.

275

CHAPTER SEVEN

1. For an example of a crude appropriation of someone else's style, see Quentin Tarantino's endless riffs on De Palma. While one appreciates Tarantino's against-the-grain love of De Palma, it is he who perpetrates, in my view, the corrupt coarsening of his predecessor's work of which so many critics have accused De Palma.

2. Neale and Krutnik, *Popular Film and Television Comedy*, 19.

3. Orr, *Hitchcock and 20th Century Cinema*, 2, 3.

4. Žižek, "Is There a Proper Way," 268–269.

5. The subject of De Palma's Catholicism is treated at length in Richard Blake's book *Afterimage: The Indelible Catholic Imagination of Six American Filmmakers*. His religious upbringing, however, is more complex than the term "Catholic" would immediately suggest. As De Palma explained to Geoff Beran, "Both of my parents are Catholic, and my grandparents are Italian-speaking Catholics on both sides. However, ironically, I was baptized Presbyterian, and went to a Quaker school for 12 years . . . So you get this sort of restrained, religious framework that you're brought up in. And that's why I think you have this sort of strange mix with me." See De Palma, *Interviews*, 180–181.

6. Bouzereau, *The De Palma Cut*, 11–12. My thanks also to Geoff Beran, who coordinates the marvelous website *De Palma A La Mode*.

7. Williams, "When the Woman Looks" (1983).

8. For a measured reading of De Palma and *Dressed to Kill* and its political reception, see Linda Ruth Williams, *The Erotic Thriller*.

9. Kael, *Taking It All In*, 36.

10. As I argue in my book *Representations of Femininity in American Genre Cinema*, De Palma's films, like many others in the post-studio era, should be read as "concealed woman's films."

11. The classic account of this concept remains Joan Riviere's essay "Womanliness as a Masquerade," collected in *Formations of Fantasy*, eds. Victor Burgin, James Donald, Cora Kaplan (London: Methuen, 1986), 35–44. The article was first published in *The International Journal of Psychoanalysis* 10 (1929): 303–313.

12. The figure of the hypocrite, as David S. Reynolds puts it in his study of nineteenth-century American culture, could be called "the oxymoronic oppressor," the embodiment of the "moral and social paradoxes" that bedeviled American life. The oxymoronic oppressor expressed the "divided natures" of the American people. Reynolds, *Beneath the American Renaissance*, 86–87.

13. Not all critics see it this way. Glen O. Gabbard and Krin Gabbard, while granting that De Palma skillfully makes use of the filmic past, find his depiction of the psychiatrist very much in keeping with the mainstream negative portrayal of psychiatrists in film. See their *Psychiatry and the Cinema*, 111.

14. The sequence on the train demonstrates De Palma's interest in adding the politics of race to the Hitchcock thriller. Eluding the killer, Liz has sidled up to a group of stereotypical "black youths," seeking safety among their ranks. Instead, they curse at, threaten, and chase her. Liz's attempt to elude her pursuers on the train, is an ugly sequence (though exhilaratingly shot and edited). If it devolves into caricature and perhaps even racism, it nevertheless speaks to De Palma's determination to incorporate the presence of African Americans within the racially whitewashed milieu of the Hitchcock thriller. Certainly, there is a race discourse encoded within Peter's manufacturing of a white fluid to combat white male psychosexual disturbance.

15. Bettelheim, *Symbolic Wounds*, 151.

16. Ibid., 10–11.

17. Ibid., 19, Bettelheim's emphases.

18. Tharp, "Transvestite as Monster," 5–6.

19. Wood, *Hollywood*, 134.

20. It is also worth noting that De Palma's *Raising Cain* (1992), which riffs on both Hitchcock and *Peeping Tom* (1960), leaves us with a transsexual version of its main character as the most appealing figure in the film. This is a significant conclusion for a film about a diabolical father who evokes the era of classical psychoanalysis. The elder Dr. Nix experimented on his own son, Carter, producing Carter's "multiples," the various personalities, some murderous, some protective, that teem within the adult Carter's mind. With dark irony, De Palma makes Carter Nix (John Lithgow, who in a bravura performance plays not only all of Carter's alter egos but also his father) a child psychologist. Carter's cruel and tyrannical father continues to dominate his son's life well into the present, but, unlike Mrs. Bates, he is still alive and actively tormenting his son.

In the final shot, the endangered mother and daughter reunite, both having survived the mayhem. Behind the reunited mother and daughter in this final image stands the shocking and smiling figure of the schizophrenic protagonist, in full womanly drag as "Margo," who protects the children. Carter has assumed, finally, the female protector-personality in his arsenal of multiple alter egos.

21. It bears mentioning that Hitchcock is not the only director that De Palma maintains an agonistic relationship toward. The stylish, elegant, irresistible, wildly inconsistent films of Dario Argento, often called the "garlic Hitchcock," bear scrutiny as important De Palma intertexts. Argento's *The Bird with the Crystal Plumage* (1970) also contains the murder of a young woman (actually, by a deranged other woman) in an elevator. The elevator murder in Argento is quite brutal in its own way, but actually this brief scene, and in a manner that contrasts with the later, more baroquely stylized Argento as well as with De Palma in his 1980 film, has a kind of documentary realism. Some would argue that *Dressed To Kill* steals its famous elevator murder sequence from the Italian *giallo* film *The Case Of The Bloody Iris* (1972), directed by Giuliano Carnimeo. Again, other than the content, De Palma's version—languorous, distended—bears little resemblance to this film's. He does, however, borrow from the *giallo*'s repertoire of killer fashions: the classic killer disguise in the *giallo* is black hat, black overcoat, and black gloves. Argento's famous predecessor Mario Bava put his stamp on this iconic image, and Argento reworked Bava's aesthetic in *Bird*. In this regard, the genre may have also influenced Hitchcock in *Family Plot*'s criminal get-up for Karen Black, as it seems to have influenced Bobbi's outfit in *Dressed to Kill*. For discussions of the killer's look in the *giallo*, see Koven, *La Dolce Morte*, 8.

22. De Palma's fusion of styles relates very deeply, of course, to De Palma's Hitchcock agon. For an excellent analysis of the relationship between expressionism and surrealism in Hitchcock's work, which I would argue that De Palma not only engages with but also takes to different places, see Richard Allen, *Hitchcock's Romantic Irony*, 219–220, especially. As Allen puts it, surrealism and expressionism both suggest that a "deeper reality" lies behind the surface appearances of the world. Surrealism, however, "displaces the hierarchy of surface reality and shadow world by rendering the unconscious or dream world coextensive or continuous with reality itself" (219). If such a surrealist aesthetic informs Hitchcock films such as *Spellbound*, *Rear Window*, *Vertigo*, and *Marnie*, it more than informs De Palma films, especially the sustained dreamlike atmospheres of *Dressed to Kill* and *Femme Fatale*.

23. Though I do not have the space to pursue it here, such odd camp effects in De Palma, along with his fascination with women characters, make his work surprisingly analogous to that of the Spanish director Pedro Almodóvar, whose films *Matador* (1986) and *Women on the Verge of a Nervous Breakdown* (1988) are readable as pastiches of De Palma's work.

24. In "The Theme of the Three Caskets," Freud considers the significance of plays, tales, and other mythic-fable narratives in which a man must make a choice amongst three options, a choice that, if successful, leads to the prize of the "right" woman. He takes his first example from Shakespeare's play *The Merchant of Venice* when Basiano must

277

choose amongst three caskets—one gold, one silver, one lead—to win the hand of the "fair and wise Portia"; the correct casket contains her portrait. Two suitors, who between them chose the gold and silver caskets, have already failed the test and left; Basiano, the third suitor, correctly chooses the lead casket and therefore wins Portia as his prize. She becomes his bride. This essay is collected in Freud, *The Standard Edition*, vol. 12.

25. Freud's 1914 essay "On Narcissism: An Introduction" is collected in vol. 14 of *The Standard Edition*. Quotations taken from 88–89.

26. The narcissistic woman has engendered a great deal of debate in psychoanalytic theory. Elizabeth Grosz challenges the view taken by Sarah Kofman in *The Enigma of Woman* that Freud's construction of the narcissistic woman is, as Grosz summarizes Kofman, "a positive and resistant femininity which refuses phallocentric circulation." In Grosz's view, the Freudian woman is much more "dependent and subordinate than she seems. Her identity as narcissistic is in fact dependent on her being desired by the other." She commands an arsenal of powers—of *semblance* and *seduction*—but these are powers of passivity. Her passivity is mistaken by her male lover for a "coolness" that always keeps her out of reach, therefore sustaining her lover's desire and allowing her to maintain an "apparent independence." Grosz, *Lacan*, 131. For a view of Freud's theory that also treats it as a plausible account of female sexuality within patriarchy, see also Kaja Silverman, *Threshold*, 33–34.

27. Žižek notes in "Is There a Proper Way to Remake a Hitchcock Film?" that Lila Crane, as played by Vera Miles in *Psycho*, is an oddly cold character (258). I admire Miles's performance and marvel at Lila's often overlooked determination and agency in this film. Alexander Doty has done a commendable job of reclaiming Lila, which he does as a lesbian heroine, in his essay "How Queer is My Psycho." Nevertheless, the Liz Blake of Nancy Allen seems to me a breath of fresh air as the "second woman" in De Palma's version of *Psycho*, and an appealing counterbalance to Miles's Lila—tough, acerbic, funny, compassionate, warm, loyal, and just as brave. I discussed Lila's ambiguities in Chapter 2.

CODA

1. Paglia, "The Dangers of the Gay Agenda."

Aldrich, Robert. *The Seduction of the Mediterranean: Writing, Art, and Homosexual Fantasy.* London: Routledge, 1993.

Allen, Richard, and Sam Ishii-Gonzales. *Hitchcock: Centenary Essays.* London: British Film Institute, 1999.

———. *Hitchcock's Romantic Irony.* New York: Columbia University Press, 2007.

Barton, Sabrina. "'Crisscross': Paranoia and Projection in *Strangers on a Train.*" In *Out in Culture: Gay, Lesbian, and Queer Essays on Popular Culture,* edited by Corey K. Creekmur and Alexander Doty, 216–238. Durham, NC: Duke University Press, 1995.

———. "Your Self Storage: Female Investigation and Male Performativity in the Woman's Psychothriller." In *The Film Cultures Reader,* edited by Graeme Turner, 311–331. 1st ed. New York: Routledge, 2001.

Basinger, Jeanine. *A Woman's View: How Hollywood Spoke to Women, 1930–1960.* Hanover, Connecticut: Wesleyan University Press, 1993.

Bellour, Raymond. "Psychosis, Neurosis, Perversion." In *The Analysis of Film,* edited by Constance Penley, 238–262. Bloomington: Indiana University Press, 2001.

Benshoff, Harry M., and Sean Griffin. *Queer Images: A History of Gay and Lesbian Film in America.* Lanham, MD: Rowman and Littlefield, 2006.

Bersani, Leo. *Homos.* Cambridge, MA: Harvard University Press, 1995.

———. "Is the Rectum a Grave?" In *AIDS: Cultural Analysis and Cultural Activism,* edited by Douglas Crimp, 197–223. Cambridge, MA: MIT Press, 1989.

Bettelheim, Bruno. *The Empty Fortress: Infantile Autism and the Birth of the Self.* New York: The Free Press, 1967.

———. *Symbolic Wounds: Puberty Rites and the Envious Male*. New York: Collier Books, 1962.

Biskind, Peter. *Easy Riders, Raging Bulls: How the Sex-Drugs-and-Rock 'n' Roll Generation Saved Hollywood*. New York: Simon & Schuster, 1998.

Blake, Richard A. *Afterimage: The Indelible Catholic Imagination of Six American Filmmakers*. Chicago: Loyola Press, 2000.

Bloch, Robert. *Psycho*. Greenwich, CT: Fawcett, 1961.

Bogle, Lori Lynn, ed. *Cold War Espionage and Spying (The Cold War, Volume 4)*. New York: Routledge, 2001.

Bonitzer, Pascal. "Notorious." In *Everything You Always Wanted to Know About Lacan (But Were Afraid to Ask Hitchcock)*, edited by Slavoj Žižek, 151–154. New York: Verso, 1999.

———. "The Skin and the Straw." In *Everything You Always Wanted to Know About Lacan (But Were Afraid to Ask Hitchcock)*, edited by Slavoj Žižek, 178–185. New York: Verso, 1999.

Bordwell, David, and Noël Carroll. *Post-Theory: Reconstructing Film Studies*. Madison: Wisconsin University Press, 1996.

Bouzereau, Laurent. *The De Palma Cut: The Films of America's Most Controversial Director*. New York: Dembner Books, 1988.

Brill, Lesley. *The Hitchcock Romance: Love and Irony in Hitchcock's Films*. Princeton, NJ: Princeton University Press, 1988.

———. "Hitchcockian Silence: *Psycho* and Jonathan Demme's *The Silence of the Lambs*." In *After Hitchcock: Influence, Imitation, and Intertextuality*, edited by David Boyd and R. Barton Palmer, 31–46. Austin: University of Texas Press, 2006.

Boyd, David, and R. Barton Palmer, eds. *After Hitchcock: Influence, Imitation, and Intertextuality*. Austin: University of Texas Press, 2006.

Butler, Judith. *Bodies That Matter: On the Discursive Limits of Sex*. New York: Routledge, 1993.

———. "Imitation and Gender Insubordination." In *Inside/Out: Lesbian Theories, Gay Theories*, edited by Diana Fuss. New York: Routledge, 1991.

Carroll, Noël. "The Future of an Allusion: Hollywood in the '70s (and Beyond)." *October* 20 (1982): 51–78.

Chion, Michel. *The Voice in Cinema*. Translated and edited by Claudia Gorbman. New York: Columbia University Press, 1999.

Clover, Carol J. *Men, Women, and Chainsaws: Gender in the Modern Horror Film*. Princeton, NJ: Princeton University Press, 1992.

Corber, Robert J. *In the Name of National Security: Hitchcock, Homophobia, and the Political Construction of Gender in Postwar America*. Durham, NC: Duke University Press, 1993.

———. *Homosexuality in Cold War America: Resistance and the Crisis of Masculinity*. Durham, NC: Duke University Press, 1997.

Crain, Caleb. "Pleasure Principles: Queer Theorists and Gay Journalists Wrestle over the Politics of Sex." *Lingua Franca* 7.8 (October 1997): 26–37.

Creed, Barbara. *The Monstrous-Feminine: Film, Feminism, Psychoanalysis*. New York: Routledge, 1993.

Creekmur, Corey K., and Alexander Doty. *Out in Culture: Gay, Lesbian, and Queer Essays on Popular Culture*. Durham, NC: Duke University Press, 1995.

Cuordileone, K. A. *Manhood and American Political Culture in the Cold War*. New York: Routledge, 2004.

Cvetkovich, Ann. "Postmodern *Vertigo*: The Sexual Politics of Allusion in De Palma's *Body Double*." In *Hitchcock's Rereleased Films: From Rope to Vertigo*, edited by Walter Raubicheck and Walter Srebnick, 147–163. Detroit, MI: Wayne State University Press, 1991.

Davidson, Guy. "'Contagious Relations': Simulation, Paranoia, and the Postmodern Condition in William Friedkin's *Cruising* and Felice Picano's *The Lure*." *GLQ: A Journal of Lesbian and Gay Studies* 11.1 (2005): 23–64.

DeAngelis, Michael. *Gay Fandom and Crossover Stardom: James Dean, Mel Gibson, and Keanu Reeves*. Durham, NC: Duke University Press, 2001.

Deleuze, Gilles. *Masochism: An Interpretation of Coldness and Cruelty*. New York: Zone Books, 1991.

D'Emilio, John. *Sexual Politics, Sexual Communities: The Making of a Homosexual Minority in the United States, 1940–1970*. Chicago: Chicago University Press, 1983.

Deutelbaum, Marshall, and Leland Poague. *A Hitchcock Reader*. Ames: Iowa State University Press, 1986.

De Palma, Brian, and Laurence F. Knapp. *Brian De Palma: Interviews*. Jackson: University Press of Mississippi, 2003.

Dixon, Wheeler Winston. *It Looks At You: The Returned Gaze of Cinema*. New York: SUNY Press, 1995.

Dollimore, Jonathan. *Sexual Dissidence: Augustine to Wilde, Freud to Foucault*. New York: Oxford University Press, 1991.

Doty, Alexander. "How Queer Is My *Psycho*." In *Flaming Classics: Queering the Film Canon*, 155–189. New York: Routledge, 2000.

Durgnat, Raymond. *A Long Hard Look at Psycho*. London: BFI, 2002.

Dyer, Richard. "Gays in Film." *Jump Cut: A Review of Contemporary Media*, no. 18 (August 1978): 15–16.

———. *The Matter of Images: Essays on Representation*. New York: Routledge, 1993.

Edelman, Lee. *Homographesis: Essays in Gay Literary and Cultural Theory*. New York: Routledge, 1994.

———. *No Future: Queer Theory and the Death Drive*. Durham, NC: Duke University Press, 2004.

———. "*Rear Window*'s Glasshole." In *Out Takes: Essays on Queer Theory and Film*, edited by Ellis Hanson, 72–97. Durham, NC: Duke University Press, 1999.

Elsaesser, Thomas, Alexander Horwath, and Noel King, eds. *The Last Great American Picture Show: New Hollywood Cinema in the 1970s*. Amsterdam: Amsterdam University Press, 2004.

Emerson, Ralph Waldo. *Essays, Lectures, and Orations*. London: William S. Orr, 1848.

Farmer, Brett. *Spectacular Passions: Cinema, Fantasy, Gay Male Spectatorships*. Durham, NC: Duke University Press, 2000.

Fink, Bruce. *The Lacanian Subject*. Princeton, NJ: Princeton University Press, 1995.

Foucault, Michel. *The History of Sexuality, Volume I*. Translated by Robert Hurley. New York: Vintage Books, 1988–1990.

281

Freud, Sigmund. *The Standard Edition of the Complete Psychological Works of Sigmund Freud.* Translated by James Strachey, in collaboration with Anna Freud, assisted by Alix Strachey and Alan Tyson. London: Hogarth Press and the Institute of Psychoanalysis, 1993. Originally published 1953–1974 by Hogarth Press.

Frost, Laura. *Sex Drives: Fantasies of Fascism in Literary Modernism.* Ithaca, NY: Cornell University Press, 2002.

Fuchs, Cynthia. "*Taxi Driver* (1976): 'I Got Some Bad Ideas in My Head.'" In *Film Analysis: A Norton Reader,* edited by Jeffrey Geiger and R. L. Rutsky, 696–714. New York: W. W. Norton, 2005.

Fuss, Diana. "Oral Incorporations: *The Silence of the Lambs.*" In *Identification Papers,* 83–107. New York: Routledge, 1996.

Gabbard, Glen O., and Krin Gabbard. *Psychiatry and the Cinema.* 2nd ed. Washington, DC: American Psychiatric Publishing, Inc., 1999.

Geiger, Jeffrey, and R. L. Rutsky. *Film Analysis: A Norton Reader.* 1st ed. New York: W. W. Norton, 2005.

Genet, Jean. *Funeral Rites.* Trans. Bernard Frechtman. New York: Grove/Atlantic, 1988.

Gilbert, James. *Men in the Middle: Searching for Masculinity in the 1950s.* Chicago: University Of Chicago Press, 2005.

Girard, René. *Deceit, Desire, and the Novel: Self and Other in Literary Structure.* Translated by Yvonne Freccero. Baltimore, MD: Johns Hopkins University Press, 1965.

Granger, Farley, and Robert Calhoun. *Include Me Out: My Life from Goldwyn to Broadway.* New York: St. Martin's Griffin, 2008.

Greven, David. "Engorged with Desire: Alfred Hitchcock Films and the Gendered Politics of Eating." In *Reel Food,* edited by Anne Bower. New York: Routledge, 2004.

———. "In a Pig's Eye: Masculinity, Mastery, and the Returned Gaze in *The Blithedale Romance.*" *Studies in American Fiction* 34, no. 2 (2006): 131–159.

———. *Manhood in Hollywood from Bush to Bush.* Austin: University of Texas Press, 2009.

———. *Men Beyond Desire: Manhood, Sex, and Violation in American Literature.* New York: Palgrave Macmillan, 2005.

———. *Representations of Femininity in American Genre Cinema: The Woman's Film, Film Noir, and Modern Horror.* New York: Palgrave Macmillan, 2011.

———. "Rereading Narcissism: Freud's Theory of Male Homosexuality and Hawthorne's 'The Gentle Boy.'" *Modern Psychoanalysis* 34, no. 2 (2009): 48–78.

Grosz, E. A. (Elizabeth A.). *Jacques Lacan: a Feminist Introduction.* New York: Routledge, 1990.

Gunning, Tom. *The Films of Fritz Lang: Allegories of Vision and Modernity.* London: BFI, 2000.

Halberstam, Judith. *Female Masculinity.* Durham, NC: Duke University Press, 1998.

———. *Skin Shows: Gothic Horror and the Technology of Monsters.* Durham, NC: Duke University Press, 2000.

Halperin, David, and Valerie Traub, eds. *Gay Shame.* Chicago: University of Chicago Press, 2008.

Hanson, Ellis. "Teaching Shame." In *Gay Shame,* edited by David Halperin and Valerie Traub, 132–165. Chicago: University of Chicago Press, 2008.

———. *Out Takes: Essays on Queer Theory and Film.* Durham, NC: Duke University Press, 1999.

Hark, Ina Rae. "Revalidating Patriarchy: Why Hitchcock Remade *The Man Who Knew Too Much.*" In *Hitchcock's Rereleased Films: From Rope to Vertigo*, edited by Walter Raubicheck and Walter Srebnick, 209–220. Detroit, MI: Wayne State University Press, 1991.

Harris, Daniel R. "Effeminacy." *Michigan Quarterly Review* 30, no. 1 (Winter 1991): 72–81.

Heilbrun, Carolyn G. *Writing a Woman's Life.* New York: Ballantine, 1989.

Hepworth John. "Hitchcock's Homophobia." In *Out in Culture: Gay, Lesbian, and Queer Essays on Popular Culture*, edited by Corey K. Creekmur and Alexander Doty, 186–197. Durham, NC: Duke University Press, 1995.

Herzog, Amy. "In the Flesh: Space and Embodiment in the Pornographic Peep Show Arcade." *The Velvet Light Trap* 62 (2008): 29–43.

Hewitt, Andrew. *Political Inversions: Homosexuality, Fascism, and the Modernist Imaginary.* Palo Alto, CA: Stanford University Press, 1996.

Hitchcock, Patricia. *Alma Hitchcock: The Woman Behind the Man.* New York: Berkley, 2003.

hooks, bell. "Eating the Other: Desire and Resistance." In *Black Looks: Race and Representation*, 21–39. Boston: South End Press, 1992.

Horrigan, Patrick E. *Widescreen Dreams: Growing Up Gay at the Movies.* Madison: University of Wisconsin Press, 1999.

Houlbrook, Matt. *Queer London: Perils and Pleasures in the Sexual Metropolis, 1918–1957.* Chicago: Chicago University Press, 2005.

Jonte-Pace, Diane E. *Speaking the Unspeakable: Religion, Misogyny, and the Uncanny Mother in Freud's Cultural Texts.* Berkeley: University of California Press, 2001.

Jeffords, Susan. *Hard Bodies: Hollywood Masculinity in the Reagan Era.* New Brunswick, NJ: Rutgers University Press, 1994.

Jensen, Paul M. *Hitchcock Becomes Hitchcock: The British Years.* Baltimore, MD: Midnight Marquee Press, 2000.

Kael, Pauline. *5001 Nights at the Movies.* 3rd ed. New York: Henry Holt, 1992.

———. *Kiss Kiss Bang Bang.* New York: Bantam Books, 1969.

———. *State of the Art.* New York: Plume, 1985.

———. *Taking It All In.* New York: Henry Holt & Co., 1984.

———. "Underground Man." In *When the Lights Go Down*, 131–135. New York: Holt, Rinehart and Winston, 1980.

Kaite, Berkeley. *Pornography and Difference.* Bloomington: Indiana University Press, 1995.

Kalugin, Oleg. *Spymaster: My Thirty-two Years in Intelligence and Espionage Against the West.* New York: St. Martin's, 1994.

Kapsis, Robert E. *Hitchcock: The Making of a Reputation.* Chicago: Chicago University Press, 1992.

Kauffman, Linda S. *Bad Girls and Sick Boys: Fantasies in Contemporary Art and Culture.* Berkeley, California, 1998.

Keane, Marian E. "A Closer Look at Scopophilia: Mulvey, Hitchcock, and *Vertigo.*" In *A Hitchcock Reader*, edited by Marshall Deutelbaum and Leland Poague, 231–249. Ames: Iowa State University Press, 1986.

Kendrick, James. *Hollywood Bloodshed: Violence in 1980s American Cinema*. Carbondale: Southern Illinois University Press, 2009.

Kibbey, Ann M. *Theory of the Image: Capitalism, Contemporary Film, and Women*. Bloomington: Indiana University Press, 2004.

Kimmel, Michael S., and Michael A. Messner. *Men's Lives*. New York: Allyn & Bacon, 2007.

King, Noel. "'The Last Good Time We Ever Had': Remembering the New Hollywood Cinema." In *The Last Great American Picture Show*, edited by Thomas Elsaesser, Alexander Horwath, and Noel King, 19–33. Amsterdam: Amsterdam University Press, 2004.

Kipnis, Laura. *Bound and Gagged: Pornography and the Politics of Fantasy in America*. New York: Grove Press, 1996.

Kofman, Sarah. *The Enigma of Woman: Woman in Freud's Writings*. Ithaca, NY: Cornell University Press, 1985.

Kolker, Robert Phillip. *A Cinema of Loneliness: Penn, Kubrick, Scorsese, Spielberg, Altman*. New York: Oxford University Press, 2000.

Koven, Mikel J. *La Dolce Morte: Vernacular Cinema and the Italian Giallo Film*. Lanham, MD: The Scarecrow Press, 2006.

Krämer, Peter. *The New Hollywood: From Bonnie and Clyde to Star Wars*. New York: Wallflower Press, 2005.

Laurents, Arthur. *Original Story: A Memoir of Broadway and Hollywood*. New York: Knopf, 2000.

Lawrence, Amy. "American Shame: *Rope*, James Stewart, and the Postwar Crisis in American Masculinity." In *Hitchcock's America*, edited by Jonathan Freedman and Richard Millington, 55–76. New York: Oxford University Press, 1999.

Lawrence, D. H. *Studies in Classic American Literature: The Works of D. H. Lawrence*. Edited by Ezra Greenspan, Lindeth Vasey, and John Worthen. New York: Cambridge University Press, 1979.

Lindsey, Shelley Stamp. "Horror, Femininity, and Carrie's Monstrous Puberty." In *The Dread of Difference: Gender and the Horror Film*, edited by Barry Keith Grant. Austin: University of Texas Press, 1996.

Lowenstein, Adam. "The Master, the Maniac, and *Frenzy*: Hitchcock's Legacy of Horror." In *Hitchcock: Past and Future*, edited by Richard Allen and Sam Ishii-Gonzales, 179–193. London: Routledge, 2004.

Mack, Jefferson. *Running a Ring of Spies: Spycraft and Black Operations in the Real World of Espionage*. Boulder, CO: Paladin Press, 1996.

MacKinnon, Kenneth. *Misogyny in the Movies: The De Palma Question*. Newark, NJ: Delaware University Press, 1990.

Marshall, Stuart. "The Contemporary Political Use of Gay History: The Third Reich." In *How Do I Look?: Queer Film and Video*, edited by Cindy Patton et al., 65–102. Seattle, WA: Bay Press, 1991.

Martin, Adrian. "*Cruising*: The Sound of Violence." http://www.fipresci.org/undercurrent/issue_0407/martin_cruising.htm.

McLaughlin, Thomas. "All in the Family: Hitchcock's *Shadow of a Doubt*." In *A Hitchcock Reader*, edited by Marshall Deutelbaum and Leland Poague. Ames: Iowa University Press, 1986.

Melendez, Frank. "Video Pornography, Visual Pleasure, and the Return of the Sublime." In *Porn Studies*, edited by Linda Williams, 401–431. Durham, NC: Duke University Press, 2004.

Menand, Louis. "Finding It at the Movies." *The New York Review of Books* 42, no. 5, March 23, 1995.

Miller, D. A. "Anal Rope." In *Inside/Out: Lesbian Theories, Gay Theories*, edited by Diana Fuss. New York: Routledge, 1991.

———. "Cruising." *Film Quarterly* 61, no. 2, (Winter 2007): 70–73.

Mitchell, Juliet. *Mad Men and Medusas: Reclaiming Hysteria*. New York: Basic Books, 2001.

Modleski, Tania. *The Women Who Knew Too Much: Hitchcock and Feminist Theory*. 2nd ed. New York: Routledge, 2005.

Mosse, George L. *The Image of Man: The Creation of Modern Masculinity*. New York: Oxford University Press, 1996.

Mulvey, Laura. "Visual Pleasure and Narrative Cinema." In *Feminist Film Theory: A Reader*, edited by Sue Thornham. New York: New York University Press, 1999.

———. "Afterthoughts on 'Visual Pleasure and Narrative Cinema' inspired by King Vidor's *Duel in the Sun* (1946)." In *Feminist Film Theory: A Reader*, edited by Sue Thornham, 122–131. New York: New York University Press, 1999.

Muñoz, José Esteban. *Cruising Utopia: The Then and There of Queer Futurity*. New York: New York University Press, 2009.

———. *Disidentifications: Queers of Color and the Performance of Politics*. Illustrated edition. Minneapolis: University of Minnesota Press, 1999.

Naremore, James. *Filmguide to Psycho*. Bloomington: Indiana University Press, 1973.

Neale, Steve, and Frank Krutnik. *Popular Film and Television Comedy*. New York: Routledge, 1990.

Nelson, Dana. *National Manhood: Capitalist Citizenship and the Imagined Fraternity of White Men*. Durham, NC: Duke University Press, 1998.

Nystrom, Derek. *Hard Hats, Rednecks, and Macho Men: Class in 1970s American Cinema*. New York: Oxford University Press, 2009.

O'Donnell, Patrick. *Latent Destinies: Cultural Paranoia and Contemporary U.S. Narrative*. Durham, NC: Duke University Press, 2000.

Orr, John. *Hitchcock and Twentieth-Century Cinema*. London: Wallflower, 2005.

Paglia, Camille. "The Dangers of the Gay Agenda." *Salon.com*. October 28, 1998. http://www.salon.com/col/pagl/1998/10/28pagl.html (accessed on May 12, 2011).

———. *Sexual Personae: Art and Decadence from Nefertiti to Emily Dickinson*. New Haven, CT: Yale University Press, 1990.

———. *Vamps & Tramps: New Essays*. New York: Vintage Books, 1994.

Peretz, Eyal. *Becoming Visionary: Brian De Palma's Cinematic Education of the Senses*. Stanford, CA: Stanford University Press, 2008.

Piso, Michele. "Mark's Marnie." In *A Hitchcock Reader*, edited by Marshall Deutelbaum and Leland Poague, 288–299. Ames: Iowa State University Press, 1986.

Rafferty, Terrence. *The Thing Happens: Ten Years of Writing about the Movies*. New York: Grove Press, 1993.

Ramakers, Micha. *Dirty Pictures: Tom of Finland, Masculinity, and Homosexuality*. New York: St. Martin's Press, 2000.

Rank, Otto. *The Double: A Psychoanalytic Study*. Chapel Hill: University of North Carolina Press, 1971.

Ray, Robert B. *A Certain Tendency of the Hollywood Cinema, 1930–1980*. Princeton, NJ: Princeton University Press, 1985.

Rechy, John. *City of Night*. New York: Grove Press, 1988.

Reich, Wilhelm. *The Mass Psychological Structure of Fascism*. Translated by Vincent R. Carfagno. New York: Noonday, 1970.

Reynolds, David S. *Beneath the American Renaissance: The Subversive Imagination in the Age of Emerson and Melville*. Cambridge, MA: Harvard University Press, 1988.

Rohmer, Eric, and Claude Chabrol. *Hitchcock: The First Forty-four Films*. Translated by Stanley Hochman. New York: F. Ungar, 1979.

Rose, Jacqueline. "Paranoia and the Film System." *Screen* 17, no. 4 (Winter 1977): 85–104.

Rothman, William. *Hitchcock: The Murderous Gaze*. Cambridge, MA: Harvard University Press, 1982.

Rosenbaum, Jonathan. "Crap Shooting." Review of *Snake Eyes*, directed by Brian De Palma. http://www.jonathanrosenbaum.com/?p=6534 (accessed July 5, 2010).

———. "Master Thief." Review of *Femme Fatale*, directed by Brian De Palma. http://www.jonathanrosenbaum.com/?p=6185 (accessed July 5, 2010).

Rosenbladt, Bettina. "Doubles and Doubts in Hitchcock: The German Connection." In *Hitchcock: Past and Future*, edited by Richard Allen and Sam Ishii-Gonzales, 37–64. London: Routledge, 2004.

Rossiter, Arthur Percival. *Angel with Horns, and Other Shakespeare Lectures*. Essex, UK: Longmans, 1961

Samuels, Robert. *Hitchcock's Bitextuality: Lacan, Feminisms, and Queer Theory*. New York: SUNY Press, 1998.

Schaefer, Eric. "Gauging a Revolution: 16-mm Film and the Rise of the Pornographic Feature." In *Porn Studies*, edited by Linda Williams, 370–400. Durham, NC: Duke University Press, 2004.

Schrader, Paul. *Transcendental Style in Film: Ozu, Bresson, Dreyer*. Berkeley: University of California Press, 1972.

Sedgwick, Eve Kosofsky. *Between Men: English Literature and Male Homosocial Desire*. New York: Columbia University Press, 1985.

———. *Epistemology of the Closet*. Berkeley: University of California Press, 1990.

Shaviro, Steven. *The Cinematic Body*. Minneapolis: University of Minnesota Press, 1993.

Shoffman, Mark. "Half a Century of Gay Progress." Pinknews.co.uk, April 28, 2006. http://www.pinknews.co.uk/news/articles/2005-1303.html (accessed on May 23, 2009).

Silverman, Kaja. *Male Subjectivity at the Margins*. New York: Routledge, 1992.

———. *The Threshold of the Visible World*. New York: Routledge, 1996.

Smith, Joseph W. *The Psycho File: A Comprehensive Guide to Hitchcock's Classic Shocker*. Jefferson, NC: McFarland & Co., 2009.

Spoto, Donald. *The Art of Alfred Hitchcock: Fifty Years of His Motion Pictures*. 2nd ed. New York: Anchor Books, 1992.

———. *The Dark Side of Genius: The Life of Alfred Hitchcock*. Boston, MA: Little Brown and Company, 1983.

Stacey, Judith. "Cruising to Familyland: Gay Hypergamy and Rainbow Kinship." In *Men's Lives*, edited by Michael S. Kimmel and Michael A. Messner. New York: Allyn & Bacon, 2007.

Stam, Robert, and Roberta Pearson. "Hitchcock's *Rear Window*: Reflexivity and the Critique of Voyeurism." In *A Hitchcock Reader*, edited by Marshall Deutelbaum and Leland Poague, 199–212. Ames: Iowa State University Press, 1986.

Studlar, Gaylyn. *In the Realm of Pleasure: Von Sternberg, Dietrich, and the Masochistic Aesthetic*. New York: Columbia University Press, 1993.

Suárez, Juan A. *Bike Boys, Drag Queens, and Superstars: Avant-Garde, Mass Culture, and Gay Identities in the 1960s Underground Cinema*. Bloomington: Indiana University Press, 1996.

Tasker, Yvonne. *Spectacular Bodies: Gender, Genre, and the Action Cinema*. New York: Routledge, 1996.

Tate, Allen. "Our Cousin, Mr. Poe." In *Essays of Four Decades*. Chicago: The Swallow Press, 1968.

Taubin, Amy. *Taxi Driver*. London: British Film Institute, 2000.

Tharp, Julie. "The Transvestite as Monster." *The Journal of Popular Film and Television* 19, no. 3 (Fall 1991): 105–113.

Theweleit, Klaus. *Male Fantasies: Volume 1: Women, Floods, Bodies, History*. Minneapolis: Minnesota University Press, 1987.

Thompson, David. *The Moment of Psycho: How Alfred Hitchcock Taught America to Love Murder*. New York: Basic Books, 2010.

Thompson, Kristin. *Storytelling in the New Hollywood: Understanding Classical Narrative Technique*. Cambridge, MA: Harvard University Press, 1999.

Toles, George E. "'If Thine Eye Offend Thee . . .': *Psycho* and the Art of Infection." In *Hitchcock: Centenary Essays*, edited by Richard Allen and Sam Ishii-Gonzales, 159–179. London: British Film Institute, 1999.

Truffaut, François, and Helen G. Scott. *Hitchcock*. New York: Simon & Schuster, 1985.

Tyler, Parker. *Screening the Sexes: Homosexuality in the Movies*. New York: Da Capo Press, 1993.

Ullén, Magnus. "Pornography and Its Critical Reception: Toward a Theory of Masturbation." *Jump Cut: A Review of Contemporary Media*, no. 51 (Spring 2009).

Waitt, Gordon, and Kevin Markwell. *Gay Tourism: Culture and Context*. Psychology Press, 2006.

Warner, Michael. "Homo-Narcissism: Or, Heterosexuality." In *Engendering Men: The Question of Male Feminist Criticism*, edited by Joseph A. Boone and Michael Cadden, 190–206. New York: Routledge, 1990.

Waugh, Thomas. "Homosociality in the Classical American Stag Film: Off-Screen, On-Screen." In *Porn Studies*, edited by Linda Williams, 127–141. Durham, NC: Duke University Press, 2004.

Weinreich, Martin. "The Urban Inferno: On the Aesthetics of Martin Scorsese's *Taxi Driver*." *Point of View: The Art of Film Editing*, no. 6 (December 1998): 1–14.

Welldon, Estela V. *Sadomasochism*. Cambridge, UK: Icon Books, 2002.

Werth, Barry. *The Scarlet Professor: Newton Arvin: A Literary Life Shattered by Scandal*. New York: Anchor, 2002.

White, Armond. *The Resistance: Ten Years of Pop Culture That Shook the World*. New York: The Overlook Press, 1995.

White, Patricia. "Hitchcock and Hom(m)osexuality." In *Hitchcock: Past and Future*, edited by Richard Allen and Sam Ishii-Gonzales, 211–229. London: Routledge, 2004.

White, Susan. "*Vertigo* and the Problems of Knowledge in Feminist Film Theory." *Hitchcock: Centenary Essays*, edited by Richard Allen and Sam Ishii-Gonzales, 279–307.

Williams, Linda. "Discipline and Fun: *Psycho* and Postmodern Cinema." In *Reinventing Film Studies*, edited by Linda Williams and Christine Gledhill. New York: Oxford University Press, 2000.

———. "Film Bodies: Gender, Genre, and Excess." In *Feminist Film Theory: A Reader*, edited by Sue Thornham, 267–281. New York: New York University Press, 1999.

———. *Hard Core: Power, Pleasure, and the "Frenzy of the Visible."* Berkeley: University of California Press, 1999.

———, ed. *Porn Studies*. Durham, NC: Duke University Press, 2004.

———. "Porn Studies: Proliferating Pornographies On/Scene: An Introduction." In *Porn Studies*, edited by Linda Williams, 1–23. Durham, NC: Duke University Press, 2004.

———. *Screening Sex*. Durham, NC: Duke University Press, 2008.

———. "When the Woman Looks." In *Re-Vision: Essays in Feminist Film Criticism*, edited by Mary Anne Doane, Patricia Mellencamp, and Linda Williams, 83–99. Los Angeles: The American Film Institute, 1984.

Williams, Linda Ruth. *The Erotic Thriller in Contemporary Cinema*. Bloomington: Indiana University Press, 2005.

Wood, Robin. "Brian De Palma: The Politics of Castration." In *Hollywood from Vietnam to Reagan . . . and Beyond*. London: Routledge, 2004.

———. *Hitchcock's Films Revisited*. 1989. New York: Columbia University Press, 2002.

———. "The Incoherent Text: Narrative in the '70s." In *Hollywood from Vietnam to Reagan . . . and Beyond*. New York: Columbia University Press, 2003.

Žižek, Slavoj. "Is There a Proper Way to Remake a Hitchcock Film?" In *Hitchcock: Past and Future*, edited by Richard Allen and Sam Ishii-Gonzales, 257–275.

———. *Looking Awry: An Introduction to Jacques Lacan through Popular Culture*. Cambridge, MA: MIT Press, 1992.

Gavin, John, 35, 65, 73
gay culture, pre-AIDS. *See* AIDS era
gender roles, compulsory, 29, 30, 57, 59, 166
Genet, Jean, 200
genre film, 9–13
Get to Know Your Rabbit (De Palma), 118, 119, 123, 139–140
Gilbert, James, 92
Gilman, Charlotte Perkins, 49
Girard, René, 49, 123
girl, the, 173, 217, 222, 232, 238–241
Godard, Jean-Luc, 112, 119, 126, 152, 208
Godfather, The (Coppola), 14, 189, 259n17
Gordon, Keith, 217, 231
gothic, 34, 227
Granger, Farley, 24, 25, 61, 63, 66, 68, 103, 187, 222, 255n26, 259n2
Grant, Cary, 25, 54, 61, 206, 212, 257n35
Greetings (De Palma), 118, 122, 123, 124, 125–129, 130, 137, 139, 141, 143, 147, 178, 227, 265n2
Gunning, Tom, 15

Halberstam, Judith (J. Jack), 8, 47, 251n9, 256n29
hands, 42, 44, 190, 198, 208
Hanson, Ellis, 8, 251n9
Hark, Ina Rae, 254n10, 258n43
Hawks, Howard, 10, 208
Hawthorne, Nathaniel, 34, 64, 208, 211, 263n20
Head, Edith, 224
Hedren, 'Tippi,' 28, 54, 68, 243, 257n35
hegemony, 28
Heiress, The (Wyler), 93, 262n9
Hepworth, John, 260n19
Herrmann, Bernard, 44, 55, 110, 157, 158, 211, 219, 230
Herzog, Amy, 100–101
heterosexuality: doubles and, 71, 79–80; in Hitchcock, 30, 62, 68, 79; mythic natural-ness of, 3–4; pornography and, 168–172; in *Taxi Driver*, 168. *See also* sexuality
Hewitt, Andrew, 199
Hi, Mom! (De Palma), 118, 123, 129–139, 147, 148, 163, 265n2

Hitchcock, Alfred, 23, 26–27, 62, 65, 83, 91, 241, 254n4; blot, 37, 254n17; and capital punishment, 67; and eating in films, 39, 42, 50; feminine versus the queer pattern, 26–27; 65, 83, 241, 254n4; and heterosexu-ality, 30, 62, 68, 79; masculinity in, 60–88; as Original Genius, 110; and shadow couple, 76–83; stereotypes in, 34; and Victorian dandy, 62; women's screams in films, 53–57. *See also specific films*
Hitchcock: The First Forty-Four Films (Chabrol and Rohmer), 28
homosexuality: 3–4, 46, 146; and the Cold War, 10, 34, 46, 91, 254n12; gay sex, 104; and murder, 103. *See also* homosociality; masculinity; sexuality; *and individual films*
homosociality, 149–155. *See also* masculinity
hooks, bell, 283
Horrigan, Patrick E., 30
horror film, 7, 65, 83, 85, 88, 238; slasher, 82, 83, 242
Houlbrook, Matt, 51
Hurt Locker, The (Bigelow), 213
hysteria, 48–49

I Confess (Hitchcock), 68, 70
In the Company of Men (LaBute), 141

James, Henry, 34, 64, 174, 211
Jaws (Spielberg), 13, 14, 174
jealousy, 18, 34, 45, 46, 146, 178, 180, 233, 256n29, 256n30
Jensen, Paul M., 45
Jourdan, Louis, 70, 260n25

Kael, Pauline, 6, 7, 16, 111–113, 121, 156, 157, 175, 184, 222, 251n6, 257n35, 258n42, 265n2
Kaite, Berkeley, 163
Kapsis, Robert E., 121, 266n13
Katz, Alex, 221
Keitel, Harvey, 150, 172, 173, 175
Kelly, Grace, 2, 6, 27, 63, 103, 162, 212, 257n35
Kibbey, Ann M., 252n10
Kill Bill: Volume 1 (Tarantino), 230

www.ingramcontent.com/pod-product-compliance
Ingram Content Group UK Ltd.
Pitfield, Milton Keynes, MK11 3LW, UK
UKHW010315240525
458861UK00003B/451